Weak Links

Weak Links

Fragile States, Global Threats, and International Security

A Council on Foreign Relations Book

Stewart Patrick

OXFORD
UNIVERSITY PRESS

OXFORD
UNIVERSITY PRESS

Oxford University Press, Inc., publishes works that further
Oxford University's objective of excellence
in research, scholarship, and education.

Oxford   New York
Auckland   Cape Town   Dar es Salaam   Hong Kong   Karachi
Kuala Lumpur   Madrid   Melbourne   Mexico City   Nairobi
New Delhi   Shanghai   Taipei   Toronto

With offices in
Argentina   Austria   Brazil   Chile   Czech Republic   France   Greece
Guatemala   Hungary   Italy   Japan   Poland   Portugal   Singapore
South Korea   Switzerland   Thailand   Turkey   Ukraine   Vietnam

Copyright © 2011 by Oxford University Press, Inc.

Published by Oxford University Press, Inc.
198 Madison Avenue, New York, NY 10016

www.oup.com

Oxford is a registered trademark of Oxford University Press

Library of Congress Cataloging-in-Publication Data
Patrick, Stewart.
Weak links : fragile states, global threats, and international security/ Stewart Patrick.
p.   cm.
Includes bibliographical references.
ISBN-13: 978- 0-19-975151-8
ISBN-10: 0-19-975151-X
1. Security, International.   2. Political stability.   3. Failed states.
4. World politics--2005-2015.   I. Title.
JZ5588.P37 2011
355'.033--dc22   2010026001

4 5 6 7 8 9

Printed in the United States of America
on acid-free paper

CONTENTS

ACKNOWLEDGEMENTS

I incurred many institutional and intellectual debts in researching and writing this book. While I can never truly repay these, I can at least try to enumerate them. I owe sincere thanks to Richard N. Haass, the president of the Council on Foreign Relations (CFR), for the opportunity he and CFR provided to complete this manuscript, alongside my other duties as director of the International Institutions and Global Governance (IIGG) program. James M. Lindsay, CFR's director of studies, offered wise advice in framing the book's argument. I am also grateful to the board of the Robina Foundation for its generous support for this book and the IIGG program's broader research and policy agenda.

This book project originated when I was a research fellow at the Center for Global Development (CGD), with initial funding provided by the Carnegie Corporation of New York. I am indebted to CGD president Nancy Birdsall and then-vice presidents Ruth Levine and Dennis De Tray for endorsing this research agenda. I thank Stephen Del Rosso of the Carnegie Corporation for finding merit in this study and Vartan Gregorian, president of the corporation, for agreeing to fund it so generously. I am also grateful to Alexander Lennon, editor of the *Washington Quarterly*, which published my 2006 article, "Weak States and Global Threats: Fact or Fiction?" That piece served as the basis for this book-length exploration of the relationship between state fragility and transnational threats.

One of the rewards of writing on such a complex and wide-ranging topic is the chance to engage with and learn from multiple experts. My biggest thanks go to Susan E. Rice, with whom I collaborated closely prior to her appointment as U.S. permanent representative to the United Nations. As a senior fellow at the Brookings Institution, Susan reached out to me upon my arrival at CGD and graciously offered to co-sponsor a joint roundtable series on security threats and developing countries. That initiative spawned a three-year partnership, culminating in our Index of State Weakness in the Developing World—upon which this book draws. I will always be grateful for Susan's friendship and her generosity in helping me get established in the Washington, DC, policy community.

In writing this book, I gained insights from leading academic and policy experts, who enriched my understanding of the nature and dynamics of state fragility and of the challenges of state-building. I am particularly indebted to Francis Fukuyama, Bruce Jones, Shepard Forman, Carlos Pascual, Carol Lancaster, Ellen Laipson, Stephen Krasner, Robert Perito, Chet Crocker, Princeton Lyman, Paul Collier, Tjip Walker, Elizabeth Kvitashvili, Marina Ottaway, Jack Goldstone, Monty Marshall, Pauline Baker, Elizabeth Cousens, Peter Lewis, Hans Binnendijk, James Dobbins, James Schear, Johanna Mendelson-Forman, Geoff Dabelko, Vijaya Ramachandran, Todd Moss, Christopher Preble, Ashraf Ghani, Rick Barton, John Agoglia, Joe Collins, Howard Wolpe, Dick Sokolsky, Clare Lockhart, Robert Rotberg, Paul Stares, Ciara Knudsen, Laura Hall, Gordon Adams, Rand Beers, Lael

Brainard, Roland Paris, Charles Call, David Carment, John Herbst, Andrew Natsios, Steve Morrison, Kathleen Hicks, Jennifer Windsor, Barnett Rubin, Thomas Carothers, Susan Woodward, Mariano Aguirre, Steven Biddle, Colin Kahl, Victoria Holt, Reuben Brigety, Bill Nash, Matthew Levinger, Michael Lund, Mark Schneider, John Sewell, Karin von Hippel, Eric Schwartz, Steve Radelet, Bill Anderson, Ken Knight, Micah Zenko, Simon Chesterman, Ramesh Thakur, Mike Dziedzic, Beth Degrasse, Jeremy Weinstein, William Durch, Stephen Stedman, Nicholas van de Walle, David Roodman, Michael Clemens, Arvind Subramanian, Kim Elliott, Robert Lamb, Harold Trinkunas, Anne Clunan, William Zartman, Kimberly Marten, Joseph Siegle, Sarah Cliffe, and Gayle Smith.

The scope of this book forced me to educate myself on several global threats—ranging from terrorism to nuclear proliferation, transnational crime, energy insecurity, and infectious disease. Fortunately, I could rely on numerous specialists whose expertise could compensate for my ignorance. I am expecially indebted to Daniel Byman, Dan Benjamin, Steve Simon, Kenneth Menkhaus, Marc Sageman, Ulrich Schneckener, Douglas Farah, David Albright, Eric Rosand, Alistair Millar, Matthew Bunn, Jeffrey Lewis, John Wolfstahl, James Forest, Amy Smithson, John Pike, David Mosher, Brian Finlay, Libby Turpen, Moises Naim, James Cockayne, Raymond Baker, Richard Cincotta, Antonio Maria Costa, Bartosz H. Stanislawski, Ted Truman, Jack Blum, Peter Andreas, Vanda Felbab-Brown, Sarah Mendelson, John T. Picarelli, Louise Shelley, Phil Williams, Donna Ninic, Jonathan Winer, Laurie Garrett, Harley Feldbaum, Jean-Paul Chretien, Fred Burkle, Maureen Lewis, David Fidler, David Gordon, and Pieter Fourie.

This book would never have seen the light of day without the dedication of several younger colleagues. I owe my greatest debts to Alex Pascal and Stephanie Gilbert, who provided extraordinary research assistance and sage advice on how to organize and present vast quantities of information in an accessible manner. They also proved to be wonderful writers and editors. I cannot thank them enough for the talent and energy which they devoted to this project. I also thank Preeti Bhattacharji, program coordinator at CFR, who worked tirelessly to prepare the manuscript for publication. With the assistance of Brian Williamson and Shelby Leighton, she helped track down stray references and format the many tables and figures. Farah Thaler, my talented assistant director, kept the IIGG program running smoothly as I completed this book. I am also grateful to Kevin Ummel, Corrinne Graff, Larry Malm, Brandon Hunt, Liana Wyler, and Papia Debroy for their work in producing the Index of State Weakness. Kaysie Brown, my wonderful colleague at both CGD and CFR, lent her support and expertise to this project from its inception.

I was fortunate to work with an excellent editorial team at Oxford University Press (OUP). I thank David McBride and two anonymous reviewers for endorsing OUP's publication of this book, and Marc Schneider for managing production of the manuscript. Patricia Dorff and her colleagues in CFR's publications division helped steer the book through to completion.

Finally, I owe a special debt to my wife Sophia and our children—Oliver, Henry, and Iona—for their forebearance and good cheer in surviving yet another time-consuming book project.

Stewart Patrick

Weak Links

INTRODUCTION
WEAK STATES, GLOBAL THREATS, AND
INTERNATIONAL SECURITY

One of the defining challenges in our world, now and for many years to come, will be to deal with weak and poorly governed states—states that are on the verge of failure, or indeed, states that have already failed. These crises create environments of anarchy, and conflict, and ungoverned space—where violence and oppression can spread; where arms traffickers and other transnational criminals can operate with impunity; and where terrorists and extremists can gather, and plot, and train to kill the innocent. In a world as increasingly connected as ours, the international state system is only as strong as its weakest links.
—*Secretary of State Condoleezza Rice, July 16, 2008*[1]

[Al-Qaeda recruits] operate freely in the disaffected communities and disconnected corners of our interconnected world—the impoverished, weak and ungoverned states that have become the most fertile breeding grounds for transnational threats like terror and pandemic disease and the smuggling of deadly weapons.
—*Senator Barack Obama, April 23, 2007*[2]

It has become commonplace to claim that the gravest dangers to U.S. and world security are no longer military threats from rival great powers but rather cross-border threats emanating from the world's most poorly governed, economically stagnant, and conflict-ridden countries. Public officials and the media—as well as many scholars— depict weak and failing states as generating or enabling a vast array of dangers, from transnational terrorism to weapons proliferation, organized crime, humanitarian catastrophes, regional conflict, mass migration, pandemic disease, environmental degradation, and energy insecurity.[3] Leading thinkers like Francis Fukuyama argue, "Since the end of the Cold War, weak and failing states have arguably become the single-most important problem for international order." Official Washington agrees. Secretary of State Hillary Rodham Clinton has spoken of the "chaos that flows from failed states," which serve as "breeding grounds, not only for the worst abuses of human beings, from mass murders to rapes to indifference toward disease and other terrible calamities, but they are [also] invitations to terrorists to find refuge amidst the chaos." Likewise, Secretary of Defense Robert Gates predicts, "Over the next 20 years, the most persistent and potentially dangerous threats will come less from emerging ambitious states, than from failing ones that cannot meet the basic needs—much less the basic aspirations—of their people."[4]

This new focus on weak and failing states represents a noteworthy shift in U.S. threat perceptions. During the 1990s, a handful of U.S. strategists began to call attention to the possible spillover consequences of weak governance in the developing world.[5] Most U.S. policymakers, however, regarded states with sovereignty deficits almost exclusively through a humanitarian lens: such countries piqued the moral conscience but appeared to have little strategic significance. This calculus shifted following September 11, 2001, when al-Qaeda attacked the United States from Afghanistan, one of the poorest and most wretched countries in the world. The assault quickly produced a consensus in U.S. policy circles that state fragility was both an incubator and vector of multiple transnational threats. President George W. Bush captured this new view in his National Security Strategy of 2002, declaring: "America is now threatened less by conquering states than we are by failing ones." In the words of Richard Haass, the State Department's director of policy planning, "The attacks of September 11, 2001, reminded us that weak states can threaten our security as much as strong ones, by providing breeding grounds for extremism and havens for criminals, drug traffickers, and terrorists. Such lawlessness abroad can bring devastation here at home. One of our most pressing tasks is to prevent today's troubled countries from becoming tomorrow's failed states."[6] This new threat perception quickly became conventional wisdom among government officials, journalists, and independent analysts at home and abroad.

Since 9/11, this preoccupation with spillovers from weak or failed states has driven a slew of U.S. policy pronouncements and institutional innovations spanning the realms of intelligence, diplomacy, development, defense, and even trade. In 2003, the Central Intelligence Agency (CIA) identified some fifty lawless zones around the world that might be conducive to illicit activity, and began to devote new intelligence collection assets to long-neglected parts of the world. The following year, Secretary of State Colin Powell established an Office of Reconstruction and Stabilization in the State Department, which worked with the National Intelligence Council to identify states at risk of collapse where the United States could launch conflict prevention and mitigation efforts. In 2006 the National Security Strategy cited "weak and impoverished states and ungoverned areas" as a critical threat to the United States,[7] and Condoleezza Rice, Powell's successor, announced a new "transformational diplomacy" initiative intended to help build and sustain democratic, well-governed states that respond to the needs of their people and conduct themselves responsibly in the international system. To advance this goal, Rice announced a sweeping plan to ensure that U.S. foreign assistance was more closely aligned with U.S. foreign policy priorities. USAID devised its own Fragile States Strategy, designed to bolster countries that otherwise might breed terror, crime, instability, or disease. The Bush administration even cast its campaign for regional trade liberalization as a means to prevent state failure and its negative externalities. These trends have continued into the Obama administration, informing the Presidential Policy Directive on Global Development issued in September 2010 and the first-ever Quadrennial Diplomacy and Development Review (QDDR), released three months later. Hillary Clinton, Obama's Secretary of State, has repeatedly depicted fragile and dysfunctional states as growing threats to global security, prosperity, and justice—and endorsed increased investments in U.S. "civilian power" resources to address these challenges.[8]

Such initiatives have been mirrored across the Potomac. The Defense Department's guiding strategy documents now emphasize military cooperation to strengthen the sovereign capacities of friendly governments in the developing world against the internal threats posed by insurgents, terrorists, and criminals. "State weakness and failure may be an increasing driver of conflict and situations that require a U.S. military response," the Undersecretary of Defense for Policy declared in spring 2009.[9] As the National Defense Strategy of June 2008 explains, "Ungoverned, under-governed, misgoverned, and contested areas offer fertile ground for such groups to exploit the gaps in governance capacity of local regimes to undermine local stability and regional security."[10] The Defense Department and its Combatant Commands—including a new Africa Command—are responding to this new mission by deploying assets to the world's rugged remote regions, uncontrolled borders, and un-policed coastlines. Defense Secretary Robert Gates has emphasized that, "Where possible, U.S. strategy is to employ indirect approaches—primarily through building the capacity of partner governments and their security forces—to prevent festering problems from turning into crises that require costly and controversial direct military intervention."[11]

The new conventional wisdom is not restricted to the United States. Other rich world governments have adopted analogous policy statements and have begun to adapt their defense, diplomatic, and development policies and instruments to help prevent state failure and respond to its aftermath—and to quarantine themselves from the presumed "spillover" effects of state weakness. The European Security Strategy identifies the "alarming phenomenon" of state failure as one of the main threats to the European Union. In Great Britain, Prime Minister Tony Blair's government pioneered a government-wide effort to help prevent failed states from generating pathologies like crime, terrorism, disease, uncontrolled migration, and energy insecurity. Blair's successor, David Cameron, has since launched a new UK National Security Strategy that prioritizes attention and resources to "fragile, failing, and failed states" around the world. Canada, Australia, and others have issued similar policy statements.[12]

Likewise at the multilateral level, international organizations depict state failure as the Achilles' heel of collective security. A unifying theme of UN reform proposals over the past decade has been the need for effective, sovereign states to contend with today's global threats. As UN Secretary General Kofi Annan declared in a December 2004 speech, "Whether the threat is terror or AIDS, a threat to one is a threat to all.... Our defenses are only as strong as their weakest link."[13] In 2006, UN member states endorsed the creation of a Peacebuilding Commission to ensure that states emerging from conflict do not collapse once again into failure. In parallel with these steps, the major donors of the Organisation for Economic Co-operation and Development

(OECD) have pursued a "Fragile States" initiative, in partnership with the World Bank's Low Income Countries Under Stress (now Fragile and Conflict Affected States) program. The underlying motivation for all of these efforts, as former Congressman Lee Hamilton has noted, is that "our collective security depends on the security of the world's most vulnerable places."[14]

What is striking, in view of this flurry of official activity, is how little empirical analysis has been undertaken to document and explore the connection between state failure and transnational security threats. Policymakers have advanced blanket associations between these two sets of phenomena, often on the basis of anecdotes or single examples (e.g., al-Qaeda operations in Afghanistan before 9/11) rather than through sober analysis of global patterns or in-depth case studies that reveal causal linkages.[15] Such sweeping generalizations provide little analytical insight or guidance for policymakers in setting priorities, since they fail to distinguish among categories of weak and failing states or to ask whether (or why) particular developing countries are associated with specific sets of threats. This book aims to fill these gaps by analyzing the relationship between state weakness and five of the world's most pressing transnational threats.

WEAK STATES AND TRANSNATIONAL THREATS: RHETORIC AND REALITY

The growing concern with weak and failing states is really based on two separate propositions: first, that traditional concepts of security such as interstate violence should expand to encompass cross-border threats driven by non-state actors (such as terrorists), activities (crime), or forces (pandemics or environmental degradation); and second, that such threats have their origins in large measure in weak governance in the developing world.

Since the Reagan administration, successive versions of the U.S. National Security Strategy have incorporated non-military concerns such as terrorism, organized crime, infectious disease, energy security, and environmental degradation. The common thread linking these challenges is that they originate primarily in sovereign jurisdictions abroad but have the potential to harm U.S. citizens. This definitional expansion has stimulated lively debate. Some national security traditionalists argue that such concerns pose at best an indirect rather than existential threat to U.S. national interests, and that the effort to lump diverse phenomena into a common analytical framework dilutes the meaning of "national security." Proponents of a wider view of national security respond that unconventional threats contribute to violence by destabilizing states and regions and generating spillover effects. More fundamentally, they argue that the traditional "violence paradigm" for national security must adapt to accommodate other threats to the safety, well-being, and way of life of U.S. citizens. Such threats include not only malevolent, purposive ones such as transnational terrorism— something many traditionalists now accept—but also "threats without a threatener": malignant forces that emerge from nature, such as global pandemics, or as by-products of human activity, such as climate change.[16] Senator Barack Obama firmly embraced this perspective in his first major foreign policy address as a presidential candidate.

"Whether it's global terrorism or pandemic disease, dramatic climate change or the proliferation of weapons of mass destruction, the threats we face at the dawn of the 21st century can no longer be contained by borders and boundaries."[17]

Today the conventional wisdom in official circles holds that poorly governed states are disproportionately linked to these types of transnational threats. Lacking even minimal levels of resilience, they are perceived as more vulnerable than rich nations to illicit networks of terrorists or criminals, cross-border conflict, and devastating pandemics. Yet traditionalists are often dubious that weak and failing states—in general—endanger U.S. national security.[18] More relevant, they contend, are a handful of pivotal weak states, such as nuclear-armed Pakistan or North Korea, whose fortunes may affect regional balances of power or prospects for large-scale destruction. It is not always easy to predict, however, where such threats may emerge. In the 1990s, few anticipated that remote, poor, and war-ravaged Afghanistan would be the launching pad for the most devastating attack on the United States in the nation's history.

The unenviable challenge for policymakers is to try to anticipate where weak governance in the developing world is likely to become strategically salient. "A failing state in a remote part of the world may not, in isolation, affect U.S. national security," Peter Bergen and Laurie Garrett explain, "but in combination with other transnational forces, the process of state failure could contribute to a cascade of problems that causes significant direct harm to the United States or material damage to countries (e.g., European allies) or regions (e.g., oil-producing Middle East) vital to U.S. interests."[19]

At least four things have been missing from the discussion of failed states and transnational threats. The first is an appreciation that state failure is not simply an either/or condition. Rather, states may fall along a broad continuum in terms of their relative institutional strength, both at the aggregate level and within individual dimensions of state function. Equally important, states' level of function (or dysfunction) may represent a variable mixture of inadequate capacity and insufficient will.[20] The second is a sophisticated understanding of the conditions under which state weakness may increase a country's propensity to fall victim to or enable negative "spillovers," ranging from terrorism to infectious disease. The third is the recognition that all weak states are embedded in a larger global system that can exert both positive and pernicious effects on their resilience and vulnerability. The fourth is an awareness of how transnational threats, such as crime, terrorism, or disease, can further undermine the capacity and will of weak states to meet their obligations to citizens and the international community.

This book seeks to fill these gaps. It begins by delving more deeply into the definition of state weakness, identifying its potential sources and expressions. Chapter 1 introduces an Index of State Weakness in the Developing World, which permits one to gauge relative state performance across 141 developing countries. Chapters 2–6 then probe the potential connections between state fragility and five of the most pressing global threats to U.S. and international security: transnational terrorism; the proliferation of weapons of mass destruction; cross-border criminal activity; energy insecurity; and major infectious disease. Where relevant, these chapters also reveal reverse linkages, that is, the role of transnational forces in weakening local governance in the developing world.

Understanding State Weakness and Its Consequences

The point of departure for assessing common claims about "weak and failed states" is clarity about the meaning of "state weakness," or "fragility" (terms that the book uses interchangeably). As chapter 1 points out, a weak (or fragile) state is one that struggles to fulfill the fundamental security, political, economic, and social functions that have come to be associated with sovereign statehood. These four core functions include: preserving a monopoly over the use of armed force within a given territory and providing its inhabitants with security from physical violence; maintaining effective, accountable, and legitimate institutions of government that protect the basic rights of citizens; creating a legal and regulatory environment conducive to private sector activity and broadly shared growth; and meeting basic social welfare needs, including in the spheres of health and education.

Particularly in the developing world, many states have difficulty fulfilling even the most basic responsibilities of statehood. The reasons are partly historical. Although state sovereignty has been a bedrock of international legal and political order since the mid-seventeenth century, it is a comparatively recent phenomenon in much of the post-colonial world, a belated effort to superimpose a Western model of the legal-rational state onto often unpromising political, geographical, social, and cultural foundations.

Generally speaking, a state's propensity to weakness or even failure is determined by dynamic feedback among four sets of variables: its baseline level of institutional resilience; the presence of long-term drivers (or "risk factors") of instability; the nature of the state's external environment (whether positive or negative); and the occurrence of short-term shocks or "triggering" events. In extreme circumstances, as in the Democratic Republic of the Congo or Liberia in the recent past, some weak states may actually fail. This typically occurs when the political legitimacy of the governing regime evaporates and the state faces an existential armed threat to its survival. The vast majority of fragile states, however, fall along a continuum of performance between the extremes of effective statehood and outright failure.

After reviewing the strengths and shortcomings of previous approaches to measuring state fragility, chapter 1 introduces an Index of State Weakness in the Developing World, which the author developed with Susan E. Rice. Using twenty widely accepted indicators as proxies for state performance, the Index ranks 141 developing and transitional countries according to how well they fulfill the four basic functions of statehood. States ranking in the bottom two quintiles of the Index are separated into three tiers: "failed," "critically weak," and "weak." The Index also identifies a number of "states to watch." These countries earn higher aggregate scores but nevertheless possess worrisome shortcomings in at least one area of state function.

The Index offers a useful picture of relative state performance at a single point in time. What it does not reveal is whether state weakness in any given case is primarily a function of (objectively) low capacity or of inadequate commitment by the ruling regime to fulfill basic state functions. Nor does the static ranking tell us whether the country is headed in a negative or positive direction. To supplement the Index, chapter 1 proposes additional taxonomies of state weakness, depending on the nature of the ruling regime and the country's trajectory. Making such distinctions is essential if policymakers hope to tailor strategies to specific fragile states.

The chapter closes by enumerating the potential implications of state weakness for three categories of interested parties: for the state's inhabitants themselves; for the surrounding region; and for the wider international community. The burden of state fragility falls hardest, of course, on the citizens of weak and failing states, which are home to the vast majority of the "bottom billion" of humanity. The regional implications of state fragility can also be immense, however, with neighboring countries suffering from additional instability and conflict, spillovers of humanitarian disasters, and years of lost economic growth. Such local and regional instability may have important strategic implications for the United States, for instance by undermining friendly governments, weakening regional anchors of U.S. foreign policy, and limiting or reversing economic and democratic gains.

By themselves, the humanitarian, economic, political, and regional implications of state fragility would be enough to warrant sustained policy attention from U.S. policymakers. It is above all the risk of transnational threats, however, that has animated U.S. and Western concern with the world's weak and failing states. Chapters 2–6 thus look more closely at recent claims by U.S. officials and others that weak and failing states are disproportionately implicated in five critical global threats: transnational terrorism; proliferation of weapons of mass destruction; transnational crime; energy insecurity; and infectious disease.

TRANSNATIONAL TERRORISM

A central motivation for recent U.S. and international attention to weak and failing states is the conviction that such countries enable transnational terrorist networks. "Weak and impoverished states and ungoverned areas are…susceptible to exploitation by terrorists," declares the 2006 U.S. National Security Strategy. Such claims seem plausible. All things being equal, terrorist groups would presumably prefer to operate within corrupt, unstable, and violent states that lack effective control over their territories. Weak states from Sudan to Pakistan have at times provided transnational terrorist organizations, including al-Qaeda, with certain benefits. These include offering sanctuary to conduct and plan operations; access to weapons, conflict experience, financial resources, and pools of recruits; supply lines, transit zones, staging grounds and targets for attack; and opportunities to gain ideological support through provision of services left by the vacuum of state capacity. Certainly, jihadist web sites have identified weak and failing states as attractive targets of opportunity for al-Qaeda and affiliated organizations.

With these presumed connections in mind, the U.S. National Strategy for Combating Terrorism commits the United States to "diminishing the underlying conditions that terrorists seek to exploit," by bolstering state capacities, alleviating poverty, and promoting good governance. A major strategic aim in the U.S.-led campaign against global terrorism is to deny terrorists access to poorly governed lands, including in Africa, where porous borders, political instability, and lawless regions are perceived as vulnerabilities.[21]

Chapter 2 takes a closer look at the connection between state weakness and transnational terrorism, focusing on the most pressing terrorist threat to U.S. and international security: the global presence and activities of al-Qaeda and the broader Salafi jihadist movement. Based on an analysis of global patterns and specific country case studies, it concludes that the links between state weakness and transnational terrorism are more complicated and tenuous than often assumed. To begin with, it is obvious that not all (or even most) weak and failed states are afflicted by terrorism. By itself, weak capacity cannot explain why terrorist activity is concentrated in the Middle East and broader Muslim world, rather than other regions like Central Africa. Clearly, other variables and dynamics—including political, religious, cultural, and geographical factors—shape its global distribution.

Nor are all weak and failing states equally attractive to transnational terrorists. Conventional wisdom holds that collapsed, lawless polities like Somalia are particularly vulnerable. In fact, terrorists are likely to find *weak but functioning* states like Pakistan or Kenya more congenial long term bases of operations. Such poorly governed states are fragile and susceptible to corruption, but they also provide easy access to the financial and logistical infrastructure of the global economy, including communications technology, transportation, and banking services.[22] Moreover, weak states may be of declining importance to transnational terrorists as the al-Qaeda threat has evolved from a centrally directed network, dependent on a "base," into a more diffuse global movement, with autonomous cells in dozens of countries, poor and wealthy alike.

Moreover, some of the supposed benefits of weak states to transnational terrorists are less important than often assumed. Among the most attractive attributes such states present to terrorists are safe havens for leadership cadres; conflict experience for terrorist fighters; opportunities for training and planning; and weak border and customs control. With important exceptions, however, weak states rarely provide large pools of recruits, attractive targets of operations, or opportunities to win popular support through the performance of para-state functions. Whether states provide lucrative sources of terrorist financing depends on the presence of exploitable resources.

Beyond these factors, two other sets of variables appear critical in determining the attractiveness of fragile states to transnational terrorists. The first are the social/cultural attributes of the country in question. Although national security experts often speak of "ungoverned" spaces, such territories are more commonly "alternatively" governed, by non-state forms of social and political arrangements, including tribes. The specific cultural and social milieu of the state (or region) in question—and the interests and ideology of local power-wielders—will often determine whether transnational terrorists are able to set up shop. The second, arguably most important, variable is the attitude of the state itself. Independent of a state's objective *capacity* to oppose terrorism, its actual *policy* may occupy a blurry middle ground between wholehearted sponsorship and clear opposition. As U.S. experiences with Pakistan in the years following 9/11 underscore, even countries designated "critical allies in the global war on terrorism" may pursue ambiguous policies, particularly if the state itself is internally fragmented.

The chapter's overall conclusion is that weak and failing states can provide useful assets to transnational terrorists, but they may be less indispensable to their operations than is widely believed. Moreover, weak state commitment may be as important as weak state capacity in determining the global distribution of transnational terrorism.

WEAPONS OF MASS DESTRUCTION (WMD) PROLIFERATION

Fears that weak and failing states may incubate transnational terrorism merge with a related concern: that poorly governed countries may—deliberately or otherwise—facilitate the global spread of weapons of mass destruction or their component parts and technology. These are not idle worries. According to the British government, beyond the five permanent members of the UN Security Council, thirteen of the seventeen states with current or suspended WMD programs are "countries at risk of instability."[23] Perhaps the most frightening prospect is that a nuclear armed weak state like Pakistan or North Korea might lose control of its weapons, placing them directly in the hands of a successor regime (or non-state actors) with little compunction about using them. Direct transfer of functioning WMD is not the only concern, however. Revelations about the international nuclear arms bazaar of Abdul Qadeer Khan have suggested that poor governance in the developing world may be the weak link in global non-proliferation efforts.

Chapter 3 identifies and evaluates five potential "proliferation pathways" by which fragile states might exacerbate the growing WMD threat. First, a fragile state could itself decide to purchase, steal, or develop weapons of mass destruction, or consciously assist other states or non-state actors in doing so. Second, state or non-state proliferators could target WMD weapons or materials located in weak states for theft or diversion, without the knowledge or consent of the host country. Third, WMD traffickers could exploit weak states as intermediaries and transshipment points for their activities. Fourth, fragile states could provide sanctuaries for non-state actors seeking to develop their own weapons. Finally, the collapse of a WMD-armed state could result in the unauthorized transfer of nuclear, biological, and chemical weapons to non-state actors.

The chapter uses a mixture of global data and case studies to suggest that not all of these scenarios are equally plausible. Weak states do possess important vulnerabilities that provide an opening for would-be proliferators. These include incomplete territorial control, weak law enforcement, poor security, and high corruption. Overall, however, the connection between state weakness and WMD proliferation is more limited than often presumed. Perhaps most significantly, few fragile states currently possess or indeed seek nuclear, chemical, and biological weapons, and thus the vast majority of countries in this cohort do not present major proliferation concerns. The two glaring exceptions are North Korea and Pakistan, both nuclear-armed states that have served as important sources of WMD-related technology and materials for other countries. Taken collectively, however, the world's fragile states pose less acute risks for WMD proliferation than do a number of countries that score more highly on the Index. These include Russia, whose vast and poorly secured nuclear stockpiles have long been considered a major proliferation risk, as well as Iran, Syria, and several other countries in the Middle East.

The apparent lesson is that the biggest WMD proliferation risks emanate less from weak states than from countries that are superficially strong. Such countries are more likely to have the capacity to seek nuclear as well as chemical and biological weapons, but still suffer from governance gaps that can be exploited by proliferators. The A. Q. Khan case is revealing in this regard. On the one hand, as David Albright and Corey Hinderstein write, "The Khan network could not have evolved into such a dangerous supplier without the utter corruption and dishonesty of successive Pakistani governments."[24] But it also could not have gone global, they add, without institutional weaknesses in more advanced middle-income countries, including Malaysia, South Africa, and Turkey, that possessed manufacturing capabilities but lacked the capacity or will to implement relevant export controls and non-proliferation laws.

TRANSNATIONAL CRIME

Transnational criminal activity has surged in the two decades since the end of the Cold War, paralleling the dramatic expansion of licit cross-border transactions. Weak and failing states are often portrayed as critical nodes in this global trend, providing convenient bases for groups involved in the production, transit, or trafficking of drugs, weapons, people, and other illicit commodities, and in the laundering of the profits from such activities. On its face, this connection seems logical. If given a choice of where to conduct operations, criminal groups would presumably be attracted to corrupt, unstable, and dysfunctional states that lack the capacity or the will to deliver impartial justice and the rule of law, provide for the safety of their inhabitants, enforce private contracts, and regulate economic activity.

Chapter 4 explores the linkages between state fragility and transnational crime, focusing on six sectors often cited as being facilitated by weak governance: narcotics production and transit, human trafficking, the illicit small arms trade, money laundering, environmental crime, and maritime piracy. As elsewhere, the book combines an in-depth analysis of global patterns along with targeted country case studies, including of Haiti, Afghanistan, Guinea-Bissau, Cambodia, and Somalia.

The resulting picture is one in which patterns of transnational crime are imperfectly correlated with state weakness. Fragile states can indeed provide criminal networks with important functional benefits. These include high levels of corruption and weak rule of law; safe havens for illicit activity; poor border and customs control; lack of licit economic alternatives; and unique criminal opportunities provided by violent conflict and its immediate aftermath.

As with transnational terrorism and proliferation, however, the relationship between state fragility and cross-border criminality is variable and complicated. To begin with, the strength of the connection depends on the nature of the criminal activity. Weak states rank high as hotbeds of certain types of narcotics production, illegal arms trafficking (as destination countries), and maritime piracy, but there is no obvious relationship when it comes to human trafficking, money laundering, drug transit, or environmental crime. Such states play only a marginal role in other realms of transnational crime, such as intellectual property theft, cybercrime, and the counterfeiting of manufactured goods.

Furthermore, as with terrorism, weaker is not necessarily better for transnational criminals. In a global economy, realizing high returns requires tapping a worldwide market to sell illicit commodities and launder the proceeds, which in turn depends on access to financial services and a modern telecommunications and transportation infrastructure—which many of the weakest states lack. Failed or critically weak states may thus be less attractive than superficially functional states, which provide a baseline level of order and easy access to international commerce while also affording opportunities to corrupt political authorities and exploit various governance gaps. Geographical location and proximity to the global marketplace may also trump the weakness of state institutions as enticements for criminals. Such considerations help account for the activities of transnational criminal groups in many middle-income and even highly developed countries.

Finally, the chapter suggests that the relationship between transnational crime and state fragility is a dynamic and parasitic one. A state's vulnerability to transnational criminals and its commitment to combating their activities are in part a function of the state's penetration by those same illicit actors. Beyond benefiting from fragility, criminals often deepen it, deploying corruption as a tool to weaken state institutions and, in extreme cases, to "capture" the state itself.

ENERGY INSECURITY

The tremendous volatility in global oil prices in the first decade of the twenty-first century helped to place energy at the top of the U.S. and global security agenda. In the first eight years of the decade, the price of a barrel of oil increased more than three and a half times. Although prices fell sharply as a result of the global financial crisis that began in late 2008, most analysts expect the upward trend to resume, given rapidly rising demand in emerging countries and dwindling reserves, investment, and production in major producing states. In such an environment, analysts and officials have argued, U.S. and global energy security will increasingly rely on supplies of oil and gas from weak and failing states, from Nigeria to Angola to Iraq.

Chapter 5 takes a closer look at the influence of state weakness on the availability, reliability, and cost of global energy. The chapter focuses primarily on oil, likely to remain the world's most important source of commercial energy and the dominant preoccupation in U.S. energy security for the foreseeable future.

In principle, countries suffering from weak or dysfunctional governance could endanger global energy security in several ways, whether these countries are suppliers, transit states, or simply situated in proximity to world energy choke points. First, political instability and violence, terrorist or insurgent attacks on energy infrastructure, widespread social unrest, and rampant criminality in some fragile states may endanger the production or transit of oil and gas. Second, poor governance in energy-rich states, including high levels of corruption and weak rule of law, may discourage or thwart productive investment in energy exploration and production, limiting the ability of such states to meet growing demand on world energy markets. Third, natural resource bonanzas may well exacerbate the pathologies of fragile states, reinforcing patterns of authoritarian governance, hindering investment in other sectors of the economy, and exacerbating the risk of violent conflict between groups competing for access to revenue streams. Chapter 5 shows how these dynamics play out in a number of developing countries, from Nigeria to Iraq to Colombia to Chad.

Although the threat posed by weak states to U.S. energy security has sometimes been overstated, it remains real and is likely to grow as global demand surges in the years ahead. As the world becomes increasingly dependent on fragile-state producers, the reliability and price of oil and gas supplies will be more and more subject to the internal dynamics of weak states.

At the same time, the chapter reveals that many of these vulnerabilities are not limited to fragile states. Indeed, the greatest threat to global energy security may come not from those countries ranked in the bottom quintile of the Index of State Weakness but rather from better-performing countries, including several classified as "states to watch," such as Venezuela, Iran, and Russia. Besides suffering from governance gaps that discourage investments in their energy sectors, such countries are also more likely to use their energy resources to pursue political ends at odds with those of the United States and its allies.

INFECTIOUS DISEASE

The rapid spread of avian influenza, with the potential to kill tens of millions of people, and the more recent emergence of H1N1 ("swine flu") have made infectious disease a first tier national security issue. At first blush, the connection between state weakness and pandemic threat would appear strong. In an age of mass travel and global commerce, a government unable or unwilling to respond to a disease outbreak with vigorous public health measures is a potential threat to countless lives across the globe. Many disease agents that have emerged in recent decades, including HIV/AIDS, Ebola, and West Nile virus, originated in developing countries; national security and public health experts alike worry that weak and failed states—which invest little in epidemiological surveillance, health information and reporting systems, primary health care delivery, preventive measures, or response capacity—lack the means to detect and contain such outbreaks. States in the bottom two quintiles of the Index are also among the main victims of the world's seven deadliest infectious diseases: respiratory infections, HIV/AIDS, diarrheal diseases, TB, malaria, hepatitis B, and measles, some of which are emerging in drug-resistant strains that pose serious challenges to global public health.

Chapter 6 takes a closer look at the purported link between state fragility and the most serious infectious disease threats, and finds that while shortcomings in state capacity and commitment can facilitate the emergence and spread of infectious disease, globally there is no consistent relationship between levels of state fragility and patterns of pandemics. A number of ecological, geographic, cultural, technological, and demographic variables having little to do with state capacity help to determine whether (and which) developing countries are susceptible to spawning and spreading infectious disease. There is no question that many infectious diseases are incubated in weak and failing states, exacting a horrific human toll. But only some of these diseases pose direct threats to U.S. national security, while a number of critical infectious diseases (including avian flu) are concentrated not in the weakest countries, but in stronger developing states. Indeed, the most promising disease vectors may be better-performing countries that are more integrated into the global economy, yet suffer from limited but critical governance gaps.

The chapter begins by analyzing the contemporary global threat of infectious disease, distinguishing among various pathogens according to their ease of transmission, mortality rates, potential economic impact, and geographic scope. Three main categories emerge from this exercise: (1) endemic diseases, including tuberculosis, malaria, measles, and hepatitis B and C; (2) diseases with short-wave, rapid-onset pandemic potential, such as influenza and Severe Acute Respiratory Syndrome (SARS); and (3) long wave pandemics, notably HIV/AIDS, which have the ability to afflict millions around the world but over the course of many years. Of these, rapid-onset pandemics pose the most immediate and alarming threat to U.S. national security, while long-wave pandemics are a serious but more manageable concern. Endemic diseases, while exacting enormous human costs at a national and regional level—and thus worthy of attention on humanitarian grounds—are least likely to have a direct impact on U.S. security.

The chapter then explores whether and how fragile states facilitate the spread of pandemic diseases. The picture is mixed. It concludes, first, that countries are more likely to serve as vectors of disease if they suffer from critical shortcomings in state capacity, particularly in the area of public health, including inadequate levels of funding, poor health infrastructure, organizational and public policy gaps, and a dearth of human services. These shortcomings not only decrease baseline levels of public health but also impair the ability of states to quickly detect and respond to disease outbreaks. The inability of many weak states to control their borders and the persistence of violent conflict within them can also serve as infectious disease multipliers. Second, insufficient will on the part of governing regimes to tackle public health problems can be an important enabling factor in the spread of disease, often trumping baseline state capacity in determining effective national and international responses. Lack of candor and resistance to external assistance can pose as great a threat to global public health as decrepit infrastructure—and such shortcomings are often most prevalent in countries of middling performance, rather than the weakest states. Finally, the chapter notes that, contrary to widespread fears that infectious disease might exacerbate instability and even state failure in the developing world, there is little evidence that endemic or long-wave disease actually leads to violence or state collapse.

CONCLUSIONS AND POLICY IMPLICATIONS

The book's Conclusion makes three main points. First, the relationship between state fragility and transnational threats is more complicated and contingent than the conventional wisdom would suggest. It depends on the threat in question, the specific sources of state weakness, and the will of a regime—not simply its inherent capacity—to assume sovereign functions. Globally, most fragile states do not present significant security risks, except to their own people, and the most important spillovers that preoccupy U.S. national security officials are at least as likely to emanate from stronger developing countries, rather than the world's weakest countries. Where such linkages do exist, the most salient governance gaps tend to be in the political and security arenas—notably high levels of corruption, weak rule of law, and a history of violent conflict—rather than in the economic and social welfare spheres (such as absence of economic growth or failure to meet basic human needs).[25] And when poor state performance is associated with transnational threats, it often reflects weak commitment by the ruling regime to meet obligations to its citizens and the international community, rather than an inherent lack of capability.

Second, the United States retains a compelling interest, for humanitarian as well as strategic reasons, in helping fragile states—as well as more stable developing countries—improve their institutional performance. Unfortunately, the U.S. government's recent approach to state fragility has been reactive, fragmented, militarized, under-resourced, and self-contained. The conclusion calls on the United States to formulate a preventive, government-wide "fragile states strategy" that can be tailored to local conditions. As part of such a strategy, the U.S. government should adapt its conventional development aid and policy to the realities of fragile states; invest in the civilian U.S. capabilities necessary to advance good governance and security in such contexts; and rebalance the military, diplomatic, and development components of its engagement. Most importantly, it must embrace a multilateral approach to the problem of state fragility, coordinating its efforts with like-minded donor governments and international institutions to share the burdens and increase the legitimacy of its state-building initiatives.

Finally, developing a generic fragile state strategy is not enough. The United States and other international actors must also formulate targeted interventions to cut connections between fragile statehood and transnational threats where these exist, shaping incentives and deploying resources that bolster the capacity and the will of vulnerable regimes to exercise responsible sovereignty, including curtailing spillovers across their borders. The Conclusion outlines specific initiatives that rich world countries can take to mitigate the risks from fragile states; these include modifying some of their own counterproductive policies (such as source control approaches to counter-narcotics) that inadvertently exacerbate state weakness and vulnerability. At the same time, policymakers must design and implement such threat-specific initiatives in a manner that complements rather than undermines more broad-based efforts to advance sustainable economic growth, promote good governance, and advance human security. Some trade-offs will be inevitable, of course. But the United States and its international partners should beware pursuing short-term "fixes" to perceived threats—like bolstering authoritarian regimes to combat terrorism or ensure steady access to oil resources—that may undercut the long-term pursuit of resilient, effective, and accountable state institutions.

1

LEFT BEHIND:
UNDERSTANDING STATE FRAGILITY

Capable states control their territory, govern justly, provide security and essential services, protect their citizens' rights, and offer their people hope for a better future. When a country cannot—or will not—perform these core functions, when a nation is wracked by war, when a state becomes a shell, its people suffer immediately. But over the longer term, a fragile state can also incubate global trouble that can spread far beyond its borders. And that is where the transnational threats of the twenty-first century too often begin.
—*U.S. Ambassador to the United Nations Susan E. Rice, August 2009*[1]

In the decades to come, the most lethal threats to the United States' safety and security—a city poisoned or reduced to rubble by a terrorist attack—are likely to emanate from states that cannot adequately govern themselves or secure their own territory. Dealing with such fractured and failing states is, in many ways, the main security challenge of our time.
—*Secretary of Defense Robert M. Gates, May 2010*[2]

The problem of state failure has risen to the top of the international security agenda over the past two decades, as the world turned its attention to terrorism, genocide, weapons of mass destruction (WMD) proliferation, and infectious diseases. The concept describes a phenomenon ignored for most of the twentieth century—that of a nation that fails to fulfill the requirements of sovereign statehood. Scholars, officials, and pundits alike point to the growing threat that such countries pose, not only to their own inhabitants but to the international community at large.

Yet there is little consensus about the number and identity of today's weak, failed, and failing states, nor about the criteria that would warrant such designations. Without greater clarity about the nature, causes, and expressions of state weakness, policymakers will be in no position to discern, map, and contain the transnational "spillovers" that may arise from it.

This chapter attempts to fill these gaps. It begins by considering the origins and motivations of contemporary concern with state weakness (or fragility, to use the currently preferred term[3]), and the analytical shortcomings of current paradigms. The chapter then provides historical context, summarizing the origins, gradual spread, and evolving functions of the sovereign state, emphasizing that the state is a relatively recent form of political organization, particularly in the postcolonial world, which helps to account for its current difficulties.

After reviewing the various definitions and measures of state failure that have guided (and at times confused) the debate among scholars and policymakers, the chapter introduces a new approach to measuring state fragility: the Index of State Weakness in the Developing World. This Index, which the author designed with Susan E. Rice (then a fellow at the Brookings Institution) permits comparisons of state strength across 141 developing and transitional countries based on their performance in providing four critical sets of goods: physical security, legitimate political institutions, effective economic management, and basic social welfare. A state is weak (or fragile) to the degree that it has deficits in one or all of these dimensions. Based on the Index, the chapter distinguishes among four categories of fragile states: a handful of truly "failed" states; a bottom quintile of "critically weak" states; a slightly stronger cohort of "weak" states; and a set of "states to watch" that suffer from important institutional gaps. The chapter underscores that state weakness is not an either/or designation but rather a relative condition, with different countries falling along a spectrum both in their overall performance and on particular aspects of state function.

The Index provides a useful snapshot of state performance at a single moment in time. It does not, however, capture critical dimensions of state fragility, including whether weakness is caused primarily by an inherent lack of capacity, or by inadequate will on the part of the ruling regime. Nor does it specify the trajectory of the state. This chapter proposes additional parameters to capture these and other dimensions of state weakness. The chapter then briefly reviews some of the factors, both internal and external, that may cause fragile states to weaken further and, in some circumstances, to fail entirely. The chapter closes by enumerating the potential consequences of state weakness for the state and its inhabitants; for the surrounding region; and for the wider international community, including the United States.

THE "FAILED STATE": UNPRECEDENTED ATTENTION, LITTLE CLARITY

Over the past decade, "failed states" have gained unprecedented attention in both official policy and popular discourse. This preoccupation reflects a confluence of security, development, and human rights concerns—and the recognition that the sovereign state remains a critical foundation of world order. In an age of globalization, building effective and legitimate states is widely seen as the key to preserving international peace and security, winning the war against global poverty, and advancing justice around the world. Of these factors, security considerations have usually been uppermost in the minds of American foreign policy officials, who perceive weak states as a growing source of threats to the lives and well-being of American citizens.

The intellectual antecedents of this perspective can be traced to the early post–Cold War years, when a shocking outburst of internal violence and state collapse from Somalia to Yugoslavia to Rwanda seemed to herald a "new world disorder." Journalist Robert Kaplan luridly portrayed state failure in West Africa as portending a "coming anarchy" that would engulf much of the developing world. The respected Harvard political scientist Samuel Huntington, meanwhile, anticipated "a global breakdown of law and order" triggered by "failed states." Within the Clinton administration, USAID administrator Brian Atwood warned that "disintegrating societies and states with their civil conflicts and destabilizing refugee flows have emerged as the greatest menace to global stability."[4] Such concerns led Vice President Albert Gore to create and chair an interagency State Failure Task Force, intended to help predict—and where possible head off—incipient state collapse.

Despite this growing attention, however, the mainstream U.S. national security establishment continued to regard the problems of weak and failed states primarily as a third-tier national security problem. Indeed, President Clinton's decisions to intervene in the affairs of weak states such as Bosnia and Haiti elicited strong condemnation from self-described foreign policy "realists," particularly in the Republican Party.[5]

This changed after the attacks of September 11, 2001. Republicans and Democrats alike quickly embraced the view that weak states could pose mortal dangers to American security. As Secretary of State Condoleezza Rice explained in 2005, in an age of transnational threats, states unable to exercise "responsible sovereignty" can generate a host of "spillover effects."[6] Four years later, the Obama administration's envoy to the United Nations, Susan E. Rice, made the same point: "In a globalized age, the troubles that ravage fragile states can ultimately menace sturdy ones. Whether the peril is terrorism, pandemics, narcotics, human trafficking, or civil strife, a state so weak that it incubates a threat is also a state too weak to contain a threat."[7] Potential responses range from development assistance to (in extreme cases) military operations, to assist local authorities in building state capacity and gaining control over "ungoverned spaces" that might otherwise be exploited by nefarious actors.[8]

In parallel with these security imperatives, the United States and other countries have come to realize that fragile states constitute "the toughest development challenge of our era," in the words of World Bank president Robert Zoellick.[9] The international community is thus devoting new attention to the dilemmas caused by states whose lack of capacity or will renders traditional models of development cooperation ineffectual. Many of these states have been left behind as the donor community directs a growing proportion of aid to "good performers," in the belief that assistance is most effective in sound institutional and policy environments.[10] Whatever the merits of this approach, the United States and other donors have struggled to engage states at the other end of the development spectrum: some fifty-odd fragile states, home to perhaps a billion of the world's inhabitants.[11]

A third main impetus for increased attention to weak and failing states is growing global attention to human rights issues—and awareness that gross abuses frequently arise in weak and failing states. In 2005, UN member states endorsed a new international norm known as the "responsibility to protect," which holds that all states have an obligation to protect their citizens from genocide, ethnic cleansing, and other crimes against humanity. The doctrine also raises the prospect of international intervention if a state fails to prevent mass atrocities—or itself commits them.

In sum, policymakers and analysts in the United States and abroad increasingly view the emergence of effective and accountable states as central to the quest for international peace and security, the alleviation of global poverty, and the spread of universal human rights.

The "Failed State" Reconsidered

Despite this unprecedented recent attention, the concept of the "failed state" remains vague and imprecise. Analytical shortcomings include the absence of clear criteria to measure weakness or define "failure," and an inattention to the specific histories, trajectories, and regimes of the countries so designated. The concept of the "failed state" also raises troubling normative questions, implicitly placing the blame entirely on developing countries for their current circumstances, and (at least potentially) privileging the preservation of domestic order over the pursuit of justice.

Perhaps the main limitation of the "failed state" concept is the lack of agreement among both policymakers and scholars about the particular characteristics that warrant such a designation. As Charles Call observes, scholars have proposed a wide range of idiosyncratic indicators to measure state failure.[12] Lacking a consensus definition, analysts tend to lump all troubled developing countries into a single, catchall "failed state" category. Besides obscuring their unique cultural legacies, historical experiences, and current challenges, this hodgepodge approach risks encouraging generic, one-size-fits-all policies instead of thoughtful interventions tailored to the unique causes and expressions of instability in a given case.

This grab-bag approach to "failed states" likewise does not distinguish among troubled countries based on the commitment—as opposed to capacity—of their regimes to deliver the basic goods associated with statehood and to engage constructively with the international community. It makes little sense, for example, to group North Korea—whose authoritarian leader Kim Jong Il fields one of the largest armies in the world while his citizens starve—or Zimbabwe—a once-promising country driven into the ground by President Robert Mugabe—with post-conflict East Timor or Liberia, whose recent governments have demonstrated the will but often lacked the capacity to meet the needs of their people.

The blanket "failed state" label also raises normative hackles. First, it is ahistorical, ignoring that many of the countries so designated have *never* been effective states in the Western territorial and bureaucratic model. Particularly in Africa, many are artificial creations of the European scramble for empire and subsequent abrupt decolonization. Such "quasi-states" possess the nominal trappings of sovereignty but little of the substance, and their arbitrary borders encompass diverse and often fractious political communities. Upon independence, many became objects of Cold War competition and patronage, further distorting their institutional development. Given such unpromising beginnings, when one of them "fails," "what has collapsed is more the *vision* (or dream) of the progressive developmental state" imagined in Western minds "than any real existing state."[13]

Second, the failed state designation lays the culpability for state weakness and its attendant spillovers squarely at the feet of dysfunctional governments and societies in the developing world. While authoritarianism and corruption are indeed often implicated in overall weak state capacity, the sources of state weakness are often *in part* a function of sins of omission or commission in the global North. These include a tendency for wealthy countries (and firms) to cast aside concerns for good governance in resource-rich countries; sustain demand for narcotics and other illicit commodities; provide financial havens for the ill-gotten gains of developing world kleptocrats; and engage in a lucrative trade in armaments that subsequently circulate freely in the world's conflict zones.[14]

Finally, the "failed state" lens arguably encourages rich world policies that promote stable but not necessarily just or equitable rule in the developing world. Just as Cold War security concerns led the United States and its allies to promote strongman rule in the periphery, there is a risk that in the context of today's "global war on terrorism" policymakers may pursue a shallow approach to state-building, encouraging regimes that promise short-term stability rather than supporting the slow and painstaking work of creating legitimate, participatory institutions of governance capable of ensuring the security of their populations.

Notwithstanding analytical flaws and normative objections in current approaches to "failed states," there is merit in attempting to distinguish among countries in the developing world on the basis of their relative institutional strength. Doing so, however, requires greater clarity about which functions states should perform—and how domestic and international expectations of those functions have changed over time.

THE SOVEREIGN STATE: ITS ORIGINS, SPREAD, AND FUNCTIONS

The starting point for understanding state weakness is an appreciation of the history of the "state" and its functions. Under the minimalist definition provided by international law (under the 1931 Montevideo Convention), the state is an independent political entity with recognized sovereignty over a specific geographic area and population, which is capable of entering into relations with other such entities. From a political and sociological perspective, the state is a territorial form of social order that enjoys legitimate authority over a given territory and its inhabitants, including a monopoly over the use of armed force, sole power to levy taxes, and the ability to enforce binding rules of governance. Statehood has both *juridical* and *empirical* dimensions. Juridical statehood is focused *outward*, implying recognition as a sovereign entity under international law. Empirical statehood, in contrast, is the ability to project administrative and regulatory power *within* defined territorial borders. This is an important distinction, since a state may have one but not the other.

The Origins of the State

The sovereign state is so taken for granted as the bedrock of the international system that it is easy to forget its relatively recent origins. For millennia, humans organized themselves into an array of different social groupings, ranging from hunter-gatherer bands to tribes, city-states, confederations, khanates, kingdoms, suzerainties, satrapies, and empires. It was only in the seventeenth century that the state—based on the principles of sovereignty, territorial integrity, and noninterference—achieved privileged status within Europe.[15]

This transformation—while more protracted than a single event would imply—is conventionally dated to the Peace of Westphalia in 1648, which ended the Thirty Years' War. That settlement, designed to put an end to the wars of religion that had convulsed the continent, established two fundamental principles for European political order. The first was *rex imperator in regno suo*—the king is emperor in his own realm. The second was *cuius regio eius religio*—whose the region, his the religion. In effect, the agreement recognized states as independent units, with supreme jurisdiction over a given territory and population, and entitled to equal treatment under international law. The triumph of state sovereignty helped stabilize European political order by making intervention the exception rather than the rule, providing a predictable foundation for diplomatic negotiation among juridically equal actors, and advancing the development of international law.[16]

Over the following three centuries, European imperial expansion exported the Western model of the sovereign territorial state to the wider world. This was a tumultuous and brutal affair, with the imposed colonial state "colliding with existing forms of political, cultural and economic order."[17] Where authoritative structures of indigenous rule were present, as in the Indian subcontinent, the superstructure of the colonial state was grafted onto existing social systems. Where such institutions did not exist or had been decimated (as in much of the Americas and in Australia), Europeans created colonial states out of whole cloth.

During successive waves of decolonization, these overseas possessions eventually became independent, sovereign states in their own right. The Charter of the United Nations, signed in 1945, enshrined the doctrines of sovereign equality and nonintervention as foundations of the postwar international order. By 1965, the number of UN member states had more than doubled, from 51 to 117, reaching 192 by the turn of the millennium. The global spread of sovereignty has not, however, always translated into effective statehood. Many UN member states enjoy *de jure* but not *de facto* sovereignty: Their status as full members of the international community is not matched by their authority, practical capacity, or in some cases willingness to control or administer their own territories, protect their populations from physical violence, or provide them with the most basic public goods. They are, in effect, states "by courtesy."[18]

The abruptness of decolonization is partly to blame. Many of today's postcolonial states, particularly in Africa and Asia, achieved independence only two or at most three generations ago—a brief window in which to accomplish the processes of state building. Particularly in sub-Saharan Africa, European powers artificially accelerated the process of state formation by imposing the trappings of sovereignty—national borders, administrative structures, bureaucratic rules, armies and the like—onto traditional institutions. They often did so arbitrarily, with little regard to patterns of political and ethnic affiliation or the economic, demographic, or geographic viability of the resulting polity. The rapid emancipation of European colonies after World War II created dozens of states that possessed sovereign equality under international law but little of the empirical substance of statehood.[19] Under these circumstances, the expectation that the former colonies, in the throes of early state formation, could somehow avoid the protracted, tumultuous and often violent upheaval that accompanied analogous processes in Europe and the United States—much less quickly deliver security, legitimate institutions, economic growth, and social welfare to their citizens—appears in retrospect both historically ignorant and hopelessly naïve.

At its core, writes Christopher Clapham, "the 'problem' of failed states" is in large measure about "whether the grafting of such states...onto unpromising rootstock can be made to take."[20] Evidence to date provides grounds for pessimism. Recent research confirms that states with artificial borders, drawn in the chancelleries of the imperial powers, remain far more vulnerable than other developing countries to violent conflict, high corruption, underdevelopment, and other negative outcomes. In some cases, the state's authority has *never* been recognized as legitimate in large swaths of its national territory. In sum, while Westerners are inclined to see state fragility "as a 'deviation' from an OECD model," it is more accurately seen as "the 'norm' across much of the world."[21]

Prior to 1945, one obvious international response to state weakness and failure would have been territorial aggrandizement by stronger powers, including overseas imperial expansion. But this "solution" has been complicated by the evolution of international norms against colonialism and for the sanctity of international borders, as well as by recognition of the expense, difficulty, and limited economic benefits of traditional conquest in the contemporary world. Before World War II, "state death" was a relatively common occurrence (as the fate of Poland between 1795 and 1919 attests). It is no longer today. States may fail but—at least in juridical terms—they remain very much alive.[22]

The State and Its Functions

As the sovereign state has spread globally over the past several centuries, so the content of its social contract has evolved. By the early twenty-first century, statehood has come to imply an obligation to provide citizens with four main categories of political goods: physical security and territorial control; legitimate, representative, and accountable governance under the rule of law; competent economic management that provides an environment conducive to growth; and basic social welfare services to meet the fundamental needs of the population.[23]

The first and arguably most fundamental function of the state is to *ensure basic social order and protect inhabitants from the threat of violence from internal and external forces.* This is the Weberian conception of the state as an entity with a monopoly over the legitimate use of armed force within a defined territory. Charles Tilly has described the emergence of this state function in early modern Europe as a form of protection racket, in which powerful elites offered security in return for resource extraction (in the form of taxation), which enabled the proto-states to wage war against external enemies while expanding political control over their own territories. (In Tilly's famous formulation, "States make war, and war makes the state."[24]) This notion that the state is ultimately responsible for the basic physical security of its inhabitants, coupled with a monopoly on taxation, remains a core tenet of modern statehood. Increasingly, and particularly within democratic nations, the expectation is that the provision of security will be applied equally to all citizens and that the use of force will be under the ultimate control of accountable political authorities.

The second core function, reflecting the rise of the constitutional state during the nineteenth century, is to *provide legitimate, representative, and accountable governance under the rule of law*. The state's leaders should have the recognized authority to rule; reflect the general will and aspirations of the citizenry; protect fundamental human rights and liberties; and govern in a transparent and honest manner. This conception of statehood as a social contract between the rulers and the ruled can be traced back to the theories of Hobbes, Locke, and Rousseau, who sought secular justifications for allegiance to European sovereigns in the aftermath of the Peace of Westphalia. But it has expanded over time, thanks to the explosive force of nationalism and the global spread of democracy, which have deepened the expectation that the sovereign state, to be legitimate, must embody the will of the people.

The state's third major role is to *create a legal and regulatory framework conducive to economic growth and development*, including through the promotion of market activity and the accumulation and investment of financial, physical, and human capital. A crucial breakthrough in the history of capitalism was the emergence in early modern Europe of a vibrant merchant class that was autonomous of political authority and not—as has happened so frequently in history—smothered by it. The state over time developed a symbiotic relationship with the market, defining the rules according to which private actors could pursue their material self-interest, while ensuring a steady revenue stream for the state. Although the economic role of the modern state ranges widely, spanning laissez-faire to deeply interventionist policies, it is generally accepted that this role should include sound management of public finances and assets, enforcement of property rights, and efficient regulation of market activity.

The final core function of the state is to *provide basic social welfare*, including through delivery of services like water and sanitation and investments in health and education. This conception of effective statehood is comparatively recent, paralleling the origins of the welfare state in Europe and North America in the late nineteenth and early twentieth century and its subsequent spread, to varying degrees, throughout much of the world. Popular expectations about the state as a provider of social welfare expanded dramatically within industrialized countries during the twentieth century, accompanied by heavier taxation as a share of national income. By the early twenty-first century, populations in developed and developing countries alike took for granted the state's obligation to ensure the provision and delivery of at least a minimal array of public goods like education, sanitation, health, and infrastructure.

As this history suggests, understandings of what states should do domestically (as well as how they should behave internationally) have changed dramatically over the past several centuries, and will likely continue to do so. A century and a half ago, for example, few even in Europe imagined that the state would provide social insurance for its elderly citizens. Needless to say, publics in most countries continue to engage in vigorous debate over the legitimate scope of state functions—that is, the range of activities that the state should govern—as well as the expense and quality of the goods that it does provide.

MEASURING STATE WEAKNESS

Based on this common understanding of the core functions of any sovereign state, we can begin to compare states according to their relative performance in delivering these essential public goods.[25] The starting point for any discussion of "weak and failed" states is a recognition that state weakness (or fragility) is *relative* rather than a binary, either/or condition. That is, each state falls along a continuum, depending on the vitality of its institutions and the commitment of its governing regime to fulfill the basic duties of statehood. Recognizing where states fall along this spectrum, both overall and in specific sectors, permits both national authorities and outside actors to pinpoint sources of institutional weakness and target their policy interventions accordingly.

Despite numerous efforts to define and measure state weakness, there is no consensus on the precise number of "weak and failing states," nor indeed about how to define and measure the phenomenon. Divergent estimates reflect differences in the criteria used to define state weakness, the indicators used to gauge it, and the relative weighting of various aspects of governance.[26] Box 1.1 below summarizes the advantages and drawbacks of some leading approaches to defining and measuring state fragility.

Box 1.1: Existing Attempts to Define and Measure State Weakness

In recent years scholars and policymakers have made a number of quantitative and analytical efforts to define and measure state weakness and failure. While valuable, none is comprehensive. Perhaps the best known is the CIA-supported **State Failure (now Political Instability) Task Force**, which uses an extensive data set to isolate variables associated with the onset of a "severe internal political crisis." Although considered the most accurate predictor of severe "state failure," it is not geared to analyzing cases of more moderate or endemic weakness.[27] In another notable effort, the Center for Global Development's **Commission on Weak States and U.S. National Security** produced a 2004 report that classified fifty to sixty countries as "weak states" based on their failure to provide physical security, social welfare, and legitimate institutions.[28] However, the report relies on only three indicators to define its cohort, omits any quantitative indicators for economic performance, and does not rank states on relative performance.

The U.S. **Agency for International Development** USAID) in 2006 produced a model proposing thirty-three indicators for measuring the capacity and legitimacy of state institutions in four critical spheres of governance: security, political, economic, and social. Unfortunately, the initiative was shelved during the second term of the Bush administration, and its country-specific findings were never released publicly. In fact, among major donor agencies, only the United Kingdom's **Department for International Development (DFID)** has taken the bold step of producing a public list of fragile states, but the forty-six countries in its data set are not ranked according to their relative degree of weakness. Meanwhile, the World Bank's **Fragile and Conflict-Affected Countries Group** identifies roughly thirty extremely impoverished countries "characterized by weak policies, institutions, and governance" as Low-Income Countries Under Stress (LICUS). However, the LICUS designation is based largely on economic components of governance, with less weight given to security, political, and social considerations; and it is limited to those countries eligible for grants from the Bank's International Development Association (IDA) financing window, thus omitting a number of other fragile countries.[29]

Several indices actually rank state capacity and performance. The **Failed States Index**, published by *Foreign Policy* magazine and the Fund for Peace, uses proprietary software to grade states according to their susceptibility to political instability. The effort focuses primarily on the risk of violence rather than other aspects of institutional strength. A more comprehensive model is the **Country Indicators for Foreign Policy** (CIFP) Project of Carleton University, funded by the Canadian International Development Agency, which measures states' ability to provide basic governance functions on the basis of seventy-four indicators across ten dimensions of statehood. A **Sovereignty Index** developed by Ashraf Ghani, Clare Lockhart, and Michael Carnahan identifies ten areas used to assess a country's sovereignty gap, placing heavy emphasis on the financial and economic components of state function. The **Mo Ibrahim Foundation's Index of African Governance**, initially produced by Harvard's Robert I. Rotberg and Rachel Gisselquist, assesses the performance of forty-eight sub-Saharan African countries in five key governance areas: safety and security; rule of law, transparency, and corruption; participation and human rights; sustainable economic development; human development; and essential political goods. In addition, Monty G. Marshall and Jack A. Goldstone of George Mason University have published a **State Fragility Index**. Much like USAID's approach, the Fragility Index ranks country performance both in terms of effectiveness and legitimacy—a potentially blurry distinction in practice—across four dimensions of state function: economic development, governance, security, and social development.[30]

At least one major quantitative effort has been made to *predict* the outbreak of conflict or state failure. The University of Maryland's Center for International Development and Conflict Management's **Peace and Conflict Instability Ledger** ranks countries according to their risk of "future state instability." Building on the work of the Political Instability Task Force (PITF), the Ledger provides an overall "risk ratio" for 160 countries using five political, economic, security, and social variables that are statistically correlated with "instability events." Rigorous and transparent, the Ledger (like the PITF) aims to provide "early warning" for violent events like war or genocide.[31]

Collectively, these approaches provide valuable insights, by (among other things) suggesting connections between institutional weakness, poverty, and political violence. At the same time, they tend to suffer from one or more shortcomings, whether by focusing on extreme cases of failure or collapse, rather than a broader spectrum of weakness; by lacking transparent data sources or complete coverage of the relevant countries; or by emphasizing one or two dimensions of state weakness (such as propensity for conflict or strength of economic institutions) while overlooking other manifestations of institutional capacity.

Building on the insights of previous efforts to devise a more balanced and transparent index, the author collaborated with Susan E. Rice of the Brookings Institution to create in 2008 an Index of State Weakness in the Developing World.[32] The Index measures the relative performance of 141 developing and transitional countries[33] in fulfilling the security, political, economic, and social welfare functions of modern statehood—the same general categories of state function now used by major development agencies to measure state fragility.[34] A state is strong (or resilient) to the degree to which its institutions are designed to meet these core responsibilities; backed by adequate material resources; perceived as legitimate by its citizens; and nurtured and supported by the ruling regime.

By contrast, a weak (or fragile) state is institutionally anemic, unable—and in some cases unwilling—to mobilize the resources required to deliver these core goods. In the security realm, it may strain to maintain a monopoly on the use of force, protect its population from external and internal threats, control its borders and territory, provide public order, and ensure safety from crime. Politically, it may lack effective and legitimate institutions of governance that can check political power, protect basic rights and freedoms, hold leaders accountable, deliver impartial justice and the rule of law, provide efficient administration, and permit broad citizen participation. Economically, it may struggle to design and implement basic macroeconomic and fiscal policies and to develop and enforce a legal and regulatory climate conducive to private enterprise and growth. Finally, it may struggle to meet the basic social welfare needs of its population, making only minimal investments in health, education, and other social services, resulting in low or abysmal human development indicators.

Indicators of State Weakness

To measure state weakness, the Index relies on twenty widely accepted proxies for the four core aspects of state performance:[35]

Indicators in the *security* basket evaluate whether a state is able to provide security for its citizens and sovereignty over its territory. The justification for these indicators is straightforward. The intensity of recent conflict provides a fair indicator of the state's ability (or inability) to maintain peace within its borders and ensure basic physical and human security. Likewise, perceptions of political violence and instability within the society provide a reasonable proxy for actual vulnerability to upheaval. A recent history of coups or other extra-constitutional regime overthrow suggests a lack of political mechanisms for the peaceful transfer of power and susceptibility to violence. Gross

Table 1.1: Indicators for State Weakness in Developing Countries

Security	Political	Economic	Social Welfare
1. **Conflict Intensity, 1992–2006** (Center for Systemic Peace, Major Episodes of Political Violence)	6. **Government Effectiveness, 2006** (World Bank, Governance Matters VI)	11. **GNI per capita, 2006** (World Bank, World Development Indicators)	16. **Child Mortality, 2005** (UNICEF, State of the World's Children)
2. **Political Stability and Absence of Violence, 2006** (World Bank, Governance Matters VI)	7. **Rule of Law, 2006** (World Bank, Governance Matters VI)	12. **GDP growth, 2002–2006** (World Bank, World Development Indicators)	17. **Primary School Completion, 2005** (World Bank, World Development Indicators)
3. **Incidence of Coups, 1992–2006** (Archigos 2.8 and Economist Intelligence Unit)	8. **Control of Corruption, 2006** (World Bank, Governance Matters VI)	13. **Inflation, 2002–2006** (International Monetary Fund, International Financial Statistics)	18. **Undernourishment, 2004** (Food and Agriculture Organization)
4. **Gross Human Rights Abuses, 1992–2006** (Political Terror Scale)	9. **Voice and Accountability, 2006** (World Bank, Governance Matters VI)	14. **Income Inequality, 2006** (World Bank, World Development Indicators)	19. **Access to Improved Water Sources and Improved Sanitation Facilities, 2004** (World Bank, World Development Indicators)
5. **Territory Affected by Conflict, 1991–2005** (Political Instability Task Force)	10. **Freedom Ratings, 2006** (Freedom House)	15. **Regulatory Quality, 2006** (World Bank, Governance Matters VI)	20. **Life Expectancy, 2005** (World Bank, World Development Indicators)

Source: Rice and Patrick (2008)

human rights abuses, likewise, are characteristic of regimes that rely on widespread oppression and terror to maintain power. Such states both have low levels of human security and are vulnerable to rebellion or violent upheaval. Finally, territory affected by conflict provides the best available measurement of the state's authority and ability to maintain a monopoly on armed force throughout its territory.

The *political* basket assesses the extent to which a government rules in a legitimate, capable, and responsive manner through accountable, effective, and representative institutions. An effective state administration is essential for the provision of public goods and the implementation of sound policy. The rule of law indicator measures a state's ability to govern on the basis of legitimate public norms and institutions and is a strong gauge of long-term stability. The corruption indicator measures the degree to which the state is able to prevent the diversion of public resources, which otherwise erodes state institutions and curtails investment in public goods. The voice and account-ability rating reflects whether the state has mechanisms in place for peaceful dissent, transfer of power through participatory (ideally democratic) processes, and policy reform. Lastly, overall freedom ratings measure the state's commitment to civil liberties and political rights, which reduce susceptibility to destabilizing events. As this set of indicators suggests, the Index does not consider authoritarian states like Burma or North Korea—whose regimes maintain their grip on power almost entirely through the use of fear and brute force—cases of "strong" governance.

The *economic* basket assesses a state's ability to provide its citizens with a stable mac-roeconomic, fiscal, and regulatory environment that is conducive to growth. The five indicators in this basket include gross national income (GNI) per capita, growth in per capita GDP, inflation, income inequality, and regulatory quality. Low per capita income and depressed economic growth are proximate causes (as well as effects) of state weakness, circumscribing state capacity to fulfill essential government functions. Inflation is another important indicator because sizable fluctuations in general price levels may indicate an economy's susceptibility to external shocks, unsustainable fiscal policy, or poor monetary policy by the government—all of which can make a country prone to political or economic instability. Income inequality is in part a symptom of the state's unwillingness or inability to generate broadly shared economic growth, and may indicate an increased likelihood of rebellion and other forms of political violence. Lastly, poor regulatory quality indicates the inability or unwillingness of the state to foster an environment that facilitates private-sector growth, which is indispensable to increasing household and national income.

The fourth, *social welfare* basket assesses how well a state meets the basic human needs of its citizens. Child mortality is widely recognized as an accurate proxy for the state's ability to provide a wide range of public services, including health care, environ-mental quality, and maternal education. Likewise, the other measures for this basket— primary school completion rates, undernourishment, access to improved water and sanitation, and life expectancy—provide a direct measure of the state's capacity or will to meet the basic requirements of its people.

Table 1.1 lists the twenty indicators included in the Index and the underlying data sources for each (with more detail in Appendix 1.3). These indicators were selected on the basis of several criteria: the relevance of the data set to state weakness in developing countries; the accuracy, currency, and transparency of the underlying data set; and the extent of data coverage for the 141 countries included in the Index. As is inevitable in assessing state performance across multiple spheres, the Index relies on a combination of "objective" indicators (e.g., measurements of child mortality or GDP per capita) and more "subjective" indicators (e.g., in assessing corruption or the rule of law). Moreover, as is often the case when it comes to developing countries, and particularly fragile states, ideal indicators are not always available. Ideally, one would like to compare tax collection as a percentage of GDP across countries as a measure of the state's economic and social performance, but existing data sets lack sufficient coverage and precision. Similarly, accurate data for national levels of unemployment and crime simply does not exist for a large proportion of developing countries. Finally, while the Index relies on the most current data sets, these are not always compiled annually, introducing potential time lags.

Although there is no standing methodology for creating an index based on country-level indicators, the Index strives to achieve analytical simplicity and accuracy. In each of the four baskets, it aggregates the underlying indicators to determine a score that reflects a country's performance in that area. Scores are then normalized on a scale from 0 (weak) to 10 (strong) within each of the four core functions, to allow comparison across different types of indicators. The four normalized basket scores are then averaged to obtain an overall score of state weakness. (This aggregation methodology implicitly assumes that each of the four core areas of state function contribute to state weakness equally—an intellectually defensible position.[36])

The results permit an assessment of the relative institutional strengths and weaknesses of 141 developing countries in the four core areas (and twenty sub-indicators) of state function. The ability to examine the unique performance profile of each country and to compare countries across four principal dimensions of weakness is a distinctive contribution of this approach.

The Index recognizes that state weakness is a relative condition, with countries falling at different places along a broad spectrum of performance, depending on how close they come to realizing empirical (as opposed to legal) sovereignty in the core areas of state function. State weakness should also be understood as a dynamic phenomenon, rather than a static condition or permanent designation. Individual states can oscillate along the continuum of performance, graduating from failure or declining into it. (However, as a descriptive model, the Index does not purport to predict which states will slide into failure, or which will emerge from it.)

The Index also suggests that there are multiple typologies of fragility, with each fragile state possessing its own complex of problems, both chronic and acute. Some of the weakest states perform poorly across the board, whereas others exhibit weakness in just one or two functions. (A comparison of the Democratic Republic of the Congo with Colombia makes the point: the DRC performs poorly in all categories, whereas Colombia scores well on political, economic, and social welfare indicators, but miserably on security, due to an ongoing insurgency and the state's inability to control huge swathes of its territory). For policymakers, this heterogeneity underlines the importance of taking each fragile state on its own terms, rather than adopting one-size-fits-all policy responses.

As discussed below, any large-scale, cross-country comparison of this nature can only be an approximation, to be supplemented by more detailed analysis of each state's circumstances and trajectory. Nevertheless, the Index provides a useful snapshot of relative state performance, both in the aggregate and across components of state function.

OVERVIEW OF THE FINDINGS

The 141 countries measured by the Index of State Weakness in 2008 can be broken down into several categories based on their relative strength or weakness. Beyond the scores of the bottom three countries, which perform markedly worse than even those in their critically weak cohort, gradations in state weakness appear as a relatively smooth continuum of performance.

Failed and Critically Weak States

The twenty-eight countries in the bottom quintile of the Index merit the designation of "critically weak states." With a few exceptions, they face challenges in virtually all categories of state function, as well as protracted violence and grinding poverty. The bottom quintile of the Index includes nine of the ten poorest countries in the world (Malawi is the one exception), and all but five of the twenty-eight failed and critically weak states are classified as low-income countries.[37] The five exceptions—Iraq, the Republic of Congo, Angola, Equatorial Guinea, and Cameroon—are oil-producers with the attendant problems of extreme inequality and corruption. Another distinctive feature of most critically weak states is a recent history of violence and political upheaval. More than 85 percent of these countries have experienced conflict in the past fifteen years.

Of the twenty-eight critically weak countries, three—Somalia, Afghanistan, and the Democratic Republic of the Congo—perform markedly worse than the rest and can be considered "failed states." All have been in conflict for years if not decades, and their governments do not control substantial portions of their territory. These countries' abysmal overall scores reflect the vicious cycle of collapsed security environments, which result in (and may sometimes be fueled by) extreme poverty, decaying political institutions, bankrupt economies, and some of the world's most appalling social conditions.

Somalia, the weakest state according to the Index, is in a class by itself. It has been without a functional central government since 1991, and its capacity to provide key public goods to citizens is nonexistent. Somalia's internationally backed interim government—which has failed to perform any critical state functions since it was installed in 2007—controlled virtually none of the country beyond the capital city in late 2010. Somalia's health care and education systems remain in shambles, as reflected in the country's rock-bottom social welfare score.

Weak States

Those countries in the second-lowest quintile can be considered "weak states." These twenty-eight countries suffer fewer severe capacity gaps than the bottom quintile, but most tend to perform poorly in more than one area of state function (and some demonstrate mediocre performance across the board). Several countries in this quintile—including Malawi, Mali, Mozambique, Tanzania, and Zambia—are relatively stable and secure, but receive extremely poor economic and/or social welfare scores. Poor political performers among weak states include Cameroon, Laos, and Turkmenistan. Like the critically weak states, most of the world's weak states are also impoverished: twenty-one out of twenty-eight in this second quintile are designated low-income countries.

States to Watch

Beyond the bottom two quintiles (the fifty-six weakest states), the Index helps identify a set of twenty-five "states to watch" (see table 1.2). Although their aggregate scores fall within the third or fourth quintiles, these states perform particularly poorly (i.e., in the bottom quintile) in at least one of the four core areas of state function, or in the second quintile in at least two core areas. States to watch include both fragile democracies and authoritarian regimes, as well as several regionally or globally significant countries like Russia, China, Egypt, India, Venezuela, and Turkey.

Patterns of State Weakness

Several clear patterns emerge from the Index's data.[38] Most failed and critically weak states are in the bottom quintile of developing countries when it comes to gross

Table 1.2: States to Watch

Country	Index Ranking	Country	Index Ranking
Algeria	57	Paraguay	75
Philippines	58	Indonesia	77
Syria	59	Egypt	78
Guatemala	60	Thailand	79
Sao Tome and Principe	61	Azerbaijan	80
Cuba	62	Belarus	81
Gabon	63	Namibia	82
Bolivia	64	Libya	86
Russia	65	Turkey	98
Iran	66	Micronesia	103
India	67	Tonga	104
Venezuela	70	Marshall Islands	106
China	74		

national incomes (GNI) per capita. This correlation is not surprising, given that poorer states with smaller tax bases generally lack the resources to effectively meet their populations' needs. Yet, even among this group we find notable "under-performers" that enjoy higher incomes but fail to use their resources to deliver essential public goods. Some of these countries are energy producers, such as Turkmenistan. Likewise, a handful of states (such as Gambia, Malawi, and Tanzania) perform better overall than their low incomes would indicate.

The weakest countries also tend to have unrepresentative or repressive forms of government. Only two of the states in the bottom two quintiles, Mali and Lesotho, are classified by Freedom House as "free," whereas only six of the top-performing quintile of countries fall short of "free." On the other hand, while the majority of the critically weak and weak states falter in the political sphere, democracy is not always associated with strong state capacity. States that are fairly well governed yet weak include Colombia and Zambia, while some autocracies like Belarus and Libya score relatively well.

Overall, the Index suggests multiple typologies of weakness. Most of the critically weak states are weak across the board. Yet a minority of developing countries exhibit extremely low scores in just one or two areas. Two second-quintile countries—Colombia and Sri Lanka—are stung by poor marks for security and conflict, dragging down their overall scores. Equatorial Guinea, one of the few upper-middle-income critically weak states, performs dismally on the political and social welfare baskets, yet above the mean in the other two areas. Likewise, Mozambique scores in the bottom 10 percent on social welfare, despite above-average scores in the other three core areas.

The Index also reveals patterns of performance across core areas of state responsibility. Developing countries that rank higher on political governance also tend to be better providers of social welfare and physical security, and those that manage their economies more successfully also tend to be better providers of social welfare. The relationship between economic and political performance is also positive, though less strong. None of these relationships is watertight, moreover. For instance, a few countries with autocratic governance, such as Syria and Cuba, perform well on social welfare, while some comparatively well-governed states, such as Namibia and Botswana, score poorly in this area. Where performance is poor overall, the Index does not tell us whether weakness across baskets is being driven by one of the components. For instance, does low social welfare cause insecurity, or vice versa? Answering this question is something that requires detailed analysis of the specific case in question.

Geographically, failed and critically weak states are concentrated in sub-Saharan Africa and, to a lesser extent, in South and Central Asia. While only about one-third of the 141 developing countries measured in the Index are in sub-Saharan Africa, twenty-two of the twenty-eight critically weak states are located there. The six exceptions are Afghanistan, Iraq, Haiti, North Korea, Burma, and Nepal. The Index also reveals other regional variations. In South Asia, countries tend to score lower on security than other core areas due primarily to ongoing or recent conflict. Likewise, countries in Central Asia typically score lower on political indicators than in the other baskets (see figure 1.1).

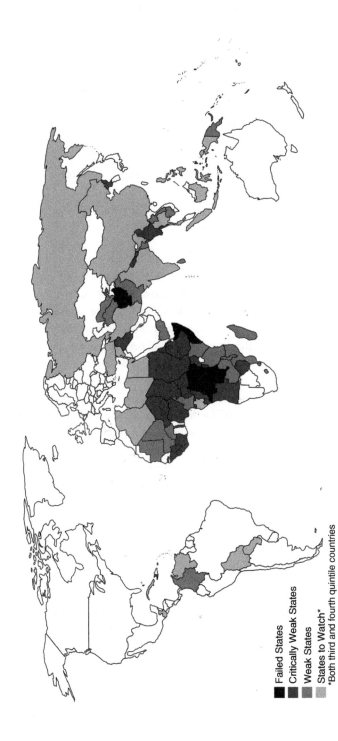

Figure 1.1: Map of the Weak States

The data for this image was taken, with permission, from the Brookings Institution.

Failed States

Critically Weak States

Weak States

States to Watch*

*Both third and fourth quintile countries

A TYPOLOGY OF PATHOLOGY: ADDITIONAL PARAMETERS OF STATE WEAKNESS

The Index of State Weakness permits cross-country comparison of institutional performance in the developing world at any moment in time. As a static snapshot of state strength, however, the Index tells us little about the internal dynamics that are driving poor (or good) state performance in any particular case, or the direction in which the country is headed. Beyond arraying states along a continuum, it may be useful analytically to distinguish among several types of weak states, based on their particular situation and current trajectory, as well as the commitment (not merely capacity) of their governing regimes to provide essential goods. The following categories of countries (which may overlap in practice) present distinctive challenges, and require differentiated approaches from would-be interveners:

Weak State Trajectories

Chronic Situations

- *State collapse:* In extreme cases, countries may experience a near-total breakdown of state institutions and functions. In the absence of state authority, sub-national institutions, local power-wielders, and traditional societal structures may provide what semblance of governance exists. Somalia since 1991 is the archetypal example, but others would include Afghanistan and Sierra Leone in the mid-1990s.
- *Endemic weakness*: This label applies to stagnant, often aid-dependent countries that are not at major risk of violent conflict but are stuck in a state of arrested development, characterized by low growth, anemic institutions, and patrimonial systems of political leadership.[39] Zambia and Bangladesh for the past two decades provide cases in point.
- *Resource-rich poor performers*: Such countries generate large natural resource rents that distort the national economy and sustain corrupt, clientelist governance.[40] Nigeria, Equatorial Guinea, and Angola provide examples of this phenomenon.
- *Brittle dictatorships:* Many of the world's "weakest" states are paradoxically ruled by strongmen. They include North Korea, Myanmar, and Uzbekistan, each of which has an authoritarian regime that appears strong but rests on a fragile foundation.

Deteriorating Situations

- *Prolonged political crisis*: This category encompasses states suffering a marked decline in institutional performance, often as a result of political standoff or economic meltdown, with increasing risk of violence and even state collapse. Zimbabwe in the first decade of the twenty-first century provides a case in point, Pakistan in 2008–2010 another.
- *Conflict-ridden countries:* This category includes states experiencing protracted conflict and, often, a breakdown in government control over large portions of the country's territory. Recent examples include Sri Lanka, Sudan, Yemen, and Chad.

Improving Situations

- *Post-conflict recovery*: States emerging from war, whether as the result of a negotiated settlement or victory by one side, face daunting challenges. As examples from Mozambique to Liberia attest, these include designing a stable framework for political reconciliation and legitimate governance, making the difficult transition from a wartime to a peacetime economy, rebuilding essential infrastructure, delivering basic needs to war-ravaged citizens, and protecting a vulnerable population from residual violence.[41]
- *Democratic transitions*: In a number of states around the world (e.g., Georgia following the "Rose Revolution" of 2003), reform-minded governments have attempted to overcome legacies of authoritarian rule and failed development policies, often in the context of a bumpy democratic transition. Such transitions present economic and political opportunities, but may also be inherently destabilizing as states face a greater risk of violence or upheaval.

Special mention should be made of Iraq, which in 2008 had dismally low scores in the security sphere, thanks to ongoing civil conflict and terrorism. Its political performance was also abysmal, earning Iraq the world's third-worst score on the rule of law indicator, and the fourth-worst score on government effectiveness. Improvements in Iraqi security and political stability since 2008, however, promise stronger performance in these scores. Iraq provides an example of how countries can move through different trajectories in a very short time, particularly if given an outside push. In a few short years, Iraq went from a brittle dictatorship under Saddam Hussein to something approaching state collapse in 2005–2006, to what today resembles prolonged political crisis in a resource-rich state. Prospects for sustained recovery and democratic consolidation remain uncertain.

Will vs. Capacity

State fragility is not merely a question of inherent capacity or current trajectory but also of *will*—namely, the willingness of the governing regime to pursue constructive policies and reforms intended to provide its citizens with fundamental goods. History provides repeated examples of corrupt, incompetent, or venal regimes—Zimbabwe under Robert Mugabe comes to mind—that have driven promising countries into the ground. Distinguishing between a governing regime's ability to deliver the goods and its commitment to do so enables us to identify four categories of states: (a) those with both the will and the way; (b) weak but willing states; (c) states with the means but not the commitment; and (d) those with neither the will nor the way (see table 1.3). Such analytical distinctions have practical utility, informing the mix of incentives that external actors can deploy in engaging poor performers. The goal is to move weak states toward the upper left quadrant, by filling capacity gaps, persuading venal elites to mend their ways, or both.

Table 1.3: Capacity and Will as Dimensions of State Weakness in Developing Countries

	Strong Will	Low Will
High Capacity	Relatively Good Performers (e.g., Senegal, Botswana)	Unresponsive/Corrupt/ Repressive (e.g., Burma, Zimbabwe)
Low Capacity	Weak but Willing (e.g., Mozambique, Mali)	Weak-Weak (e.g., DRC; Haiti before 2006)

WHAT CAUSES STATES TO WEAKEN AND FAIL?

State "failure" is an extreme condition of fragility or weakness, characterized above all by an evaporation of political legitimacy of the governing regime and the state's loss of a monopoly on the use of armed force. The question of why states fail is the subject of a voluminous and growing literature,[42] and a definitive answer is beyond the scope of this chapter. In general, those seeking a single causal explanation will be disappointed: there is no single pathway to this destination.

What we can say is that state instability and failure is the outcome of the dynamic interplay among four sets of variables that, collectively, determine a state's capacity to peacefully manage and adapt to change: (1) the state's baseline level of institutional resilience or strength; (2) the presence of long-term risk factors or "drivers" of insta-bility, which increase strains on the state; (3) the nature of the external environment, which can either exacerbate or mitigate these drivers; and (4) short-term shocks to the system (or "triggers").

The most important factor is the state's *underlying resilience*, reflecting the strength (or fragility) of its institutions, as well as the vigor of its civil society. As noted earlier, a healthy, strong, and resilient state is one that is capable of and willing to provide—in a legitimate and effective manner—the fundamental goods of physical security, sound economic management, accountable and responsive governance, and basic social welfare.

The second set of variables consists of those *underlying internal risk factors* that deter-mine how vulnerable a country is to sudden upheaval or crisis. The risk factors include incomplete transitions to democracy; ethnic and communal cleavages; poverty and underdevelopment; international isolation; recent civil war; extensive natural resource endowments; and heavy dependence on primary commodities. States are seven times more likely to fail if their ruling regime is a partial democracy rather than a full democ-racy or autocracy. Regimes that institutionalize policies of exclusion, discrimination, and repression against particular communal groups are likewise vulnerable, as are states suffering from underdevelopment (as reflected in high infant mortality), and which have low levels of trade openness (measured by imports and exports as a percentage of GDP).[43] Unsurprisingly, violence also tends to beget more violence: countries emerging from conflict have a 44 percent chance of relapsing within five years. Less intuitively, a rich natural resource endowment is more apt to be a curse than a blessing, warping a state's political economy, driving out domestic investment, encouraging corruption, and providing incentives for armed opposition. Likewise, dependence on primary commodities for current account balance and foreign exchange leaves developing nations exposed to price shocks and currency fluctuations, which can have destabilizing social and political effects.[44]

Third, a country's *external environment* can either mitigate or exacerbate the state's vulnerability. Stabilizing factors include membership in regional organizations, the provision of security guarantees by outside actors, access to foreign markets, sustained foreign direct investment, generous and well-designed foreign assistance, and sizable flows of remittances. Destabilizing factors, which are often overlooked in Western diagnoses of state fragility, are even more numerous. They include the geopolitics of more powerful states; location in a "bad neighborhood" populated by other weak states; inflow of small arms; exploitation by transnational criminal networks; foreign demand for illicit commodities; foreign political support for authoritarian regimes; corrupt practices by foreign-domiciled corporations; availability of offshore financial havens; commercial barriers to global markets; long-term declines in terms of trade; provision of foreign assistance in a manner that substitutes for rather than builds local capacity; and growing vulnerability to global warming and its secondary effects. Moreover, developing countries' growing integration into the globalized economy has exposed them to the vicissitudes of global financial markets, as demonstrated during the global financial crisis (see Box 1.2). In this context, international expectations of what a "responsible" developing country should be able to deliver are far more demanding than the obligations of today's OECD countries "at equivalent levels of economic development and income."[45]

Box 1.2: The Global Financial Crisis: Its Impact on Fragile States

In late 2008, as the world's financial markets bottomed out and global trade shrank for the first time in decades, many observers predicted that the world's poorest countries would escape relatively unscathed. Largely marginalized from the global economy, these countries had limited exposure to the subprime mortgages, toxic assets, and risky derivatives that had doomed rich-world banks and stock markets. As the downturn deepened, however, it became apparent that the effects of the economic crisis on poorer developing countries—while mostly indirect—would nonetheless be significant.[46] Among other negative consequences, the global recession drove down the prices of commodities that prop up the economies of some of the world's poorest countries; dampened inflows of foreign investment, aid, and remittances; and raised the specter of harmful protectionist policies in developed countries. Many feared these dynamics would lead to worsening poverty, unemployment, and inequality in fragile states, generating mounting social unrest and political instability in many regions.

Falling commodity prices. Many of the world's weakest states lack sophisticated manufacturing sectors and are heavily dependent on commodity exports, making them especially vulnerable to falling prices in the wake of slumping global demand. Falling prices for cobalt,

---

(*continued*)

Box 1.2: Continued

copper, and other minerals devastated once robust mining sectors in the Democratic Republic of the Congo and Zambia, for instance. The economic impact of falling commodity prices forced some developing country governments in Latin America, Asia, and Africa to cut spending on desperately needed infrastructure and social programs.[47]

Declining investment inflows. The global credit crunch led to a sharp contraction in investment levels worldwide. The effects of tighter credit were particularly pronounced in weak states, which are among the riskiest investment targets even in the best of times. Indeed, the sharpest decline in foreign direct investment (FDI) to developing countries came in Africa, with stock markets tumbling in South Africa, Kenya, and Nigeria (which saw the world's biggest decline—31 percent—in the month of January 2009 alone). Perhaps most damaging in the long term, hundreds of major investments in critical infrastructure— including roads, electricity, and communications projects—stalled.[48]

Dwindling Remittances. Remittances from workers abroad totaled at least $280 billion in 2008, a figure that dwarfs total foreign aid transfers from rich to poor countries. In many weak states remittances constitute a significant proportion of GDP, filling critical public sector gaps and perhaps even helping maintain social stability. As the recession drove up unemployment levels in developed and emerging host countries, migrant workers were often among the first to lose their incomes. By some estimates, remittances worldwide were projected to fall by 5 or 6 percent in 2009.[49]

Rising protectionism. Increased regional and international trade is critical to prospects for poverty-reduction and long-term development in the poorest countries. Yet in the midst of global recession, international trade levels declined in 2009 for the first time in nearly three decades, and protectionist pressures rose in wealthy countries. The impact on exports from low-income countries was substantial. Former UN Secretary-General Kofi Annan warned, "As global trade contracts and protectionist instincts are emboldened, the danger is that those least responsible for the present crisis will be hardest hit."[50]

In view of these trends, many of the weakest states confronted grim economic prospects— and increased likelihood of political instability. Amid economic stagnation, rising unemployment, and fraying social safety nets, deprivation and desperation could generate turmoil and violence. This would represent a replay, on a much grander scale, of the global food crisis of 2008, when skyrocketing food prices led to demonstrations and violent protests in more than thirty countries—and toppled at least one government, in Haiti. Thanks to the worldwide economic crisis, *Foreign Policy* magazine predicted, the successor to the "axis of evil" in U.S. national security policy could well be an "axis of upheaval."[51]

Taken together, a country's baseline fragility (or resilience), its internal risk factors, and the external environment determine its overall vulnerability to instability and failure—metaphorically, how dry the "kindling" is. What typically sets this tinder alight are more proximate *triggering events.* Such unpredictable, rapid-onset shocks can include natural disasters; assassinations, coups, or other succession crises; commodity price shocks; and global or regional financial crises resulting in capital flight. Such events are often externally generated, but they may be caused or exacerbated by the decisions of a misguided or predatory regime. They are particularly destabilizing when they alter the relative fortunes of different social groups. Even if sudden shocks do not lead to state failure, they tend to exacerbate underlying risk factors, weakening the state's resilience and increasing susceptibility to future shocks.

WHY SHOULD WE CARE ABOUT WEAK AND FAILING STATES?

State weakness and failure can have numerous consequences for the affected country and its inhabitants; for the country's immediate neighbors; and for the wider international community. The United States and other wealthy nations have a clear interest, on both humanitarian and strategic grounds, in helping mitigate the local, regional, and global impact of state fragility.

Cost for the Affected Country and Its People

When states struggle to discharge their basic functions, the price is paid most heavily by their inhabitants. States with weak governance are disproportionately vulnerable to internal conflict and civil violence, and are particularly susceptible to humanitarian catastrophes, both man-made and natural. The World Bank estimates that fragile states are fifteen times more prone to civil war than OECD countries, and such violence is on average both more extreme and longer lasting than conflict in other developing countries.[52] The legacy of war, moreover, often lasts far longer than the violence itself. Beyond reducing national incomes by an average of 15 percent, civil wars undermine subsequent development by depleting social capital, accelerating brain drain and capital flight, elevating mortality and morbidity levels, entrenching criminalized economies, and empowering corrupt and unaccountable leaders.[53]

Because they are prone to violent internal conflict, weak states are also the overwhelming source of the world's refugees and internally displaced persons. Six of the seven top source countries for refugees in 2007—in order, Afghanistan, Iraq, Sudan, Somalia, Burundi, and the DRC—are also the six lowest-ranking states on the Index. (The exception is Colombia, the third-largest source of refugees, and also a weak state). These seven states accounted for more than two-thirds of the world's 11.4 million refugees in 2007.[54]

Some of the world's worst human rights abusers are found in weak and failing states, which are also the most likely settings for genocide and mass atrocities. All five countries scoring a "5" (the worst score) on the 2007 Political Terror Scale—Afghanistan, DRC, Iraq, Burma, Somalia, and Sri Lanka—fall in the bottom two quintiles of the Index, as do more than half the countries scoring a "4" (the second worst rating).[55]

Compared to other developing countries, fragile states are on balance more prone to suffer low or negative growth, and to be farthest from the Millennium Development

Table 1.4: Fragile States and the Millennium Development Goals[59]

MDG	Relevance to Fragile States
1. Eradicate extreme poverty and hunger	Fragile states are home to more than one-third of the world's people living on less than $1 a day (two-thirds if one removes China and India) and one-quarter of the world's malnourished. One-third of all residents of fragile states are malnourished.
2. Achieve universal primary education	Fragile states are home to one-third of the world's primary age children not in school. On average, primary school enrollment is only 70 percent, versus 86 percent in other developing countries.
3. Promote gender equality and empower women	Women face greater gender discrimination, on average, in fragile states and are far more likely to die in childbirth than in other developing countries (734 per 100,000 versus 270 in other developing countries).
4. Reduce child mortality	Children in fragile states are more than twice as likely to die before their fifth birthdays as those in other developing countries (138 vs. 56 per 1,000), with one-third of all children that fail to reach this landmark living in fragile states.
5. Improve maternal health	Of countries with the world's worst maternal mortality rates (i.e., more than 1,000 per 100,000 live births), all are fragile states. The average maternal mortality rate in the developed world is 9 per 100,000; in the broader developing world, the average is 450 per 100,000—less than half the figure in the weakest states.
6. Combat HIV/AIDS, malaria, and other diseases	Fragile states contain nearly half (44 percent) of the developing world's HIV/AIDS burden and twelve times the malarial death rate as other developing countries.
7. Ensure environmental sustainability	Fragile states contain almost one-third of the number of people in developing countries without sustainable access to safe drinking water. They are also responsible for 43 percent of global deforestation annually, with a forested area approximately the size of Hong Kong being destroyed each week.

Goals (MDGs)—a set of concrete development objectives (e.g., eradicating extreme poverty and hunger, achieving universal primary education, and reducing child mortality) endorsed by UN member states in 2000. Indeed, Britain's Department for International Development (DFID) considers fragile states to represent the "single biggest challenge" to making progress on the MDGs[56] (see table 1.4). Former World Bank economist Paul Collier has coined the term "bottom billion" to refer to the one-sixth of humanity living in dire circumstances within fragile states.[57] The inhabitants of these states are more likely than their counterparts in other developing countries to be poor and malnourished; endure gender discrimination; lack access to education, basic health care, and modern technology; and die young or suffer chronic illness.[58]

Clearly, advancing human development, security, and rights requires dealing with the plight of those living in fragile states. Yet despite their glaring human needs and rising strategic salience, fragile states receive on average much lower levels of foreign aid per capita than do other developing countries. Moreover, that assistance tends to be less reliable, concentrated in a few high-profile or strategic countries (sometimes leaving the remainder to languish as "aid orphans"), and targeted to debt relief and humanitarian assistance, rather than development.[60]

Costs for the Region

Outside the affected state, the main consequences of state fragility are typically borne by neighboring states. Violent conflict, large quantities of arms, massive refugee flows, disease, and decreased economic growth can all spread from weak states. The risk of contagion is compounded when weak, vulnerable, or collapsed states are adjacent to countries with similar characteristics and few defenses against spillovers.[61] As the following table suggests, there is a positive correlation between numbers of weak states in a given region and the overall level of conflict within it (see table 1.5).[62]

Weaknesses in one state can thus contaminate the surrounding region, sparking or perpetuating civil wars, insurgencies, and cross-border military incursions. Such a pattern emerged in West Africa during the 1990s, as insurgents, guns, and

Table 1.5: Fragile States and Warfare Trends by Region[63]

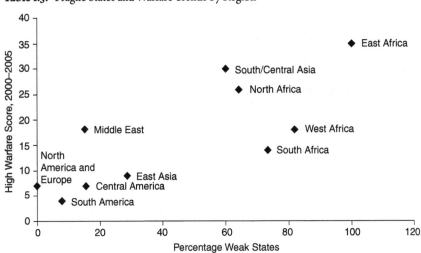

conflict diamonds from Liberia poured across national borders, undermining Sierra Leone, Guinea, and Côte d'Ivoire. Likewise, Rwanda's collapse in 1994 led to the extreme violence that has plagued Africa's Great Lakes region for more than a decade and a half. In reciprocal fashion, bad neighborhoods can undermine governance and encourage violence in individual states, so that even "islands of good performance" have difficulty preserving stability when surrounded by dysfunctional, conflict-affected countries.[64] In some cases, contiguous countries have actively fomented civil war by offering support for armed groups that share their political goals, or providing them with safe haven. In other cases transnational networks—whether based on ethnic identity, political affinity, or economic interest—have undermined central governments and fueled conflict by facilitating illicit traffic in small arms, drugs, people, or lootable commodities.

Even in the absence of violence, failing states impose startling economic hardship on their neighbors. By one calculation, merely being adjacent to what the World Bank calls a Low-Income Country Under Stress (LICUS) reduces a country's annual growth by an average of 1.6 percent. Since each LICUS country has, on average, three neighbors, the overall economic cost of a state falling into LICUS status is actually greater for its neighbors (4.8 percent) than for the state itself (2.3 percent). Indeed, analysis by World Bank researchers suggests that when costs to its neighbors are included, the average annual cost of a state falling into LICUS status amounts to a staggering $82.4 billion. This begins to rival the total global foreign aid budget, which was roughly $103 billion in 2007. In other words, deterioration in a single state can nearly erase an entire year's worth of official development assistance worldwide.[65]

Potential Cost for International Peace and Security—and for the United States

Beyond generating domestic misery and regional instability, fragile states have the potential under certain circumstances to endanger international peace and security. In addition to the compelling humanitarian considerations discussed above, the United States has certain strategic and financial stakes in bolstering and promoting reform in fragile states. (See table 1.6)

To begin, some fragile states have intrinsic strategic importance to the United States by virtue of their size, location, and population. The collapse of a large weak state that serves as a regional anchor (such as Nigeria or Kenya), or has a pivotal geographical location (such as Yemen on the Arabian Peninsula), could threaten U.S. security. Sixteen of the world's most populous fifty countries are fragile states, with populations of more than 20 million each.[66] The collapse of any of these states could have significant international repercussions.

Whether or not a weak state is considered strategically important, its failure may carry financial costs to the United States, particularly if military personnel are deployed to evacuate U.S. citizens, protect U.S. property, or prevent a total state collapse.

Between 1990 and 2007, the United States deployed military forces in thirty-two countries, of which more than two-thirds are classified as weak states in the Index.[67] Such operations ranged from full-scale military intervention (Iraq), to counterterrorism operations (Yemen), to humanitarian missions (Somalia), to protection of U.S. civilians (Republic of Congo), to the prevention of total state collapse (Haiti).[68] The United States has also expended tens of billions of dollars to support UN peace operations, including in fifteen of the twenty weakest states on the Index.[69] As of September 2009, the annual cost of the sixteen ongoing UN operations totaled nearly $8 billion (of which the United States paid about one-quarter), with more than 90 percent of the budget going to operations in weak states.[70] Thus the United States would, at the least, have a strong financial incentive to prevent the violent conflict that often goes hand in hand with state failure.

At the same time, the dangers and challenges that weak states pose to the United States should not be overstated. Illegal migration is a case in point. Notwithstanding the data on refugees examined above, of the top twenty source countries for illegal migrants into the United States in 2007, only four (Colombia, Haiti, Pakistan, and Nigeria) were weak states—and together they accounted for only 0.4 percent of the aliens deported from the United States that year. Rather than state weakness, regional proximity seems to be the overwhelming factor in migration patterns, as far as the United States is concerned. Mexico alone accounted for nearly 90 percent of aliens deported in 2007, for instance.[71]

Similarly, most weak states possess little obvious geopolitical importance to the United States. The U.S. Department of Defense owns or uses 823 publicly known military facilities in thirty-nine foreign countries. Only eight of these sites—less than 1 percent—are located in weak states.[72] Arguably, the only weak states that could pose a direct military threat to the United States are North Korea and Pakistan. None of the fifty-six weakest states on the Index was a part of the U.S.-led coalition in Iraq between 2003 and 2010, and none except Pakistan is classified as a major non-NATO ally. Weak states that do garner strategic attention from the United States do so not because of their weakness, but because of specific issues, like terrorism, proliferation, and energy.

But the United States nonetheless has significant security, economic, and humanitarian stakes in some of the world's weakest states, and in the past two decades has expended significant diplomatic, military, and financial resources to counter threats or resolve conflicts in many of them, from Haiti to Sudan. Moreover, because certain weak states—including Iraq, Nigeria, Pakistan, and North Korea—are strategically significant (and given the possibility that governance gaps in other key states, such as Saudi Arabia, could over time lead to greater weakness and instability), it is critical for U.S. policymakers to understand the dynamics of state failure and reconstitution.

The global costs of state fragility—particularly its negative consequences for international security—have elevated the problem of weak and failing states to the top of the U.S. foreign policy agenda. Beyond human suffering and regional instability, policymakers and commentators have implicated weak and failing states in a wide range of

Table 1.6: Potential U.S. Stakes in Fragile States

Country	Index Rank	Population[73]	U.S. Foreign Aid request, FY08 ('000)[74]	Major Source of Refugees in 2007[75]	Gross Human Rights Abuses in 2007[76]	U.S. Military Facilities	U.S. Sanctions In Place Since 1990	U.S. Use of Force Since 1990[77]	UN PKO Since 1990	Total U.S. Stakes in Fragile States (of 8)
Somalia	1	Medium (9,558,666)	Low (12,300)	Highest	Yes	No	No	Yes	Yes	4
Afghanistan	2	High (32,738,376)	Highest (1,406,050)	Highest	Yes	Yes	Yes	Yes	Yes	8
DR Congo	3	High (66,514,504)	Medium (80,200)	Highest	Yes	No	Yes	Yes	Yes	6
Iraq	4	High (28,221,180)	Highest (1,331,800)	Highest	Yes	Yes	Yes	Yes	Yes	8
Burundi	5	Medium (8,691,005)	Low (28,550)	Highest	Yes	No	No	Yes	Yes	4
Sudan	6	High (40,218,456)	Highest (679,200)	Highest	No	No	Yes	Yes	Yes	6
Central African Rep.	7	Low (4,444,330)	Low (100)	Medium	Yes	No	No	Yes	Yes	3
Zimbabwe	8	Medium (11,350,111)	Low (21,010)	Medium	Yes	No	Yes	No	No	2
Liberia	9	Low (3,334,587)	Medium (115,575)	Medium	No	No	Yes	Yes	Yes	3
Cote d'Ivoire	10	High (20,179,602)	Medium (96,100)	Medium	No	No	Yes	Yes	Yes	4
Angola	11	Medium (12,531,357)	Low (34,950)	High	No	No	Yes	No	Yes	3
Haiti	12	Medium (8,924,553)	Highest (222,900)	Low	Yes	No	No	Yes	Yes	4
Sierra Leone	13	Medium (6,294,774)	Low (16,550)	Medium	No	No	No	Yes	Yes	2
Eritrea	14	Medium (5,502,026)	Low (0)	High	No	No	No	Yes	Yes	3

Country	#									
North Korea	15	High (23,479,088)	Low (89)	Low	Yes	No	Yes	No	No	3
Chad	16	Medium (10,111,337)	Low (5,300)	Medium	Yes	No	No	No	Yes	2
Burma	17	High (47,758,180)	Low (4,630)	High	Yes	No	Yes	No	No	4
Guinea-Bissau	18	Low (1,503,182)	Low (3,193)	Low	No	No	No	Yes	No	1
Ethiopia	19	High (82,544,840)	Highest (507,430)	Medium	Yes	No	No	Yes	Yes	5
R. Congo	20	Low (3,903,318)	Low (100)	Medium	No	No	No	Yes	No	1
Niger	21	Medium (13,272,679)	Low (21,497)	Low	No	No	No	No	No	0
Nepal	22	High (29,519,114)	Low (26,625)	Low	No	No	No	No	No	1
Guinea	23	Medium (9,806,509)	Low (15,593)	Low	Yes	No	No	No	No	1
Rwanda	24	Medium (10,186,063)	Medium (142,202)	Medium	No	No	No	Yes	Yes	2
Equatorial Guinea	25	Low (616,459)	Low (45)	Low	Yes	No	No	No	No	1
Togo	26	Medium (5,858,673)	Low (2,895)	Medium	No	No	No	No	No	0
Uganda	27	High (31,367,972)	High (33,099)	Medium	Yes	No	No	No	Yes	4
Nigeria	28	Highest (146,255,312)	Highest (533,550)	Medium	Yes	No	No	No	No	3
Cameroon	29	Medium (18,467,692)	Low (4,703)	Medium	No	No	No	Yes	No	0
Yemen	30	High (23,013,376)	Low (23,059)	Low	Yes	No	No	No	No	3
Comoros	31	Low (731,775)	Low (100)	Low	No	No	No	No	No	0
Zambia	32	Medium (11,669,534)	High (339,793)	Low	No	No	No	[78]	No	1
Pakistan	33	Highest (172,800,048)	Highest (785,000)	Medium	Yes	(Alleged)	No	Yes	Yes	4
Cambodia	34	Medium (14,241,640)	Low (42,285)	Medium	No	No	No	Yes	Yes	2
Turkmenistan	35	Medium (5,179,571)	Low (8,430)	Low	No	No	No	No	No	0

(continued)

Table 1.6: Continued

Country	Index Rank	Population[73]	U.S. Foreign Aid request, FY08 ('000)[74]	Major Source of Refugees in 2007[75]	Gross Human Rights Abuses in 2007[76]	U.S. Military Facilities	U.S. Sanctions In Place Since 1990	U.S. Use of Force Since 1990[77]	UN PKO Since 1990	Total U.S. Stakes in Fragile States (of 8)
Uzbekistan	36	High (27,345,026)	Low (9,374)	Low	No	No	No	No	No	No	1
Mauritania	37	Low (3,364,940)	Low (10,358)	Medium	No	No	No	No	No	No	0
Djibouti	38	Low (506,221)	Low (7,090)	Low	No	No	No	Yes	No	No	1
Mozambique	39	High (21,284,700)	High (283,929)	Low	No	No	No	No	No	Yes	3
Papua New Guinea	40	Medium (5,931,769)	Low (2,360)	Low	No	No	No	No	No	No	0
Swaziland	41	Low (1,128,814)	Low (9,033)	Low	No	No	No	No	No	No	0
Tajikistan	42	Medium (7,211,884)	Low (32,120)	Low	No	No	No	No	No	Yes	1
East Timor	43	Low (1,108,777)	Low (10,050)	Low	No	No	No	Yes	Yes		2
Burkina Faso	44	Medium (15,264,735)	Low (13,314)	Low	No	No	No	No	No	No	0
Laos	45	Medium (6,677,534)	Low (4,571)	Medium	No	No	No	No	No	No	0
Malawi	46	Medium (13,931,831)	Medium (61,578)		No	No	No	No	No	No	1
Colombia	47	High (45,013,672)	Highest (589,710)	Highest	Yes	No	No	No	No	No	4
Bangladesh	48	Highest (153,546,896)	Medium (119,790)	Low	Yes	No	No	No	No	No	2
Madagascar	49	High (20,042,552)	Low (35,657)	Low	No	No	No	No	No	No	1
Kenya	50	High (37,953,840)	Highest (543,511)	Low	Yes	No	No	Yes	No	No	4

Gambia	51	Low (1,735,464)	Low (2,008)	Medium	No	No	No	No	No	0
Mali	52	Medium (12,324,029)	Low (32,875)	Low	No	No	No	No	No	0
Lesotho	53	Low (2,128,180)	Low (10)	Low	No	No	No	No	No	0
Solomon Islands	54	Low (581,318)	Low (177)	Low	No	No	No	No	No	0
Tanzania	55	High (40,213,160)	High (344,303)	Low	Yes	No	No	Yes	No	3
Sri Lanka	56	High (21,128,772)	Low (6,950)	Low	No	No	No	No	No	2

LEGEND: Indicates a U.S. Stake in the Fragile State

potential threats to the security and well-being of the international community. These include providing safe havens, training grounds, and recruits for transnational terrorists; offering bases for transnational criminal enterprises involved in the production and trafficking in drugs, weapons, people, and other illicit commodities; facilitating the proliferation of weapons of mass destruction and associated technology; serving as breeding grounds for ongoing pandemics and emerging infectious diseases; and increasing the cost and volatility of global energy supplies. The remaining chapters of this book examine the degree to which state fragility is actually linked to these pressing concerns.

INDEX OF STATE WEAKNESS IN THE DEVELOPING WORLD

The 141 weakest states with their overall and basket scores are presented below. A basket score of 0.00 represents the worst score in the 141-country sample, a score of 10.00 signifies the best.	**Color Coding Key** Color coding and quintiles are based on full sample of 141 countries.	Bottom quintile
		2nd quintile
		3rd quintile
		4th quintile
		Top quintile

Rank	Country	Overall Score	Economic	Political	Security	Social Welfare	GNI per capita
1	SOMALIA	0.52	0	0	1.37	0.7	226
2	AFGHANISTAN	1.65	4.51	2.08	0	0	271
3	CONGO, DEM. REP.	1.67	4.06	1.8	0.28	0.52	130
4	IRAQ	3.11	2.87	1.67	1.63	6.27	1134
5	BURUNDI	3.21	5.01	3.46	2.95	1.43	100
6	SUDAN	3.29	5.05	2.06	1.46	4.59	810
7	CENTRAL AFRICAN REP.	3.33	4.11	2.9	5.06	1.25	360
8	ZIMBABWE	3.44	1.56	1.56	6.81	3.84	350
9	LIBERIA	3.64	3.39	3.91	6.01	1.25	140
10	COTE D'IVOIRE	3.66	5.23	2.12	3.71	3.56	870
11	ANGOLA	3.72	5.42	2.67	5.32	1.45	1980
12	HAITI	3.76	3.9	2.62	5.21	3.31	480
13	SIERRA LEONE	3.77	5.04	3.87	5.43	0.76	240
14	ERITREA	3.84	3.09	2.78	7.01	2.48	200
15	NORTH KOREA	3.87	0.52	0.95	7.28	6.73	n/a
16	CHAD	3.9	5.8	2.42	6.18	1.21	480
17	BURMA	4.16	4.72	0.89	3.96	7.07	n/a
18	GUINEA-BISSAU	4.16	5.22	3.83	5.96	1.69	190
19	ETHIOPIA	4.46	6.14	4.03	5.91	1.75	180
20	CONGO, REP.	4.56	5.08	2.77	6.45	3.95	1100
21	NIGER	4.6	5.45	4.69	7.33	0.94	260
22	NEPAL	4.61	5.17	3.84	2.94	6.5	290
23	GUINEA	4.67	5	2.64	7.43	3.61	410
24	RWANDA	4.68	5.33	4.26	6.62	2.51	250
25	EQUATORIAL GUINEA	4.77	7.51	1.73	7.95	1.91	8250

(continued)

Rank	Country	Overall Score	Economic	Political	Security	Social Welfare	GNI per capita
26	TOGO	4.8	4.78	2.68	7.38	4.38	350
27	UGANDA	4.86	5.78	4.55	4.89	4.23	300
28	NIGERIA	4.88	5.39	3.51	5.37	5.24	640
29	CAMEROON	5.12	5.78	3.09	7.54	4.07	1080
30	YEMEN	5.18	5.8	3.64	6.43	4.85	760
31	COMOROS	5.2	4.24	4.2	8.18	4.2	660
32	ZAMBIA	5.23	5.08	4.59	8.15	3.11	630
33	PAKISTAN	5.23	6.58	3.52	4.69	6.13	770
34	CAMBODIA	5.27	6.33	3	7.18	4.57	480
35	TURKMENISTAN	5.27	5.05	1.4	7.88	6.75	1700
36	UZBEKISTAN	5.3	5.2	1.78	6.66	7.54	610
37	MAURITANIA	5.3	6.23	4.34	6.38	4.24	740
38	DJIBOUTI	5.31	5.05	3.69	8.21	4.29	1060
39	MOZAMBIQUE	5.32	5.6	5.33	8.35	1.98	340
40	PAPUA NEW GUINEA	5.32	5.13	4.62	7.45	4.08	770
41	SWAZILAND	5.33	5.57	3.65	8.28	3.8	2430
42	TAJIKISTAN	5.35	6.18	3.03	6.39	5.82	390
43	EAST TIMOR	5.51	3.93	4.41	7.74	5.98	840
44	BURKINA FASO	5.51	6.3	4.87	8.3	2.59	460
45	LAOS	5.53	5.88	2.56	7.98	5.71	500
46	MALAWI	5.6	5.68	4.83	8.11	3.77	170
47	COLOMBIA	5.63	5.84	5.79	1.78	9.11	2740
48	BANGLADESH	5.64	6.08	3.97	6.55	5.98	480
49	MADAGASCAR	5.65	5.24	5.95	7.65	3.76	280
50	KENYA	5.65	5.77	4.72	6.95	5.15	580
51	GAMBIA	5.79	5.26	4.54	8.29	5.06	310
52	MALI	5.85	6.33	6.16	8.49	2.43	440
53	LESOTHO	5.88	4.59	6.4	8.35	4.18	1030
54	SOLOMON ISLANDS	5.92	4.59	5.05	7.66	6.39	680
55	TANZANIA	5.94	6.38	5.41	8.08	3.89	350
56	SRI LANKA	5.94	6.32	5.47	3.38	8.59	1300
57	ALGERIA	6.07	6.83	4.27	4.04	9.13	3030
58	PHILIPPINES	6.08	6.18	5.59	4.16	8.4	1420

Rank	Country	Overall Score	Economic	Political	Security	Social Welfare	GNI per capita
59	SYRIA	6.14	4.62	2.76	7.49	9.67	1570
60	GUATEMALA	6.15	5.63	4.66	6.65	7.65	2640
61	SAO TOME & PRINCIPE	6.17	4.86	5.77	7.95	6.12	780
62	CUBA	6.17	3.6	2.94	8.28	9.88	n/a
63	GABON	6.18	6.51	3.93	8.36	5.94	5000
64	BOLIVIA	6.19	4.64	5.01	7.77	7.34	1100
65	RUSSIA	6.2	7.14	3.81	4.83	9.04	5780
66	IRAN	6.25	5.51	3.32	6.91	9.28	3000
67	INDIA	6.28	6.72	6.72	4.87	6.79	820
68	SENEGAL	6.28	6.38	5.97	7.96	4.82	750
69	HONDURAS	6.33	5.3	4.86	7.68	7.47	1200
70	VENEZUELA	6.33	6.01	3.76	7.12	8.44	6070
71	BENIN	6.36	6.25	5.82	8.51	4.86	540
72	NICARAGUA	6.37	5.61	4.79	8.14	6.94	1000
73	KYRGYZSTAN	6.39	6.27	3.62	7.53	8.14	490
74	CHINA	6.41	6.89	3.69	6.85	8.21	2010
75	PARAGUAY	6.44	4.78	4.5	8	8.5	1400
76	FIJI	6.47	5.99	5.19	6.32	8.37	3300
77	INDONESIA	6.49	6.46	5.25	5.92	8.34	1420
78	EGYPT	6.5	6.34	4.09	6.55	9.03	1350
79	THAILAND	6.5	7.14	5.3	5.07	8.51	2990
80	AZERBAIJAN	6.54	7.85	3.36	7.06	7.89	1850
81	BELARUS	6.63	6.57	2.31	8.24	9.41	3380
82	NAMIBIA	6.66	5.21	7.26	8.93	5.23	3230
83	VIETNAM	6.66	6.33	3.67	8.35	8.31	690
84	GHANA	6.72	5.92	7.02	8.44	5.48	520
85	ECUADOR	6.78	5.55	4.53	7.47	9.56	2840
86	LIBYA	6.8	6.84	2.45	8.12	9.77	7380
87	GUYANA	6.83	5.56	5.71	7.89	8.15	1130
88	MOLDOVA	6.89	6.41	4.69	7.93	8.54	1100
89	KAZAKHSTAN	6.92	7.43	3.59	8.33	8.31	3790
90	GEORGIA	6.99	6.58	5.66	7.15	8.58	1560
91	DOMINICAN REPUBLIC	7.01	5.83	5.89	8.18	8.14	2850
92	PERU	7.01	6.58	5.69	7.25	8.54	2920

(continued)

Rank	Country	Overall Score	Economic	Political	Security	Social Welfare	GNI per capita
93	LEBANON	7.02	7.05	4.86	6.77	9.4	5490
94	BHUTAN	7.08	6.04	6.16	9.78	6.33	1410
95	EL SALVADOR	7.1	6.03	6	8.13	8.23	2540
96	MOROCCO	7.11	6.77	5.5	8.01	8.15	1900
97	MONGOLIA	7.16	6.68	6.01	8.78	7.17	880
98	TURKEY	7.18	7.32	6.53	5.83	9.06	5400
99	BRAZIL	7.22	6.12	6.42	7.32	9.01	4730
100	MALDIVES	7.25	7	4.77	8.96	8.29	2680
101	JAMAICA	7.26	6.28	6.39	7.78	8.6	3480
102	BOTSWANA	7.27	6.59	8.41	9.29	4.78	5900
103	MICRONESIA	7.28	4.65	7.77	9.81	6.9	2380
104	TONGA	7.32	4.9	5.25	9.52	9.63	2170
105	ARMENIA	7.34	7.97	4.73	8.23	8.44	1930
106	MARSHALL ISLANDS	7.37	4.2	6.66	9.82	8.82	3000
107	UKRAINE	7.38	6.92	5.34	7.9	9.34	1950
108	SERBIA	7.43	7.14	5.89	7.39	9.29	3910
109	SURINAME	7.49	5.86	6.63	8.72	8.74	3200
110	SOUTH AFRICA	7.5	6.89	8.07	7.72	7.33	5390
111	ALBANIA	7.59	7.42	5.33	7.95	9.65	2960
112	TUNISIA	7.61	7.12	5.57	8.22	9.53	2970
113	BOSNIA-HERZEGOVINA	7.63	7.52	5.63	7.87	9.51	2980
114	MACEDONIA	7.66	7.04	5.84	8.09	9.66	3060
115	ARGENTINA	7.67	6.18	6.17	8.54	9.77	5150
116	VANUATU	7.7	6.06	7.21	10	7.52	1710
117	BELIZE	7.71	6.49	6.92	8.54	8.88	3650
118	JORDAN	7.74	7.26	6.16	8.03	9.5	2660
119	KIRIBATI	7.75	5.65	7.61	10	7.75	1230
120	MEXICO	7.83	7.82	6.38	7.63	9.51	7870
121	ROMANIA	7.91	7.91	6.77	8.42	8.54	4850
122	PANAMA	7.94	7.06	7.02	9.05	8.64	4890
123	CAPE VERDE	7.96	6.6	8.46	9.49	7.3	2130
124	MALAYSIA	8.2	7.64	7.06	8.49	9.61	5490
125	SAMOA	8.21	5.87	7.77	9.86	9.33	2270

Rank	Country	Overall Score	Economic	Political	Security	Social Welfare	GNI per capita
126	SEYCHELLES	8.23	7.33	6.54	9.52	9.55	8650
127	BULGARIA	8.38	8.05	7.21	8.61	9.64	3990
128	OMAN	8.46	8.67	6.26	9.42	9.48	9070
129	GRENADA	8.48	7.03	7.87	9.49	9.52	4420
130	COSTA RICA	8.65	6.89	8.31	9.62	9.79	4980
131	CROATIA	8.67	9.26	7.27	8.46	9.7	9330
132	URUGUAY	8.76	7.14	8.67	9.43	9.79	5310
133	MAURITIUS	8.79	7.34	8.49	9.67	9.68	5450
134	DOMINICA	8.9	7.47	8.92	9.57	9.66	3960
135	POLAND	9.01	8.95	8.17	8.98	9.95	8190
136	LATVIA	9.08	9.18	8.54	9.45	9.16	8100
137	SAINT LUCIA	9.11	8.01	9.6	9.25	9.59	5110
138	LITHUANIA	9.27	9.33	8.44	9.63	9.69	7870
139	CHILE	9.35	7.99	10	9.43	10	6980
140	HUNGARY	9.41	10	8.92	9.01	9.69	10950
141	SLOVAK REPUBLIC	9.41	9.95	8.68	9.32	9.68	9870

Appendix 1.2: Top Five Worst Performers on Each Indicator

	GNI per capita	GDP growth	Income Inequality	Inflation	Regulatory Quality
Economic	1. Burundi (#5) 2. Dem. Rep. of Congo (#3) 3. Liberia (#9) 4. Malawi (#46) 5. Ethiopia (#19)	1. Zimbabwe (#8) 2. East Timor (#43) 3. Liberia (#9) 4. Micronesia (#103) 5. Seychelles (#126)	1. Namibia (#82) 2. Lesotho (#53) 3. Central African Republic (#7) 4. Botswana (#102) 5. Bolivia (#64)	1. Zimbabwe (#8) 2. Angola (#11) 3. Burma (#17) 4. Guinea (#23) 5. Eritrea (#14)	1. Somalia (#1) 2. North Korea (#15) 3. Burma (#17) 4. Zimbabwe (#8) 5. Turkmenistan (#35)

	Government Effectiveness	Rule of Law	Voice & Accountability	Control of Corruption	Freedom (equal score of 0.0)
Political	1. Somalia (#1) 2. North Korea (#15) 3. Comoros (#31) 4. Iraq (#4) 5. Dem. Rep. of the Congo (#3)	1. Somalia (#1) 2. Afghanistan (#2) 3. Iraq (#4) 4. Zimbabwe (#8) 5. Dem. Rep. of the Congo (#3)	1. Burma (#17) 2. North Korea (#15) 3. Somalia (#1) 4. Turkmenistan (#35) 5. Libya (#86)	1. Somalia (#1) 2. North Korea (#15) 3. Burma (#17) 4. Equatorial Guinea (#25) 5. Afghanistan (#2)	1. Somalia (#1) 1. North Korea (#15) 1. Burma (#17) 1. Turkmenistan (#35) 1. Uzbekistan (#36) 1. Libya (#86) 1. Syria (#59) 1. Cuba (#62)

	Conflict Intensity	Gross Human Rights Abuses (tie for first and third)	Territory Affected by Conflict	Incidence of Coups	Political Stability & Lack of Violence
Security	1. Sudan (#6) 2. Somalia (#1) 3. Sri Lanka (#56) 4. Dem. Rep. of the Congo (#3) 5. Afghanistan (#2)	1. Sudan (#6) 1. Iraq (#4) 3. Dem. Rep. of the Congo (#3) 3. Colombia (#47) 5. Afghanistan (#2)	1. Colombia (#47) 2. Afghanistan (#2) 3. Somalia (#1) 4. Nepal (#22) 5. Dem. Rep. of the Congo (#3)	1. Fiji (#76) 2. Thailand (#79) 3. Guinea-Bissau (#18) 4. Mauritania (#37) 5. Sao Tome & Principe (#61)	1. Iraq (#4) 2. Somalia (#1) 3. Dem. Rep. of the Congo (#3) 4. Afghanistan (#2) 5. Nepal (#22)

	Child Mortality	Access to Improved Water and Sanitation	Under-nourishment	Primary School Completion	Life Expectancy
Social Welfare	1. Sierra Leone (#13) 2. Angola (#11) 3. Afghanistan (#2) 4. Niger (#21) 5. Liberia (#9)	1. Ethiopia (#19) 2. Chad (#16) 3. Somalia (#1) 4. Niger (#21) 5. Guinea (#23)	1. Eritrea (#14) 2. Dem. Rep. of the Congo (#3) 3. Burundi (#5) 4. Comoros (#31) 5. Tajikistan (#42)	1. Central African Republic (#7) 2. Guinea-Bissau (#18) 3. Niger (#21) 4. Burkina Faso (#44) 5. Chad (#16)	1. Botswana (#102) 2. Lesotho (#53) 3. Zimbabwe (#8) 4. Zambia (#32) 5. Central African Republic (#7)

Number in parenthesis indicates the country's overall rank.

Appendix 1.3: Methodological Note on Indicators

(1) **Conflict Intensity:** Measures the scale of violent conflict within a country, drawing from the Major Episodes of Political Violence data set maintained by the Center for Systemic Peace at the University of Maryland. Available at http://members.aol.com/cspmgm/warlist.htm. The indicator uses the "magnitude of societal-systemic impact (Mag)" variable from that data set, which measures "destructive impact, or magnitude, of the violent episode on the directly affected society or societies on a scale of 1 (smallest) to 10 (greatest)." The Index draws on data from 1993–2007, weighted toward the most recent data. Data is available for all countries in the Index.

(2) **Political Instability and Absence of Violence:** Measures "the perceptions of the likelihood that the government will be destabilized or overthrown by unconstitutional or violent means, including domestic violence or terrorism." This indicator is compiled from 12 different data sources. See *Governance Matters VI 2007*. Data is available for all countries in the Index. Available at http://papers.ssrn.com/sol3/papers.cfm?abstract_id=999979.

(3) **Incidence of Coups:** Indicator measures whether a leader was removed through irregular means, including by domestic rebel forces, military actors, or other government actors. This indicator draws on the Archigos data set, supplemented by Economist Intelligence Unit reports. Years included in the Index are 1992–2004 (Archigos), 2005–2006 (EIU), weighted toward most recent. Data is available for all countries in the Index.

(4) **Gross Human Rights Abuses:** Measures a state's scores on the Political Terror Scale, a ranking compiled by Mark Gibney of the University of North Carolina based on reports from the State Department and Amnesty International. The Index codes states as experiencing gross human rights abuses if they attain Level 4 or Level 5 on the Political Terror Scale. Level 4 is defined as practices of "imprisonment for political activity;" "politically-motivated executions;" "political murders, disappearances, and torture" that affect a "large portion of the population" and are a "common part of life;" and common unlimited detention, with or without trial, for political views. Level 5 is defined as including all the Level-4 terror characteristics that "encompass the entire population;" in addition, "the leaders of these countries place no limits on the means or thoroughness with which they pursue personal or ideological goals." Data coverage includes 2002–2006, weighted toward the most recent scores. Data is available for 135 countries in the Index.

(5) **Territory Affected by Conflict:** Draws on the "MAGAREA" variable of the Political Instability Task Force, which measures the "scaled portion of [a] country affected by fighting" in ethnic or revolutionary wars, ranging in score from 0 (less than one-tenth of the country and no significant cities directly or indirectly affected) to 4 (more than one-half of the country directly or indirectly affected). The indicator draws on data from 1991–2005, weighted toward the most recent. Data exists for all countries in the Index.

(6) **Government Effectiveness**: Measures the "quality of public services, the quality of the civil service and the degree of its independence from political pressures, the quality of policy formulation and implementation, and the credibility of the government's commitment to such policies." The indicator, which draws on 18 underlying data sources, is taken from the World Bank's *Governance Matters VI* (2007) data set. Data is available for all countries in the Index.

(7) **Rule of Law**: Indicator measures the "extent to which agents have confidence in and abide by the rules of society, in particular the quality of contract enforcement, the police, and the courts, as well as the likelihood of crime and violence." Taken from the World Bank's *Governance Matters VI* (2007) data set, it draws on 24 different sources. Data is available for all 141 countries in the Index.

(8) **Control of Corruption**: Measures the "extent to which public power is exercised for private gain, including petty and grand forms of corruption, as well as 'capture' of the state by elites and private interests." It comes from the World Bank's *Governance Matters VI* data set and draws on 23 different sources. Data is available for all 141 countries in the Index.

(9) **Voice and Accountability**. Measures the "extent to which a country's citizens are able to participate in selecting their government, as well as freedom of expression, freedom of association, and a free media." The indicator, which draws on 19 underlying sources, is taken from the World Bank's *Governance Matters VI* data set. Data is available for all 141 countries in the Index.

(10) **Freedom**: Measures the quality of "political rights and civil liberties" in each country. Scores range from 1 to 7, "with 1 representing the most free and 7 the least free." The source is Freedom House, *Freedom in the World* 2007. Data is available for all 141 countries in the Index.

(11) **GNI per Capita**: Measures gross national income per capita, converted into current U.S. dollars by using the World Bank Atlas method (which smoothes exchange rate fluctuations by using a three-year moving average, price-adjusted conversion factor). The source is World Bank, *World Development Indicators* 2007. Data is available for 138 countries in the Index.

(12) **GDP Growth**: Measures the growth of real gross domestic product (GDP) at market prices based on constant (inflation-adjusted) local currency. The source is World Bank, *World Development Indicators*. Years included in the Index are 2002–2006, weighted toward the most recent. Data is available for 138 countries in the Index.

(13) **Inflation**: Measures annual absolute percentage change in consumer prices. The Index uses the absolute value of the annual change in consumer prices, so that cases of deflation and inflation are treated in same manner. Years included in the Index are 2003–2007, weighted toward the most recent. Data is available for 135 countries in the Index.

(continued)

Appendix 1.3: Continued

(14) **Income Inequality:** The Gini coefficient. Measures "the extent to which the distribution of income . . . among individuals or households within an economy deviates from a perfectly equal distribution," with values ranging from 0 (perfect equality) and 100 (perfect inequality). Data is taken from World Bank, *World Bank Development Indicators, 2007*. Data is available for 99 countries in the Index.

(15) **Regulatory Quality:** Measures the "ability of the government to formulate and implement sound policies and regulations that permit and promote private sector development." The indicator, which is drawn from 15 different sources, including international business and bank country analysis surveys, is taken from the World Bank data set, *Governance Matters VI, 2007*. Data exist for all 141 countries in the Index.

(16) **Child Mortality:** Measures the annual probability (per 1,000 live births) of a child dying before reaching five years of age. The data source is a 2005 estimate "based on the work of the Interagency Group for Mortality Estimation, which includes UNICEF, the World Health Organization, the World Bank and the UN Population Fund," published in UNICEF's State of the World's Children 2007. Data exists for all 141 countries.

(17) **Primary School Completion:** Reports the proportion of pupils starting grade 1 who reach grade 5. The Index uses the most recent figures between 2000 and 2005, with data available for 126 countries.

(18) **Prevalence of Undernourishment:** Measures the "percentage of the population whose food intake is insufficient to meet dietary energy requirements continuously." The source is FAO, which has data for 130 countries in the Index.

(19) **Access to Improved Water Sources and Improved Sanitation Facilities:** Averages two data points: (a) the percentage of people in each country that are "using improved drinking water sources," which may include "household water connection, public standpipe, borehole, protected dug well, protected spring, rainwater collection and bottled water—if a secondary available source is also improved"; and (b) the percentage of people in that country "using improved sanitation facilities (including flush to piped sewer system, flush to septic tank, flush/pour flush to pit, flush/pour to flush elsewhere)." The source is World Bank, *World Development Indicators, 2007*. Data is available for 130 countries in the Index.

(20) **Life Expectancy:** Estimates predicted years of life at time of birth. The source is the World Bank, *World Development Indicators 2007*, which has data for 130 countries in the Index.

2

TRANSNATIONAL TERRORISM

From Africa to Central Asia to the Pacific Rim, nearly sixty countries stand on the brink of conflict or collapse. These failed states are the perfect incubators for extremism and terror.
—*Senator Barack Obama, August 2007*[1]

We must help raise up the failing states and stagnant societies that provide fertile ground for terrorists.
—*President George W. Bush, September 2005*[2]

Since the terrorist attacks of September 11, 2001, it has become commonplace to assert that weak states are ideal breeding grounds for transnational terrorism. The *New York Times* argued in a July 2005 editorial, "Failed states that cannot provide jobs and food for their people, that have lost chunks of territory to warlords, and that can no longer track or control their borders, send an invitation to terrorists."[3] At face value, such claims seem compelling. All things being equal, we would expect terrorists to be attracted to poorly governed or ungoverned states in which they can hatch plans without scrutiny; recruit and train without hindrance; and raise funds through illicit channels. This chapter reviews the evidence for the connection between state fragility and transnational terrorism, focusing on al-Qaeda and its affiliated organizations, which pose the most acute global terrorist threat. It concludes that the links between these two phenomena are more complex and contingent than conventional wisdom would have us believe.

First, fragile states *do* offer some benefits to transnational terrorists, including conflict experience, weak border control, and safe havens for training and planning. But other ostensible advantages of state weakness are less salient than frequently assumed. With the important exceptions of Iraq, Afghanistan, and Pakistan, weak states do not appear to have provided disproportionately large pools of recruits or targets for recent terrorist operations. Resources and financing may be found in weak states but are as (or more) likely to come from wealthier countries. Nor do most weak states offer significant opportunities for terrorists to win local political support by performing para-state functions, such as the provision of social welfare services. In fact, most weak states that have been named as potential havens for transnational terrorists, from Uzbekistan to Mali, have failed to emerge as such—while al-Qaeda and its affiliates are increasingly exploiting developed countries in Europe and North America.

Second, transnational terrorist groups require a certain baseline level of political order. Territories that are truly "ungoverned" may present insuperable obstacles to terrorist operations, since they fail to provide minimal operational security and lack the normal trappings of sovereignty (which might otherwise discourage external intervention). For these reasons, a middle-ranking group of weak—but not yet failing—states (e.g., Pakistan, Kenya) may offer more long-term advantages to terrorists than either anarchic zones or strong states. Such weak states are less chaotic than failed states and have the transportation and communications infrastructure terrorists need to operate, but are less likely than developed countries to have the will or capacity to carry out serious counterterrorism efforts.

Finally, the evidence suggests that a critical, if not determinative, factor in whether a country at any point along the spectrum of state fragility becomes a terrorist haven is whether transnational terrorist groups enjoy *active* support from national or local power brokers. Such support is most often based on cultural and religious factors that make leaders and populations sympathetic to terrorist aims, as has occurred in Yemen, or where indigenous radical Islamist groups have come to power or are contesting power, as in Somalia in 2010. By contrast, transnational Islamic terrorists are unlikely to be attracted to non-Muslim failed states (such as the Democratic Republic of the Congo) or even unstable Muslim ones where local power wielders are opposed to their goals (such as Iraq following the Sunni Awakening). Given the importance of local support for terrorist groups, a state's will is arguably more important than its capacity when it comes to providing safe haven to terrorists.

THE GLOBAL THREAT OF TRANSNATIONAL TERRORISM

Terrorism has emerged as one of the most daunting global security challenges of the twenty-first century. The phenomenon itself is nothing new, however. Politically motivated violence against noncombatants has been a hallmark of the modern age. From Guy Fawkes's efforts to blow up the Houses of Parliament in 1605 to Gavrilo Princip's assassination of Archduke Franz Ferdinand in 1914, individuals and groups have planned and executed terrorist acts to advance political and ideological agendas. What *have* changed are the potential scale of such attacks and the sweeping objectives of some perpetrators. Terrorist groups have emerged that aspire not merely to local goals but to undermine global order and transform the international system, and the diffusion of new technologies of mass destruction could provide them with the means to accomplish their ends.

Terrorism is a contested concept that lacks a universally accepted meaning. A serviceable definition is *the deliberate use or threat of violence against noncombatants by a nonstate actor for the achievement of political ends, typically with the intent of creating a wider psychological impact.*[4] Terrorists have earthly goals, even when they find inspiration from religion. A brief glance at the U.S. list of officially designated "Foreign Terrorist Organizations" reveals enormous variation in the motivations of such groups and the geographic scope of their ambitions.[5] Most pursue distinctly local agendas (e.g., the Liberation Tigers of Tamil Eelam in Sri Lanka and the Revolutionary Armed Forces of Colombia). For most developing countries, the main terrorist threat is posed not by transnational terrorists but by local armed groups launching politically motivated attacks against unarmed civilians.

Transnational terrorists are a unique subset of terrorists with a distinctive profile. First, they plan and carry out attacks across international borders, and their logistical arrangements typically span national frontiers. Second, although they may exploit local insurgencies, their motivations and objectives are global (or at least regional) in scope. Third, their ideology focuses on the transformation of international power and political relationships. Fourth, their membership crosses national, cultural, and ethnic backgrounds, often including veterans of nationally based conflicts. Finally, they are typically organized as decentralized networks of affinity groups, with cells in multiple countries and flexible alliances with local extremists.[6] Given these criteria, the cohort of transnational terrorist organizations represents a small fraction of terrorist groups worldwide, notwithstanding the growing overlap in some countries and the tendency of some local actors to adopt a transnational brand.

Al-Qaeda and its Evolution

The world's leading terrorist network remains al-Qaeda, spearhead of the global jihadist movement and the primary target of U.S. counterterrorism efforts. Formed around 1988 in Afghanistan, by the Saudi extremist Osama bin Laden, al-Qaeda represents the most significant terrorist challenge the world has ever known. The organization is distinguished by its global and revolutionary goals, which include the acquisition and use of weapons of mass destruction. Following 9/11, the George W. Bush administration made the "global war on terrorism" the central focus of its foreign policy, and the Obama administration continues to maintain that "bin Laden and al-Qaeda are our number one threat when it comes to American security."[7]

Al-Qaeda's agenda is grounded in religious fundamentalism, namely a *salafi* interpretation of Sunni Islam. But the group's objectives are earthly rather than apocalyptic: it seeks to eliminate Western influence from the Islamic world, particularly the Arab Middle East. Among the world's Muslims, a minority seek to make Islamic law, or sharia, the primary source of law. The *salafis* represent a further subset of Islamic extremists who demand a return to the original practices of the *salaf* (the founding fathers of Islam) by making the Quran and the example of Mohammed the sole basis for governance in Muslim states. Al-Qaeda and its affiliates represent an even smaller subset of *salafis* engaged in a violent struggle against the enemies of Islam. Al-Qaeda and the broader *salafi* jihad seek to depose Western-backed Muslim regimes and create a unified Caliphate spanning the entire Islamic world. Al-Qaeda's distinctive contribution is the conviction that a key to defeating the "near enemy"—the corrupt Muslim governments of Egypt, Jordan, Saudi Arabia, and Pakistan—is to simultaneously attack the "far enemy"—the United States and its Western allies, who sustain and protect the apostate regimes.[8] Bin Laden announced his intentions to lead this struggle in 1997, when he declared war on the West, and the following year, when he signed a fatwa justifying the killing of Americans and their allies, including civilians.

Bin Laden has decreed it a "religious duty" for Muslims to acquire nuclear and chemical weapons—and as a networked organization lacking a specific "return address," al-Qaeda will not be easily deterred. The network has made numerous attempts to acquire WMD, including experimentation with chemical weapons, efforts to develop ricin and anthrax, attempts to procure highly enriched uranium, and meetings with Pakistani nuclear scientists. While al-Qaeda's use of nuclear weapons would be catastrophic, the network has already demonstrated the ability to inflict great damage on the West. As bin Laden has boasted, the 9/11 attacks cost the U.S. economy some $500 billion, for a cost to al-Qaeda of only $500,000—a million-to-one return on its investment. The 9/11 attacks were followed by a string of horrific (if less spectacular) attacks, including bombings of trains in Madrid, mass transit in London, and various Western targets in locations ranging from Bali to Istanbul.

Although its leaders retain a safe haven in the poorly policed borderlands of Afghanistan and Pakistan, al-Qaeda has morphed since 9/11 from a monolithic organization into a "networked constituency" of affiliated "franchises," as well as local groups that undertake anti-Western attacks without apparent support or direction from al-Qaeda itself.[9] A global *jihadi* subculture is mobilized and linked through video and the Internet. While some analysts believe the organization has been significantly degraded in recent years, others note that al-Qaeda "might well regroup if left unmolested in a lawless region in Pakistan, Afghanistan, or Somalia."[10] Meanwhile, the threat from affiliated groups may be growing. Despite enormous expenditures by the United States in the "global war on terrorism," Director of National Intelligence Dennis Blair testified in February 2009 that "al-Qaeda and its affiliates and allies remain dangerous and adaptive enemies...intent on attacking U.S. interests worldwide, including the U.S. Homeland."[11]

Al-Qaeda and Company: Mapping the Global Salafi Jihad

Al-Qaeda cannot be considered in isolation.[12] Alongside "al-Qaeda central," one finds a diffuse and decentralized network of local and regional actors inspired by a common *salafi* ideology and perceived enemy. These include transnational groups like Jemaah Islamiyah in Southeast Asia, and al-Qaeda in the Islamic Maghreb (AQIM), which is active across North Africa and the Sahel. Al-Qaeda "franchises" have been established in Iraq, Saudi Arabia, and Yemen.[13] Other groups, such as the Islamic Movement of Uzbekistan (IMU) and Egypt's al-Gama'a al-Islamiyya, have strong institutional and personal ties to al-Qaeda. Still other organizations may cooperate tactically with al-Qaeda members but do not share its *salafi* ideology or target list. These would include, for example, the Pakistan-based terrorist groups Jaish-e-Mohammed (JeM), Lashkar-e-Taiba (LeT), Lashkar-e-Jhangvi (LeJ), and Harakat ul-Mujahedin (HUM); and the Philippines-based Abu Sayyaf Group (ASG).

The evolving relationship between al-Qaeda and AQIM illustrates the fluid nature of the global *salafi* jihad. AQIM originated in 1998 as a splinter group of Algerian rebels under the name Salafist Group for Preaching and Combat (GSPC). On the second anniversary of 9/11, GSPC pledged its fealty to bin Laden, broadening its aspirations from the overthrow of the Algerian government to promote sharia-based states across the Maghreb and Sahel. The arrangement was fruitful for both al-Qaeda and AQIM: the former gained a North African foothold and an opportunity to demonstrate the vigor of its "brand." AQIM, meanwhile, benefited financially and in recruitment from the affiliation, which it believed would translate into easier fundraising.[14]

Table 2.1 identifies some thirty-four groups that currently comprise the "global jihadist network," defined as al-Qaeda and affiliated terrorist groups. The table draws on three authoritative sources: the State Department's 2008 Country Reports on Terrorism, which list Foreign Terrorist Organizations (FTOs), and its Terrorist Exclusion List; the MIPT Terrorism Knowledge Base (TKB); and the RAND Corporation's 2006 study, *Beyond al-Qaeda: The Global Jihadist Movement*.[15] For each affiliate group, the table summarizes the extent and nature of the presumed connection with al-Qaeda central, and the group's primary countries of operation. (Inevitably, this list is at best a time-bound approximation of what is a fluid, evolving global jihadist movement).

Material support, personal ties, and ideological affinity have played an important role in building and sustaining the transnational jihadist network. As shown in table 2.1, a "top tier" of al-Qaeda-linked terrorist groups may receive financial support and training from al-Qaeda, conduct joint operations and planning sessions, and have extensive leadership ties. Other groups are more loosely affiliated with al-Qaeda; in their case, shared ideology becomes the most prevalent linkage. At least ten groups have pledged support to al-Qaeda, either through "official" mergers, implicit or explicit adoption of the al-Qaeda brand, or public statements.

As table 2.1 indicates, al-Qaeda-linked terrorist groups are geographically centered in South Asia, the Middle East, and North Africa, with lower concentrations in the periphery of these regions, including sub-Saharan Africa, Central Asia, and Southeast Asia. A few groups have an operational presence in Western Europe. (The table notes primary areas of operation; it does not reflect the significant fund-raising and logistical networks of many of these groups throughout Europe, North America, and the Middle East.) Particularly striking is the number of "top tier" groups—ten of nineteen—operating in Afghanistan, Pakistan, or Kashmir. Other countries that appear particularly attractive to *salafi* groups include Algeria, Morocco, Yemen, Somalia, and Iraq.

Table 2.1: The Global Jihadist Network - Al Qaeda Affiliates

Group	Type of Affiliation								Primary Area of Operation
	Ideology	Public Support	Finance	Operations	Training	Planning	Sanctuary	Leadership Ties	
Al-Qaida (AQ)	-	-	-	-	-	-	-	-	Pakistan, Afghanistan
Al-Jihad (AJ)/Egyptian Islamic Jihad (EIJ)	Officially merged with al Qaeda								Egypt, Pakistan
Al-Qaida in the Islamic Maghreb (AQIM)*	Officially merged with al Qaeda								Algeria, Mali, Mauritania
Al Qaeda in the Arabian Peninsula (AQAP)	x	?	x	x	x	x	x	x	Saudi Arabia, Yemen
Jemaah Islamiya Organization (JI)	x		x	x	x	x	x	x	India, Malaysia, Philippines
Lashkar-e-Jhangvi (LeJ)	x	x	x	x	x	x	x	x	Pakistan
Lashkar-e-Taiba (LeT)	x		x	x	x	x	x	x	Pakistan, Kashmir
Jaish-e-Mohammed (JeM)	x		x	?	x	x	x	x	Pakistan, Kashmir
Harakat ul-Mujahedin (HUM)	x	x	x	x	x	x	x	x	Pakistan, Kashmir, Afghanistan
Islamic Movement of Uzbekistan (IMU)	x	?	x	x	x	?	?	?	Afghanistan, Pakistan, Iran, Kyrgyzstan, Tajikistan, Kazakhstan, Uzbekistan
Harakat ul-Jihad-I-Islami/Bangladesh (HUJI-B)	x	x	x	x	x	x	x		Bangladesh, India, Burma
Moroccan Islamic Combatant Group (GICM)	x		x	x	x	x	x	?	Morocco, Europe, Afghanistan, Canada

Group							Countries of Operation
Libyan Islamic Fighting Group (LIFG)	x		x	x	x	x	Libya, UK
Al-Qaida in Iraq (AQI)**	x	x	?	x	x	x	Iraq
Al-Ittihad al-Islami (AIAI)	x	x	x	x	x		Somalia
Al Shabab	x	x	?	x		x	Somalia
Taliban	x	x	x	x	x	x	Afghanistan, Pakistan
Hizb-I Islami Gulbuddin (HIG)	x		?	?	?	x	Afghanistan, Pakistan
Abu Sayyaf Group (ASG)	x		x	x	x	x	Philippines, Malaysia
Gama'a al-Islamiyya (IG)	x	x	x	?	?		Afghanistan, Yemen, Iran, Germany, UK
Tunisian Combatant Group (TCG)	Recruiting, logistics for Afghan training camps; ties to global jihadist network						Tunisia
Islamic Jihad Union (IJU)			x				Uzbekistan, Afghanistan, Pakistan, Germany
Islamic Int'l Peacekeeping Brigade (IIPB)							Russia (Chechnya and North Caucasus)
Riyadus-Salikhin (RSRSBCM)***	?		?	x		x	Russia (Chechnya)
Salafia Jihadia	x		x	?	x	?	Morocco
Dhamat Houmet Dawaa	x		?	?	?		Algeria
Salafia							
Ansar al-Islam	x		x				Iraq
Hizbul Mujahideen (HM)			?	?		?	Pakistan, Kashmir

(continued)

Table 2.1: Continued

Group	Type of Affiliation								Primary Area of Operation
	Ideology	Public Support	Finance	Operations	Training	Planning	Sanctuary	Leadership Ties	
East Turkistan Islamic Movement (ETIM)			?		?				China, Kyrgyzstan, Afghanistan
Eastern Turkistan Liberation Organization			?		?				China, Kyrgyzstan, Pakistan
Armed Islamic Group (GAI)	x								Algeria
Islamic Army of Aden (IAA)†	x	x							Yemen
Abu Nayaf al-Afghani	x								Spain
Takfir wa Hijra	x			?					Egypt, Sudan, Algeria; cells throughout Middle East and Europe

LEGEND:

* Formerly Salafist Group for Preaching and Combat (GSPC)

** Formerly Tawhid and Jihad

*** Riyadus-Salikhin Reconnaissance and Sabotage Battalion of Chechen Martyrs

? Insufficient data/information

† a.k.a. Aden Abyan Islamic Army (AAIA)

‡ a.k.a. Battalion of the Martyr Abdullah Azzam (named after Osama bin Laden's mentor)

	Definitively linked with al-Qaeda
	Member of the broader Jihadi Network

Sources: Compiled from State 2008 Country Reports on Terrorism; RAND Report: Beyond al-Qaeda (Part 1): The Global Jihadist Movement; MIPT Terrorism Knowledge Database

THE CONVENTIONAL WISDOM ABOUT TRANSNATIONAL TERROR AND WEAK AND FAILED STATES

It is above all the danger posed by al-Qaeda and its affiliates that explains the growing U.S. and international preoccupation with weak and failing states. As President Bush explained in his introduction to the 2002 U.S. National Security Strategy, the terrorist attacks of 9/11 showed the United States that it is "now more threatened by weak and failing states than we are by conquering ones."[16] That same year, an independent study of postconflict reconstruction agreed: "One of the principal lessons of the events of September 11 is that failed states matter—not just for humanitarian reasons but also for national security as well."[17] More recently, terrorist expert Bruce Hoffmann asserted: "Al-Qaeda is aggressively seeking out, destabilizing, and exploiting failed states and other areas of lawlessness. While the United States remains preoccupied with trying to secure yesterday's failed state—Afghanistan—al-Qaeda is busy staking out new terrain."[18]

On its face, the connection between state weakness and transnational terrorism seems plausible. Weak and failing states could theoretically provide a range of benefits, including access to sanctuaries, bases, weapons, recruits, financing, transit routes, staging grounds, conflict experience, and opportunities to secure ideological support through local propaganda and the provision of services. Data on global terrorist attacks from 1991 to 2001 suggest that most deaths due to terrorism could be attributed to perpetrators from economically stagnant, conflict-ridden, authoritarian countries.[19] Similarly, as shown in table 2.1, many terrorists use poorly governed, unstable, and violence-prone countries as their primary base of operations. Al-Qaeda, for example, enjoyed the hospitality of Sudan and Afghanistan, where it built training camps and enlisted new members; exploited Somalia and Yemen to launch attacks on the U.S. embassies in Nairobi and Dar es Salaam, as well as on the *USS Cole*; and allegedly financed its operations in part through illicit trade in gemstones from African conflict zones. Thus the British government has argued that lack of access to weak and failed states "would be a severe impediment" to terrorist operations.[20]

STATES AND TERRORISM

The decision by a transnational terrorist group to set up shop in a particular state is presumably shaped by a variety of considerations. Although weak capacity may enable terrorism in some circumstances, it is obvious that not all weak and failed states are afflicted by terrorism.[21] A country's attractiveness to global *salafi* jihadists is at least partly a function of the size and ideological (or political) orientation of its Muslim population. Africa is a case in point. In principle, the region should be attractive to transnational terrorist groups, given its many ungoverned spaces, conflict zones, porous borders, refugees, social cleavages, corrupt and authoritarian governments, stagnated economies, and ready supply of small arms and light weapons. And yet we find enormous variation in al-Qaeda's presence and influence on the continent, which

Table 2.2: State Capacity versus State Policy to Oppose Terrorism[22]

		STATE CAPACITY	
		High	Low
STATE POLICY	*Opposes Terrorism*	State capable of acting, opposes terrorism	State incapable of acting, opposes terrorism (**exploitable weak state**)
	Supports Terrorism	State capable of acting, supports terrorism (**classic state sponsor**)	State incapable of acting, supports terrorism

is greatest in North Africa and the Horn, moderate in the Sahel, and quite weak in Central and Southern Africa.

A second critical factor is whether the state in question has either the inclination or capacity to prevent the terrorist group from setting up shop. It is common to make firm distinctions between states that oppose terrorism and those that actively support it. In fact, the connection between states and transnational terrorists may encompass a wide range of relationships between wholehearted sponsorship and unequivocal antipathy. Chapter 1 introduced a distinction between types of weak states according to their capacity to provide essential political goods versus their will to do so. Borrowing from the work of Daniel Byman, consider a similar matrix (table 2.2) that divides states into four quadrants, based on whether the state supports or opposes terrorism as a matter of policy, and whether it possesses or lacks the inherent capacity to act against terrorists.

Disentangling shortcomings in capacity and will to explain poor performance in combating terrorism can be difficult. Counterterrorism assistance from the United States and other donors is predicated on the belief that fragile states are poor but well-intentioned: they simply lack the resources and tools to do the job. This is undoubtedly true for many poor countries, which find it difficult to police mountainous terrain, jungles, mangrove swamps, desert wastes, and chaotic urban environments. Mali, for instance, is a relatively well-governed country and a willing partner in U.S. counterterrorism efforts—but it is one of the poorest countries in the world, with only 10,000 security forces and two functional helicopters. Mali also faces a low-level insurgency among the nomadic Tuareg people, who may cooperate with terrorists for financial or tactical reasons. Despite the government's efforts (and a U.S.-led program to build the capacity of Malian forces), AQIM militants operate in the country's remote northern deserts, a lawless region along the Algerian border inhabited by tribes and smugglers.

In an era of nonstate, networked terrorism, some observers believe the relevance of "state sponsors" will continue to wane.[23] As a practical matter, however, state policy may occupy a blurry middle ground between overt support and clear opposition. A handful of states, including Iran and Syria, actively support terrorist groups (e.g., Hezbollah) by providing money, arms, passports, training, diplomatic backing, organizational assistance, ideological direction, or sanctuary. More common is passive state acquiescence to the presence of transnational terrorists, due to ignorance, weak capacity, or a lack of political will. A regime's irresolution may reflect official and/or public sympathy with terrorist goals; a perception that such groups do not represent a direct threat; fears of reprisal from terrorist groups; or constraints imposed by local norms, laws, or customs.[24] Yemen, discussed at the end of this chapter, shows how desultory counterterrorist policies can provide openings for such groups to flourish. In some instances, state policy itself may be fragmented, with some regime components supporting terrorist activities, while others are either unaware or powerless to stop it. The murky relationship among Pakistan's Inter-Services Intelligence Directorate (ISI), the Taliban, and al-Qaeda since 9/11 offers a case in point (see Box 2.1).

In a similar manner, a state's *capacity* to combat terrorism may vary considerably across functional areas (e.g., intelligence collection, border control, law enforcement, provision of justice, or financial regulation) or regions. In some of the weakest states, the governing regime has difficulty controlling its own capital city, much less its borders and periphery. Weak-state governments may simply lack the resources to devote to counterterrorism capabilities, or they may choose not to invest in such capabilities due to other policy or security priorities. In many developing countries, pervasive corruption may further impede border control and law enforcement efforts. State-terrorist linkages thus reflect gradations of capability and commitment.[25]

Box 2.1: Capacity vs. Will: The Case of Pakistan

Despite the repeated U.S. official descriptions of Pakistan as a "staunch ally in the global war on terrorism," the country's record in taking on al-Qaeda and its affiliates in the country has been uneven. Al-Qaeda's senior leadership is believed to have fled to Pakistan following the collapse of the Taliban in late 2001. By 2006, the State Department reported, the country's Federally Administered Tribal Areas (FATA) had become "a safe haven for al Qaida terrorists and other extremists."[26] Al-Qaeda's continued ability to operate in this region appears to reflect a lack of both capacity and will on the part of successive regimes in Islamabad.

There are clearly enormous obstacles to the suppression of al-Qaeda and its allies in the FATA. The Pakistani state has never effectively controlled the 1,500-mile-long border region, where power is held by local Pashtun tribes (many of whom have close ethnic, ideological, or familial ties to the Taliban). Pakistan's neocolonial system in the FATA is arbitrary, and the region's tribes have long resisted central authority from both Islamabad and Kabul. Until 2009, Pakistan's primary military presence in the region was the under-equipped and poorly trained Frontier Corps paramilitary force. (The Pakistani army did not enter the FATA at all between the country's founding in 1947 and October 2001.) As a result, the government of President Pervez Musharraf was forced to acquiesce to Taliban advances in and beyond the FATA, negotiating several truces that allowed the Taliban to escalate attacks against North Atlantic Treaty Organization (NATO) forces and other targets in Afghanistan.

Even aside from these constraints, however, and notwithstanding the arrest of several hundred terrorists, successive Pakistani regimes have largely turned a blind eye toward al-Qaeda

(continued)

Box 2.4: Continued

and its affiliates. Since the 1980s, Pakistan has deployed radical Islamist terrorist groups in Kashmir. Until 9/11, Pakistan also supported the Taliban, and some observers claim the military and intelligence services have maintained ties to Taliban leaders (and other al-Qaeda-linked groups) as potential allies in the region if and when NATO withdraws from Afghanistan. In 2009, Secretary of State Hillary Clinton publicly questioned whether Pakistan's government was fully on board in tracking down al-Qaeda members believed to be active in its territory.[27] In October 2010, the White House confirmed to Congress that Pakistan's military had "continued to avoid military engagement that would put it in direct conflict with Afghan Taliban or [al Qaeda] forces in North Waziristan."[28]

The civilian government under President Asif Ali Zardari, who replaced Musharraf in August 2008, initially appeared more willing—though perhaps even less able—to suppress Pakistan's *jihadi* groups. In late 2009, the government undertook significant operations against militants in the country's North West Frontier Province as well as the FATA. But through autumn 2010 it remained far from certain that the government's efforts to bring the military and the ISI in line would be either sustained or successful. The Zardari government remained highly unpopular and faced numerous security and economic crises—difficulties exacerbated by the catastrophic floods that inundated much of the country in summer 2010. Pakistani public opinion remained largely anti-American (if not in widespread sympathy with the *jihadi* movement, particularly since the latter targeted major Pakistani cities in a wave of terrorism). And the Zardari government, like its predecessor, had done little to counter the Afghan Taliban leadership believed to operate from Quetta, "viewing it as a strategic asset rather than a domestic threat."[29] It is hardly surprising, then, that more than nine years after the Taliban was driven from Afghanistan, Pakistan remained a safe haven for bin Laden and his associates.

WHY TERRORISTS MIGHT BE ATTRACTED TO WEAK AND FAILING STATES

How might transnational terrorism be linked to state weakness? In principle, fragile states could provide terrorists with functional benefits. Beyond forthright sponsorship, these include safe havens, bases, conflict experience, recruits, fund-raising opportunities, transit routes, targets, staging grounds, and opportunities to secure ideological support through propaganda and local services.[30]

American civilian and military officials have repeatedly stressed the value of weak and failing states to transnational terrorists.[31] More interestingly, terrorists themselves have made similar assertions. Identifying frontline bastions for the creation of a sharia-based Islamic caliphate, the *jihadi* strategist Abu Bakr Naji names Yemen, Saudi Arabia, Pakistan, Nigeria, Jordan, and North Africa. In elaborating on "the factors considered when selecting countries," Naji discussed the presence of rugged topography and geographically remote regions; a weak system of political governance, both "in the peripheries of the borders of its state" and in "overcrowded" urban regions; and a ready availability of weapons. He also mentions two features less directly related to governance: the presence of extremist ideas of "jihadi Islamic expansion" and amenable cultural traits that predispose inhabitants to jihad.[32]

Conflict Experience and Weapons

History suggests that states racked by civil war or insurgency can habituate future terrorists to extreme violence, while providing them with the skills they need to take human life and survive attacks. Beginning with Afghanistan in the 1980s, and extending through subsequent conflicts in Bosnia, Chechnya, Algeria, Kashmir, Iraq, and Somalia, foreign fighters have flocked to defend other Muslims, with the veterans of these conflicts subsequently carrying their ideology and skills to other struggles (or returning home to form part of a global *jihadi* network). Veterans of the Afghan war were at the vanguard of the terrorist campaign in Egypt from 1990 to 1997, and carried out the bombing of the World Trade Center in 1993. Similarly, the collapse of Iraq following the U.S.-led invasion transformed that country into a magnet for thousands of foreign fighters. Indeed, the invasion was a gift of incalculable proportions for bin Laden, allowing him to depict its struggle as a "defensive" jihad against "crusaders" in the heartland of the Islamic world.[33] By early 2009, the government of Afghanistan reported that Taliban ranks were swelling with foreign fighters from Iraq.[34] Somalia has more recently played a similar role, drawing "a fresh flow of foreign fighters," including Americans and Europeans of Somali origin, Arabs, Afghans, Pakistanis, Chechens, Uzbeks, and Sudanese.[35]

Zones of turmoil and insecurity can also serve as laboratories for innovative terrorist techniques that migrate from one conflict to the next. One example is suicide bombing, which was pioneered in Beirut during the 1980s, perfected in Sri Lanka by the LTTE, and adopted by terrorist groups around the world. A more recent example is the improvised explosive device (IED) and its various permutations, which became a hallmark of the insurgency in Iraq but has since spread to Afghanistan.

Beyond providing useful experience in the administration of violence, many weak and failing states offer ready access to the instruments of violence. Yemen provides a startling example. The country is awash in small arms and light weapons. According to Yemen's Interior Ministry, the number of firearms in private hands may exceed 60 million, for a population of 20 million. This implies a dozen small arms for every adult male. Outside the capital—where weapons possession is banned, but not uncommon—most men carry weapons, and arms trafficking is rampant. Beyond small arms, anti-tank rockets and other heavy weapons are occasionally used in intertribal and tribe-state conflicts and, disconcertingly, are often sold by corrupt military commanders to tribesmen.[36]

The record suggests that transnational terrorist groups benefit from ready access to means of violence, a cadre of battle-hardened operatives prepared to engage in ruthless acts, and innovations in the art of destruction. All things being equal, such conflict experience, available weaponry, and practical knowledge is most likely to be found in the unstable and conflict-ridden countries that dominate the bottom two quintiles of the Index of State Weakness in the Developing World.

Pools of Recruits

Weak and failing states are often described as rich recruiting grounds for terrorists for two reasons. First, such countries often suffer from high levels of conflict, suggesting a large number of individuals trained in and accustomed to the use of extreme violence. Second, the poor economic prospects and high unemployment rates of many fragile states, particularly those experiencing youth bulges, can reduce the opportunity costs of joining a terrorist organization.[37] The Sahel is a case in point: The region's countries are among the very poorest in the world, with Mali, Chad, and Niger ranking among the bottom twelve (out of 179) countries on the UNDP's 2008 Human Development Index (and Mauritania not much better at 140). As the head of the USAID mission in Mali told a reporter in 2008: "Young men...are looking for jobs or something to do with their lives. These are the same people who could be susceptible to other messages of economic security."[38]

However, looking at the nationalities of known or captured transnational terrorists, we find a more complex picture. None of the nineteen 9/11 hijackers came from a fragile state (fifteen were from Saudi Arabia, and one was from Lebanon, a middle-ranking state). In a broader survey of known al-Qaeda operatives, terrorism expert Marc Sageman found the top countries of origin to be Saudi Arabia, Egypt, France, Algeria, Morocco, and Indonesia—none a weak or critically weak state.[39]

A similar pattern appears to hold among known and captured foreign fighters in Iraq during the height of U.S. military involvement there. Among the many source countries, only Sudan and Yemen can be described as fragile states[40] (see tables 2.3 and 2.4).

Table 2.3: Nationality of Captured Foreign Fighters in Iraq (2005) (weak, critically weak and failed states bolded)

Egypt: 78	Tunisia: 10	United Arab	Somalia: 1
Syria: 66	Algeria: 8	Emirates: 2	**Yemen: 1**
Sudan: 41	Libya: 7	India: 2	Indonesia: 1
Saudi Arabia: 32	Turkey: 6	Denmark: 1	Ireland: 1
Jordan: 17	Lebanon: 3	France: 1	Kuwait: 1
Iran: 13	Great Britain: 2	Macedonia: 1	United States: 1
Palestine: 12	Qatar: 2	Moroco: 1	
		Israel: 1	

Table 2.4: Nationalities of Foreign Fighters in Iraq, Based on Biographical Data (2007) (Weak states in bold)

Saudi Arabia: 305	Algeria: 64	Tunisia: 38	Egypt: 2
Libya: 137	Syria: 56	Jordan: 14	France: 2
Yemen: 68	Morocco: 50	Turkey: 6	

To be sure, a handful of weak and critically weak Islamic states do provide a significant percentage of terrorist recruits. A list of 759 U.S. prisoners in Guantanamo Bay, Cuba, shows that nearly fifty percent came from Pakistan, Yemen, or Afghanistan (the last of these hardly surprising, given that U.S. forces had been engaged there since 2001). And some recent reports from Somalia and Pakistan have cited the presence of numerous fighters from Uzbekistan, which is certainly a weak state as well.[41] (See figure 2.1).

With a few exceptions, however, the contribution of weak and failing states to transnational terrorist organizations seems fairly modest. Why? To begin, the skills and sophistication required for transnational terrorism, including the ability to exploit information, pass undetected through border controls, and navigate foreign societies, are not common in many of the weakest states. Combat skills may also be in high demand locally, particularly in conflict-ridden states. Other variables, including low affinity to jihad, lack of shared cultural links or historical narratives, geographic distance, individual preoccupations with basic survival, and the absence of *jihadi* networks to facilitate travel, may also play a role.

Possibly for this reason, a large percentage of the known members of al-Qaeda and affiliated members of the global *salafi* movement have been drawn from the Muslim diaspora, particularly living in Western Europe, where they often experience discrimination.[42] One scholar found that 84 percent of the al-Qaeda members in his sample joined terrorist networks while living in the diaspora, and 87 percent of these while in Western Europe.[43] The problem may not be limited to Europe, however, despite the widely held belief that Muslims in the United States tend to be less susceptible to

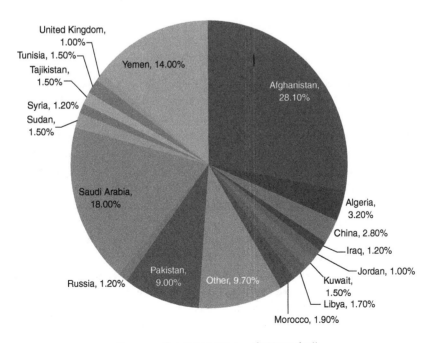

Figure 2.1: Guantanamo Detainees by Nationality[44]

extremism. A number of Somali youths from the Minneapolis area (many of them refugees) were recruited to join a "jihad" against the Ethiopian troops who invaded Somalia in 2006. Many of them are believed to have joined the al-Qaeda-linked al-Shabab group, and at least one has carried out a suicide bombing. As of late 2010, these recruits had not succeeded in attacking the United States, but as the *New York Times* observes, "FBI officials worry that with their training, ideology and American passports, there is a real danger that they could."[45]

Porous Borders That Facilitate Transit and Logistical Support

To sustain themselves and prepare for complex transnational operations, terrorist groups need to be able to move people and materials across borders unimpeded. Fragile states are often attractive to such networks by virtue of their poorly policed borders. For instance, Yemen's unmonitored frontiers, unregulated ports, and weak customs control make it a natural transit point for militants traveling to and from the Horn of Africa and the Persian Gulf, as well as a trading post for illicit arms and other contraband. Similarly, AQIM has moved with ease across the largely undemarcated Sahel, a region that one journalist believes "may be the most lawless zone on the planet."[46] Similar dynamics play out in other regions, such as the Afghan-Pakistan borderlands, the Caucasus, and the maritime borders of Malaysia, Indonesia, and the Philippines. In sum, anecdotal evidence suggests that porous frontiers in weak states—as well as urban centers and internal transit routes—can prove invaluable for terrorist operatives. At the same time, stronger states can provide transit opportunities as a matter of policy, a role that Syria periodically played in permitting the infiltration of foreign fighters into Iraq.

Targets for Operations

As targeting the U.S. homeland becomes increasingly difficult, the global *salafi* network may turn to Western as well as government targets in weak states, where shortcomings in local intelligence and law enforcement reduce the cost and risks of launching attacks. Al-Qaeda attacks against U.S. targets in Kenya, Tanzania, and Yemen prior to 9/11 are illustrative examples. Indeed, analysis of attacks by Sunni Islamic extremists shows that most have occurred in a handful of states, several of which are in the bottom two quintiles of the Index of State Weakness (see figure 2.2).

On the other hand, this association decreases significantly if one omits from consideration Afghanistan, Iraq, and Pakistan, on the grounds that these three countries have been the sites of massive insurgencies, and "insurgent" attacks are often conflated with "terrorist" ones that have more global objectives.[47] By contrast, some of the high-profile attacks of recent years by transnational (as opposed to domestic) terrorist groups have occurred in states in the top quintiles (e.g., Indonesia, Turkey, Jordan) or the West (Spain, England, the United States). This may suggest that targets are as much a function of the terrorists' goals as of the permissiveness of the operating environment.

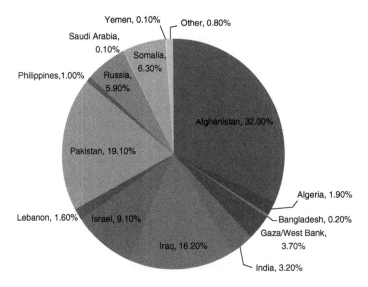

Figure 2.2: Attacks by Sunni Islamic Extremists, 2004–2009

Resources

To support their operations, transnational terrorists need to raise funds. Weak, failing, and postconflict settings can give terrorists opportunities for both legitimate money-making ventures and lucrative illicit activities, such as smuggling, looting, kidnapping, drug trading, and extortion. According to the U.S. Drug Enforcement Administration (DEA), eighteen of the forty-two U.S. designated terrorist groups have links to drug trafficking.[48] In late 2009, authorities arrested several AQIM operatives for allegedly helping move South American cocaine through West Africa to European markets.[49] One of the most cited (if still disputed) examples of terrorists exploiting weak states' resources is al-Qaeda's alleged trafficking in African gemstones and conflict diamonds in the years prior to 9/11. According to investigative journalist Douglas Farah, al-Qaeda operatives established relationships with former president of Liberia Charles Taylor and his client rebels in Sierra Leone to transfer the terrorist group's financial assets into an easily portable, untraceable store of value: rough diamonds. A central lesson of al-Qaeda's involvement in West Africa, writes Farah, is that terrorist groups can exploit "gray areas" in weak states, where "corruption is rampant, and the rule of law nonexistent."[50]

Financing

Terrorists need secure means to transfer value across national borders to support their operations and infrastructure. A state's capacity to combat terrorism financing depends on its ability to disclose suspicious transactions to competent authorities, freeze funds, make arrests, and prosecute violators. Despite unprecedented international attention to the issue since 9/11, many fragile states struggle to combat terrorist financing, as they are obligated to do under UN Security Council Resolution 1373.[51]

Fragile states give terrorist financiers distinct advantages because they typically possess weak banking sectors and lax regulation of cross-border transactions. Terrorists operating in weak states can smuggle cash; trade in gold, diamonds, and other valuable commodities; launder the proceeds from illicit activities; use offshore accounts and tax havens; rely on legal import/export firms, shell companies, and mailbox firms to arrange financial transfers; utilize Islamic charitable enterprises; and employ informal mechanisms of transfer, such as *hawala*, which in many cases are entirely legal.[52] The use of *hawala* and other alternative remittance systems, which are commonly employed in poorer countries with undeveloped banking sectors, allows brokers to transfer money across countries into different currencies without leaving a trace, complicating financial forensics.[53]

At the same time, truly failed states pose significant limitations for terrorist fund-raising. For this reason, only 13 percent of the "specially designated terrorist entities" in the U.S. Treasury Department's list operated in failed states in 2004. Some transnational terrorist groups have raised money in failed states, such as Sierra Leone, but "the amounts are dwarfed by the sums raised through crime and drug trafficking in non-failed states."[54] Meanwhile, patterns of terrorist financing have emerged from strong states in the West, as well as in the diversion of contributions to the extensive network of Wahhabi charitable organizations domiciled in Saudi Arabia and the Persian Gulf.

Extremist-Filled Gaps in Public Services

Finally, the inability of many fragile states to provide core goods to their people— including security, jobs, and basic social services—provides openings for extremists to fill the void. But there is little evidence that transnational terrorist groups have attempted to do so; in fact, there seems to be something antithetical about being a transnational terrorist movement and functioning as a para-state. Hamas and Hezbollah, which often use terrorist methods, have won popular support in the Palestinian Territories and Lebanon, respectively, by providing social services—but neither is a global *jihadi* organization.[55] The Taliban has played a similar role in parts of Afghanistan and Pakistan, but the Taliban, although harboring al-Qaeda, is not a transnational terrorist group.[56]

Nonetheless, by providing services where governments cannot, radical Islamic groups (including charities) facilitate the spread of violent ideologies and win adherents who may ultimately feed into the global *jihadi* network. In the Sahel, for example, fundamentalists have attracted local constituencies by building mosques, schools, and orphanages in poverty-stricken regions.[57] In Pakistan, anti-Western groups have provided food, medical care, and other services that the Pakistani state fails to supply. Just as alarming has been the proliferation of radical Quranic schools in Pakistan, where the public education system is abysmal.[58] The more extreme schools have provided a steady stream of Taliban recruits. At the same time, the vast majority of these graduates do not possess "the technical and linguistic skills necessary for effective terrorism". Robert Pape's own analysis of suicide terrorism would appear to corroborate this claim. He estimates that fewer than half a dozen of the hundreds of suicide bombers in his sample were educated in madrassas.[59]

Some terrorist-linked movements have come to power at least in part because they could provide one critical state function: law and order (albeit of an extremely brutal variety). Collapsed states such as Afghanistan in the early 1990s and Somalia today are so violent and miserable that they may enable even the most extreme groups to come to power—and be popularly accepted—if they can impose order. Many people initially welcomed the Taliban, as they did the Union of Islamic Courts in Somalia in 2006. Indeed, counterinsurgency analysts have attributed the resurgence of the Taliban in much of Afghanistan to their ability to fill the governance vacuum in many parts of the country, where the Taliban's brutal but effective system of justice has been welcomed as an alternative to the government's corruption and ineptitude. "When people are given a choice between an oppressive but effective administration and anarchy and corruption, they tend to go to effective administration," says counterinsurgency expert David Kilcullen.[60]

WEAK STATES AS SAFE HAVENS?

The perpetration of major terrorist acts is the product of months, if not years, of preparation. Al-Qaeda's haven in Afghanistan was critical to its ability to stage the 9/11 attacks. More recently, some observers have suggested that physical havens are no longer central to the operations of transnational terrorists, given al-Qaeda's increasingly decentralized network and what one analyst calls "the explosive potential of the internet" as a terrorist tool.[61] Yet safe havens appear to be critical over the long haul, helping terrorists survive counterterrorism efforts and permitting them to recruit, plan, and train for multiple operations far from the prying eyes of hostile intelligence services.[62] They also offer space to develop the complex logistics needed to carry out a major attack. For these reasons, the 9/11 Commission concluded that the importance of terrorist sanctuaries cannot be overstated.[63] Al-Qaeda's continued vitality has been largely due to its base in Pakistan's border regions, where the organization's long-standing ties to local tribes and militant groups has enabled it to establish a "virtual mini-state."[64]

Ungoverned Spaces as Safe Havens?

What makes a good safe haven for terrorists? For most U.S. national security officials, the lack of effective state presence is paramount. According to this view, terrorist havens are most likely to arise in the "ungoverned spaces" of weak or failing states. The initial and still dominant conception posits such "ungoverned areas" as remote, inaccessible, and unpatrolled spaces in the developing world, ranging from rugged mountains to impenetrable jungles, desert wastes, far-flung archipelagos, and ill-defined, undefended, or disputed border regions. Ideally, the National Intelligence Council argues, such havens should be sufficiently isolated to ensure operational security, yet also afford some access to commerce and communication, as well as proximity to population centers, borders, or coasts.[65]

In fact, the "ungoverned" spaces concept is somewhat misleading.[66] Its focus on harsh terrestrial locations ignores other areas that terrorists find attractive. Crowded refugee camps from Pakistan to Lebanon have provided opportunities for extremists to recruit, organize, and arm new members. Urban havens work as well: Transnational terrorists can often move undetected by state authorities within teeming slums, shantytowns, and apartment complexes in mega-cities like Nairobi, Dhaka, Manila, Casablanca, Cairo, or Jakarta.[67] Maritime havens, including the open sea, coastal littorals, island chains, and riparian systems also merit concern. And advances in global electronic infrastructure have created a sort of virtual "ungoverned space"—one that governments are hard-pressed to monitor and control.[68] Moreover, *jihadi* groups have proven adept at using Western states (which have fewer problems controlling their physical territory) to recruit, raise funds, and plan attacks, too. Based on these trends, the "safe havens" of global terrorists are as likely to be the *banlieues* of Paris as the wastes of the Sahara or the slums of Karachi.

Nonetheless, identifying—and if possible eliminating—the world's so-called "ungoverned spaces" remains a major focus of U.S. and international counterterrorism efforts. U.S. agencies and officials commonly cite several such regions as being of particular concern as current or potential safe havens for transnational terrorists. These include Afghanistan and Pakistan (particularly the FATA); the Ferghana Valley spanning parts of Uzbekistan, Tajikistan, and Kyrgyzstan; remote areas of Saudi Arabia and Yemen; Lebanon's Bekaa Valley; portions of the Caucasus, including the Pankisi and Kodori Gorges in Georgia; the Sulu archipelago in the Philippines, Indonesia, and Malaysia; southern Thailand; the Tri-Border area where Paraguay, Brazil, and Argentina come together; the Horn of Africa; and the Trans-Sahel region. (Appendix 2.1 summarizes actual and potential terrorist safe havens identified by the U.S. State Department.) Sub-Saharan Africa has emerged as a special arena of concern. U.S. military officials warn that "terrorists could take advantage of Africa's little-policed deserts and jungles to set up shop. The regions are so remote and vast that Africa's relatively small, under-equipped and underpaid security forces have difficulty controlling them."[69]

Yet the vast majority of U.S.-designated "ungoverned areas"—as well as failing states and conflict zones—have not emerged as major sanctuaries for al-Qaeda or other transnational (as opposed to local) terrorists. There are a few exceptions, including potentially Somalia and Yemen today. The most notable examples of terrorist safe havens, of course, are Afghanistan and Pakistan. Leaders or recruits trained in Pakistan have been involved in virtually every major al-Qaeda attack against a Western target in the last two decades, including bombings in Istanbul and London, as well as a disrupted 2006 plot to blow up at least seven airliners.[70]

The myriad weaknesses of the Afghan and Pakistani states have undeniably facilitated al-Qaeda's emergence and continued presence in the region: Long-running conflicts in Afghanistan and Kashmir have provided al-Qaeda recruits with weapons and combat experience, while the organization has exploited the region's entrenched criminal and smuggling networks for financial and operational purposes. The failure of successive governments in both countries to provide basic services, education, and rule of law has enabled al-Qaeda-linked extremists to flourish by filling in these gaps in state function.

But the centrality of these two states to global terrorism is also the result of specific historical, cultural, and geopolitical factors only partially related to state weakness. These include the historical influence of hard-line Deobandi ideology in the subcontinent; the personal, ideological, and tactical alliances that al-Qaeda has developed with local leaders over the past two decades; and support to *jihadi* groups for strategic ends from the Pakistani military and intelligence services (and, in the 1980s, from the United States and Saudi Arabia).

As the cases of Afghanistan and Pakistan show, a true haven requires more than the absence of the state. In fact, even for areas that fit the traditional conception of "ungoverned space," the term is a misnomer. A state may not control its borders or administer its territory, but the affected region is rarely the anarchical, Hobbesian zone of Western imagining. Within such "sovereignty-free areas," an alternative form of sociopolitical order generally takes hold. Indeed, some of the world's so-called "ungoverned" spaces, such as the tribal zones of Yemen or the rebel regions of Colombia, exist because the inhabitants make themselves ungovernable from the capital.[71] Less "ungoverned" than "alternatively" governed, such regions are regulated by entrenched laws, customs, and norms regarding the use of violence, mediation of conflict, and dispensation of justice.[72]

Terrorists can take advantage of these alternative local orders, brokering arrangements with relevant powers that control entry and exit, offer protection from state authority, and provide access to resources and revenue. They can enter into tactical alliances with other illicit groups, ranging from drug lords to insurgents to smugglers, to gain access to secure locations, transport, and communications. But the more durable alliances between transnational terrorists and local tribes or insurgents have been grounded in common ethnic, linguistic, cultural, or ideological affinities. The conservative brand of Islam widely practiced in South Asia, shaped by decades of fundamentalist Deobandi and more recent Wahhabi influence, has proven conducive to al-Qaeda's operations, for instance. Long-standing Sunni-Shiite tensions have been exploited by al-Qaeda-linked extremists in countries such as Pakistan, Yemen, and Iraq. The Taliban have proven more stalwart hosts to al-Qaeda than Sudan's opportunistic Omar al-Bashir, who quickly agreed to expel bin Laden when faced with significant U.S. pressure.

By contrast, al-Qaeda has been mostly unsuccessful in establishing fronts in the Balkans and Central Asia, where Muslim communities are largely secularized. Likewise, while observers have warned for years that the Muslim-majority countries of the Sahel are becoming increasingly radicalized,[73] the dominant brand of Islam in the region falls within a moderate and peaceful Sufi tradition at odds with the puritanical, fundamentalist tradition propagated by Wahhabis. This may be one reason why the lawless Sahel region (including Mali, Mauritania, Niger, and Chad) has failed to emerge as "the next Afghanistan," as some U.S. officials have warned it could.[74] Similarly, cultural dictates against the more extreme forms of Islam seem to have—at least so far—inoculated sub-Saharan Africa against the emergence of large *jihadi* movements. With a very few exceptions (notably Kenya and Somalia), there is little indication that al-Qaeda or its affiliates have built a significant presence on the continent south of the Sahel.

Ultimately, state weakness appears to be less important in enabling terrorist safe havens than the question of whether (and where) transnational terrorist groups can build and exploit local alliances. In its entire history, al-Qaeda has operated openly and without interference in only two countries: Afghanistan under the Taliban and Sudan under Bashir. Both were weak states—but, far from choosing to operate in "ungoverned" areas, al-Qaeda enjoyed the active support of a sovereign government in both cases (see box 2.2 on Afghanistan). Al-Qaeda's haven in Pakistan's FATA is the exception that proves the rule—it sits in an area in which the *state* has failed, but where the strength of traditional Pashtun systems of tribal self-government has enabled al-Qaeda to flourish thanks to its ideological, financial, and even familial ties to local power brokers (including possibly even elements of Pakistan's state and military). In contrast, although al-Qaeda-linked groups have built a presence in the lawless areas of countries such as Iraq, Algeria, and Somalia, none of these countries has (so far) been a primary planning or training base for the organization. In fact, rejection of al-Qaeda by the Sunni tribes of Iraq's Anbar province proved a decisive setback to the group's ability to operate in the country.

Ultimately, "ungoverned" spaces may be less appealing to transnational terrorists than "mis-governed" areas where the state (or a local alternative) allows illicit actors to act freely.[75] Indeed, there is little evidence that al-Qaeda has ever successfully exploited a truly "ungoverned"—that is, anarchic—region (see "The Bottom Line: Weaker is Not Always Better," below). Instead, the organization has adeptly exploited like-minded insurgent groups that come to power in the context of state collapse or civil war. In this context, the consolidation of power by the al-Qaeda-linked Shabab in Somalia in 2009 was alarming. While their ability to actually govern remains doubtful, the Shabab need not take over the entire country to offer safe haven to al-Qaeda in the territory they do control.

Box 2.2: Afghanistan as a Terrorist Haven: Failed State or Functional Ally?

Al-Qaeda is often depicted as a "postmodern" terrorist network that does not rely on state sponsorship but rather flourishes in failed states. The historical record points to a more complicated relationship, in which al-Qaeda both benefited from the explicit sponsorship of the Taliban regime *and* exploited the state's weaknesses.

Al-Qaeda was born out of the anti-Soviet jihad that swept Afghanistan in the 1980s. Yet as Afghanistan collapsed into warlordism during the early 1990s, Osama bin Laden relocated to Sudan at the invitation of Omar al-Bashir's regime. It was not until 1996, as the Taliban consolidated its hold on power in Afghanistan and *restored* statehood to much of the country, that bin Laden returned there, this time as an honored guest of the Taliban government.

Active state sponsorship gave al-Qaeda carte blanche to enter and exit the country, to mobilize recruits and resources, and to train, plan, and stage attacks—a degree of freedom to operate "rare in the annals of state-terrorist group relations."[76] U.S. officials estimate that al-Qaeda trained 10,000–60,000 foreign fighters during the Taliban era.

Despite the Taliban's oppressive governance and the country's abysmal social conditions, Afghanistan under the Taliban was not really a failed state in security terms: the regime imposed a (brutal) rule of law and controlled at least half the country fairly effectively, and thus could guarantee security for al-Qaeda's leaders and operations. To some degree, Afghanistan became a "terrorist-sponsored state," with al-Qaeda channeling tens of millions of dollars a year to the Taliban, and with the influence of the terrorist group in some ways exceeding that of its host. Thus the value of Afghanistan to al-Qaeda derived not from the absence of state institutions, but from the organization's ability to harness and exploit the resources and sovereignty of a sympathetic state.

In recent years, the extreme weakness of the Afghan government and a growing Taliban insurgency have led some observers to question whether the Taliban's return to power would necessarily result in al-Qaeda regaining its foothold in Afghanistan.[77] If the government were to collapse and the country plunge again into full-scale civil war, the Taliban might become merely one warlord faction among many—or could itself fragment. The historical evidence suggests that al-Qaeda would have difficulty exploiting such a chaotic scenario. On the other hand, if a unified Taliban consolidated power even in part of the country, al-Qaeda might indeed find ample room to operate: As one expert noted in late 2009, "The kind of separation that existed between the Taliban and al-Qaeda in 2001 really doesn't exist anymore."[78]

UNDERSTANDING THE WEAK STATE-TRANSNATIONAL TERRORISM CONNECTION

How does the conventional wisdom about state weakness and transnational terrorism square with the empirical evidence? To get a better grasp on this question, table 2.5 compares the Index of State Weakness introduced in chapter 1 with evidence regarding the activities of the global *salafi* jihad. It is based on data contained in the National Counterterrorism Center's Worldwide Incidents Tracking System and the U.S. State Department's Country Reports on Terrorism, 2002–2009. The first column lists the countries in the bottom three quintiles of the Index of State Weakness. The second and third columns identify, respectively, the number of major attacks and total attacks in each country perpetrated by Sunni Islamic extremists between 2004 and 2009. Based on State Department reporting, the fourth and fifth columns identify, respectively, countries in which al Qaeda-linked jihadi groups have been active, and that have provided sources of terrorist finance. The sixth column identifies whether countries have been cited as cooperating with U.S. counterterrorism efforts. The final column identifies sources of recruits for global jihad, using the admittedly problematic measure of the nationalities of detainees at the U.S. base in Guantanamo Bay, Cuba.[79] (Among other issues, using Guantanamo evidence presumes that all detainees are involved in jihadist terrorism, which is unproven.)

Table 2.5: Links between State Fragility and Transnational Terrorism[80]

Rank	Country	Major Attacks (2004–2009)[i]	All Attacks (2004–2009)[ii]	Jihadi Presence[iii] (including transit)	Terrorist Finance[iv]	Government Cooperation[v]	Recruits[vi]
Bottom Quintile in Overall Index							
1	Somalia	40	813	X	X		0.5
2	Afghanistan	73	4133	X	X	+	28.1
3	Congo, Dem. Rep.				X		
4	Iraq	294	2098	X	X	+	1.2
5	Burundi				X		
6	Sudan			X		+	1.5
7	Central African Rep.						
8	Zimbabwe					+	
9	Liberia				X	+	
10	Cote D'ivoire				X		
11	Angola					-	
12	Haiti				X	+	
13	Sierra Leone						
14	Eritrea		1	X		X	
15	North Korea						
16	Chad			X			0.1
17	Burma						
18	Guinea-Bissau						
19	Ethiopia	3	11		X	+	0.1

No.	Country					
20	Congo, Rep.			X		
21	Niger		3		+	
22	Nepal					
23	Guinea					
24	Rwanda				+	
25	Equatorial Guinea					
26	Togo					
27	Uganda			X	+	0.1
28	Nigeria	2	12	X	+	

Second Quintile in Overall Index

No.	Country					
29	Cameroon					
30	Yemen		19	X	+/-/X	14.0
31	Comoros				+	
32	Zambia				+/-	
33	Pakistan	61	2474	X	+/-/X	9.0
34	Cambodia				+	
35	Turkmenistan					0.1
36	Uzbekistan		11	X	+/-/X	0.9
37	Mauritania	1	7	X	+	0.4
38	Djibouti				+	
39	Mozambique				+	
40	Papua New Guinea				+	
41	Swaziland					
42	Tajikistan		6	X	+	1.5

(continued)

Table 2.5 Continued

Rank	Country	Major Attacks (2004–2009)[ii]	All Attacks (2004–2009)[iii]	Jihadi Presence[iii] (including transit)	Terrorist Finance[iv]	Government Cooperation[v]	Recruits[vi]
43	East Timor						
158 344	Burkina Faso					+	
45	Laos					+	
46	Malawi						
47	Colombia					+	
48	Bangladesh	1	26	X		+	0.1
49	Madagascar					+	
50	Kenya		3	X		+/-	0.1
51	Gambia						
52	Mali		2	X		+	
53	Lesotho						
54	Solomon islands						
55	Tanzania			X	X	+	0.1
56	Sri Lanka					+	
Third Quintile in Overall Index							
57	Algeria	8	245	X		+	3.2
58	Philippines	3	126	X		+	
59	Syria	1	4	X	X	+/X	1.2
60	Guatemala						
61	Sao tome & Principe					+	

62	Cuba					X	
63	Gabon						
64	Bolivia						
65	Russia	7	762	X	X	–	1.2
66	Iran	1	1	X	X	+	0.4
67	India	17	417	X	X	X	
68	Senegal					+	
69	Honduras					+	
70	Venezuela				X	X	
71	Benin						
72	Nicaragua					–	
73	Kyrgyzstan			X		+	
74	China	1	6	X	X	+	2.8
75	Paraguay				X	+/–	
76	Fiji						
77	Indonesia	1	5	X	X	+	0.1
78	Egypt	2	7	X	X	+	0.8
79	Thailand		8	X		+	
80	Azerbaijan		2	X		+/–	0.1
81	Belarus						
82	Namibia					+	
83	Vietnam						
84	Ghana						

(continued)

Table 2.5 Continued

Rank	Country	Major Attacks (2004–2009)[i]	All Attacks (2004–2009)[ii]	Jihadi Presence[iii] (including transit)	Finance[iv]	Government Cooperation[v]	Recruits[vi]
Totals—Critically Weak States		412 attacks (**78.5%** of total) (**28.5%** excluding Iraq and Afghanistan)	7071 attacks (**54.8%** of total) (**12.6%** excluding Iraq and Afghanistan)	9 states, including 6 of major concern	11 states, including 4 of major concern	11 states cited as cooperative, versus 1 uncooperative.	**30.1%** of Guantanamo prisoners (**2.3%** excluding Afghanistan and Iraq)
Total–Weak States		63 attacks (**12.0%** of total) (**40.0%** excluding Iraq and Afghanistan)	2548 attacks (**19.7%** of total) (**38.1%** excluding Iraq and Afghanistan)	10 states, including 7 of major concern	2 States, both of major concern	14 states cited as cooperative, versus 3 uncooperative.	**26.2%** of Guantanamo prisoners
Total–3rd Quintile States		42 attacks (**8.0%** of total) (**26.6%** excluding Iraq and Afghanistan)	1583 attacks (**12.3%** of total) (**23.7%** excluding Iraq and Afghanistan)	12 states, including 9 of major concern	8 states, including 4 of major concern	12 states cited as cooperative, versus 4 uncooperative.	**7.4%** of Guantanamo prisoners

i   *Major Attacks:* Attacks perpetrated by Sunni Islamic extremist groups in which more than 10 people were killed, 2004–2009. National Counterterrorism Center Worldwide Incidents Tracking System, as of January 23, 2010. According to the NCTC/WITS, there were 525 such attacks from 2004–2009.

ii   *All Attacks:* Attacks perpetrated by Sunni Islamic extremist groups, 2004–2009. National Counterterrorism Center Worldwide Incidents Tracking System, as of January 23, 2010. According to the NCTC/WITS, there were 12,912 total attacks from 2004–2009.

iii   *Jihadi Presence:* The **darkest** countries are those for which the State Department concludes that a sizable jihadi element is or has been present in recent years, with or without the consent of the host government. Countries in gray are those which may have previously been used as transit states or safe havens for individual operatives, but were not major bases of operations.

iv   *Finance:* The **darkest** countries are those known to have served as major sources of funding or money laundering for transnational terrorist groups. Countries in gray are specifically cited in the State Department reports as "potential" safe havens or centers of terrorist financing.

v   *Government Cooperation:* Data based on State Department reporting, and thus potentially determined by broad bilateral relations. For "government cooperation," a "+" indicates that a country is cited as actively cooperating with U.S. and/or international counterterrorism efforts. A "-" means the State Department report mentions continuing gaps in a country's efforts unrelated to capacity (e.g., failure to pass relevant anti-money laundering legislation). An "X" means the country is specifically mentioned as not cooperating with the United States in this area.

vi   *Recruits:* Data on recruits is given as the percentage of 778 current or former detainees from the state in question held at Guantanamo Bay, Cuba, since 2001. (This is admittedly a highly imperfect proxy for recruits linked to global salafist groups).

Analyzing the Findings

The findings presented in table 2.5 suggest that state weakness correlates only imperfectly with exploitation by transnational terrorists. Only twenty-four of the fifty-six weakest states (42.9 percent) are known to have had any connection to at least one dimension of transnational terrorist activity—and in many cases these links are fairly minor.[81] The quintile with the highest percentage of states that have (willingly or otherwise) played host to *jihadi* groups is actually Quintile 3 (12 of 28 states, or 43 percent), rather than the weakest states in Quintile 1 (9 of 28 countries, or 32.1 percent) or the slightly stronger states in Quintile 2 (10 of 28 countries or 36 percent). When Iraq and Afghanistan are excluded, only about 12 percent of attacks perpetrated by Sunni extremists in 2004–2009 occurred in the weakest quintile of states, compared to about one-quarter in 3rd-Quintile states. (Some 40 percent of attacks occurred in 2nd-Quintile states, although this data is skewed by the conflict in Pakistan.) If one accepts the number of foreign fighters in Afghanistan and Iraq (i.e. not including Afghans or Iraqis) detained as "enemy combatants" at Guantanamo Bay as a rough proxy for terrorist recruits, Quintile 2 has the greatest number (26.2 percent) versus only 2.3 percent from the weakest states and 7.4 percent from Quintile 3 countries (excluding Saudi Arabia, from where nearly 20 percent of Guantanamo detainees originate).

At the same time, a number of strong Western states and other wealthy countries outside the Index suffer from exploitation or attack. Western and Gulf states have suffered more than forty attacks since 1990, with notable attacks on France, Saudi Arabia, the United States, the United Kingdom, and Spain. Terrorists have been recruited from France, Spain, the United Kingdom, the United States, Canada, Australia, Denmark, Sweden, Belgium, and Israel, as well as all of the Persian Gulf states. It is also clear that European countries and the Gulf states play a disproportionately significant role in facilitating the raising and movement of funds for groups in the global jihadist network. Where weak states assist in terrorist financing, they tend to do so in one of two ways: (1) by hosting Islamic charities and nongovernmental organizations (NGOs), some of which siphon off the money to support terrorist activities (particularly in East Africa, the Middle East, South Asia, and Southeast Asia); and (2) by enabling criminal enterprises like narcotics and commodities smuggling that terrorists have used to earn operating funds (as in Western and Southern Africa, and Central Asia).

Table 2.6 seeks to summarize the advantages that weak and failing states provide to transnational terrorists.

Which Governance Gaps Matter?

Although all four governance gaps associated with weak and failing states—political, security, economic, and social—may contribute to transnational terrorism, political and security gaps may be the most important. In the absence of peaceful outlets for political expression, frustrated groups are more likely to adopt violence against repressive regimes and their perceived foreign sponsors. Likewise, states

Table 2.6: Summary of Benefits of Weak and Failing States to Terrorists

Functional Benefit	Relative Importance of State Weakness	Details
Conflict Experience	High	Historical experience suggests jihadists flock to conflict zones in fragile states (Afghanistan, Iraq, Somalia).
Training and Planning	Moderate-High	Training requires space out of view of authorities, easier in weak state; planning less reliant on state weakness.
Transit and supply	Moderate-High	Weak border control and customs facilitate entry and exit of personnel and materiel.
Safe Haven/ Sanctuary	Moderate-High	Leadership cadres of transnational terrorist organizations can exploit remote "ungoverned" (and "alternatively governed") spaces in remote regions and chaotic urban settings; but reception depends heavily on socio-cultural factors and attitudes of local or national power brokers.
Resources and Financing	Mixed	Connection varies with presence of illicit resources (e.g., gemstones, opium) and smuggling opportunities; presence of Islamic charities (dominated by Saudis, Gulf, more than weak states); and availability of formal infra-structure and informal channels (hawala) of financial transfer.
Targets of Operations	Moderate	Omitting Afghanistan, Pakistan and Iraq (where insurgent and terrorist attacks are often conflated), correlation between attacks and state weakness is modest.
Pools of Recruits	Low-Moderate	Recruitment patterns show little correlation with state weakness, beyond Afghanistan, Pakistan, Yemen.
Win Popular Support by Filling State Vacuum	Low	Although terrorist groups do seek to exploit public opinion wherever possible, cells are less likely than insurgents to seek support by providing social services, something that generally requires local roots and a local political agenda. In rare cases al-Qaeda or its affiliates may develop exceptionally strong relationships with local insurgent groups that perform such para-statal functions.

that do not control their borders or territory facilitate terrorist infiltration and operations. On the other hand, many states that have suffered attacks, such as Morocco and Algeria, are authoritarian regimes with effective, if often ruthless, security forces.

The two other gaps associated with state weakness—poor provision of social welfare and economic management—may play supporting roles. When states do not meet basic social needs, as in Pakistan and Yemen, they provide openings for charitable organizations or educational systems linked to radical networks. Likewise, mass joblessness can breed bitterness and a sense of inadequacy that, in certain cultural contexts, can lead people to extremism and terror. The relative roles of repression and lack of economic opportunity in stimulating terrorist activity remain a matter of intense scholarly dispute (see box 2.3).

Box 2.3: "Root Causes" of Terrorism: Poverty vs. Repression

The common assertion that weak and failing states provide fertile recruiting grounds for terrorists rests on two alternative but unproven hypotheses about individual motivations—one connected to poverty, the other to political grievance. Since 9/11, political leaders have frequently linked economic misery to transnational terrorism. "We fight against poverty because hope is an answer to terror," President Bush declared in 2002. Prime Minister Tony Blair made the same link in 2005, saying, "Where there is extremism, fanaticism, and appalling forms of poverty in one continent, the consequences no longer stay fixed on that continent."[82]

In fact, there is little evidence of a direct or even indirect connection between poverty and transnational terrorism, at either the micro or macro level. Individual terrorists, far from being dispossessed, tend to come from privileged classes and be more educated than most of their compatriots.[83] Nor is there evidence that poorer countries generate disproportionate numbers of terrorists. Growth rates in the Arab Middle East have been higher than in sub-Saharan Africa, which, despite its greater poverty, has experienced relatively little terrorism (albeit significant violence), even in Muslim-majority countries.[84]

There is stronger evidence that terrorism reflects *political* grievances. Several studies have found a strong empirical basis to argue that repression—in the form of restricted civil and political liberties and human rights violations—is a strong predictor of a country's propensity to generate terrorist activity. In analyzing the nationalities of 312 foreign fighters captured in Iraq during 2005, one study found the absence of civil liberties was strongly correlated with their radicalization.[85] This helps explain the vulnerability of Arab countries to al-Qaeda's brand of transnational terrorism. As the Arab Human Development Report observed in 2002, collectively the region ranks lowest in the world on political freedom, civil liberties, and gender empowerment. Its regimes are authoritarian and corrupt; open dissent is often impossible; and prospects for the future are dim. Beyond domestic repression, political grievances generated by foreign occupation are another frequent motivation in terrorist attacks, particularly when it comes to suicide terrorism.[86]

This is not to suggest that economic factors are entirely irrelevant to the incidence of terrorism. But the dynamics of modernization, as opposed to poverty per se, provide the structural preconditions for terrorism by generating economic and social upheaval. Modernizing countries are characterized by rapid change and rising expectations. Stalled transitions can shatter these hopes and lead to alienation, particularly among disappointed men. At the same time, the number of aggrieved individuals who actually join terrorist groups remains relatively small. A growing body of network analysis suggests that these individual decisions are shaped by "intimate social forces" or small group dynamics that cannot be reduced to the shortcomings of the state.[87]

THE BOTTOM LINE: WEAKER IS NOT ALWAYS BETTER

(Un)safe Havens: Failed versus Weak States

Conventional wisdom contends that failed states are potentially attractive, even essential, for the operations of transnational terrorist organizations. In fact, as the evidence shows, truly failed states are less attractive to terrorists than merely weak ones. While anarchical zones can provide certain niche benefits, they do not offer the full spectrum of services available in weak states. Instead, failed states tend to suffer from a number of security, logistical, geographic, and political drawbacks that make them inhospitable to transnational terrorists.

To begin, failed states may lack even minimal levels of security or predictability. Where anarchy prevails, terrorists must spend precious resources, energy, and time ensuring their own protection—or obtaining it from others. In the FATA, by contrast, the support of local power brokers has enabled al-Qaeda to survive more than nine years of U.S. counterterrorism efforts. Likewise, rugged, desolate, or inaccessible settings can pose monumental logistical hurdles, since they are often far removed from the transportation, communications, and financial infrastructure need to support complex terror operations (to say nothing of Western targets). Even when the Taliban was in power in Afghanistan, al-Qaeda's "main logistical support came from Pakistani extremist groups, who could provide the kinds of supplies and means of communication with the outside world not available in Afghanistan."[88]

Accordingly, rather than truly failed states, what terrorists and other illicit transnational groups find most conducive are weak but functioning states, where formal state structures and trappings of sovereignty exist in a rudimentary form but are fragile and susceptible to corruption—that is, settings where "states are governed badly, rather than not at all."[89] For instance, an area of particular concern for terrorist financing activities (and broader money laundering) has been the Tri-Border region where Brazil, Paraguay, and Argentina intersect—an "under-governed" zone of otherwise functional states.

Furthermore, collapsed states cannot provide a key benefit offered by slightly stronger ones: the shield of state sovereignty, behind which terrorists can operate unmolested. Regardless of their ability to control their own territories, governments strenuously resist military incursions by outside powers, and such interventions are not undertaken lightly. In early 2005, the United States called off a special operations mission against al-Qaeda leaders meeting in Pakistan.[90] As Deputy Director of National Intelligence Thomas Fingar testified to Congress in summer 2007, "It's not that we lack the ability to go into that space [the Pakistani tribal belt], but we have chosen not to do so without the permission of the Pakistani government."[91] Such diplomatic qualms can erode over time, of course; after taking office in 2009, the Obama administration stepped up remote drone attacks in Pakistan's tribal regions. Nevertheless, the United States refused through 2010 to publicly acknowledge that it was conducting such attacks, or to seriously consider insertion of U.S. ground forces into Pakistan to conduct sustained military operations.

But when a state has collapsed, the international norm of nonintervention relaxes, providing greater scope for the United States and its allies to interdict and destroy terrorist cells, either by remote strikes or the insertion of Special Forces. Indeed, "the idea of a 'safe haven' in a failed state or ungoverned territory is a bit of an oxymoron."[92] The limitations of Somalia as a safe haven, for instance, have been exposed by a series of U.S. air strikes on suspected al-Qaeda militants in the country, and by a U.S. commando raid in September 2009 that killed one of the most wanted Islamic militants in Africa, Saleh Ali Saleh Nabhan. Somalia's status as a completely collapsed state and the weakness of its nominal government (which acquiesced in the U.S. strikes) facilitated U.S. action. According to the Combating Terrorism Center at West Point, "Such attacks are much less likely to occur against operatives working under the umbrella of state sovereignty."[93]

Case Study: Somalia vs. Kenya

A review of al-Qaeda's experiences in the Horn of Africa since 1990 would tend to reinforce these points. After 9/11, Somalia quickly emerged in official U.S. thinking as a potential haven for al-Qaeda operatives fleeing Afghanistan.[94] On the surface, Somalia would appear attractive to al-Qaeda. After two decades of political instability and violence, the country has large quantities of weapons in circulation and no security services. It has a long unpatrolled coastline conducive to smuggling, as well as long, porous, unpoliced borders that can be crossed without a visa. Somalia also has homegrown Islamic extremists. However, a fascinating study by the Combating Terrorism Center at West Point—based on captured communications between bin Laden and his lieutenants in Sudan and al-Qaeda operatives in Somalia during the 1990s—suggests that truly failed states such as Somalia may pose significant, even insuperable operational challenges to transnational terrorist networks.[95]

In the 1990s, from al-Qaeda's headquarters in Sudan, bin Laden made a major effort to establish a regional presence in the Horn, dispatching several hundred operatives to the region in the hopes that it could provide a launching pad for operations against

Western targets. Bin Laden presumed that the region, and particularly Somalia, would offer an ideal base, providing a combination of operational security, logistical needs, ideological support, an inexpensive pool of recruits, and sources of financing for al-Qaeda activities.

But none of these assumptions was borne out. Like participants in the ill-fated UN intervention that same local decade, al-Qaeda operatives arrived in Somalia with a poor understanding of the local sociocultural, political, and economic context, and seriously underestimated the costs of operating in a completely nonfunctional state. Cultural barriers complicated al-Qaeda's plans; most Somalis practice a moderate form of Sufi Islam, and the attraction of the *jihadi* cause could rarely compete with the more powerful pull of clan identification in Somali society. The Somalis also proved suspicious of outsiders, and even al-Qaeda's relationship with homegrown Somali jihadists was fractious.

The activities of transnational terrorists require at least a baseline level of security, and Somalia's utter lawlessness left al-Qaeda's Africa Corps at the mercy of bandits and local warlords. Similarly, Somalia's near-total lack of physical infrastructure presented al-Qaeda with logistical nightmares, forcing the network to procure supplies from distant markets and journey over rudimentary transportation routes to remote training sites. Al-Qaeda's Africa Corps also struggled to fund its far-flung and expensive operations. It lacked revenue streams to finance its activities, and even informal mechanisms of financial transfer, including *hawaladars*, proved more frustrating to use than anticipated. Indeed, a captured al-Qaeda document proposed a strategy for Somalia that resembled a full-fledged, *jihadist*-led, state-building project. Beyond calling for the "(1) expulsion of the foreign international presence," it envisioned: "(2) rebuilding state institutions; (3) establishment of domestic security; (4) comprehensive national reconciliation; and (5) economic reform and combating famine."[96]

In contrast, al-Qaeda found Kenya—a weak but not failing state—to be a much better operational base throughout the 1990s. This was thanks to its (relative) stability and decent infrastructure, on the one hand, and its poor governance on the other. The terrorist network found ample transportation and communications networks, financial channels, and Western targets for attack. Al-Qaeda cells were able to move unimpeded within and across the country's borders, raise funds through legitimate businesses and Islamic charities, transfer money around the world, and gain access to weapons from nearby conflict zones. Al-Qaeda's activities were facilitated by a culture of corruption among the worst in the world. It also encountered disaffected and sympathetic Muslim minorities among Kenya's Arab, Swahili, and Somali populations, as well as weak security, law enforcement, and criminal justice capabilities.

Not all of these conditions obtain today, of course. Somali society is more radicalized than it was a decade ago. As the *Economist* reported in 2009, "[M]any young Somalis now seem to take solace from the idea of a global jihad."[97] Most concerning has been the emergence of the al-Qaeda-linked al-Shabab movement, whose steady military gains across southern Somalia has raised concerns that Somalia could still emerge as a haven for global jihadists. As of late 2010, al-Shabab and its affiliates controlled much of southern Somalia, where they imposed sharia law and earned significant revenues from taxes, piracy, extortion, and donations from the diaspora. Like the Afghan Taliban, the Shabab were welcomed by some Somalis as a force of law and order. However, infighting and ideological disagreements among al-Shabab factions raised doubts about its ability to govern. Reported tensions between al-Shabab and al-Qaeda leaders, as well as the Shabab's focus to date on Somalia rather than attacking the West, may prevent an al-Qaeda haven even in al-Shabab-controlled territory. Continued anarchy seemed a likelier outcome than the emergence of functional terrorist state like Afghanistan in the 1990s. But if Somalia does emerge as a major al-Qaeda base, such a development would probably owe more to the success of the Shabab as a ruling force and its active support for the organization, than to al-Qaeda's (heretofore limited) ability to exploit a truly collapsed state.

Even if the Shabab do prove willing and able hosts to al-Qaeda, Somalia's extreme weakness effectively negates the principle of nonintervention, making al-Qaeda operatives there much more vulnerable to intervention from the United States and other external powers. In 2006, the Bush administration supported an Ethiopian invasion that toppled the regime of the Union of Islamic Courts, a group calling for sharia law and potentially linked to al-Qaeda. (In retrospect, the group appears more moderate; its leader, Sharif Sheikh Ahmed, is now president of the U.S.-backed Transitional Federal Government.) More recently, a number of U.S. missile strikes (and at least one raid) on suspected al-Qaeda members in the country have prompted only muted international response. In contrast to the constraints on U.S. military action in other countries, the "free rein granted to the Pentagon in carrying out attacks in Somalia's largely ungoverned spaces"[98] has made Somalia a less-than-ideal haven.

CONCLUSION

Despite the conventional wisdom about a nexus between failed states and terrorism, the reality appears considerably more complex. Failed and collapsed states may provide certain services, including conflict experience and havens for leaders. But transnational terrorists are perhaps decreasingly reliant on weak and failing states. Attacks have been planned from weak states such as Yemen and Somalia—but also from Western countries like Germany and Spain. By most accounts, the resources that *salafi* groups earn in weak states are dwarfed by the revenues raised through charities, fund-raising, and diaspora groups centered in wealthy countries. And terrorists do not want to operate at the complete mercy of warlords or in unstable security conditions.

Generally speaking, the most attractive states for transnational terrorists are *weak but functioning* states where state structures have not collapsed but remain minimally effective, in the context of a permissive cultural and ideological environment. Such badly governed states allow terrorists to operate relatively undisturbed from the scrutiny of local law enforcement and interdiction efforts of foreign actors, while enjoying a basic level of order and infrastructure (including communications technology, transportation, and banking services). A collapsed state such as Somalia or Afghanistan may provide jihadists with arms, conflict experience, and recruits—but the real danger to the West from such anarchic zones occurs only if and when they give rise to an indigenous *salafi* movement that is both able to impose order and willing to work with al-Qaeda to deploy these assets against Western targets.

In fact, historical evidence suggests that the weakest states or "ungoverned" areas will be conducive to terrorism only insofar as national or local power brokers support (or ignore) the presence of transnational terrorist groups. Al-Qaeda has been most successful when it can secure the protection and material support of locals, as in Afghanistan, parts of Pakistan, and perhaps Somalia. (A similar dynamic could be occurring in Yemen; see box 2.4). In this context, a state's will is arguably more important than its capacity to conduct counterterrorism efforts. Sudan is an illustrative case: al-Qaeda found a haven there in the mid-1990s with the active support of President Bashir—whose regime then proved more than capable of quickly expelling the group when international pressure made it convenient to do so.

Overall, the connection between failing states and transnational terrorism does not appear that strong. Still, the governance gaps of a few weak states do have an outsized influence on the capabilities of transnational terrorists. The enduring presence of al-Qaeda in Afghanistan and Pakistan certainly owes something to the weaknesses of their central governments (although, given the evolution of al-Qaeda in the region and the group's exceptionally strong ties to local tribes, developments in these countries do not necessarily portend a broader pattern for weak states). Most notably, the Taliban and other extremist groups—though not necessarily al-Qaeda—have gained support by providing employment, security, and rule of law in the impoverished and war-torn areas along the Afghan-Pakistan border. Consequently, the Obama administration's initial strategy for the region equated counterterrorism with nation-building, saying the United States must "promote a more capable and accountable government," to "prevent Afghanistan from becoming the al-Qaeda safe haven that it was before 9/11."[99]

In fact, the frequent assumption that state-building is a critical component of counterterrorism efforts may be misconceived—a point belatedly acknowledged by the Obama administration in Afghanistan.[100] To gain the upper hand against the Taliban, U.S. forces will have to assist at least some state functions. But they should also work with local actors, including tribal leaders and militias, on whose support Afghanistan's future truly balances. Given local tribes' historical resistance to governments in Kabul and Islamabad, "state-building" projects (particularly in the economic and security arenas) may be more realistic and more successful in the long run if they occur at the local rather than the national level.

More broadly, the above analysis indicates that a too-broad focus on "failed states" as potential terrorist havens is inappropriate and inefficient. There are many chaotic states in the world, but only a handful (even among Muslim-majority countries) that are likely to give rise to an indigenous salafi movement both capable of and willing to support al-Qaeda. Indeed, after the Afghan jihad ended in 1989, al-Qaeda fighters scattered into many of the world's weakest and most conflict-ridden states. Yet with the partial exceptions of Yemen (see Box 2.4) and perhaps Somalia, none has yet emerged as a major terrorist haven akin to Afghanistan or Pakistan—where local historical, cultural, and geopolitical factors facilitated the rise and integration of al-Qaeda.

Box 2.4: State Weakness and the Terrorist Threat in Yemen

America's stakes in the fortunes of poorly governed developing countries are starkly apparent in Yemen, the poorest and most unstable country on the Arabian Peninsula. At least since the *USS Cole* bombing in the Yemeni port of Aden in 2000, U.S. officials have worried that the country could emerge as a major haven for al-Qaeda. In February 2009, the U.S. Director of National Intelligence warned, "Yemen is reemerging as a jihadist battleground and potential regional base of operations for al-Qaeda to plan internal and external attacks, train terrorists, and facilitate the movement of operatives."[101] Indeed, ten months later, the foiled Christmas day bombing of a U.S. airliner was traced to al-Qaeda in the Arabian Peninsula (AQAP). In October 2010, the United States dodged a second AQAP plot: an effort to blow up U.S.-bound planes with explosive packages.[102]

Yemen's vulnerability to exploitation by transnational terrorist groups is accentuated by a weak state that struggles to provide its citizens with physical security, the rule of law, accountable and representative government, sound economic management, and basic social services.[103] Perhaps just as important, however, are Yemen's particular socio-cultural characteristics, as well as its government's ambivalent attitude toward Islamic extremism.

A weak state. The sources of state weakness in Yemen are partly historical. As Sheila Carapico reminds us, Yemen is not (yet) a failed state but rather a "new state,"[104] created in 1990 by the amalgamation of North and South Yemen (which subsequently fought a brief civil war). Modern state institutions have been grafted onto a traditional, tribal society that has long resisted state control. The central government makes no pretense of policing its borders or maintaining a monopoly over the use of armed force inside its territory, large swathes of which are effectively outside state control. In the north, the powerful Houthi tribe has waged an insurgency since 2004, while the formerly independent south is increasingly restive.

The government of President Ali Abdullah Saleh has retained its grip on power through a corrupt system of patronage and co-optation. Economic governance is also abysmal. The regime has made little effort to diversify a national economy heavily dependent on remittances, foreign assistance, and (rapidly diminishing) oil revenues. Yemen's anemic economic growth cannot keep up with the country's brisk population growth rate (with nearly half the nation under the age of fourteen). Poverty and illiteracy rates are among the highest in the region. The country's prospects for economic and human development are further threatened by ecological degradation and the rapid depletion of the country's water resources. Meanwhile, the regime's favoritism, corruption, and mismanagement have fueled regional resentments in the country. The *Economist* predicted in September 2009 that Yemen may be "the world's next failed state."[105]

A hotbed of terrorism? Yemen's rugged terrain and lawlessness has proven congenial to terrorists and militants, who travel freely across Yemen's border with Saudi Arabia. Al-Qaeda has established training camps in sanctuaries provided by sympathetic tribes of northern Yemen. From the Afghan-Soviet war to the Iraq conflict, Yemen has a long tradition of sending *jihadi* warriors to foreign campaigns—and reabsorbing these radical elements. An estimated two thousand veterans of the Iraq war have returned to Yemen, and Yemenis have been heavily represented among detainees held at Guantanamo Bay. Since the *Cole* bombing in 2000, militants based in Yemen have launched more than twenty attacks against Western targets in Yemen, including the U.S. embassy in Sana'a in 2008.[106] During 2009, radical Islamic groups were in the ascendant in Yemen. U.S. officials reported increased communication and coordination between al-Qaeda militants in Yemen and their counterparts in Pakistan and Somalia.[107]

Weakness or Welcome? Perhaps the most important factor in al-Qaeda's toehold in Yemen may be the government's historic ambivalence in taking on the terrorist groups and its local allies. Yemen is a conservative Muslim country, where a longstanding Sunni-Shiite divide has helped fuel radicalism and militancy. Islamic extremists are "a crucial domestic constituency" in Yemen, and figures such as Osama bin Laden are popular.[108]

The Saleh regime largely acquiesced to U.S. pressure to cooperate in counterterrorism efforts following the *Cole* bombing and 9/11, bolstering intelligence-sharing and accepting U.S. military assistance. But its support remained halfhearted at best. In fact, the Saleh regime has periodically embraced Islamic militants, particularly during the 1994 civil war when they were welcomed as ideological allies in the ongoing struggle against the more secular, formerly Marxist South Yemen. In recent years the government has supported hard-line Sunni Islamists in an effort to contain the rebellion among the Houthi (who are Shiite).

Unsurprisingly, given this double game, Yemen's counterterrorism efforts have produced mixed results. Successful raids on militant hideouts have been offset by failures, such as the escape of dozens of U.S. terror suspects from Yemeni jails (likely with official complicity, due either to corruption or to ideological sympathies). In early 2009, the government released more than one hundred prisoners said to be linked to al-Qaeda— possibly to deploy them against the Houthi. The *New York Times* quotes one Yemeni analyst as saying, "Yemen is like a bus station—we stop some terrorists, and we send others on to fight elsewhere. We appease our partners in the West, but we are not really helping."[109]

Whether Yemen becomes an enduring sanctuary for al-Qaeda remains to be seen. It will depend primarily on whether its government shows resolve in taking on the rising terrorist threat—something it began, belatedly, to do in 2010. If the country were to weaken further, or disintegrate into a full-scale civil war, al-Qaeda and its affiliates could build on their alliances with local tribes to extend their presence and operations in the country

(continued)

Box 2.4 Continued

with impunity. More than many other weak states, Yemen's cultural, social, and political makeup could make it an ideal haven for al-Qaeda. One Western journalist writes, "Yemen is rapidly approaching an economic and political crisis that could result in its becoming a failed state." Already "a longtime haven for jihadists," the country "could collapse into another Afghanistan."[110]

Appendix 2.1: Potential or Actual Safe Havens in Fragile States Identified by the U.S. Government

Potential Terrorist Safe Havens	Terrorist Threat	Index Ranking	Governance Gaps
Somalia	Al-Qaeda-linked groups operate in Somalia, including al Shabab	Somalia: 1	"Somalia remains a concern given the country's long, unguarded coastline, porous borders, continued political instability, and proximity to the Arabian Peninsula, all of which provide opportunities for terrorist transit and/or safe haven."
Trans-Sahara	Al-Qaeda in the Islamic Maghreb; Libyan Islamic Fighting Group (officially merged with al-Qaeda)	Chad: 16 Niger: 21 Mauritania: 37 Mali: 52	"Remote areas of the Sahel and Maghreb regions in Africa serve as terrorist safe havens because of limited government control in sparsely populated regions.... AQIM taps into already existing smuggling networks in the Sahel to obtain weapons, explosives, and supplies."
Sulu/Sulawesi Seas Littoral	Jemaah Islamiya; Abu Sayyaf Group	Philippines: 58 Indonesia: 77 Malaysia: 124	"Although Indonesia, Malaysia, and the Philippines have improved their efforts to control their shared maritime boundaries, this expanse remains difficult to control. Surveillance is partial at best, and traditional smuggling and piracy groups provided an effective cover for terrorist activities."

(continued)

Appendix 2.1: Continued

Potential Terrorist Safe Havens	Terrorist Threat	Index Ranking	Governance Gaps
Southern Philippines	Jemaah Islamiya; Abu Sayyaf Group	Philippines: 58	"The government's control in this area is weak due to rugged terrain, weak rule of law, poverty, and local Muslim minority resentment of central governmental policies."
Iraq	Al-Qaeda in Iraq (AQI); Ansar al-Islam (AI); and Ansar al-Sunna (AS).	Iraq: 4	"Iraq is not currently a terrorist safe haven, but terrorists…as well as Shia extremists and other groups, view Iraq as a potential safe haven."
Lebanon	Hezbollah; Sunni extremist groups. "An increasing number of AQ-associated Sunni extremists are also operating within the country"	Lebanon: 93	Hezbollah and Sunni extremists both use "refugee camps as staging grounds for recruitment, training, planning, and facilitating transit of foreign fighters to and from Iraq. The camps, run by Palestinian authorities inside the camps, continue to be no-go zones for the Lebanese Armed Forces."
Yemen	Al-Qaeda in Yemen (now AQ in the Arabian Peninsula)	Yemen: 30	"The security situation in Yemen continued to deteriorate in 2008.…the Government of Yemen has been unable to disrupt other AQY cells and its response to the terrorist threat was intermittent.…land border security along the extensive frontier with Saudi Arabia remained a problem."

Afghanistan	Al-Qaeda activity, particularly in the border region with Pakistan	Afghanistan: 2	"Criminal networks and narcotics cultivation remained particularly prevalent in the south and east of the country, constituting a source of funding for the insurgency in Afghanistan."
Pakistan	Al-Qaeda and affiliated groups	Pakistan: 33	"Islamist Deobandi groups and many local tribesmen in the FATA and the NWFP continue to resist the government's efforts to improve governance and administrative control at the expense of longstanding local autonomy."
Colombia border region	Revolutionary Armed Forces of Colombia (FARC)—a non-jihadi group	Colombia: 47 Venezuela: 70 Ecuador: 85 Peru: 92 Brazil: 99 Panama: 122	Colombia's border regions "include rough terrain and dense forest cover. These conditions, coupled with low population densities and weak government presence, create potential areas of safe haven for insurgent and terrorist groups."
Venezuela	Revolutionary Armed Forces of Colombia (FARC)—a non-jihadi group	Venezuela: 70	"Corruption within the Venezuelan government and military; ideological ties with the FARC; and weak international counternarcotics cooperation have fueled a permissive operating environment for drug traffickers and an increase in drug transit to the United States and Europe."

(continued)

Appendix 2.1: Continued

Potential Terrorist Safe Havens	Terrorist Threat	Index Ranking	Governance Gaps
Tri-Border Area	No known activity by al-Qaeda affiliates; Hezbollah and other groups may raise funds in the region.	Paraguay: 75 Brazil: 99 Argentina: 115	"Suspected supporters of Islamic terrorist groups, including Hizballah, take advantage of loosely regulated territory and the proximity of Ciudad del Este, Paraguay and Foz do Iguaçu, Brazil to participate in a wide range of illicit activities and to solicit donations from within the sizable Muslim communities in the region." The region's governments "have long been concerned with arms and drugs smuggling, document fraud, money laundering, trafficking in persons, and the manufacture and movement of contraband goods through this region."

INDEX LEGEND:

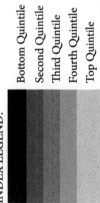

Bottom Quintile
Second Quintile
Third Quintile
Fourth Quintile
Top Quintile

Source: State Department 2009 Country Reports on Terrorism

3

PROLIFERATION OF WEAPONS OF MASS DESTRUCTION

I ask you to stop and think for a moment what it would mean to have nuclear weapons in so many hands—in the hands of countries large and small, stable and unstable, responsible and irresponsible—scattered throughout the world. There would be no rest for anyone then, no stability, no real security, and no chance of disarmament.
—*John F. Kennedy, July 1963*[1]

The proliferation of nuclear, biological, and chemical weapons poses perhaps the greatest threat to U.S. national security in the early twenty-first century. The development of nuclear arsenals by "rogue states" could set off regional arms races and destabilize strategic areas. Successful proliferation by rival states in volatile regions could even lead to nuclear war. Terrorist attacks with biological, chemical, nuclear, or radiological weapons could kill hundreds of thousands of people and cause catastrophic economic damage. Unfortunately, recent revelations about clandestine nuclear programs in North Korea and Iran—as well as the nuclear black market run by Pakistani scientist A.Q. Khan—have served as sobering reminders that state and nonstate actors alike have many avenues for pursuing weapons of mass destruction (WMD).

Many observers fear that the proliferation risk is increasing as more states pursue WMD-related technologies, even if only for civilian purposes (such as nuclear energy or biotechnology). Weak states in particular are often perceived as less willing or able to prevent WMD materials from falling into the hands of terrorists or other rogue actors.[2] Even if they do not pursue such weapons themselves, their porous borders and ungoverned spaces could provide havens and smuggling routes for state or nonstate actors attempting to build or acquire WMD. Of perhaps greatest concern is the possibility that political turmoil or state collapse in a nuclear-armed country could allow terrorists or others to gain access to the world's deadliest weapons.

However, as with transnational terrorism, the connection between weak states and WMD proliferation is more complicated than the conventional wisdom would suggest. This chapter explores those links, examining the threat of WMD proliferation, outlining various avenues by which both state and nonstate actors might attempt to acquire WMD, and exploring ways that state weakness could facilitate each proliferation pathway. It focuses primarily on nuclear weapons, but also discusses chemical and biological weapons.

The chapter argues, first, that weak states do have certain vulnerabilities that proliferators might attempt to exploit, including high levels of corruption, poor security, and weak law enforcement capabilities. Two fragile states in particular—North Korea and Pakistan—clearly pose a serious proliferation threat. Globally, however, state fragility does not uniformly correlate with proliferation potential. In fact the most problematic group of countries may be relatively strong "states to watch" that have or seek nuclear weapons capabilities. States in this category—unlike the weakest states—have the resources and capacity to develop WMD, which in some cases could pose a direct threat to the United States. They also are characterized by certain governance gaps that may make them deliberate or inadvertent sources of WMD materials for nonstate actors. Similarly, poorly governed but relatively stable states in regions with high concentrations of WMD materials—particularly the former Union of Soviet Socialist Republics (USSR)—are the likeliest transit states for traffickers and smugglers.

THE GLOBAL THREAT OF WMD PROLIFERATION

Weapons of mass destruction are instruments of violence intended to generate massive casualties, including among civilian populations. While civilizations have used variants of chemical and biological warfare since classical antiquity, the term "weapons of mass destruction" was first employed in 1937 to describe the German bombing of Spanish cities. In 1947, the United Nations Security Council defined "weapons of mass destruction" in a narrower sense, to refer to "atomic explosive weapons, radioactive materials, lethal chemical and biological weapons, and any weapons developed in the future which have the characteristics comparable in destructive effect." Although conventional weapons can also create "mass destruction," as the death tolls at Verdun (250,000), the Somme (more than 1 million), and Stalingrad (1.5 million) attest, a "true" WMD causes similar devastation with a single weapon.[3]

The WMD Threat

Nuclear Weapons

Nuclear weapons possess an awesome power to destroy lives and infrastructure, both in their immediate detonation and long-term radioactive effects. The 15-kiloton (KT) bomb dropped on Hiroshima on August 6, 1945, killed 70,000 people instantly; tens of thousands more succumbed within months. The 21-KT weapon dropped on Nagasaki three days later resulted in more than 60,000 dead. Both metropolises were laid to waste by the blasts' shock waves and fires. Today, there are approximately 30,000 nuclear weapons worldwide, the vast majority in the stockpiles of advanced nuclear weapons states. These devices average more than 100-KT yields apiece, so an attack on a major city could instantly kill tens or hundreds of thousands. It would also disrupt international commerce and travel, with unprecedented political, social, and economic implications within and beyond the target country.

There is very little defense against nuclear weapons once launched or detonated, so prevention is critical. For nearly four decades, the Nuclear Nonproliferation Treaty (NPT) has been at the center of the global nonproliferation regime. It targets state actors, although recent initiatives have sought to prevent nonstate actors from acquiring nuclear material as well. The NPT recognizes five nuclear weapons states (China, France, Russia, the United Kingdom, and the United States) and prohibits them from sharing weapons-related technology with non-nuclear weapons states. The latter are guaranteed the right to civilian nuclear technology, subject to international safeguards. However, four states that are not NPT members—India, Israel, Pakistan, and North Korea—have nuclear weapons. And several NPT members, including Libya, Iraq, Iran, and Syria, have today or in the past pursued weapons programs in violation of their treaty obligations.

Some experts perceive the dawn of a "second nuclear age," as volatile oil prices, rapid population growth, and fears about global warming increase the incentives for countries to develop civilian nuclear energy programs.[4] Approximately thirty countries have nuclear reactors, and dozens of new reactors are being planned, many in developing countries. In some cases, civilian nuclear technologies can be converted into weapons programs fairly easily. Proliferation experts worry about "dual use" technology that can be used to produce fuel for nuclear weapons as well as civilian reactors. Already, some forty-nine nations have the know-how to produce nuclear arms.[5] Even if most states' intentions are peaceful, the spread of nuclear technology may present opportunities to sophisticated terrorist groups such as al-Qaeda to pursue their own nuclear ambitions.

Radiological Devices

Given the hurdles of procuring a functioning nuclear weapon, terrorists or other rogue actors might well opt for the cheaper alternative of creating a "dirty bomb" out of radiological materials, which lack the catastrophic destructive power of nuclear weapons. The damage would vary greatly depending on the material used, the nature and topography of the target, and wind and other climatic conditions. Nevertheless, radiological weapons might serve as "weapons of mass disruption," with harmful psychological, physical, social, and economic effects. According to one analyst, a crude radiological weapon "detonated at the lower tip of Manhattan would render most of the borough virtually uninhabitable for decades."[6]

Biological Weapons

Biological weapons are infectious agents, including viruses, bacteria, and other dis-ease-causing organisms that are consciously employed as instruments of war. An ideal candidate is a pathogen that is easily manufactured, highly infectious, lethal, unpreventable, and deliverable in aerosol form.[7] Some of the most feared agents include anthrax and the smallpox virus, which killed more than 300 million people in the twentieth century alone and remains lethal in some 30 percent of those infected.

If the nuclear age dates from 1945, the age of biological warfare is considerably older. The Hittites of the eastern Mediterranean may have sent rams infected with tularemia into the villages of their enemies. Later civilizations, including the Assyrians, Greeks, and Romans, poisoned the wells of their enemies with fungi, poisonous herbs, carrion, and human corpses.[8] The European age of exploration that began in the late fifteenth century revealed the potential of germ warfare to decimate human populations— although largely inadvertent, exposure to smallpox and other diseases endemic to Europe had catastrophic effects on the inhabitants of the New World.[9] More recently, during World War II, the armed forces of imperial Japan conducted grisly experiments with plague, anthrax, and other infectious agents on prisoners of war. Subsequently, both the United States and the Soviet Union amassed giant bioweapons stockpiles. Both countries signed the Biological and Toxin Weapons Convention in 1972, but the Soviet Union continued clandestine biological weapons programs throughout the remainder of the Cold War.

Although there have been more recent uses of biological weapons, most notably the U.S. anthrax scare in the wake of 9/11, no state or nonstate actor has successfully launched a massive bioweapons attack. The risk of such an event may seem unlikely, given that there are probably fewer than a dozen countries with active biological weapons programs. However, modern biotechnology creates the potential for the creation of novel "designer bugs"; the weaponization of infectious diseases like tuber-culosis or the Ebola virus; or the production of eradicated diseases like smallpox and polio. Steady advances in biotechnology will "almost inevitably place greater destructive power in the hands of smaller groups of the technically competent."[10]

Given these relatively low barriers to entry, and the fact that biological weapons stockpiles tend to be less secure than nuclear ones, most experts consider the risk of bioterrorism greater than that of nuclear terrorism. Although such an attack would likely be less devastating than a nuclear one, biological weapons could still kill massive numbers of people and cripple public health systems, inducing widespread fear and causing catastrophic economic shocks. The relatively minor 2001 anthrax attacks in New York and Washington, DC, which killed five people, forced thousands to seek treatment and cost the U.S. economy an estimated $6 billion.[11]

Chemical Weapons

Chemical weapons employ the toxic properties of chemicals to kill, injure, or incapac-itate enemies. The main categories of chemical weapons agents are nerve agents, mustard agents, hydrogen cyanide, tear gases, arsines, psychotomimetic agents (causing delusions or hallucinations), and toxins.

Like biological weapons, chemical weapons have been used for centuries. Chinese cookbooks from the first millennia B.C.E. contain recipes for producing poisonous smoke from toxic vegetation and chemical substances like lime. During the seventh and eighth centuries C.E., the Byzantines and Arabs perfected the art of "Greek fire," a precursor to napalm, which was rediscovered during the Renaissance and featured in pivotal engagements like the siege of Malta (1565).[12] The first full-scale deployment of chemical weapons in the modern era occurred in World War I, in which 85,000 were killed and more than 1 million harmed by chemical agents, including chlorine, phosgene, and mustard gas. During the Cold War, both superpowers amassed, but never deployed, large stocks of chemical weapons. Iraq under Saddam Hussein is the most notorious case in recent years of a country deploying chemical weapons against its own people as well as external foes (Iran).[13]

Only six countries have declared possession of chemical weapons, although some twenty states have possessed or pursued them. As of 2006, there were more than six thousand chemical plants worldwide that could serve as sources for chemical weapons agents. The Chemical Weapons Convention, which came into effect in 1997, bans the production, acquisition, stockpiling, transfer, and use of chemical weapons, and obliges all state parties to destroy existing holdings by 2012. Unfortunately, Russia and the United States, among others, will probably fail to meet this deadline.

In general, chemical weapons are easier to acquire, weaponize, and use than biological or nuclear weapons. Instructions for their production and use exist on the Internet, including on *jihadi* web sites. However, chemical weapons are also more limited in their impact than other types of WMD. Experts calculate that the deaths from such an attack would probably be limited to, at most, several thousand. Nonetheless, the economic impact of a chemical device could be severe, and any such attack would sow panic.[14]

The WMD Threat from State and Nonstate Actors

Two major proliferation threats confront the United States: the risk that a "rogue" state might acquire WMD—particularly nuclear weapons—and the possibility that a terrorist group or other nonstate actor might acquire and/or use such a weapon.

State Actors

States might seek nuclear weapons for a variety of reasons. Some believe that nuclear weapons will protect them from invasion or attack (a view arguably borne out by the U.S. decision to invade Iraq to prevent it from acquiring WMD, while pursuing negotiations with North Korea once it was known to have them).[15] The political and psychological value of nuclear weapons should also not be underestimated as a motive for pursuing WMD programs.

None of these motivations suggests that a state actor would be likely to actually use nuclear weapons if it were able to acquire them. To do so would invite massive retaliation and almost certain regime change. However, for financial or political reasons, a nuclear-armed rogue state might provide nuclear technology—or even a weapon—to other pariah regimes or terrorist groups with fewer qualms about using one. And even if they did not intentionally do so, as former U.S. senator and co-chairman of the Nuclear Threat Initiative Sam Nunn has pointed out, "The more countries that have this fissile material, the more likely the risk of a diversion or theft of fissile material becomes."[16]

Beyond direct threats to the United States, the acquisition of nuclear weapons by hostile states would dramatically change global and regional power dynamics in negative ways. In the Middle East, nuclear possession might actually encourage aggressive behavior, by "making it 'safe' to engage in such activities."[17] Successful proliferation efforts by one state could spark regional arms races, and perhaps even nuclear conflict. If Iran develops a nuclear weapon, for example, rival regional powers such as Saudi Arabia, Egypt, and Turkey might follow. Aggressive posturing by North Korea could prompt Japan and South Korea to quickly develop their own nuclear weapons—a feat they are easily capable of—unsettling China and potentially upending the entire East Asian security architecture. Unfortunately, the successful efforts of India, Pakistan, Israel, and North Korea to acquire WMD, and ongoing efforts by Iran and perhaps Syria to do so, suggest that more and more states may seek nuclear capabilities.

Nonstate Actors

The second proliferation threat centers on nonstate actors. Transnational terrorists have actively sought weapons of mass destruction, including nuclear, biological, chemical, and radiological devices and their raw materials. Whereas state actors can be deterred, nonstate actors would probably use such weapons. Today's major nuclear threat thus "comes from a direction unforeseen in 1945, that this technology might now pass into the hands of the new stateless guerrillas, the jihadists, who offer none of the targets that have underlain the nuclear peace—no permanent infrastructure, no capital city, no country called home."[18]

It would be difficult, but not impossible, for terrorists to get their hands on a functioning nuclear weapon. More likely, a well-organized and well-financed terrorist group might steal or buy enough fissile material to build a simple bomb, which would require just a few kilograms (25 kg and 8 kg, respectively) of either weapons-grade uranium (U-235) or plutonium (Pu-239). A December 2008 report by the bipartisan U.S. Commission on the Prevention of WMD Proliferation and Terrorism found that without serious U.S. action to prevent such an outcome, a terrorist attack with WMD is "more likely than not" to occur by 2013.[19]

Probably the greatest WMD threat involving a nonstate actor comes from al-Qaeda. In 1998, Osama bin Laden declared the pursuit of WMD a "religious duty." Al-Qaeda has sought biological weapons and expertise, and apparently met with Pakistani nuclear scientists prior to September 11, 2001. A July 2007 U.S. National Intelligence Estimate stated that al-Qaeda "will continue to try to acquire and employ chemical, biological, radiological, or nuclear material in attacks and would not hesitate to use them."[20]

Other nonstate actors, such as organized criminals or militant groups, could also attempt to acquire WMD materials for political leverage, or to sell them to rogue states or terrorist groups. In some cases they might actually use them. The Japanese cult Aum Shinrikyo experimented with biological warfare, including numerous attempts to spread anthrax and botulism. The group botched at least a dozen biological attacks, but in 1995 carried out a sarin gas attack on the Tokyo subway that killed twelve and harmed more than six thousand people. In the 1990s, Chechen rebels with ties to al-Qaeda twice attempted to use a radiological device, and in 2002 reportedly considered launching an attack on a Russian nuclear research reactor.[21]

PROLIFERATION PATHWAYS

There are at least five ways by which state or nonstate actors could conceivably acquire weapons of mass destruction: (1) through the illicit purchase of a functional weapon; (2) by stealing weapons from government or private stockpiles; (3) through (authorized) state-sponsored transfers; (4) through unauthorized acquisition during state failure; or (5) by developing their own capacity to produce WMD. The following section elaborates on these pathways to WMD proliferation.[22]

Purchases on the WMD Black Market

One of the greatest WMD threats to the United States is what former International Atomic Energy Agency (IAEA) director-general Mohamed ElBaradei has referred to as the "Wal-Mart of private sector proliferation."[23] The extent and sophistication of the A.Q. Khan arms bazaar highlighted the variety of avenues by which a government or nonstate actor could purchase chemical, biological, radiological, or nuclear (CBRN) know-how, material, or weapons (see box 3.1). Potential sellers include corrupt government or military officials, individuals within private companies or research facilities, and criminal groups. (Khan himself was apparently motivated by profit.) And there is no shortage of would-be customers: the Khan network sold nuclear technology to Iran, Libya, and North Korea (and may also have worked with Algeria, Syria, and Saudi Arabia). Terrorist groups such as al-Qaeda are also actively seeking WMD.[24]

Some experts consider the threat of WMD smuggling overstated. Khan's apparent willingness to sell nuclear warhead designs notwithstanding, it is unlikely (though not impossible) that complete weapons of mass destruction—particularly nuclear weapons—could be purchased through illicit channels. Although thousands of tactical nukes in the former Soviet Union are unaccounted for, there has not been a single documented case of a functional nuclear weapon being sold on the black market. Indeed: "The dim realm of nuclear trafficking…is littered with rumors and outright scams. When actual material is involved, it often turns out to be radioactive detritus barely useable in a so-called 'dirty bomb.' "[25]

And yet, because the illicit trade in weapons of mass destruction is "furtive, murky, utterly nimble and ultimately elusive," it is impossible to know the true scope of the WMD black market.[26] Since the early 1990s there have been more than 1,300 confirmed incidents of lost, stolen, or unauthorized use of nuclear and radiological materials, at least fifteen of which involved weapons-grade fissile material. Between July 2007–June 2008 alone, there were 243 reported incidents of lost, stolen, or trafficked fissile material, a figure ElBaradei called "disturbingly high." Such reported incidents are only "the tip of the iceberg," believes Lyudmila Zaitseva of Stanford University, who estimates the real amount of missing weapons-grade material could be ten times higher than is officially known.[27]

Many experts predict transnational criminal groups will inevitably become heavily involved in the WMD black market. To date, there is little evidence that this is actually occurring; those engaged in nuclear and radiological trafficking appear to have been mostly smaller criminal groups, amateurs, and shady businessmen. Nonetheless, if major criminal syndicates decide trafficking in WMD is lucrative, they would be able to exploit existing smuggling routes and money-laundering networks. Of particular concern are poorly governed states of the former Soviet Union, long havens and transit points for organized criminal groups involved in narcotics and human trafficking. (There have been reports of nuclear materials being smuggled together with narcotics in South and Central Asia.[28]) Ties between organized crime bosses and state officials are especially alarming, given the latter's knowledge of security measures at WMD facilities.[29]

Box 3.1: A.Q. Khan and the WMD Black Market

Pakistani nuclear scientist Abdul Qadeer Khan is revered in his country as the "father of the Islamic bomb," but for some twenty years he also ran a transnational nuclear proliferation network that spanned at least three continents. Khan and his affiliates marketed what the *Economist* has called "a build-it-yourself bomb catalog"[30] to customers such as Iran, Libya, and North Korea, exporting everything from equipment for building uranium enrichment technology to nuclear weapons blueprints. If a nuclear terrorist attack occurs, write journalists Douglas Frantz and Catherine Collins, "there is a strong likelihood that the trail of devastation will lead back to Abdul Qadeer Khan."[31]

The central node of this proliferation network was Khan Research Laboratories (KRL) in Islamabad, but Khan's organization was global in scale and reach, leveraging resources from Europe to Southeast Asia. Primary intermediaries included a Malaysian manufacturing firm that produced centrifuge components; a Dubai-based Sri Lankan businessman; and South African and Turkish companies. Khan also drew on the resources of his former European colleagues. Before his downfall, Khan visited at least eighteen countries, including Egypt, Niger, Nigeria, Sudan, Syria, and Saudi Arabia. Although Khan's network was ostensibly dismantled after centrifuge shipments to Libya were intercepted in 2003, much about the network is still unknown. According to one expert: "It is naïve to think that somehow these guys aren't still doing business. These networks lay around like a loaded gun for anyone to use."[32] Experts debate the extent to which Pakistani officials were aware of or involved in the network's activities.[33]

Theft or Diversion of CBRN Material

Rather than relying on corrupt insiders and WMD traffickers, terrorists or state agents might themselves attempt to steal chemical, biological, radiological, or nuclear (CBRN) material or a ready-to-use weapon (or its component agents and delivery system). The possibility of terrorists acquiring poorly secured "loose nukes" is one of the most terrifying proliferation threats—but it is also one of the least likely. Although the world's tens of thousands of nuclear weapons would appear to give terrorists "a target-rich environment," the vast majority (about 95 percent) are located in Russia and the United States and are generally well guarded. (Since the end of the Cold War, U.S. assistance has helped secure some 75 percent of Russia's nuclear facilities). Of course, "being difficult to steal does not mean impossible."[34]

While a functional nuclear weapon might be hard to obtain, poorly secured fissile material is highly vulnerable to theft. Only about 25 percent of the world's scores of facilities that use or store weapons-usable uranium are adequately protected against theft or insider diversion.[35] In a number of cases, the most "unsophisticated thieves, sawing through padlocks and clipping alarm wires, [have been] able...to divert weapons-usable materials without detection and were caught only weeks or months later."[36]

Another target is civilian research reactors. Although these generally contain less fissile material, they have "some of the world's weakest security measures" for stocks of highly enriched uranium. Disturbingly, in 2007, thieves broke into a South African nuclear facility that was much better protected than most civilian reactors using highly enriched uranium.[37] And even if nuclear facilities are relatively well secured, nuclear and radioactive sources are vulnerable to theft during transit. Over the next fifteen years, some 500 tons of weapons-grade plutonium will be transported within or across national boundaries for commercial purposes—only eight kilograms of which would be adequate to produce a bomb.

Facilities housing radiological material that could be used in a dirty bomb are less well secured than nuclear sites, and biological pathogens would probably be even easier to steal. There are at least 1,500 "germ banks" worldwide, including at universities, veterinary research centers, medical businesses, and government laboratories—at least 1,000 of which may inadequately secure or regulate culture collections. And throughout the former USSR, Soviet-era bioweapons facilities and "anti-plague" laboratories contain vast stockpiles of pathogens, including anthrax, cholera, and tularemia, few of which are inventoried and many of which are vulnerable to theft.[38]

State-Sponsored Transfer

A third way by which a terrorist group or state could gain access to WMD is through the authorized transfer of a functional weapon or CBRN material from a state sponsor. Some states might do so for financial reasons; this is probably the motivation behind North Korea's nuclear-related sales to Syria, for instance. Others might provide WMD to state or nonstate allies for political or strategic reasons. A nuclear-armed Iran might conceivably transfer a weapon to a proxy such as Hezbollah. If the Pakistani government were replaced by Islamic hardliners, it could in theory do the same for al-Qaeda or Kashmiri terrorist groups.[39]

But while the danger of state-sponsored transfers should not be ruled out, nor should it be exaggerated, given the limited number of countries that would likely consider this option. Even if a state were ideologically inclined to provide WMD to terrorists or other rogue states, it is unclear whether any self-interested regime would assume such a tremendous level of risk. Given advances in nuclear, biological, and chemical forensics, the odds are fairly good that a WMD attack could be traced back to its original source—thus providing a "return address" for massive retaliation by the target state and its allies. Beyond this deterrent effect, it is unclear that even a radical "rogue" regime would as a matter of state policy share WMD with nonstate actors whose behavior they cannot, in the final analysis, control.

Unauthorized Transfer during State Failure

A fourth pathway for WMD proliferation could arise in the context of state collapse in a country with nuclear, chemical, or biological weapons. The resulting fragmentation of political authority and breakdown of public order could cripple WMD safeguards, opening the door to theft or unauthorized transfers by rogue elements within the state. Although only two nuclear-armed countries—North Korea and Pakistan—are plausible candidates for state failure, the risk is still significant, representing a national security threat of the highest order for the United States.[40]

Develop Indigenous Capacity

Finally, rogue states or nonstate actors could acquire WMD by developing—likely with assistance from another state or illicit network—their own ability to produce CBRN material and/or weapons. Manufacturing sufficient fissile material for a nuclear weapon is a daunting and costly undertaking: processing weapons-grade plutonium requires constructing large, technologically advanced facilities that are difficult to conceal, while producing sufficient quantities of highly enriched uranium involves spinning one thousand costly and carefully calibrated centrifuges an entire year. For states, the sophisticated technology required is extremely expensive; nonstate actors almost certainly would lack the necessary resources.[41]

However, terrorists could build a simple delivery device for nuclear materials acquired through theft or other means.[42] Contrary to popular belief, complete nuclear bomb schematics are not on the Internet. But in 2008, a design for a sophisticated nuclear weapon was discovered on A.Q. Khan network computers in Switzerland; in electronic form, it would be easy to copy and disseminate. If terrorists or others acquired such a design, it "would significantly shorten the time needed to build a weapon."[43] Frighteningly little money or space is required to do so: a Hiroshima-type gun-trigger atomic bomb could be built in a facility the size of a garage.[44] If, to date, even the most capable and motivated groups have lacked the functional competence to carry out such an operation, it is not for lack of interest; groups such as al-Qaeda and Aum Shinrikyo have tried on several occasions to purchase nuclear or radiological material.

Given enough time, resources, and sanctuary, terrorist groups (or state actors) could more easily develop the capability to produce weapons-grade biological and, especially, chemical agents. Aum Shinrikyo's chemical facilities, destroyed by the Japanese government in the late 1990s, apparently contained large stockpiles of sarin gas, VX, and phosgene. Terrorist plots involving chemical and biological agents, including ricin, have been disrupted in Britain. It would also be relatively simple to manufacture a device for delivering toxic chemicals or biological agents acquired through other channels. Likewise, constructing a radiological weapon or "dirty bomb" is technically straightforward, and probably within the capability of a determined nonstate actor.

A review of these proliferation scenarios suggests that all are not equally plausible, but some low-probability scenarios could nevertheless have devastating consequences.

ASSESSING THE WEAK STATE–WMD PROLIFERATION NEXUS

Particularly since 9/11, attention has increasingly focused on the threat that weak or failed states could pose for WMD proliferation. After all, al-Qaeda assiduously (if unsuccessfully) pursued WMD capabilities from its haven in Afghanistan—a critically weak if not failed state at the time. Weak states themselves might also pursue WMD, leading to the emergence of "proliferation rings" in the developing world that enable CBRN know-how and technology to spread uncontrollably to state and nonstate actors alike. In principle, the many governance gaps of weak states—particularly poor security and intelligence capabilities, corruption, and weak rule of law—could make them disproportionately likely to facilitate the spread of WMD, deliberately or otherwise.

The pathways outlined above suggest five major ways in which weak or failed states could enable the acquisition of WMD by state or nonstate actors. First, weak states could themselves seek to purchase, steal, or develop WMD, or assist others in doing so. Second, CBRN materials in weak states could be targeted by proliferators for illicit sale, theft, or diversion, without the state's knowledge or consent. Third, weak states could be used as intermediaries for WMD traffickers. Fourth, critically weak states or ungoverned spaces could serve as havens for nonstate actors attempting to develop WMD capability. Finally, the collapse of a country with WMD could result in their unauthorized transfer to nonstate actors. This section examines the plausibility of each scenario and the particular governance gaps that might make weak states likely to serve such a role.

Weak States as Deliberate WMD Proliferators

Conventional wisdom suggests that as the technology, equipment, and know-how to produce WMD diffuse, weaker states will inevitably gain access to them. "Pariah" regimes in weak states could seek WMD to shore up domestic political support, gain international prominence, or bolster their position against regional or international rivals. In turn, a weak state that acquired such capacity might be more willing than developed countries to sell related technology to other state or nonstate actors. Collaboration among developing countries could speed up the development of weapons technology for all involved. Chaim Brown and Christopher F. Chyba point to the danger of "second-tier nuclear proliferation," whereby "states in the developing world with varying technical capabilities trade among themselves to bolster one another's nuclear and strategic weapons efforts."[45] Such proliferation rings have already emerged among Pakistan, North Korea, Iran, Libya, and possibly Syria and others.

These trends pose a major threat to U.S. and global security. For starters, allowing nuclear weapons to fall into the hands of "states with weak command and control procedures and safeguards increases the probability of accidental or unauthorized nuclear use."[46] Such countries might also deliberately transfer weapons or related materials to other state or nonstate actors for ideological reasons or financial gain. Given the deplorable state of its economy, North Korea's nuclear deals were probably motivated by financial rather than strategic imperatives (see box 3.2). In the case of Pakistan, it seems likely that some state and military officials assisted Khan (though some experts would disagree). Journalist David Sanger argues that regardless of official involvement, "Khan's proliferation business thrived when Pakistan's leadership was at its weakest and most corrupt."[47]

Box 3.2: North Korea: Critically Weak Proliferator

North Korea's nuclear program dates to the 1960s, when the government established a nuclear research complex at Yongbyon with Soviet assistance. The regime began pursuing nuclear weapons during the 1980s, and by 1989 was able to process plutonium. In 1992, IAEA inspections revealed that several kilograms of plutonium had been diverted—enough for at least two nuclear weapons. Despite its pledge under the 1994 Agreed Framework to halt plutonium reprocessing, the regime has continued to seek nuclear weapons capability, likely with the assistance of the A.Q. Khan network. In 2003, North Korea withdrew from the NPT, expelled IAEA inspectors, and restarted plutonium reprocessing. Since North Korea's first underground nuclear test in 2006, several rounds of the Six Party Talks have failed to produce a verifiable agreement that would force the country to dismantle its nuclear arsenal or facilities. As of early 2010, North Korea was believed to have enough plutonium for at least half a dozen bombs, and may have already produced several weapons.

North Korea looms large in two major proliferation scenarios. First, if the state were to collapse, opportunistic military leaders could make off with nuclear assets, or well-organized foreign groups might exploit the chaos to steal or buy a nuclear weapon. The second, and probably greater risk given recent history, is that the regime of Kim Jong-Il itself may sell WMD technology. Cash-strapped North Korea has a long history of involvement in counterfeiting, illicit arms transfers, and narcotics trafficking, and has apparently supplied Syria and Iran with nuclear know-how. Experts fear that "now nuclear weapons or fissile material could take their place in its shopping catalogue,"[48] including making such weapons available to terrorists.

On the whole, however, concerns that weak states—particularly the weakest states—will acquire or transfer WMD are probably overblown. Poor countries generally do not have the financial resources or human capital to develop or purchase the technology and equipment needed to produce a nuclear weapon. Saddam Hussein's effort to acquire nuclear weapons lasted more than a decade and cost his regime more than $10 billion[49]—far beyond the resources of most weak states (or any nonstate actor). The exception that proves the rule is North Korea, a totalitarian regime willing to starve its population in order to pursue nuclear, biological, and chemical weapons.

With the two major exceptions of North Korea and Pakistan, no state in the bottom two tiers of the Weak States Index is even close to having nuclear weapons capability (see table 3.1). Only four other states in the bottom two tiers (Bangladesh, Uzbekistan, Colombia, and the Democratic Republic of Congo) even have civilian nuclear facilities on their territory. Of some forty developing countries that in recent years have expressed interest in establishing civilian nuclear power programs, only two—Nigeria and Yemen—are weak or critically weak states.[50]

Likewise, few weak states seem to be pursuing biological or chemical weapons, even though these would be much cheaper and easier to acquire than nuclear weapons. Of about a dozen countries with biological weapons programs or research facilities, only two—North Korea and Pakistan—rank in the bottom two quintiles on the Index. Perhaps twenty countries have ever pursued or acquired chemical weapons. Only five of these—Iraq, Sudan, North Korea, Pakistan, and Burma—are weak states (and only North Korea is known to definitely have a chemical weapons program; Iraq's has been dismantled).[51]

In fact, the greatest proliferation threat, in terms of states acquiring WMD, may come from a handful of relatively strong states in the third quintile of the Index, all classified as "states to watch." These countries—primarily Syria, Russia, Iran, India, China, and Egypt—all have civilian nuclear programs as well as known or suspected WMD stockpiles. Russia, India, and China all have nuclear weapons; Iran is almost certainly pursuing them; and Syria is suspected of attempting to secretly acquire some kind of nuclear-related technology. In all, fifteen of the twenty-eight states in the third quintile have some type of civilian nuclear program; all but two of these are classified as "states to watch."[52] These states are particularly problematic in terms of proliferation because they are developed enough to acquire or maintain civilian WMD programs, but often have serious governance gaps—including high levels of corruption, weak security and intelligence capabilities, and in many cases authoritarian and unaccountable governance—which may make them more likely to proliferate, deliberately or otherwise.

Some middle-ranking countries on the Index, as well as some of the world's developed countries, may be as likely to supply allies or partners with nuclear technology (if not weapons) as states like North Korea and Pakistan. The Chinese are said to have "made a policy decision to flood the developing world with atomic know-how" in the 1980s, and their clients may have included Algeria and North Korea as well as Pakistan.[53] Russian and Chinese civilian nuclear assistance to Iran may have inadvertently been used for weapons purposes. Argentina also sought to supply technology related to uranium enrichment to Iran in the 1990s, although U.S. pressure blocked the sale. The United States' recent civil nuclear deal with India has been criticized as enabling proliferation, since it could allow India, if so inclined, to divert its own civilian nuclear resources to its weapons program. And France has caused irritation in nonproliferation circles by pursuing civilian nuclear deals with countries in the Middle East (including Libya) and other "proliferation-prone regions."[54]

On the other hand, weak states do appear somewhat less likely than developed countries to adhere to international nonproliferation conventions. The two weak or critically weak states that do have nuclear weapons are not members of the NPT—Pakistan was never a member, while North Korea withdrew in 2003—or other nuclear export control regimes, such as the Nuclear Suppliers Group. Of thirty-three countries that have not acceded to the Biological and Toxin Weapons Convention, twenty-one (63.6 percent) are in the bottom two tiers of the Index, as are four of only seven countries in the world that are not signatories to the Chemical Weapons Convention.[55] This may be of minimal importance as long as these states lack the capacity to acquire WMD, but it is a troubling indicator that they are not overly concerned with the transfer of WMD capabilities to dangerous actors.

Weak States as Inadvertent WMD Source Countries

Even if official state policy does not sanction such transfers, weak states could in principle become inadvertent suppliers of WMD to state or nonstate actors. Under this scenario, would-be proliferators would gain access to CBRN stockpiles by exploiting capacity gaps in weak states' security, or by bribing insiders in societies that face pervasive corruption or economic hardship.

Yet such a scenario appears unlikely—mostly because the vast majority of weak states (those in the bottom two tiers of the Index) have no weapons-usable nuclear, chemical, or biological materials. Of the thirty-nine countries that possess significant quantities of weapons-grade fissile material, only four are weak states: North Korea, Nigeria, Pakistan, and Uzbekistan, which together possess less than 0.05 percent of the world's highly enriched uranium and 0.05 percent of weapons-grade plutonium. Conversely, all of the countries possessing more than 100 kilograms of highly enriched uranium are relatively developed countries. Likewise, over 90 percent of the world's weapons-grade plutonium is found in the United States and Russia; most of the rest is in the United Kingdom, France, China, India, Israel, North Korea, and Pakistan.[56] While those weak states that do have weapons-grade fissile material may be tempting targets for nuclear thieves, the overwhelming concentration of such materials in relatively strong states means that corrupt officials in the latter countries pose at least as great a proliferation threat.

Fears about radioactive materials being stolen or diverted from weak states are also probably overstated. This possibility gained widespread publicity in early 2003, when the Bush administration revealed intelligence (subsequently discredited) that Saddam Hussein had attempted to purchase five tons of yellowcake uranium from Niger, a critically weak state. In fact, there has been only one publicly reported incident of radiological theft in a critically weak state. In 1998, members of several Italian mafia clans were arrested for attempting to sell a low-enriched uranium fuel rod stolen from a research reactor in the Democratic Republic of Congo.[57]

As was the case with potential state proliferators, several third-tier "states to watch" are the likeliest potential sources of stolen or diverted CBRN material. These include Russia, China, India, and Iran, all of which possess large quantities of fissile material that may be inadequately secured (see box 3.3). Little is publicly known about Iranian nuclear security, in particular. Worryingly, China's nuclear material controls resemble those of the Soviet Union—a system of "guards, guns, and gates" rather than sophisticated safeguards—and may be similarly vulnerable.[58] In third-tier states with growing biotechnology industries, such as Cuba and Indonesia, dangerous pathogens are produced for medical research rather than offensive purposes, but could nonetheless fall into the wrong hands through corruption, theft, or diversion.[59] Radiological materials have been stolen from Kazakhstan, Azerbaijan, and Thailand, the latter two of which are "states to watch."[60]

A handful of relatively strong states ranking in the top two tiers of the Index—and thus not classified as "states to watch"—may also present inviting targets for terrorists or others seeking WMD materials. South Africa—which ranks 110th on Index—is a case in point. Two nuclear experts have argued, "South African technical mercenaries may be more dangerous than the underemployed scientists of the former Soviet Union."[61] More dramatically, in November 2007, South Africa's Pelindaba nuclear facility—which stores enough weapons-grade uranium for an estimated twenty-five bombs—was the scene of "the boldest raid ever attempted on a site holding bomb grade uranium."[62] The attempted burglary was apparently an inside job.

The states of the former Soviet Union are likely sources of stolen fissile or radiological material. Although state weakness overall would not seem to be the overriding factor in whether a country's CBRN materials end up on the WMD black market, most of these states do suffer from a few critical governance gaps that could make their stockpiles vulnerable to diversion. In particular, high levels of corruption, economic distress, weak rule of law, and poor security conditions make them attractive targets for those seeking to steal or buy WMD materials. Approximately 40 kilograms of weapons-usable uranium and plutonium have been stolen from poorly protected nuclear facilities in the region over the last decade.[63] Nevertheless, with both relatively strong states (e.g., Latvia and Kazakhstan) and weak ones (e.g., Turkmenistan and Uzbekistan) having been the site of nuclear theft, proliferation risk in the former Soviet Union may have as much to do with the availability of WMD materials as with state weakness. Both Aum Shinrikyo and al-Qaeda have tried to purchase nuclear assets in the region.

Corruption

WMD trafficking almost always requires the involvement of insiders, from employees and security guards to customs and transport officials. Indeed, as international efforts to physically secure CBRN materials and weapons accelerate, insider knowledge and access will be even more critical to nuclear thieves. Nuclear, biological, and chemical expertise may also be for sale to the highest bidder. Thus societies in which corruption is rampant make tempting targets to anyone seeking to purchase CBRN materials, equipment, or expertise.

Former Soviet facilities employ thousands of poorly paid experts whose knowledge of deadly weaponry could be exploited. In Tajikistan, for instance, two former government officials were tried for attempting to sell canisters of plutonium and cesium-137 on the black market.[64] In weak states such as North Korea, a lack of modern nuclear control means that there are significant risks of insider diversion. In Pakistan, Moises Naim points out, A.Q. Khan "knew, as any savvy businessman would, both the importance and the art of purchasing government approval by cutting deals with the key individuals within the system: judges, generals, ministers."[65] Obviously, individuals in any country may be susceptible to bribery, but the scope of corruption that would enable repeated WMD transfers over many years is less likely to occur in a stronger state with stricter accountability measures and rule of law.

Economic Distress

At the macro level, some developing countries may simply lack the resources to provide even basic security at WMD facilities. Likewise, individuals in developing countries experiencing economic hardship or crisis could be especially susceptible to bribery, or could themselves decide to steal and sell WMD material. Analysis of hundreds of cases of theft of nuclear and radiological materials by civilian insiders suggests that the major motive for such "inside jobs" was financial. On the other hand, at least one of the two nuclear scientists known to have worked with al-Qaeda was a hard-line Muslim probably motivated by ideology, not greed.[66]

The impact of economic distress is apparent in the case of the former Soviet Union, where economic turmoil produced dangerous effects in the region's nuclear sector— and where most illicit nuclear incidents have originated. During the 1990s, nuclear and biological facilities' budgets dropped so quickly that their employees—who had enjoyed high salaries and prestige throughout the Cold War—found themselves working in dilapidated facilities for stagnant or declining wages. By some accounts, workers went months without pay, guards left their posts to forage for food, and alarm systems shut off due to unpaid electricity bills.

Unsurprisingly, such conditions led to a number of security breaches. In 1994, an employee of a major Russian producer of reactor fuel walked out of the gates with 3 kilograms of weapons-grade uranium hidden in his protective gloves. The following year, another employee at the same plant smuggled some 1.7 kilograms of enriched uranium out of the facility in a bag of apples. There were also several reported incidents of nuclear and radiological theft involving ex-Soviet military personnel and former security service (KGB) officials with access to materials such as cesium-137, strontium-90, and cobalt-60.[67]

By contrast, as the Russian economy grew rapidly after the 1998 financial crisis, investment in nuclear security increased significantly. According to Harvard University's Matthew Bunn, "the improving Russian economy, increased revenues from nuclear electricity and nuclear exports, and huge Russian government investments in the nuclear industry have largely eliminated the 1990s-era desperation that created additional incentives and opportunities for nuclear theft."[68] However, in the aftermath of the financial crisis and collapsing oil prices of 2008, some analysts are concerned that a repeated downturn in Russia could have detrimental effects for nuclear security. Others point to China as a country that, were a major economic crisis to occur, could face problems similar to those of Russia in the early 1990s.[69]

Weak Rule of Law

Even in relatively strong states like Russia, South Africa, and many countries in Eastern Europe, weak rule of law ensures that where WMD theft or smuggling does occur, perpetrators are not dealt with effectively. In South Africa, for instance, investigations into the break-in at the Pelindaba nuclear facility have stalled—and South African officials have not been particularly transparent or cooperative with Western officials in the matter.[70] Weak rule of law also facilitates a large transnational organized criminal presence (see chapter 4), which as described above could facilitate WMD trafficking. The WMD-organized crime threat is particularly acute in Russia, Central Asia, and Eastern Europe—regions with vast quantities of fissile materials where "powerful organized crime groups...have established smoothly running mechanisms for smuggling drugs and weapons that could easily be adapted to nuclear material trafficking."[71] At least one prominent Russia criminal figure is known to have sold fissile material to North Korea, and FBI investigations have raised concerns that arms trafficking rings in Russia and the Caucasus may sell sophisticated weapons and even WMD to terrorists.[72]

Conflict and Insecurity

Only a handful of states with nuclear arsenals or significant CBRN stockpiles face serious instability or conflict, or lack control over part of their territory. But the consequences of widespread violence in a nuclear-armed state, or an insurgent attack on a facility housing CBRN materials, could be catastrophic. In China's Xinjiang region, site of a long-running insurgency by members of the minority Uighur group, "the possibility that separatists might attempt to sabotage a nuclear facility or obtain fissile materials for terrorist purposes cannot be ruled out."[73] Uzbekistan has both weapons-grade material and a significant Islamic insurgent movement, and an al-Qaeda leader claimed to have had access to radiological material obtained by the radical Islamic Movement of Uzbekistan.[74] Radiological materials have been stolen from Chechnya, a highly unstable part of a moderately strong state, Russia. Algeria, which may now annually produce enough plutonium for a bomb,[75] faces an ongoing terrorist threat. Of course the most worrying state is Pakistan (discussed in detail later in this chapter), where escalating insurgent and terrorist violence could threaten the security of the country's nuclear weapons arsenal.

Corruption, economic distress, weak rule of law and poor security thus make certain states in the middle tiers of the Index—developed enough to have significant stockpiles of CBRN material, but weakened by these particular governance gaps—likely targets for proliferators seeking "loose nukes" or CBRN material. These include Algeria, Russia, India, Indonesia, and Turkey (as well as the perennial weak-state problem children, North Korea and Pakistan).

However, as table 3.1 indicates, a clear majority of countries with weapons-usable fissile material are not among the world's most corrupt or insecure states. And developed

---

Box 3.3: Russia: Proliferation Risks in a State to Watch

As one journalist puts it, of the many countries in which weapons-grade fissile material might be acquired by rogue actors, there is "probably none better than Russia."[76] At the end of the Cold War, massive stockpiles were scattered across hundreds of poorly secured facilities throughout the former Soviet Union. By late 2008, despite significant Russian investment as well as U.S.-sponsored efforts, as much as one-quarter to one-third of Russia's vast nuclear arsenal had not been secured in line with U.S. safeguards (which may in any case be inadequate to protect against a determined insider or terrorist group).

Given its ready supply of WMD materials, rampant corruption, weak security services, volatile economy, and political instability, Russia is both a state to watch and a prime target for proliferators. Terrorist groups are known to have undertaken reconnaissance at Russian nuclear storage sites, and significant quantities of weapons-grade fissile materials that were smuggled through Georgia have been traced to Russia. And Russia's security forces are poorly equipped to protect the country's nuclear infrastructure, given their generally low pay and morale, and high alcoholism and suicide rates. Experts have documented a dysfunctional security culture at many facilities, with guards and officials failing to follow even basic procedures for safeguarding nuclear material.[77] Moreover, Russia scores in the bottom quintile of the Weak States Index for security, largely as a result of ongoing violence in the north Caucasus region where Islamic extremists have been active—and where several important nuclear facilities are located. Thus the general consensus among experts appears to be that, despite progress since the early 1990s, Russia remains one of the likeliest potential sources of illicit WMD material.

countries' CBRN programs, though generally well secured, are not invulnerable to penetration by proliferators. Weapons-grade highly enriched uranium has gone missing in Japan, for instance. A.Q. Khan stole classified information on uranium enrichment from a Dutch research facility where he was employed in the 1970s.[78]

Even the United States' CBRN stockpiles are vulnerable to diversion. By one account most of the civilian reactors that "arguably do not meet IAEA physical protection recommendations are within the United States."[79] While U.S. nuclear security is among the best in the world, it is hardly infallible: in August 2007, a B-52 bomber was inadvertently loaded with six nuclear warheads, which were not noticed as missing for thirty-six hours. Investigations have discovered "a long-term decline in the Air Force's focus on providing appropriate controls for nuclear weapons, and reportedly concluded that as many as 1,000 sensitive nuclear weapons components are unaccounted for."[80] The United States' hundreds of laboratories and chemical storage sites are also potential targets for nonstate actors. The Commission on the Prevention of WMD Proliferation and Terrorism has described how at several U.S. biological laboratories, undercover government agents testing out the facilities' security were able to "walk right up to the building housing these deadly pathogens."[81]

Stronger states are also those with the sophisticated technological firms and industries to supply the WMD black market. North Korean intermediaries may have purchased materials related to the manufacture of nuclear weapons from Chinese, British, German, and other European firms.[84] Moreover, nuclear materials and weapons are probably most vulnerable to theft during transit, which occurs primarily in Europe and other relatively developed regions. Every year, there are roughly one hundred commercial plutonium shipments, each often containing well over 100 kilograms of weapons-usable plutonium; this number could grow to about 1,500 commercial shipments containing about 500 tons of un-irradiated plutonium over the next fifteen years.[85] Just eight kilograms of weapons-grade plutonium would be enough for a single bomb.

Moreover, it is moderately strong developing countries—rather than the weakest states—that may be most resistant to U.S. or international efforts to guarantee the security of their CBRN stocks and facilities. The aspirations to regional or global influence of countries like Russia, China, India, and South Africa may complicate bilateral relations with the United States and increase their reluctance to grant access to nuclear facilities or share sensitive military information. For instance, despite significant U.S.-Russian cooperation through programs such as Cooperative Threat Reduction (CTR), Russian officials have not granted the United States access to its most sensitive nuclear sites. Meanwhile in Kazakhstan, Ukraine, and Belarus, U.S.-led efforts to remove or blend down highly enriched uranium have progressed only slowly.[86]

If CBRN materials are vulnerable even in the strongest states, some characteristics of the worst governed states may actually make them *less* likely to be targeted for theft. Totalitarian regimes such as North Korea pose especially significant hurdles to unauthorized transfers. As long as the regime is stable, "in such a garrison state, the possibility of an armed group of terrorists attacking and seizing any of this material seems vanishingly small."[87] Conversely, and ironically, some experts have pointed to the increasing political and economic liberalization of Chinese society and the relaxation

Table 3.1: Countries with weapons–usable fissile material

	Quantity of HEU (kg)[82]	Weapon Equivalents from Plutonium[83]	Security (Index Score)	Corruption (Index Score)	Economics (Index Score)	Territory Affected by Conflict (Index Score)
Australia	76 kg		n/a	n/a	n/a	n/a
Austria	5–20 kg		n/a	n/a	n/a	n/a
Belarus	170–370 kg		8.24	3.01	6.57	10.00
Belgium	700–750 kg	225–450	n/a	n/a	n/a	n/a
Canada	1,350 kg		n/a	n/a	n/a	n/a
Chile	5 kg		9.43	10.00	7.99	10.00
China	1,000 kg	600–1,200	6.85	4.01	6.89	9.29
Czech Republic	0–40 kg		n/a	n/a	n/a	n/a
France	6,392 kg	6,619–13,238	n/a	n/a	n/a	n/a
Germany	890 kg	3,200–6,400	n/a	n/a	n/a	n/a
Ghana	1 kg		8.44	5.36	5.92	10.00
Hungary	0–95.5 kg		9.01	7.41	10.00	10.00
India	0–10 kg	170–340	4.87	5.08	6.72	6.32
Iran	7 kg		6.91	3.84	5.51	10.00
Israel	34 kg	70–140	n/a	n/a	n/a	n/a
Italy	100–200 kg		n/a	n/a	n/a	n/a
Jamaica	1 kg		7.78	4.57	6.28	10.00
Japan	2,000 kg	4,825–9,650	n/a	n/a	n/a	n/a

Kazakhstan	10,590–10,940 kg		8.33	2.76	7.43	10.00
Libya	5 kg		8.12	2.85	6.84	10.00
Mexico	12 kg		7.63	4.62	7.82	10.00
Netherlands	730–810 kg		n/a	n/a	n/a	n/a
Nigeria	1 kg		5.37	1.56	5.39	10.00
North Korea	42 kg	5–10	7.28	0.24	0.52	10.00
Pakistan	17 kg	5–10	4.69	2.71	6.58	9.56
Poland	441 kg		8.98	6.21	8.95	10.00
Romania	0–5 kg		8.42	5.16	7.91	10.00
Russia	15,000–30,000 kg	16,650–33,300	4.83	3.29	7.14	6.80
Serbia	13 kg		7.39	4.61	7.14	8.71
South Africa	610–760 kg		7.72	7.56	6.89	9.56
Switzerland	5–10 kg	250–500	n/a	n/a	n/a	n/a
Syria	1 kg		7.49	3.61	4.62	10.00
Taiwan	3–10 kg		n/a	n/a	n/a	n/a
Turkey	8 kg		5.83	5.94	7.32	7.21
Ukraine	160–250 kg		7.90	3.56	6.92	10.00
United Kingdom	1,437 kg	9,250–18,500	n/a	n/a	n/a	n/a
United States	176,000 kg	11,875–23,750	n/a	n/a	n/a	n/a

(continued)

Table 3.1: Continued

	Quantity of HEU (kg)[82]	Weapon Equivalents from Plutonium[83]	Security (Index Score)	Corruption (Index Score)	Economics (Index Score)	Territory Affected by Conflict (Index Score)
Uzbekistan	Less than 56 kg		6.66	2.44	5.20	10.00
Total in bottom 2 quintiles	Less than .05% of HEU	10–20 weapons could be produced from Pu–239 in weak states	8 of 38 (21.1%)	9 of 38 (23.7%)	5 of 38 (13.2%)	7 of 38 (18.4%)

LEGEND: Index Scores

Bottom Quintile
Second Quintile
Third Quintile
Fourth Quintile
Top Quintile

of Mao-era social controls—and a corresponding rise in corruption—as a proliferation problem: Given the central government's absolute control, "Until recently there were few reasons to worry about thefts of fissile materials from Chinese facilities." But today, "local government officials routinely evade government directives," making it "possible that an insider might be tempted to steal nuclear materials for sale on the black market or for other purposes."[88]

Thus, somewhat contrary to the conventional wisdom, it is far from impossible that terrorists or criminals could target WMD materials in relatively strong states. It is precisely the most developed countries that generally have the resources to pursue civilian nuclear programs and advanced biotechnology or biodefense programs—and so are more likely to have large stores of radiological, nuclear, and hazardous biological material that could be used in an attack.

Weak States as Transit Points or Intermediaries for WMD Traffickers

Even weak states that have no nuclear, biological, or chemical weapons programs for proliferators to target may be used as transit states for WMD traffickers. Although it would be difficult to smuggle an assembled nuclear weapon overland, it is relatively easy to transport weapons-grade highly enriched uranium or plutonium across an international border. Naturally, the states likeliest to serve as transit states are those that border countries with CBRN materials or stockpiles, particularly the countries of the former Soviet Union, Eastern Europe, and South Asia. For instance, on several occasions, radioactive materials have been detected on trains leaving Kyrgyzstan (one of which was bound for Iran).[89]

Certain aspects of state weakness could facilitate WMD trafficking, including poor regulatory regimes or import/export controls, corruption, and porous borders. Security officers and border guards in developing countries often have limited surveillance capability and difficulty tracking and monitoring nonstate actors. Without sophisticated equipment and specialized training, it is practically impossible for customs officers to verify the contents of supposedly legal shipments of radioisotopes. Moreover, guards may be vulnerable to corruption. A 2006 U.S. Government Accountability Office (GAO) report cites corruption among border guards as a serious problem in several countries where the United States has installed detection equipment.[90] In 2006, weapons-grade uranium was successfully transported from Russia to Georgia despite radiation detectors at the border, thanks to bribery of a Georgian customs officer. As one Georgian official noted, "If there are high levels of bribes, in the end you can turn off the technical [radiation detection] equipment."[91]

Weak states are also more likely to lack full control of their territory and borders. In regions such as the former Soviet Union, where WMD materials are widespread, this can lead to a "toxic combination of routine smuggling, stateless zones...and the essential ingredients of nuclear weapons."[92] One expert says such ungoverned (or criminally ruled) territories have been the "Achilles' heel" for U.S. efforts to combat nuclear smuggling[93] (see box 3.4 on Georgia).

In some cases weak states may lack the will, not merely capacity, to prevent WMD trafficking across or on their territory. The UN Security Council monitors implementation of Resolution 1540, which requires all UN member states to prevent the proliferation of nuclear, chemical, and biological materials. As of July 2008, more than 70 percent of UN member states had passed implementing legislation—but only twenty-one of the fifty-six weakest states (37.5 percent) had done so. Of only thirty-four countries which by 2009 had not submitted an initial report to the 1540 Committee, twenty-six (76.5 percent) ranked in the bottom two quintiles on the Index of State Weakness.[94]

Box 3.4: Georgia Case Study: Porous Borders, Ungoverned Spaces, and WMD Proliferation

Several high-profile incidents in recent years have raised concerns that the former Soviet republic of Georgia has become "a hotbed of nuclear smuggling."[95] The country's porous borders, breakaway regions, high (though falling) levels of corruption, and proximity to Russia's vast nuclear stockpiles make it particularly attractive to nuclear traffickers.

Since 2003, there have been at least eight reported incidents of nuclear and radiological materials being smuggled into or through Georgia. The materials involved include weapons-grade highly enriched uranium, plutonium, and beryllium, most of it traced to Russia or Azerbaijan. In one of the more spectacular incidents, a Russian national named Oleg Khinsagov and three Georgian associates were arrested in January 2006 by Georgian security officials working with the CIA. Khinsagov was carrying 100 grams of uranium, smuggled from North Ossetia and enriched to nearly 90 percent, which he planned to sell for $1 million. He claimed to have another 2–3 kilograms available for purchase—"which in expert hands is enough to make a small bomb."[96]

As former U.S. Ambassador to Georgia John F. Tefft noted, the 2006 incident "highlights how smuggling and loose border control, associated with Georgia's separatist conflicts" are a threat "not just to Georgia but to all the international community."[97] The ungoverned regions of Abkhazia and South Ossetia broke away from Georgia in the early 1990s and have served as havens for criminals and corrupt officials ever since. Even before the August 2008 war between Russia and Georgia, Georgian authorities were effectively barred from both provinces, where separatist governments are backed by nominal Russian peacekeepers. Journalist Michael Bronner has described South Ossetia as "a nest of organized crime," a "smuggler's nirvana" where the economy is driven by smuggling in cigarettes, arms, people, and counterfeit U.S. dollars.[98]

Georgia's own nuclear and radiological materials are also vulnerable to theft or diversion. Although Georgia has not had nuclear weapons on its territory since the end of the Cold War, it does have three nuclear research facilities—including one in Abkhazia, which is not under IAEA safeguards. Georgian authorities have claimed that radioactive materials from the Abkhaz site, including highly enriched uranium, have been sold to terrorists, although these reports have not been confirmed.[99] The United States has made securing Georgia's borders and nuclear facilities a top priority.[100]

Again, however, the weakest states are not necessarily the likeliest transit routes for WMD smugglers, primarily because most of them are not located anywhere near CBRN stocks. Instead, major trafficking routes and intermediary states have been primarily middle-ranking countries with the governance gaps described above, including in the former Soviet Union, Asia, and Eastern Europe. Turkey, which ranks in the fourth quintile on the Weak States Index, has been the site of some two dozen seizures of CBRN material since 1993. Slovakia's border with Ukraine is considered a frequent entry point for WMD materials into the European Union, and in recent years there have been several arrests of alleged nuclear traffickers in Slovakia, Hungary, and the Czech Republic.[101] Even the United States is vulnerable to nuclear smuggling—in 2005, GAO officials demonstrated weaknesses in U.S. border security by successfully using falsified documents to bring nuclear materials into the United States from Canada. Two ABC News teams have also managed to smuggle depleted uranium into the United States from Canada.

Table 3.2 is based on data from the IAEA Illicit Trafficking Database, which has confirmed sixteen incidents involving the theft or unauthorized use of weapons-grade fissile material since 1993. As the table shows, strong states appear at least as likely as weak ones to play a role in CBRN smuggling. None of the known incidents

Table 3.2: Confirmed Nuclear Smuggling Incidents

Date	Material	Location	Index Ranking
May 1993	150 g HEU	Lithuania	138
March 1994	2.972 kg HEU	Russia	65
May 1994	6.2 g Pu	Germany	
June 1994	0.795 g Pu	Germany	
July 1994	0.24 g Pu	Germany	
August 1994	363.4 g Pu	Germany	
December 1994	2.73 kg HEU	Czech Republic	
June 1995	1.7 kg HEU	Russia	65
June 1995	0.415 kg HEU	Czech Republic	
June 1995	16.9 g HEU	Czech Republic	
May 1999	10 g HEU	Bulgaria	127
December 2000	0.001 g Pu	Germany	
July 2001	0.5 g HEU	France	
June 2003	170 g HEU	Georgia	90
February 2006	79.5 g HEU	Georgia	90
March 2006	47.5 g HEU	Germany	

Source: IAEA Illicit Trafficking Database

occurred in a weak or critically weak state. By contrast, more than half of the sixteen incidents occurred in two (highly) developed countries: Germany and the Czech Republic.[102]

Beyond serving as transit states, there have been a few reported cases of individuals, officials, and companies in critically weak states serving as intermediaries for WMD traffickers. Al-Qaeda reportedly sought to purchase South African uranium in Sudan, although the deal was apparently a scam. However, WMD traffickers also operate in some of the world's more developed countries: The A.Q. Khan network, for instance, transported equipment produced in Malaysia on German-registered ships through Dubai using a British-owned shell company. Chinese firms have facilitated North Korean nuclear purchases—possibly enabled by China's weak export controls.[103]

Weak States as Havens for Proliferators

Weak states that do not control all of their territory may provide havens in which terrorists or other nonstate actors could attempt to actually build a weapon of mass destruction, or to organize and acquire the financing to buy one. To construct a nuclear bomb, terrorists would need a sophisticated procurement organization to acquire the needed equipment and fissile material on the black market; a transport and logistical system to move these illicit goods; and space in a remote area to assemble a device and conduct tests without attracting attention. A few weak states, especially those with a known terrorist presence in regions outside formal state control—notably Pakistan—pose the greatest threat.[104]

Al-Qaeda's activities in pre-9/11 Afghanistan provide one of the most alarming illustrations of the potential threat from the nexus of terrorism, WMD proliferation, and state weakness. From its Afghan sanctuary, al-Qaeda pursued a "major biological [weapons] effort" and made "meaningful progress on its nuclear agenda."[105] The veneer of sovereignty and legitimacy afforded by the Taliban made al-Qaeda well-placed to conduct transnational transfers of illicit materials. The organization reportedly attempted to import dual-use equipment, including lathes, for nuclear weapons development, and worked with a Pakistani veterinarian and a Malaysian terrorist to develop a deadly anthrax strain. CIA operatives have also discovered that al-Qaeda was conducting experiments with chemical and biological weapons at its Afghan training camps.[106]

In 2001, al-Qaeda reached out to nuclear scientists in neighboring Pakistan, who apparently provided "advice and crude diagrams" for building a weapon.[107] Al-Qaeda is not believed to have made any significant progress toward either a biological or a nuclear weapon, but it may well have done so if its plans had not been disrupted by the U.S. invasion following the attacks of 9/11, which occurred only a month after the meetings with the Pakistani scientists. The Afghan case shows that terrorists may seek to build WMD even in countries lacking the most rudimentary industrial capacity.[108]

Sudan provides another example of a weak state serving as an operating base for terrorist groups seeking WMD. By some reports, al-Qaeda supported the Sudanese regime's attempts to develop chemical weapons, while (unsuccessfully) attempting to broker a uranium deal from its base in the country. Like Afghanistan, however, Sudan is not only a critically weak state but one whose government was ideologically allied with al-Qaeda; it actively supported the organization, rather than tacitly condoning it. Most of the weakest states are unlikely to serve a similar role.

Perhaps more likely havens for nonstate proliferation rings are states that are not critically weak, but which have isolated conflicts or breakaway regions. Particularly dangerous are the conflict-ridden, under- (or alternatively) governed spaces of the former Soviet Union, including Transdniester, Abkhazia, South Ossetia, and Nagorno-Karabakh—all of which are near Soviet-era nuclear facilities. One scholar has written, "Should a transnational terrorist group such as al-Qaeda ever get its hands on former Soviet nuclear material, it is almost a given that a territory such as Karabakh will be involved."[109]

Yet the conventional wisdom about terrorists assembling WMD in weak or failed states may be overstated—and ignores the role that more developed countries can play in proliferation efforts. In 1993, Aum Shinrikyo attempted to mine uranium in Australia—not a weak state by any measure. Moreover, ungoverned spaces or critically weak states may be too insecure to serve as safe havens for proliferators. David Albright concludes that "operating in a weak state can ease the terrorists' task of building a nuclear weapon," but "the production of separated plutonium or enriched uranium by a terrorist group appears possible only under special conditions in a weak state."[110]

Collapsed States and WMD Proliferation

Some experts have raised concerns about the possibility of terrorists acquiring WMD from a collapsing state.[111] Currently, such an outcome is plausible in only two nuclear states: Pakistan and North Korea. However, a political crisis or major conflict in a nuclear-armed "state to watch" could create similarly dramatic problems. Russia, India, and nuclear aspirant Iran have all faced significant political turmoil or internal security challenges in recent years. In China, although a Soviet-style collapse is unlikely, severe social unrest or a turbulent political transition could cause the government to lose control over some of its nuclear stockpiles, at least temporarily. As one analyst points out, "China's nuclear controls have been affected during political upheavals in the past," including during the Tiananmen crisis. Because China's nuclear controls resemble the Soviet Union's, many observers believe it "could reveal the same weaknesses during domestic crisis that the Soviet system has exhibited since 1991."[112]

The specter of instability or state collapse in a nuclear-armed country may become more likely if more third-tier states acquire WMD. According to the U.S. National Intelligence Council, "The continued spread of nuclear capabilities in the greater Middle East, where several states will be facing succession challenges over the next 20 years, also will raise new concerns over the capacity of weak states to maintain control over their nuclear technologies and arsenals."[113] (see box 3.5 for a potential scenario involving on Pakistan) The historical record provides some grounds for optimism that this risk can be contained: as far as is known, even during the most unstable moments of the Soviet Union's collapse, not a single nuclear weapon was transferred or stolen. On the other hand, al-Qaeda and the global *salafi* jihad were in their infancy in 1991. Today, there may be far more demand from "customers" seeking to acquire weapons of mass destruction.

Box 3.5: Case Study: Pakistan

Perpetual instability, Islamic extremism, and an arsenal of several dozen nuclear weapons make Pakistan, in the words of the *Economist*, "the world's most dangerous place." There are several serious—and plausible—proliferation risks associated with Pakistan: the government could deliberately transfer nuclear technology to another state or nonstate actor; rogue elements within or close to the regime could make similar transfers for financial or ideological reasons (as has already occurred in the A.Q. Khan case, and in the reported cooperation between Pakistani nuclear scientists and al-Qaeda); or, if the Pakistani state were to collapse, terrorist groups active in the region could gain access to nuclear materials or weapons. As the 2008 report of the U.S. Commission on the Prevention of Weapons of Mass Destruction, Proliferation, and Terrorism remarked, "Were one to map terrorism and weapons of mass destruction today, all roads would intersect in Pakistan."[114]

Pakistan's nuclear program was initiated in 1972 under Prime Minister Zulfikar Ali Bhutto, and was assisted by the Chinese. Pakistan conducted its first nuclear test in 1998, and today is believed to have 60–100 nuclear weapons. Following the attacks of 9/11 and the discovery of the A.Q. Khan network, Pakistan came under U.S. pressure to upgrade its nuclear security. Partly as a result of recent efforts, fissile material and delivery devices are stored separately; a U.S.-designed system of controls, locks, and sensors protects against theft; and nuclear personnel are now screened and monitored to identify potential extremists. Thus, the possibility of terrorists seizing a nuclear weapon may still be unlikely—although few U.S. experts probably share former President Pervez Musharraf's confident assertion in 2005 that "There is no doubt in my mind that they [Pakistan's nuclear weapons] can ever fall into the hands of extremists."[115]

Indeed, despite the recent upgrades there are plenty of causes for concern. In a 2007 survey of terrorism experts by *Foreign Policy* magazine, three-fourths said Pakistan is the country most likely transfer WMD to a terrorist group.[116] Even if transfers are not deliberate, Pakistan expert Stephen P. Cohen points out that the country "has a dismal record of control over its own nuclear facilities."[117] Poor institutionalization of safeguard procedures at nuclear facilities and weak monitoring of nuclear personnel could enable the deliberate proliferation of nuclear knowledge or technology. As two U.S. nuclear experts have noted, "In the current climate, with Pakistan's leadership under duress from daily acts of violence by insurgent Taliban forces and organized political opposition, the security of any nuclear materials produced in [Pakistan's] reactors is in question."[118] In 2009, the Taliban advanced within sixty miles of some of Pakistan's nuclear facilities.

But most experts' greatest concern is that political turmoil in Pakistan could cause a split within the military or intelligence services, which share oversight and management of the country's nuclear facilities. Elements within the military sympathetic to radical Islamists could transfer nuclear weapons or materials to al-Qaeda or another terrorist group. (Terrorists would not need to acquire a functional weapon; if they gained access to Pakistan's large quantities of highly enriched uranium, it would probably be fairly easy to assemble a simple trigger device.) Even if there were no deliberate transfer, a power struggle could sufficiently undermine Pakistan's nuclear controls to facilitate theft or rogue insider diversion of nuclear assets. As journalist David Sanger notes, even if the Pakistani government was not complicit in the A.Q. Khan ring, "The leaking of much of the technology to Iran, North Korea, and Libya, starting in the late 1980s, often coincided with times of political turmoil when Pakistan's leadership was weak and its attention elsewhere."[119]

According to former CIA (and current senior White House homeland security) official John Brennan, the U.S. government believes that Pakistan's current nuclear safeguards are adequate to survive a "fair amount of political commotion." But in fact, American officials have minimal knowledge of the locations and conditions of many of Pakistan's nuclear weapons, and cooperation on nuclear security has been spotty. As Brennan has remarked, "If there is a collapse in the command-and-control structure—or if the armed forces fragment—that's a nightmare scenario."[120]

CONCLUSIONS

In principle, weak states can pose two distinct types of proliferation threats to U.S. and international security. First, the state itself may pursue such weapons. Second, the state—through incapacity or as a matter of policy—may assist efforts by nonstate actors to develop such weapons.

In fact, this chapter suggests, the connection between state weakness and WMD proliferation is more limited and contingent than often believed. Few weak and failed states have—or seek—nuclear, chemical, or biological weapons, and thus are unlikely to present direct proliferation problems. Indeed, the weakest states almost universally lack the resources to make a concerted effort to develop such programs. Although high levels of corruption, weak law enforcement, and poor border control could in theory make weak states likely transit or intermediary states for WMD traffickers, most weak states do not border countries with large WMD stockpiles, and are therefore unlikely to play such a role. With the exception of Afghanistan for a brief period, there is also little evidence that any weak state has ever served as a base of operations for nonstate actors seeking to develop WMD independently.

There are two current exceptions to this general rule, however. Of the countries that pose a serious proliferation threat to the United States—both directly, as unstable and unreliable nuclear-armed states, and indirectly given their potential to supply (intentionally or otherwise) WMD materials to nonstate actors—two are very weak states: North Korea and Pakistan. Both have been the source of nuclear-related technology and materials supplied to countries the United States considers "rogue states." Instability or collapse in either country could result in nuclear weapons falling into the hands of nonstate actors, or coming under the control of a regime inclined to either use or distribute them.

In general, however, the states that pose the greatest WMD proliferation dangers may actually fall in the middle tier of the Index, particularly among "states to watch." This category includes many of the world's known nuclear powers, including Russia, China, and India; the most problematic nuclear aspirants from the U.S. perspective, such as Iran and perhaps Syria; as well as countries such as Algeria, Egypt, Saudi Arabia, Turkey, and South Africa, which have or are seeking civilian nuclear capacity that could leave nuclear technology and material vulnerable to diversion or theft (and could be fairly easily converted to weapons programs).

Such countries are superficially strong but possess important gaps in governance that might be exploited by rogue elements. Potential vulnerabilities include the presence of poorly secured WMD materials (a function of weak security, high corruption, and parlous economic conditions that might encourage theft or illicit transfers); the potential for political instability and violence; the presence of organized criminal groups; and weak regulatory, export, and border controls. Of greatest concern may be potential future nuclear energy producers such as Algeria and Saudi Arabia, which face violent extremist movements who might infiltrate or exploit the weaknesses of these states' nuclear programs (or even, in the event of state collapse or regime change, seize control of the state and its WMD arsenals).

Thus it appears, based on the analysis provided in this chapter, that proliferation is less a weak state problem than an issue of individual "problem states"—a few (but not most) of which are weak states. However, even if weak states as a general category are not *now* at the center of proliferation concerns, within ten to twenty years they may pose a much greater threat. As described above, as the financial and environmental incentives for developing nuclear energy grow, more developing countries will seek such capability—and, like today's "states to watch," their nuclear programs will be particularly vulnerable to insider corruption, theft, diversion, and the consequences of political instability or state collapse.

4

TRANSNATIONAL CRIME

Organized crime is greatly facilitated by the weakness of the state in many parts of the world. Weak financial regulatory systems, lax enforcement measures, and high levels of corruption are key factors that make certain countries particularly attractive to international criminals as safe havens.

—*UN Secretary-General's High Level Panel, 2004*[1]

Beyond facilitating terrorism and WMD proliferation, fragile states are said to threaten international security by providing hospitable environments for transnational crime. "Failing states are inextricably linked to the increasing power of international criminal networks and 'illegal' economies," the United Kingdom's Prime Minister's Strategy Unit contends.[2] This connection makes intuitive sense: Weak regimes may lack the capacity or will to combat crime, while the corruption, insecurity, and weak rule of law found in many fragile states play to criminals' advantage. This chapter evaluates the connection between state weakness and transnational crime, paying special attention to six sectors of crime: (1) narcotics production and trafficking; (2) human trafficking; (3) small arms trade; (4) money laundering; (5) environmental crime; (6) and maritime piracy. It argues that the relationship between transnational crime and weak states is more complicated than popular mythology suggests.

Fragile states can indeed provide advantages to transnational criminals, including high levels of corruption; "under-governed" areas; weak law enforcement; poor border control; and large black or "grey" markets, particularly during and after conflict. But the connection between weak states and transnational crime is far from straightforward. First, as with terrorism, weaker is not necessarily better—most criminals prefer to operate in countries with at least a modicum of political order. Truly failed states present their own set of obstacles. Second, the connection between state weakness and transnational crime depends on the nature of the illicit activity. Weak states are much less central to global cybercrime and intellectual property theft, for instance, than to narcotics production, illegal arms trafficking, and maritime piracy. Finally, the causal relationship flows in two directions. Just as weak institutions may facilitate transnational crime, so the latter can render already fragile states weaker. Whether or not they explicitly target the state, criminals exacerbate dysfunctional governance, which may reinforce cycles of crime and fragility.

THE GLOBAL THREAT OF TRANSNATIONAL CRIME

Transnational crime is illegal activity that occurs, is conceived, or has effects across national boundaries. Under the terms of the UN Convention on Transnational Organized Crime (2000), a criminal offense is deemed transnational if it meets one of four criteria: (1) it is committed in more than one state; (2) it is planned, directed, or controlled in more than one state; (3) it involves an organized criminal group that operates in more than one state; or (4) it has "substantial effects" on another state.[3]

Crime, of course, is a legal concept—national and international law determines what acts are permitted within and across sovereign borders, respectively. The law, moreover, evolves. Many of today's major global "crimes"—from money laundering to drug trafficking to trade in endangered species—were permissible as recently as a century (or, in some cases, a few decades) ago.[4] Transnational crime today encompasses a vast array of activities, including but not limited to economic espionage, smuggling, illicit technology transfer, counterfeiting, piracy, environmental crimes, intellectual property violations, money laundering, and trafficking in humans, narcotics, small arms, and gems. Such crimes are undertaken by a diverse set of illicit groups, ranging from hierarchical syndicates to networks of cells.

It is commonly (but incorrectly) assumed that transnational crime is an upshot of the modern, globalized age. In truth, such a golden age of unchallenged sovereignty never existed. Smuggling, for example, has a venerable history, with legislation governing the practice dating to fourteenth-century England. In Russia, Peter the Great was forced to legalize tobacco to tax a thriving trade in that smuggled commodity. Nor is the global drug trade new—Chinese authorities outlawed opium in 1729 (but American and British merchants continued to export it to China through the nineteenth century).[5] Multilateral efforts to combat the narcotics industry date back a century, to the 1909 International Opium Commission in Shanghai and the 1912 Hague International Opium Convention.

What *is* new is the expanding scope and scale of illegal cross-border activity, which has surged dramatically in the two decades since the end of the Cold War. Given the clandestine nature of these activities, statistics on the magnitude of transnational crime are notoriously unreliable (see box 4.1). But law enforcement officials agree that illicit commodities and services are being exchanged in unprecedented variety, volume, and velocity. The total revenue generated by global organized crime—the world's "gross criminal product"[6]—has been estimated at perhaps $1.5 trillion. The worldwide narcotics trade alone is estimated to be a $300–500 billion business—a figure greater than the GDP of all but thirty-eight nations.[7]

Box 4.1: A Note on Data Limitations

Estimates of the magnitude of illicit transnational flows should be treated with caution. Unlike corporations, criminal actors do not publish quarterly statistics of their operations, and many states lack the capacity—and often the desire—to provide an honest accounting of criminal activities within their borders. The process by which official agencies generate precise figures— for example, for drug production, money laundering, or human trafficking—is generally opaque and often classified; ostensibly authoritative numerical estimates of criminal activity may be based on considerable guesswork and are vulnerable to distortion or manipulation for political, institutional, budgetary, or public relations purposes. Many estimates are suspiciously round. Moreover, pressure on international (and domestic U.S.) agencies to quantify global illicit flows can lead to "a prioritization of bad data over no data." Similar caveats should apply to UN and U.S. assessments of illicit activity in particular countries. The thresholds for including some countries but not others as "major" source, transit, and destination countries are often vague or arbitrary, and the criteria for ranking countries relative to one another tend to be underspecified. Despite these data limitations, such "facts" are quickly entrenched in conventional wisdom.[8]

Table 4.1 includes rough estimates of the value of various illicit transactions, based on published (if inherently problematic) sources.

Criminal enterprises have been among the biggest beneficiaries of globalization, exploiting the disjunction between global economic integration, on the one hand, and the persistence of sovereign state jurisdictions, on the other. Over the past two decades, the world economy has been transformed by technological advances, the removal of trade barriers, the liberalization of finance, and the privatization of many state-owned enterprises. The economic benefits have been dramatic. At the same time, these changes have created unprecedented opportunities for criminals to profit from illicit

Table 4.1: Published Estimates of Global Scale of Some Major Organized Criminal Activities[9]

Activity	*Annual Revenues*
Illegal drugs	$300–500 billion
Counterfeit goods	$200 billion
Money laundering	$1.1–$2.7 trillion
Human trafficking	At least $10 billion
Illegal small arms and conventional weapons	$3–10 billion
Cigarette smuggling	$5–10 billion
Unrecorded oil sales	$8 billion
Illegal timber trade	$15 billion in lost revenues globally
Traffic in endangered species	$10 billion
Art and antiquities theft	$6 billion

activities. A prime example is the container revolution: global commerce now relies on millions of shipping containers, but only a tiny fraction are ever checked for contraband. Likewise, the liberalization of capital movements and foreign exchange transactions has facilitated money laundering.

Meanwhile, the triumph of neoclassical economics in the developing world, embodied in the "Washington consensus," encouraged governments to downsize their public sectors, reduce regulation, and implement fiscal austerity. While eliminating some impediments to growth, these steps sometimes deprived the state of critical resources to combat crime. Perhaps most dramatically, the transition from a socialist command system to a free market economy in the countries of the former Soviet Union and its satellites—often referred to as a period of "grabitization"—facilitated the rise of shadow economies as criminal organizations exploited collapsing state structures, weakening property laws, privatizing state assets, and relaxing regulatory scrutiny.

The persistence of national borders and independent jurisdictions hamstrings state authorities in combating transnational criminals. These "sovereignty free actors" can hopscotch across national frontiers, exploiting asymmetries in the criminalization and policing of particular activities. States, alas, have no such flexibility, and must respect one another's sovereignty in conducting law enforcement operations.

Who Are the Transnational Criminals?

Thousands of independent groups engage in transnational crime. There is in no sense a unified transnational criminal "movement," analogous to the global *salafi* jihad. However, like terrorists, transnational criminals are shifting from traditional, hierarchical organizations to more adaptable, decentralized networks involving strategic partnerships among smaller groups dispersed across many countries. This horizontal model makes it harder for law enforcement to decapitate their senior leadership. Transnational criminal groups from Russia, China, Central America, and elsewhere exploit diaspora communities to market products and launder profits. The proliferation of organized Nigerian criminal groups—present in some sixty countries and involved in activities ranging from financial scams to illicit trafficking—shows how fluid networks can operate over multiple jurisdictions.[10]

Like multinational companies, transnational criminals adopt sophisticated strategies to maximize profit and hedge risk. For example, they diversify product lines to insulate themselves from market fluctuations. They shift production sites and distribution channels in response to changing input costs and law enforcement efforts. And they engage in legal arbitrage across sovereign jurisdictions.[11] The epicenters of global crime are thus more fluid than ever, and long-term specialization in a single field or commodity is rare. Once a criminal "pipeline" has been established, criminals can use the same conduit for new illicit commodities, as well as expanding into two-way trade (for instance, running cocaine from Latin America through West Africa to Europe, then arms back to West Africa).

Transnational Crime as a Threat to U.S. and International Security

Transnational crime threatens U.S. national security in at least three ways: (1) by directly endangering the well-being of U.S. citizens; (2) by destabilizing areas of strategic importance; and (3) by facilitating the spread of other threats to U.S. security. The cross-border trade in narcotics has the most devastating direct impact, causing an estimated 17,000 drug-related deaths in the United States each year and costing some $180.9 billion annually, including health care costs and productivity losses. (These costs do not account for the role that the global trade in heroin plays in funding anti-U.S. forces in Afghanistan.) Counterfeiting and other intellectual property crimes cost U.S. businesses some $200–250 billion annually. So-called "419" (advance fee fraud) scams are believed to cost citizens in developed countries at least $3 billion each year.[12]

Second, transnational crime undermines long-term U.S. national security by thwarting good governance and encouraging violence in affected countries. Criminal enterprises undermine government legitimacy by challenging the state's monopoly on the use of force, moving illegal goods across its borders, and corrupting officials and public institutions. They erode the rule of law by flouting legal prohibitions and corroding regulatory institutions. Transnational crime can also distort economic development by channeling commercial activity in illicit directions and discouraging licit foreign investment. More dramatically, from Colombia to Afghanistan, the activities of transnational criminals have helped sustain devastating insurgencies and thwart state-building efforts, endangering both the security of civilians and the very integrity of the state.

Third, transnational crime can abet and amplify other global threats. Cooperation between criminal and terrorist groups, for instance, appears on the rise (see box 4.2). Many U.S.-designated Foreign Terrorist Organizations—including al-Qaeda—fund their activities in part through the trafficking of drugs and other illicit commodities. Likewise, illicit transactions feature prominently in plausible scenarios for WMD proliferation, as evinced by the nuclear bazaar run by A.Q. Khan (discussed in the previous chapter). Illegal cross-border activities also contribute to global epidemics, with one-quarter of the HIV/AIDS cases in Central Asia, China, and Russia stemming from intravenous drug use.[13] Finally, transnational crime contributes to the degradation of the world's environment, from illegal logging and fishing to toxic waste dumping and trade in endangered species.

The United States has been at the forefront of efforts to define transnational crime as a security threat. In its International Crime Control Strategy (1998) the Clinton administration described surging levels of global crime as "a formidable and increasing threat to national and international security." Official concern with transnational crime rose to even higher levels after 9/11, which revealed how illicit non-state actors could grievously damage U.S. national interests. In 2007, the Bush administration released an International Organized Crime Threat Assessment,

---

Box 4.2: A Criminal-Terrorist Connection?

For years, Western officials have worried that transnational criminals and terrorists would join forces, allowing (for example) terrorists to use smuggling routes to inject personnel or weapons into the United States. Both terrorists and criminals are drawn to unstable and under-governed regions, where borders are open and official authority is weak. As the two sets of actors adopt more decentralized structures, they may begin to cooperate more frequently.

Terrorists have turned to crime to secure resources and carry out their operations. Members of the al-Qaeda affiliate AQIM, for example, worked with narcotics traffickers to move drugs from Latin America to Europe through West and North Africa.[14] Criminals may likewise use terrorist methods to secure their ends. Mexican drug gangs, for example, are essentially waging a domestic terror campaign in response to the government's counternarcotics offensive. The distinctions between terrorists, insurgents and criminal groups have blurred in conflict zones like Colombia, the Balkans, Afghanistan, Pakistan, and Sri Lanka.

At the same time, there may be inherent limits to these arrangements. The two groups have fundamentally different orientations: terrorists are motivated by political (and sometimes religious) concerns, criminals by greed. And whereas terrorists generally seek to overthrow the established order, criminals who profit from the existing system have an interest in its perpetuation (and often have deep ties to the governments terrorists are targeting). Thus despite much hype, a full-blown criminal-terrorist "nexus" has yet to materialize.[15]

---

accompanied the following year by a Law Enforcement Strategy to Combat International Organized Crime.[16]

Rising U.S. concern has been mirrored internationally. In 2004, Secretary-General Kofi Annan's High-Level Panel on Threats, Challenges, and Change identified transnational crime not only as a direct "menace to states and societies" but as a contributing factor to terrorism, WMD proliferation, poverty, disease, and state failure. The European Security Strategy takes a similar stance, identifying organized crime as one of the five "key threats" facing EU members.[17]

TRANSNATIONAL CRIME AND WEAK STATES: THE CONVENTIONAL WISDOM

The premise that transnational criminal groups rely on fragile states is widely shared among national governments, international organizations, and independent analysts. The 2006 U.S. National Security Strategy argues, "Weak and impoverished states and ungoverned areas are...susceptible to exploitation by terrorists, tyrants, and international criminals." The British government likewise believes that "drugs, arms smuggling, people trafficking, organized crime and counterfeiting" all "emanate from areas of weak governance, including failed states." The United Nations portrays state weakness as the soft underbelly of global anti-crime efforts.[18]

Academics and journalists hit similar notes, identifying poorly governed states as ideal "criminal enclaves"[19] and major sources of illicit commodities, trafficking routes, financial services, and underground markets. Criminals are naturally drawn to "black spots" in the global economy, where "weak state structures and high levels of corruption provid[e] a lawless and relatively sovereignty free environment." Such "pockets of lawlessness" arise not only in failed states but also in repressive nations like Burma or North Korea—where governance has been subverted by an abusive regime—and in the chaotic regions of many developing countries.[20]

In reciprocal fashion, crime can further reduce state capacity. Criminals use their fortunes to degrade already weak institutions, bribing law enforcement officials, neutralizing courts, purchasing or intimidating politicians and journalists, and engaging business leaders in criminal activities. The cumulative effect is to tear at the social fabric, undermine the legitimacy of the state, drive out licit economic activity, endanger public security, and (often) fuel insurgency and disorder. Over the longer term, the U.S. government believes, such "unconstrained criminal activity may so corrupt and compromise the integrity of the law enforcement and other institutions that a country becomes a 'failed state' incapable of meeting many of the accepted standards and responsibilities of sovereign control over its territories."[21]

States and Crime

The relationship between criminal groups and states is variable and dynamic, a function of both the commitment and the capacity of the state to combat illegal activity. Some developing countries are well placed to meet this threat. But others have the will without the way. In West Africa, for example, drug trafficking "comes to some states who are so fragile that, despite their good faith and their willingness to do something, they just cannot," says UN Special Representative Ahmed Ould Abdullah.[22] Other regimes have the means but not the desire. The government of Turkmenistan, for instance, has refused to work with the United Nations Office on Drugs and Crime (UNODC), despite the fact that the country is a major trafficking route for Afghan heroin.[23] A similar pattern holds in Burma, where the government has taken virtually no action against the country's drug rings. On the other hand, a sufficiently determined regime in a poor, weak state may make major inroads on transnational criminal activity. For instance, Liberian President Ellen Johnson Sirleaf has taken significant steps to combat illegal logging and promote sustainable forest management.

Of course, the relative role of capacity versus will in facilitating transnational crime varies with the degree of state "capture." As crime becomes entrenched, a compromised political elite is less likely to deploy the capacities at its disposal to fight it. Depending on the resilience of the state—particularly its levels of corruption—the relationship between authorities and criminal groups can range from antagonistic (with the two effectively at war) to synergistic (with criminal elements empowering the ruling regime). Given this fluid spectrum of potential relationships, "the dominant imagery of nation-states fighting valiantly against global criminal networks is far too simplistic and even misleading."[24] Box 4.3 presents one possible way of thinking about state-criminal "ecologies."

Box 4.3: Criminal-State "Ecologies"

Borrowing from the field of biology, one might identify several distinct criminal-state "ecologies,"[25] spanning a spectrum of adversarial to collusive relationships. These permutations are admittedly ideal types that tend to overlap in practice.

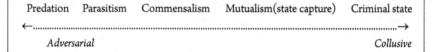

Predation   Parasitism   Commensalism   Mutualism(state capture)   Criminal state

←⋯⋯⋯⋯⋯⋯⋯⋯⋯⋯⋯⋯⋯⋯⋯⋯⋯⋯⋯⋯⋯⋯⋯⋯⋯⋯⋯⋯⋯⋯⋯⋯→

Adversarial   *Collusive*

Predation is a highly adversarial scenario in which criminals stand in violent, even existential opposition to the state (although individual state officials may be complicit in crime). One example is the war waged between the Mexican government and drug cartels in northern Mexico in 2009–2010. Many cases of "predation" involve insurgent groups enmeshed in crime. Prominent examples of this phenomenon include the Shining Path in Peru and the FARC in Colombia, which both became systematically involved in all levels of the coca trade. Most transnational criminals, however, do not seek the collapse of their host, which would greatly increase the costs of doing business. Far better to keep the state on life support, neutralizing its defenses while exploiting its weaknesses.

Symbiosis describes a relationship between two organisms in which at least one benefits. As in the natural world, a symbiotic relationship between organized criminal groups and states comes in three generic variants. The most one-sided arrangement is *parasitism*, whereby the invasive criminal organism penetrates and weakens the host state, although (unlike predation) it does not challenge the state's formal authority. One example is Kyrgyzstan, where a majority of members elected to parliament in 2005 had criminal backgrounds that helped them buy political influence.[26] A more neutral relationship is one of *commensalism*, in which the criminal group benefits from its host but has little appreciable impact on the latter's overall health. This status quo approach is characteristic of many traditional criminal groups, such as the Sicilian mafia or the Japanese *yakuza*. The third scenario is one of *mutualism*, a mutually beneficial arrangement whereby high-ranking officials offer protection to illicit actors in return for a share of the profits. Historical examples include Panama under General Manuel Noriega, Colombia during the presidency of Ernesto Samper, and the regime of Sani Abacha in Nigeria. The regimes of Cambodian dictator Hun Sen and the junta ruling Burma provide contemporary cases.

Criminal State. At the most collusive end, the state becomes a fully criminal enterprise, subverting the institutions of governance to enrich itself and abusing "the very institutions of the international system—such as sovereignty, diplomatic immunity, and judicial comity" to provide a cover for transnational crime.[27] Slobodan Milosevic's Serbia and Charles Taylor's Liberia are examples of such outlaw regimes. In Liberia, Taylor sold the emblems of sovereignty to the highest bidder, providing criminal groups with passports, visas, end-user certificates, and access to aircraft and shipping registries. The current archetype is North Korea, which Kim Jong-Il has transformed into a front for crimes like methamphetamine production and trafficking, and the counterfeiting of cigarettes, pharmaceuticals, and bogus U.S. currency.[28]

Why Criminals Might Find Weak and Failing States Congenial

Fragile states present an array of security, political, legal, economic, and social vulnerabilities that transnational criminals can, in principle, exploit. These include high levels of corruption among government officials; inept and compromised law enforcement and judicial systems; ill-equipped border control; extensive under-governed spaces (including both remote lawless regions and urban "no-go" areas); large black and gray markets; limited employment opportunities in the licit economy; and inadequate state provision of social services, which provides an opening for criminal groups to build local legitimacy through parallel systems of social welfare.

High Corruption and Weak Rule of Law

Once viewed as a domestic problem, corruption—the abuse of public office for private gain—is now understood to have global consequences by enabling all forms of transnational crime. Corruption undermines the will of law enforcement agencies to investigate, prosecute, and judge alleged violators in a transparent manner—helping to account for the common discrepancy between what is legally proscribed and what is actually enforced. When states are weak and yet behave as if they were strong by "spewing out laws and regulations" that they lack the will or capacity to enforce, they create openings for illicit actors.[29] From Central America to Central Asia, widespread corruption has created havens for organized criminals and has compromised states' ability to combat criminal activities. Recognizing these "spillover" effects, the international community in 2003 negotiated a United Nations Convention against Corruption.

Weak states often are prime targets for criminals that seek corrupt countries (see box 4.4). Of the bottom 20 percent of countries in Transparency International's 2008 Corruption Perceptions Index (CPI), nearly four-fifths (twenty-eight of thirty-six countries) are weak states—and the eleven worst-ranking countries in the CPI are all critically weak states.[30] To be sure, corruption also affects a number of authoritarian and resource-rich states that rank above the two bottom quintiles of the Index of State Weakness, and corrupt individuals in relatively well-governed states may also facilitate major transnational crime. Still, the association between corruption and state weakness is strong.

Safe Haven

Like terrorist organizations, criminal networks require some minimum level of operational security to plan, prepare, and conduct their illicit activities. Transnational networks are thus drawn to "sovereignty free" areas where state presence is minimal. Especially attractive are border regions remote from the state's coercive powers, but close enough to trade corridors to connect to the global economy.

Such zones are often found in weak states, but even in relatively strong countries, the government's authority may not extend to remote areas. The CIA has identified some fifty regions "over which central governments exert little or no control."

One is the remote region around Ciudad del Este, where the borders of Paraguay, Brazil, and Argentina converge. This seedy crossroads has become a hub for narcotics trafficking, money laundering, smuggling, and the piracy of video and compact discs. Although none of the tri-border countries is a weak state, Ciudad del Este is attractive to criminals because "regulations are weak, governments are passive, and law enforcement is irrelevant or on the take." There are more than one hundred airstrips in the region beyond state control.[31]

Particularly hospitable to transnational crime are breakaway regions and "statelets" that do not accept the sovereign authority of any national government. Separatist enclaves known to be havens for organized crime include Abkhazia and South Ossetia in Georgia, Nagorno-Karabakh in Azerbaijan, and Transdniester in Moldova. As Ronald Asmus and Bruce Jackson write, "These unresolved fragments of the Soviet Empire now serve as shipment points for weapons, narcotics, and victims of trafficking and as breeding grounds for transnational organized crime."[32]

Poor Border Control

Worldwide, more than 226,000 kilometers of land border divide sovereign states.[33] Transnational criminals would logically choose shipment routes where law enforcement and customs control are lax.

There is no authoritative, publicly available database to assess the relative strength of border control systems and customs procedures among the world's 192 countries. We do know that many developing countries suffer from severe shortcomings in their ability to regulate their national frontiers. In assessing the capacities of one hundred developing nations, the Secretariat of the World Customs Organization (WCO) identified a slew of crippling performance gaps, including rampant corruption, inadequate legal frameworks, minimal risk analysis and strategic planning, inattention to illicit flows of contraband, low levels of human and financial resources, and inadequate coordination with neighboring countries and the private sector.[34]

Beyond terrestrial borders, spotty state control over coastlines and waters provides an opening for the transit of illegal commodities. The world's weakest littoral states rarely have surveillance capabilities for ship and air traffic, much less adequate coast guard vessels and aircraft to interdict criminals operating in their national waters or airspace. In West Africa, UNODC Executive Director Antonio Maria Costa observed in 2008: "Drug planes don't have to fly below the radar, because in most cases there is no radar.... There are no local navies to intercept the ships coming from Latin America or to chase the 2,000-horse-power boats that speed drugs up the coast to Europe."[35]

As with terrorism, social variables can influence the hospitality of "ungoverned" areas to criminal networks. In many parts of the developing world, remote borderlands are grey zones whose economies and societies have been organized for centuries around informal (and often illegal) cross-border activities. For many local populations, the physical border may be essentially meaningless, as it is in much of the Sahel region of north-central Africa, among the Pashtun tribes of Pakistan and Afghanistan, or in the Ferghana Valley of Central Asia. At the same time, criminals are sensitive to the imperatives of time and cost. They may well reject a roundabout or remote route through a weak state in favor of a riskier, but more direct avenue that presents fewer logistical hassles while promising timely delivery and high volumes.

Lack of Licit Economic Alternatives and Gaps in Public Services

Some argue that weak states attract transnational criminals because their lack of legal opportunities encourages locals to participate in illegal activity. "Poverty is the biggest problem," says Costa, in explaining the spread of cocaine trafficking in West Africa.[36] In Afghanistan, where UNODC estimates that more than 14 percent of the population is involved in opium production, the top reasons that farmers cite for cultivating poppies are poverty alleviation, the high sale price of opium, the possibility of getting a loan, and the high cost of weddings. As Ahmed Rashid contends, opium provides "a support system for farmers that the state could not match."[37] At the same time, as discussed later in this chapter, the biggest opium-producing regions in Afghanistan are not the poorest, but the most insecure.

The link between economic distress and rising crime is not restricted to the weakest states. Throughout the 1990s, organized crime was rampant in much of the former Soviet Union, particularly in Russia, Ukraine, Moldova, and the Central Asian republics. Most were not critically weak states, but all experienced a sharp economic downturn in the wake of the Soviet Union's collapse that likely contributed to the rise in crime.

The state's poor performance in delivering public services may also create openings for criminals (including transnational ones) to gain local support by providing social welfare to communities in which they operate. Criminals have played such a "para-state" function in many settings, from the favelas of Brazil to Japan, where members of the *yakuza* delivered assistance in the aftermath of the Kobe earthquake. Perhaps the most celebrated instance in recent memory was Pablo Escobar, who as head of the Medellin drug cartel cultivated a Robin Hood image by sponsoring health care, education, soccer clubs, and other initiatives in local communities. At the same time, there are inherent limits to criminal involvement in such social welfare provision, given both the dangers of exposure to state law enforcement and disincentives to cut into illicit profits.

War Economies and Their Legacies

Like zones of contested sovereignty, war-torn countries present lucrative opportunities for crime, both domestic and transnational. Protracted, large-scale violence undermines the state's capacity to regulate private activity, disrupts traditional patterns of production and exchange, and rewards those who can provide goods and services that are in short supply. It also expands the ranks of criminals to include entrepreneurs who emerge to meet black market demand, and otherwise law-abiding citizens who must survive amidst uncertainty, deprivation, and turmoil. Upheaval may cause displacement, and transnational gangs can exploit refugee and diaspora populations. For instance, refugees from the Balkan wars of the 1990s are believed to have facilitated drug trafficking in Western Europe.[38]

In today's civil wars, the line between warrior and criminal is often blurred, with fighters becoming felons. As Peter Andreas writes, "Military success on the battlefield can significantly depend on entrepreneurial success in the illicit economy."[39] Rebel groups often form tacit alliances with (and tax) criminal actors to secure the financial resources they need to consolidate military and political control. Armed groups have supported themselves through illicit trafficking in a range of commodities, including opium (e.g., Afghanistan, Burma), smuggled cigarettes (e.g., Hezbollah), gemstones (e.g., Angola, Sierra Leone), timber (e.g., Liberia), and oil (e.g., Iraq, Nigeria). In some cases profit itself is—or becomes—the ultimate goal of fighting. Rebel movements, from Liberia to Burma, have at times been little more than criminal organizations. (On the other hand, full-scale war may actually hinder certain types of crime; Côte d'Ivoire was the major West African transit hub for heroin until the outbreak of civil war in 2002 disrupted trafficking routes.)[40]

The end of armed struggle may do little to overcome the criminalized economy. Countries emerging from violence typically lack public security, given wartime degradation of the state's coercive powers, judicial apparatus, and administrative machinery. Criminal groups thrive in these lawless vacuums, their ranks swelled by former combatants whose skills (including a capacity for violence) may be most rewarded in the illicit sector. As Serb forces withdrew from Kosovo in June 1999, organized criminal groups—many linked to elements of the Kosovo Liberation Army—established a vast network of trafficking in narcotics and stolen goods. Nor do postconflict governments generally make tackling crime an immediate priority, which allows it to become entrenched.[41]

Box 4.4: Haiti: State Fragility and Transnational Crime

Haiti, long a shipment point for cocaine en route to the United States, offers one of the clearest connections between state weakness and transnational crime. The drug trade through Haiti reflects multiple dimensions of the state's fragility, which were readily apparent well before the devastating earthquake of January 2010. These weaknesses include endemic corruption, weak law enforcement, an anemic judiciary, minimal border control, lack of licit economic alternatives, and the legacy of two centuries of political violence. As Haitian National Police commissioner Mario Andresol acknowledged in 2007, "The drug traffickers chose Haiti because they like to operate in countries where there are weaknesses."[42]

The failure of the state to provide basic services in much of the country provides ordinary Haitians with incentives to seek both protection and livelihoods from armed gangs often enmeshed in the drug trade. After remittances, trafficking in drugs and other contraband provides the second-largest flow of resources into Haiti, where 78 percent of the population lives on less than $2 per day.[43] Unsurprisingly, Haitian officials are frequently involved in the drug trade, helping make Haiti the fourth most corrupt state in the world.[44] Corruption has further weakened the country's notoriously dysfunctional judicial, law enforcement, customs, and corrections systems, enabling organized criminal groups to operate with relative impunity.

Corruption aside, Haitian law enforcement is extremely weak, and much of the country is effectively un-policed. As of 2008, the country had fewer than 10,000 (often poorly trained) police officers, and only fifty devoted to narcotics trafficking. The Haitian coast guard consisted of just ninety-five personnel, two patrol boats, and no airplanes or helicopters. The country had minimal customs capacity at its seventeen official ports, and the 225-mile-long border with the Dominican Republic was entirely porous.[45]

The continued, nearly unobstructed transit of large quantities of narcotics through Haiti undermines the effectiveness of the already fragile state and the democratically elected government; reinforces gang violence and pervasive corruption; and discourages licit commerce and foreign investment. In the words of former Prime Minister Jacques-Edouard Alexis, "This is a very important issue, connected to the survival of democracy and sustainable development in the country."[46]

WEAK STATES AND PARTICULAR TRANSNATIONAL CRIMINAL ACTIVITIES

The governance gaps of weak states offer multiple benefits to transnational criminals, but some types of transnational crime have little connection with weak states. A prime example is the trade in counterfeit goods—that is, articles that violate existing trademarks, patents, and copyrights—from Gucci handbags to pharmaceuticals. Most of these goods are neither produced in nor shipped through the world's weakest states. Instead, the majority are produced in Asia (particularly China, Taiwan, and Vietnam). Other major counterfeiting hotspots include emerging and developed countries like Russia, Ukraine, Chile, Turkey, Thailand, Malaysia, Indonesia, the Philippines, Brazil, Argentina, Paraguay, and South Korea.[47]

Other types of transnational criminal activities, however, *are* conventionally associated with fragile and failing states. The following sections examine six such categories: (1) the production and trafficking of illegal drugs; (2) human trafficking; (3) money laundering; (4) arms trafficking; (5) environmental crime; and (6) maritime piracy. Each is evaluated in terms of the threat it poses to U.S. and international security, the degree to which it is linked to state weakness, and the specific governance gaps most likely to facilitate each type of crime.

Production and Transit of Illegal Drugs

UNODC estimates the global narcotics market at $322 billion—an amount greater than the GDP of all but thirty-seven countries, and three-quarters of the entire GDP of Sub-Saharan Africa.[48] In addition to health care and crime-related expenditures, the "war on drugs" costs the United States more than $40 billion per year in spending at the federal and state levels.[49] Although the United States is a large producer of illegal drugs, at least 80 percent of the illicit drugs Americans consume, including all heroin and cocaine, originate internationally. Narcotics production and trade can also be highly destabilizing in source countries (including in neighboring Mexico), creating illicit revenue streams that may fund repression, insurgency, and terrorist activity.

What Do Global Patterns Tell Us about the Weak State Connection?

Production. The correlation between state weakness and drug production varies with the drug in question. As table 4.2 suggests, opium is produced almost exclusively in some of the world's weakest states, with Afghanistan accounting for more than 90 percent of global production, and Burma and Laos most of the rest. Coca production is also dominated by a weak state, Colombia, with significant production in under-governed areas of Peru and Bolivia. In both cases, global prohibition regimes have pushed drug cultivation and refinement into poorly governed locations, often plagued by instability and violence. Historically, such areas have also included the "Golden Triangle" of Southeast Asia and the Bekaa Valley of Lebanon.

In contrast to opium and coca, neither cannabis nor amphetamine production is significantly correlated with state weakness. According to the UNODC, cannabis is grown in at least 172 countries. Indeed, U.S. domestic production of marijuana "may rival that of foreign sources."[50] Likewise, amphetamine production is concentrated in developed countries, as is the manufacture of the precursor chemicals used to make heroin. No country classified by the U.S. State Department as a major source of precursor chemicals is a weak state.[51]

Global patterns of narcotics production are a function of many factors, including geography and climate. But the high production of coca and opium in weak states suggests that governance gaps may also play a role. Contrary to conventional wisdom, it may be the state's failure to provide stability—more than economic deprivation—that explains this association. While the financial rewards of cultivating illegal drugs may outstrip licit economic opportunities in the world's poorest countries, instability seems to trump penury in determining coca and opium production. In Afghanistan, UNODC reported in 2008, poppy cultivation "increased most in areas notable for their exposure to the [Taliban] insurgency, not the depth of their poverty." Opium production actually declined dramatically in northern Afghanistan, where average incomes were lower, while rising rapidly in the lawless south and east, where incomes were higher but the Taliban insurgency was stronger (see box 4.5).[52] In fact, all five of the world's major opium- and coca-producing states (Afghanistan, Burma, Colombia, Peru, and Bolivia) are either ravaged by conflict, unable to control their entire territory, or experiencing political instability.

Transit. As with other types of contraband, transit routes for illegal drugs shift in response to global demand and interdiction efforts. Drug traffickers may exploit state weakness, but illegal trafficking is hardly limited to weak states. At least 110 countries are known transit states, including some relatively strong developing nations and

Table 4.2: Illicit Narcotics Production and Weak States[53]

	Index Ranking	*Percent of Global Production*
Opium Producers		
Afghanistan	2	92%
Burma	17	5%
Laos	45	<1%
Colombia	47	<1%
Mexico	120	<1%
Peru	92	<1%
Coca Producers		
Colombia	45	55–60%
Peru	92	30%
Bolivia	64	10–15%
Cannabis Exporters[54]		
Mexico	120	18%
USA	—	11%
Paraguay	75	14%
Colombia	47	n/a
South Africa	110	6–10%
Afghanistan	2	n/a
Morocco	96	n/a
Albania	111	n/a
Netherlands	—	n/a
Nigeria	18	n/a

LEGEND: Index Rank

	Bottom Quintile
	Second Quintile
	Third - Fifth Quintile, or Not in Index

OECD members. Of twenty countries designated as major-drug producing or transit states, only seven (35 percent) are in the bottom two tiers of the Index of State Weakness.[55] Moreover, a 2009 UNODC report on the Afghan opium trade found, "counter-intuitively, [that] interdiction rates decline as the drugs move closer to lucrative, and more opulent markets." Whereas Iran and Pakistan intercept an estimated 20 percent and 17 percent of the opiates crossing their territories, Central Asian states and Russia interdict only 5 percent and 4 percent, respectively. As UNODC observes, "It should be the other way around, as richer countries can afford better law enforcement."[56]

Box 4.5: Afghanistan: Drugs, Insurgency, and Threats to International Security

Not since the mid-nineteenth century, when China dominated the global trade in opium, has a single country been responsible for nearly the entire production of a single illicit drug. But today, more than 90 percent of the world's heroin emanates from Afghanistan, a desperately poor country that ranks among the worst in the world in virtually every category of human development. The consequences for the Afghan people—and the world—are dire. Since 2001, the international community's military and financial efforts to rebuild the Afghan state have been undermined by the opium trade, which has distorted the national economy, corrupted politics, and fueled instability.

By 2009, the opium industry represented one-third of the Afghan economy. Huge profits from the opium trade had corroded Afghanistan's already fragile political system. Senior officials in all branches of government—cabinet ministers, members of parliament, judges, governors, police chiefs, and high-level officials in the Ministry of Interior—were rumored to be involved, including some ostensible allies of the United States and President Karzai. The culture of impunity for major traffickers undermined the legitimacy of the government, raising the danger that Afghanistan would become a "narco-state," effectively controlled by the drug trade.

The narcotics trade also fueled a vicious insurgency, providing the Taliban with what Defense Secretary Robert Gates conservatively estimated is $60–$80 million annually.[57] Besides taxing the production and trade of opium, the Taliban has sold protection to traffickers. Instability and opium cultivation have reinforced one another: It is no accident that the region producing the most opium—Helmand province—is also one of the most violent. In fact, there are signs that many "Taliban" factions are increasingly motivated less by ideology than by drug profits. According to the UNODC, as in Colombia and Burma, "The drug trade in Afghanistan has gone from being a funding source for insurgency to becoming an end in itself."[58]

Overall, the evidence suggests that drug traffickers value geographic convenience, exploitable infrastructure, and easy access to global markets at least as highly as they do the benefits of state weakness. A number of European states (including Spain, Portugal, Greece, the Netherlands, Belgium, and Austria) serve as shipment points for cocaine and/or heroin, in part because they are hubs for international commerce. Turkey and Iran—neither a weak state—are transit hubs for heroin en route to Europe. Despite Iran's generally robust border control and strong interdiction record, some 60 percent of Afghanistan's opium transits Iran—more than transits the weak state of Tajikistan. Similarly, many relatively capable, well-governed countries in the Caribbean, such as the Bahamas, Costa Rica, and the Dominican Republic, are ideal for cocaine trafficking, less as weak states than because they are situated between southern suppliers and northern markets, possess long coastlines, and have heavy shipping traffic that provides "ample cover."[59]

Drug traffickers require at least minimal infrastructure, so rather than being among the weakest states, the ideal drug hub has one foot in the developing world and another in the modern economy. Panama's attractiveness as a major transit state reflects its "well-developed transportation infrastructure, such as containerized seaports, the Pan-American Highway, a rapidly growing international hub airport (Tocumen), numerous uncontrolled airfields, and relatively unguarded coastlines." Likewise, too much instability makes a transit route unattractive. Balkan heroin trafficking routes were severely disrupted during the wars of the 1990s, causing the trade to shift to the "Silk Road" routes through Central Asia. There is also evidence that Syria has emerged as an important transit state for heroin due to instability along historical trafficking routes in Iraq and Lebanon.[60]

Of course, drug traffickers clearly do frequently operate in very weak states. Perhaps one-third of Afghan opium transits Pakistan. In 2007, an estimated one-third of the world's amphetamines were smuggled through weak states in Africa and the Middle East, including Burundi, the Democratic Republic of Congo (DRC), Ethiopia, Ghana, Nigeria, Somalia, Sudan, and Iraq. In recent years, cocaine trafficking has also increased dramatically in some of West Africa's weakest states, including Nigeria, Niger, Burkina Faso, and Mauritania, and the case of Guinea-Bissau is a dramatic example of how state weakness can facilitate such trade (see box 4.6).[61] As with drug production, traffickers may target weak states because of their poverty, ungoverned areas, high levels of corruption, and weak law enforcement. Police corruption and complicity in the drug trade is endemic in Central Asia, for instance. Likewise, three of the most corrupt countries in South America are Venezuela, Ecuador, and Paraguay—all major drug trafficking centers.

Whether or not traffickers target weak states disproportionately, drug trafficking can further weaken fragile states by undermining the rule of law and judicial and security institutions. It can destabilize entire regions, fueling violence and drug use in transit states. In the Caribbean, expansion of the narcotics trade has coincided with skyrocketing crime, now among the worst in the world. Along opium transit routes in the Caucasus, drug-related crime "spawns extraordinary levels of violence" as well as "political and economic insecurities." In West Africa, UN officials have cited drug trafficking as the greatest threat to regional stability.[62] The drug trade has been so destabilizing to Mexico (discussed at the end of this chapter) that in 2008, the U.S. Joint Forces Command cited Mexico as one of two states that "bear consideration for a rapid and sudden collapse."[63]

Box 4.6: Transit of Drugs: Guinea-Bissau

The connection between state weakness and narcotics trafficking is starkly evident in Guinea-Bissau, a tiny, impoverished country of just 1.6 million people. Directly across the Atlantic from northern South America, in recent years Guinea-Bissau has become a leading transshipment point for Colombian drug traffickers. In 2008, Western officials estimated that every month approximately $300 million worth of cocaine flowed into Guinea-Bissau, equivalent to the country's entire annual gross domestic product.[64]

(*continued*)

Box 4.6: Continued

Guinea-Bissau has several economic, political and geographical attributes that make it an ideal transit point for narcotics trafficking. As the *Economist* notes, "Take a long jagged coastline, a collapsed state, a collection of powerful politicians and soldiers keen to make a buck or more and you have a drug peddler's paradise."[65] The fifth-poorest country in the world, Guinea-Bissau has an extraordinarily low baseline capacity to police a sophisticated drug trade. A civil war from 1998–1999 destroyed much of the country's infrastructure and institutions. National law enforcement and interdiction capabilities remain rudimentary. There is no navy or air force to prevent drug traffickers from exploiting the country's 350 miles of coastline, which includes an archipelago of hundreds of islands and multiple watercourses, or the country's scores of abandoned air fields. The judiciary police charged with addressing the drug trade numbers only seventy, and lacks even the most basic equipment (as well as a reliable prison). One military official stationed in Guinea-Bissau says, "This is an open space where you can do anything. There is no plane. No radar. Nothing."[66]

Guinea-Bissau's coup-prone government barely functions, and it is extremely vulnerable to corruption. Salaries for civil servants and the police are often in arrears for months. Unsurprisingly, many public officials and members of the security services are on the take from traffickers, who operate openly. When in 2006 authorities (in a rare occasion) seized a $30 million shipment of cocaine, it simply disappeared from government offices.

Worried that the country might become Africa's first narco-state, the UN Security Council voted to place Guinea-Bissau on the agenda of the UN Peacebuilding Commission—only the third country to be so designated. At the same time, Guinea-Bissau's extreme weakness may actually have undermined its long-term attraction as a drug transit point, suggesting there are limits to what even traffickers will put up with in terms of lawlessness. In 2009 the country's president was assassinated, and several high-ranking current or former military and political figures were attacked or killed. According to Antonio Mazzitelli, head of UNODC programs in West Africa, the country is now "so fragile it is being abandoned even by the drug traffickers." The traffickers, he says, "need a certain stability. They don't need a failed state...They need a weak state."[67]

Human Trafficking

Among the most shocking assaults on the world's conscience is the persistence of human bondage in the twenty-first century. "Trafficking in persons" generally refers to the coerced recruitment, transfer, and harboring of persons for the purposes of sexual exploitation or forced labor, generally for little or no financial recompense.[68] Despite international conventions against human trafficking, the U.S. government believes that 800,000 people are trafficked across borders each year—some 80 percent of them women and children. Victims of trafficking may endure horrific psychological trauma and physical violence, and exposure to sexually transmitted diseases like HIV/AIDS.[69]

By some estimates, human trafficking is the third most lucrative form of transnational crime (after the narcotics and arms trades), with annual profits in the tens of billions of dollars. In some regions, particularly Eastern Europe, the trade has been co-opted by criminal organizations involved in other forms of transnational crime, including drug trafficking, arms smuggling, and money laundering. Accordingly, Secretary of State Condoleezza Rice declared in 2008, "The movement to end trafficking in persons is more than a human rights object; it is a matter of global security."[70]

What Do Global Patterns Tell Us about the Weak State Connection?

All things being equal, it is logical to anticipate that weak states would be over-represented as source and transit countries for human trafficking. Poor countries may provide targets for traffickers, and may lack effective legal systems (or the political will) to protect victims, prosecute perpetrators, and control cross-border movements. Conflict and post-conflict zones might also appear particularly conducive to trafficking, given the surge in crime, smuggling, and levels of sexual violence that accompany many conflicts, the economic desperation of many households, and the large populations of displaced persons vulnerable to exploitation.

Surprisingly, closer analysis shows there may in fact be little direct correlation between human trafficking and state weakness (see appendices 4.4–4.6). Several states known as major trafficking hubs, such as Russia and Turkey, score relatively high on most indicators in the Index. A 2006 report by the UNODC identified countries of origin, transit, and destination for human trafficking based on the incidence of reporting by various sources, including national governments, nongovernmental organizations, and the media (admittedly an imperfect measure of the severity of the problem in any given state).[71] The report named 127 origin countries, most poor but not necessarily weak. Of the eleven countries named as having "very high" reporting as origin states, only one—Nigeria—ranks in the bottom two quintiles of the Index. (When "high" reporting countries are included, fewer than one-third ranked in the bottom two quintiles.)

Instead, most major origin countries are transitioning states in Eastern Europe and the former Soviet Union. Likewise, all but two of the twenty countries listed by the UNODC as major (i.e., "very high" and "high") transit countries for trafficked persons are in Europe, while only one—Burma—is classified by the Index as a weak state.[72] There also does not appear to be a strong link between poverty and origin countries, as measured by the UNODC and Index of State Weakness data: of thirty-eight major ("very high" or "high") origin countries, only five (13.2 percent) scored in the bottom two economic quintiles in the Index. Finally, destination countries for trafficking victims are overwhelmingly in the developed world.

On the other hand, there is some link between poor governance and countries that are unwilling to take steps to address trafficking. State performance in the battle against trafficking depends on willingness to implement anti-trafficking legislation, invest in law enforcement and the judiciary, battle entrenched corruption, educate citizens, and partner with civil society. Of the seventeen states designated by the U.S. State Department in 2009 as the worst offenders in the area of human trafficking, fifteen are ranked in the Weak States Index. Of these fifteen, twelve score in the bottom two quintiles for the political basket.[73] This may indicate a correlation between low political freedom and lack of cooperation on human trafficking (although some critics have charged that the State Department politicizes its rankings based on bilateral relations with each country).

Illegal Arms Trafficking

The illicit arms trade poses a grave threat to international security, fueling conflicts, terrorism, and criminality around the world. Smugglers and organized criminals have trafficked in everything from small arms to nuclear material (as described in the previous chapter). This section will focus on illegal trade in small arms and light weapons (SALW).

There is no clear definition of what constitutes an illegal arms transfer. Most "illicit" arms transfers begin as legal trade, with weapons then diverted to illegal channels through theft, smuggling, falsification of end-user documents, and other means. So-called "gray market" transfers are authorized by a government but are "nevertheless of doubtful legality" since they may be obviously directed to conflict zones or groups under embargo.[74] (Governments may also use gray-market channels to supply weapons to certain groups, as Iran has done with Hezbollah.) Even some clearly illegal transfers by international standards may not violate any national laws of the countries concerned. Given its covert nature and the vast overlay between legal and illegal trade, measuring the scale of illicit trafficking in weapons raises daunting data problems.[75]

For most of the world, the spread of deadly conventional weapons poses the greatest threat to human security and civil peace. SALW are responsible for 90 percent of casualties in armed conflict. Moreover, the illicit arms trade is often linked to other global "bads" such as terrorism, narcotics trafficking, the illegal exploitation of natural resources, and human rights abuses—all of which contribute to state weakness and may fuel instability and violence in regions of vital interest to U.S. security. Unfortunately, the few international instruments to combat the illicit arms trade are hamstrung by weak implementation measures and a general lack of political will to enforce them.[76]

What Do Global Patterns Tell Us about the Weak State Connection?

Many weak, failing, and postconflict states are awash in SALW. The same factors that enable other illicit activities—porous borders, high corruption, economic hardship, and ungoverned spaces—make weak states attractive source and transit states for arms dealers. The tiny, breakaway statelet of Transdniester, for example, possesses one of the largest weapons arsenals in Europe and has been described as "a family-owned and operated criminal smuggling enterprise," in effect "the Wal-Mart of arms trafficking."[77]

There is little solid data on major source, transit, or destination countries for illegal arms transfers, but an overwhelming percentage of illegally trafficked arms end up in critically weak countries. At least twelve of the fifteen weakest states in the Index have been or are currently destination countries for illegal arms deals.

In a handful of cases, state collapse has resulted in large-scale theft from government stockpiles, as occurred in Albania in 1997 or Iraq in 2003. But the black market in illicit arms is fueled by weapons from relatively strong states, particularly in Eastern European states. After the Soviet Union collapsed, stockpiles throughout the former Eastern bloc remained, creating opportunities for businessmen, organized criminal groups, and corrupt officials in the newly independent states. Albania, Bulgaria, Moldova, Serbia, Ukraine, and others have (with or without government complicity) supplied illicit actors.

Overall, then, the connection between state weakness and illegal arms transfers is more nuanced than generally suggested. Although weak states are the primary destination for much of the illicit arms trade, source countries are likely to be stronger states that, according to *Small Arms Survey*, lack adequate controls to protect their arms exports from diversion by traffickers.[78] Beyond Eastern European nations, the United States, Germany, France, the United Kingdom, South Africa, Singapore, Israel, and others have at times been important suppliers. In contrast, weaker states generally do not have sizeable domestic armaments industries. (Illicit manufacture, such as occurs at Pakistan's notorious Dera Adam Khel arms bazaar, makes up only a very small percentage of global arms production.)[79] Illicit arms shipments often follow convoluted routes, transiting several countries before reaching recipients. Corruption fuels the entire system as arms traffickers bribe guards and forge bills of lading, end-user certificates, flight schedules, and other documents. Across Africa, "semiliterate civil aviation officials [make] their livings by collecting landing fees and bribes while keeping virtually no records" of the flights and cargoes transiting their airstrips.[80] However, while weak states such as Liberia, Togo, and Pakistan have been transit states for weapons en route to nearby conflict zones, other, relatively strong states have also played this role. Slovakia and Côte d'Ivoire, for example, were major transit states for arms to Bosnia and Sierra Leone, respectively, in the 1990s. Thus proximity to conflict may be as important as the degree of state weakness.

Moreover, international arms dealers involved in the illicit weapons trade often base their operations in developed countries, which offer sophisticated financial systems and infrastructure. Notorious arms dealers such as Viktor Bout and Leonid Minin may have supplied arms to conflict zones like Afghanistan and the DRC, but their hubs were in entrepôts like South Africa, Belgium and the United Arab Emirates. Arms dealers also use the financial infrastructure of "strong" states (e.g., Hungary, Israel, and the United States) to launder money.

Money Laundering

Money laundering—"the act of converting money gained from illegal activity, such as drug smuggling, into money that appears legitimate and in which the source cannot be traced to illegal activity"—is the circulatory system of transnational crime.[81] The globalization of international finance has created enormous opportunities for money launderers. As countries abandoned exchange controls, the daily volume of currency exchanged surged from $590 billion in 1989 to $3.2 trillion in 2007. With a click of a mouse, funds can be transferred instantly around the world, including to "brass plate" banks and shell companies in obscure island nations like Nauru or Tuvalu.[82] The world's legal financial infrastructure has been used to launder money for dictators, drug lords, and terrorists.

Estimating the volume of money laundered on an annual basis is fiendishly complex, since there is no direct measurement and proposed proxies are controversial.[83] A decade ago, IMF Managing Director Michel Camdessus cited the "consensus range" for money laundering as 2–5 percent of global GDP. In 2007, this amounted to $1.1–$2.7 trillion worth of activity. The World Bank has estimated total cross-border flows from the proceeds of criminal activities, corruption, and tax evasion at between $1 trillion and $1.6 trillion a year. The laundering of proceeds for narcotics alone has been pegged at a minimum of $200 billion.[84]

Beginning in 2000, the multilateral Financial Action Task Force (FATF) began a "name and shame" effort to identify "non-cooperative countries and territories"—or jurisdictions that fail to meet minimum anti-money laundering standards. Although it has not seriously impeded the laundering of funds from transnational criminal activities, the FATF strategy succeeded in sharpening distinctions between those jurisdictions willing and unwilling to accept their international responsibilities.[85]

What Do Global Patterns Tell Us about the Weak State Connection?

Although there is little reliable, country-level data, there does not seem to be a strong correlation between weak states and money laundering. The U.S. State Department's 2008 list of major money-laundering countries included only eight weak states out of a total of fifty-seven nations (or 14 percent).[86] Of the twenty-three countries listed on the FATF non-cooperative list since 2000, only two—Burma and Nigeria—are weak states. Instead, money laundering seems more likely to occur in relatively developed (if remote) offshore havens such as Dominica, Antigua, and Grenada; and in countries with "under-regulated banking systems," such as Panama, Israel, and the Philippines.[87] Moreover, money laundering (including through *hawala* systems) frequently occurs in the world's major financial centers, including Belgium, Switzerland, Cyprus, the United Arab Emirates, Great Britain and even the United States.

According to Peter Reuter and Edwin M. Truman, who reach similar findings, "This lack of association between money laundering and failed states should not be particularly surprising," inasmuch as "money launderers or their clients attach high importance to keeping their money safe and like to exploit legal protections to do so, which is not an easy task in politically or economically failed, or failing states."[88] In fact, the UNODC's description of an "ideal financial haven" includes several characteristics not generally associated with weak states, including strong corporate and bank secrecy laws; excellent electronic communications; a large tourist trade that can help cover major cash inflows; use of a major world currency; a relatively insulated government; and a heavy dependence on the financial services sector. As Moises Naim points out: "Laundering havens must also possess some modicum of a financial and telecommunications infrastructure. Where there are no banks, no ties to the global market, money laundering prospects dwindle severely."[89]

Nevertheless, money laundering may actually contribute to state weakness by depriving developing countries of revenue and private investment. Today, half of all illicit financial flows—worth perhaps $500–800 billion—represent transfers from developing and transitional countries to wealthy economies. These transfers outpace total foreign assistance by a ratio of nearly ten to one.[90] Moreover, corrupt officials stash roughly $40 billion of stolen assets abroad each year,[91] reducing government revenues and hollowing out any domestic institutions that remain. Such dynamics were apparent in Abacha's Nigeria, Suharto's Indonesia, and Mobutu's Zaire, but continue today. One of the most striking current examples of kleptocratic asset-stripping is that of oil-rich Equatorial Guinea, whose autocratic president (Teodoro Obiang Nguema) has stashed away at least $700 million in U.S. banks while the majority of his citizens live in grinding poverty.

Environmental Crime

One of the shadier sidelights of globalization is the growing trade in environmental contraband, from hazardous waste and ozone-depleting substances to endangered species and illegal timber. Despite multinational instruments to combat environmental crime, it remains a serious—and growing—economic, security, and ecological threat. This section examines the connections between state weakness and three types of environmental crime: (1) toxic waste dumping; (2) the illegal timber trade; and (3) trade in endangered species.

There are significant limitations in measuring and assessing environmental crimes, given uneven reporting by UN member states and the clandestine nature of these activities. However, it is clear that transnational criminal groups make enormous profits trafficking in environmental contraband. A U.S. government study suggests that environmental crime is the fastest growing illicit activity, valued at $22–31 billion a year. Annual profits from toxic waste dumping may reach $12 billion. The illicit trade in some 1,000 endangered species is worth perhaps $10 billion annually, with the ivory smuggling business alone generating hundreds of millions of dollars each year.[92] The growing involvement of major organized crime groups in illicit environmental trade is reflected in recent seizures of huge consignments of wildlife contraband—some of the largest in history.

Environmental crimes despoil the global commons and endanger biodiversity; reduce food security and prospects for sustainable development; and harm human health. They can also feed other global "bads", as groups involved in environmental crime engage in other types of transnational crime, from drug smuggling to piracy to money laundering. The economic costs are also significant: The illegal timber trade, for instance, costs governments some $15 billion annually in lost revenues (and may cost American timber companies some $460 million each year).[93] The potential human costs of such activities came tragically to light in Cote d'Ivoire in 2006, when a massive body of toxic sludge from the Netherlands dumped near Abidjan caused at least twelve deaths and perhaps 30,000 illnesses.[94]

What Do Global Patterns Tell Us about the Weak State Connection?

Environmental crimes occur in developed as well as developing countries. For instance, illegal timber is shipped through ports in both relatively weak states, like Vietnam, and developed countries, like Singapore.[95] Even when such crimes occur in weak states, rich-world governments, corporations, and other private actors are often complicit. European criminal groups play a particularly large role in the toxic waste trade, illegally transporting waste generated in wealthy countries—the "effluent of the affluent"[96]—to poor ones. And Western demand fuels the illicit trade in many environmentally sensitive commodities. The illegal timber trade makes up perhaps 10 percent of the $50 billion U.S. import market, and in 2006, the American Forest and Paper Association estimated that as much as 80 percent of Europe's imported tropical timber is of illegal origin.[97]

But if the developed world is the primary "market" for environmental crime, weak states seem disproportionately likely to facilitate it. Weak states (like Somalia, Sudan, Nigeria, Eritrea, Algeria, and Mozambique) are typically lax about environmental regulations and are likely to be dumping sites for hazardous wastes. Although several relatively strong states (including Brazil, the Philippines, Indonesia, Russia, and Ecuador) have had serious problems with illegal logging, the practice is rampant in countries such as Burma, Cambodia, DRC, Laos, Liberia, and Papua New Guinea. Weak states are also likely to be source countries for illegally poached wildlife: according to TRAFFIC, an international nongovernmental organization, the six main countries involved in the illicit ivory trade are China, Thailand, Cameroon, DRC, Ethiopia, and Nigeria. Poaching is so prevalent in the critically weak states of the Congo basin that experts have warned that the region's rain forests could be totally depleted of large mammals within a decade, and great apes could become extinct in Africa. The poaching of tigers and other endangered species is also widespread in Southeast Asia, India, and Nepal.[98]

Weak states with ocean coastlines are also vulnerable to illegal fishing, a multibillion-dollar industry that thrives where governments lack the capacity or will to enforce fishing regulations. Illegal fishing is particularly common in the pirate-infested waters off Somalia, Kenya, and Tanzania, and in the waters off West Africa. Illegal, unregulated, and unreported fishing results in losses of more than $1 billion a year for governments in sub-Saharan Africa.[99]

Weak states may be less likely than wealthier countries to regulate their environmental sectors, particularly "where corruption, poverty, war, and other social problems are perceived as greater and more immediate threats."[100] In the DRC, for instance, the forestry sector is virtually unregulated. Likewise, according to the director of the watchdog agency charged with monitoring the Convention on International Trade in Endangered Species (CITES), only about one-quarter of the 173 states party have even minimum legislation in place to implement the treaty.[101]

Even having laws on the books in weak states does not guarantee that they will be implemented, given generally weak law enforcement capacity and high levels of corruption. (Of course, officials in wealthier countries have also been complicit in environmental crimes.) As much as one-fifth of global timber comes from "countries that have serious problems enforcing their timber laws."[102] The Basel Convention regulates trade in hazardous wastes, but one-third of its 158 states party are unable to enforce their treaty obligations due to inadequate border controls, financial resources, technical expertise, staff, or public awareness.[103] Repressive regimes in weak states such as Burma, Cambodia, and Cameroon may themselves profit from environmental crime (see box 4.7).

By contrast, even very weak states can make progress against environmental crime if the government is committed to doing so. For instance, Indonesia's democratic transition over the past decade has coincided with increasingly strong measures against the illegal timber industry—more than 1,600 people were arrested in 2005 for crimes related to illegal logging. More stable countries, even if poor, appear less vulnerable to ivory smugglers. While elephant populations have declined precipitously in the fragile states of East and Central Africa, they are increasing in the relatively well-governed countries of South Africa, Namibia, and Botswana.[104]

Like other illicit activities, certain environmental crimes make weak states weaker, fueling conflict, corruption, and the erosion of state authority. Environmental crimes deprive governments of revenue and deplete key natural resources, damaging local economies, stunting agricultural output, and triggering natural disasters in countries least equipped to cope. Illegal logging, in particular, contributes to deforestation, pollution, soil depletion, erosion, drought, and flooding, and costs some $15 billion worth of lost revenue in developing countries. Environmental crime also contributes to repression and conflict; the poaching and smuggling of endangered species, for example, has funded armed militias from the DRC to Sudan.[105]

Box 4.7: Illegal Logging in Cambodia

Illegal logging has been a serious problem in Cambodia since at least the early 1990s. But in the last decade, both the licit and illicit logging industries have been brought under the control of the kleptocratic regime of Prime Minister Hun Sen. Illegal logging in Cambodia primarily consists of felling protected forests, cutting more timber than legally allowed, or operating in areas where there are no legal harvesting operations. Senior officials, military officers, and members of Hun Sen's family reap enormous profits from the practice.

Meanwhile, the livelihoods of thousands of Cambodians who use trees for resins, medicines, and construction materials have been perhaps irrevocably damaged. Cambodia has lost 29 percent of its primary tropical forest in a five-year period, and now faces the prospect of total deforestation. In response to international donor pressure, the Cambodian government suspended all logging concessions in 2002 and imposed a moratorium on timber exports. Global Witness, an NGO assigned to monitor these regulations on behalf of the international community, reported that they were routinely violated—often by the very officials charged with implementing them. Global Witness has since been expelled from the country.[106]

Maritime Piracy

From the advent of oceanic trade, shipping vessels have been vulnerable to pirate attacks. Though conjuring images of buccaneers, piracy remains a thriving profession in the modern world. Equipped with assault rifles, grenade launchers, satellite phones, and night vision goggles, pirates use high-speed boats to attack tankers, trawlers, and container ships. In fact, the number of pirate attacks is higher than at any time since at least 1945. After a record 293 reported incidents in 2008, attacks surged to 240 in the first half of 2009 alone—a rate of one every eighteen hours.[107] The rise in global piracy is likely a function of three factors: (1) the end of the Cold War, which reduced policing presence in many parts of the developing world; (2) the spread of sophisticated weapons and GPS technology; and (3) the surging volume of international trade, providing a tempting target for any would-be freebooter.

Piracy represents a significant economic and security challenge to both weak states and wealthy ones. It adds time to shipping routes and raises insurance and shipping rates. Oil tankers are highly vulnerable to pirates, who could potentially disrupt global energy supplies. The hijacking of a Saudi oil tanker in October 2008, for instance, caused a short-term spike in world oil prices. The U.S. government is also concerned that pirates may link up with terrorist networks in East Africa and the Gulf states; by some accounts "terrorist groups have come to view piracy as a potentially rich source of funding."[108] Piracy can fuel other types of transnational crime too, including smuggling, and has hindered the distribution of humanitarian aid to Somalia, where nearly one-third of the population depends on food aid transported by sea.

What Do Global Patterns Tell Us about the Weak State Connection?

Intuitively, state weakness is conducive to piracy. All things being equal, the presence of a well-functioning state—able and willing to enforce the rule of law, patrol its coasts, and meet the basic welfare of its inhabitants—reduces both the opportunity and incentive to adopt such a violent livelihood. By contrast, high levels of poverty in weak states may force some to turn to piracy out of dire necessity, while endemic corruption enables pirates to bribe their way past officials. Other weak states may simply lack the capacity to do anything about piracy. A Tanzanian navy chief has pointed out that his fleet's operational range is only twenty nautical miles.[109] Certainly, the perception that piracy thrives in dysfunctional states with ungoverned (or misgoverned) maritime spaces has inspired the Pentagon to focus its interdiction and capacity-building efforts off the coast of Africa, including creating the Africa Partnership Station in the Gulf of Guinea and stepping up patrols with NATO allies in East Africa and the Horn.

Close analysis suggests that state weakness is indeed a contributing—arguably necessary—condition for sustained maritime piracy. The vast majority of piracy incidents occur off the coasts of a handful of developing countries with significant governance gaps. In recent years, piracy has surged off the coasts of Nigeria and Somalia, two of the world's weakest states. In 2008, more than 60 percent of attacks occurred in waters near states in the bottom two tiers of the Index of State Weakness. By contrast, as governance and economic indicators have improved in Indonesia and Malaysia, both countries have taken greater steps to combat piracy, with considerable success. There have been virtually no attacks in Europe or North America since 2003 (see table 4.3).[110]

Perhaps no country better illustrates the connection between state weakness and maritime crime than Somalia, where the absence of state institutions and a climate of lawlessness has contributed to a dramatic spike in piracy. Lawlessness off the Somali coast is closely correlated with anarchy onshore. Somalia has had no national army, police, navy, or coast guard since 1991, leaving the waters off its 1,900-mile coast—the

Table 4.3: Main Locations of Piracy[111]

Country/Region	Index Ranking	Confirmed Incidents of Piracy					
		2008	2007	2006	2005	2004	2003
Somalia	1	111	31	10	35	2	3
Nigeria	28	40	42	12	16	28	39
Indonesia	77	28	43	50	79	94	121
Tanzania	55	14	11	9	7	2	5
Bangladesh	48	12	15	47	21	17	58
Malaysia	124	2	9	10	3	9	5
India	67	7	11	5	15	15	27
Peru	92	1	6	9	6	5	7
Philippines	58	8	6	6		4	12
Guyana	87		5	1	1	2	6
Vietnam	83	6	5	3	10	4	15
Brazil	99	1	4	7	2	7	7
DR Congo	3		4	3			
Guinea	23		4	5	1	4	2
Kenya	50	4	4			1	1
Sri Lanka	56		4	1			2
Other Africa	—	10	13	10		26	23
Europe	—		1			1	1
North America	—					1	1
Total		293	263	239	276	329	445

LEGEND: Index Rank

Bottom Quintile
Second Quintile
Third–Fifth Quintile, or Not in Index

longest in Africa—uniquely vulnerable. The recent rise in pirate attacks coincided with escalating violence in Somalia proper following the overthrow of the Islamic Courts Movement in December 2006. Many pirates are now paid by Somali warlords, who fund their militias through ransom funds. According to Andrew Mwangura, program coordinator for the Mombasa-based Kenya Seafarers Association, piracy will remain a problem "until there is a legitimate government in Somalia that can control its coast."[112]

But while state weakness may be a necessary condition for piracy, it is not a sufficient one. Of twenty-two littoral African states in the bottom two quintiles of the Index, only three experienced significant piracy in 2008. This suggests that a country's attractiveness to pirates is also contingent on factors that have little to do with the quality of governance, including proximity to major shipping lanes and hubs. Somalia is a hotbed of piracy in part because of its location off the Gulf of Aden, through which 10 percent of global shipping passes.

Overall, a country's level of security may be the most relevant consideration for pirates. Of the seventeen countries experiencing three or more attacks in 2007, twelve (70.6 percent) are in the bottom two tiers for security in the Index. In 2008, more than half of all incidents occurred off of Somalia and Nigeria, two conflict-ridden countries where warlords and insurgents have been widely involved in piracy. In turn, profits from piracy, like other types of transnational crime, have fueled conflicts onshore.[113]

CONCLUSION: UNDERSTANDING THE WEAK STATE–TRANSNATIONAL CRIME CONNECTION

Patterns of transnational crime are imperfectly correlated with state weakness. To begin, the link varies by sector. Piracy, arms trafficking, coca and opium production, and certain types of environmental crime (especially poaching and, to a lesser extent, illegal logging) seem to occur predominantly in very weak states. But other transnational crimes, such as money laundering, fraud, cybercrime, and intellectual property theft, rarely do. The production of some narcotics, including cannabis and amphetamines, seems at least as likely to occur in strong states as in weak ones—as does the trafficking of drugs, people, and other contraband.

Several other conclusions can be drawn. First, a country's attractiveness to criminal groups is partly a function of variables that have nothing to do with the weakness of state institutions. Among the most important is geographic location, including proximity to the global marketplace. Trafficking routes in particular reflect geography as much as overall state weakness; thus traffickers in all types of contraband exploit both very weak states like Haiti and Tajikistan, and relatively strong ones like Turkey and Iran.

Second, like terrorists, transnational criminals often find that weaker is not always better when it comes to host states. Even more than a low-risk operating environment, criminals seek the opportunity to secure profits. They can reap large returns by selling illicit commodities and laundering the proceeds, but that requires access to modern financial services and infrastructure. Thus many of the world's hubs for transnational crime, such as Israel and the United Arab Emirates, are not by any measure weak states. Such considerations may also help explain why Nigeria has become a magnet for organized crime, while Niger has not. Ironically, this means that efforts to improve transportation infrastructure and facilitate regional trade could unwittingly assist transnational criminals.

Third, some gaps in governance are especially likely to facilitate transnational crime. Corruption, for example, seems to facilitate illicit transnational activity. Of the twenty-eight countries ranking in the bottom quintile of the Index for corruption, for example, all but four[114] are major centers for at least one type of transnational crime (see appendix 4.1). Equally important to transnational criminals are physical instability, porous borders, and under-governed zones. Of the states ranking in the bottom quintile for security and territory affected by conflict, all except one (Egypt) have been centers of transnational crime (see appendix 4.2). Likewise, war-torn countries almost exclusively comprise the world's opium and coca producers, pirate havens, and illicit arms destinations.

On the other hand, certain factors that might be assumed to facilitate transnational crime, such as poverty, do not actually appear to be highly correlated with such activity. In part, this is because the poorest countries tend to lack the necessary infrastructure. Of the poorest states on the Index, only about one-quarter can be considered major centers for transnational criminal operations, and these are mostly countries in conflict such as Somalia and Afghanistan (see appendix 4.3). The bottom line seems to be that weakness is not enough to foster transnational crime—and states that are too weak may actually discourage it.

South Africa, a major emerging economy, shows how a state can rank high on the Index and yet present critical weaknesses that are easily exploited. It is a country where "the first and the developing worlds exist side by side," notes Misha Glenny. "The first world provides good roads, 728 airports ..., the largest cargo port in Africa, and an efficient banking system.... The developing world accounts for the low tax revenue, overstretched social services, high levels of corruption throughout the administration, and 7,600 kilometers of land and sea borders that have more holes than a secondhand dartboard."[115]

But regardless of whether transnational criminals disproportionately target weak states, transnational crime makes weak states weaker. By exploiting already high levels of corruption, organized criminals further undermine the rule of law in regions from the Caucasus to Afghanistan to West Africa. On the United States' own border, drug rings—and trafficked U.S. guns—have turned northern Mexico into a "war zone" (see box 4.8).[116] Illegal poaching and logging have damaged ecosystems and livelihoods throughout the developing world. Money laundering allows corrupt dictators and officials to siphon their countries' resources into private bank accounts. And the profits from all types of transnational crime have fueled conflict and insurgency around the world.

But the "blame" for transnational crime cannot be placed exclusively at the feet of the world's weakest states, even when these are the source or conduits for illicit commodities and services. In most cases, wealthy countries are the primary markets for internationally trafficked contraband, from drugs to ivory to people. Global prohibition regimes, such as those for narcotics, can create huge incentives for criminal groups and place enormous burdens on source countries. Private firms domiciled in OECD states are sometimes complicit in illicit trafficking, and funds generated by transnational crime are often stashed in rich-world banks. As globalization continues to challenge the sovereign state and empower nonstate actors, the United States and other developed countries will need to take transnational organized crime more seriously.

Box 4.8 Mexico as a Failed State?

Mexico has long been a conduit for illegal drugs into the United States, and for years the border area has been the site of drug-related crime. But today, the conflict between the Mexican government and the region's drug cartels has escalated to a low-intensity war. The current violence dates to 2006, when President Felipe Calderon initiated a military crackdown on the cartels. Two years later, more than 6,000 people were killed in drug-related violence. There were also signs that the violence had begun to spread into the United States, and by early 2009, the U.S. government estimated that Mexican cartels had operations in more than 230 U.S. cities.[117]

By January 2009, the drug trade in Mexico had become so destabilizing that the U.S. Joint Forces Command cited Mexico as one of two "weak and failing" states that "bear consideration for a rapid and sudden collapse." This characterization offended many Mexican officials, and in many respects the claims are exaggerated. Mexico, which ranks in the top quintile of the Index of State Weakness, is a consolidated democracy with robust institutions, functioning public services, and no major ethnic cleavages or secessionist problems. The U.S. Director of National Intelligence declared that "Mexico is in no danger of becoming a failed state."[118]

At the same time, Mexico's current crisis is in fact an outgrowth—at least in part—of institutional shortcomings. Corruption has hollowed out state institutions from within: the cartels spend perhaps $20 billion annually to infiltrate the police, customs, judicial system, prisons, ministries, and (to a lesser extent) the military. So many police officers are on the take that "entire forces in cities across Mexico have been disbanded and rebuilt from scratch." Mexico's top organized crime prosecutor and the head of Interpol in the country have been arrested for receiving bribes from the cartels. Nearly half a million Mexicans—including as many as 100,000 former soldiers—may be involved in some way in the drug trade, including cultivation and trafficking. In some areas, the heavily armed cartels constitute an emerging state-within-a-state, "levying taxes, throwing up roadblocks and enforcing their own codes of behavior."[119]

But the United States also bears a significant share of the responsibility for Mexico's drug crisis—as the principal market, and the primary supplier of weapons, for the cartels. Secretary of State Hillary Clinton has acknowledged that the United States' "insatiable demand for illegal drugs fuels the drug trade."[120] But it remains to be seen whether the rhetoric will be matched by a realistic and well-resourced plan to address the problems on both sides of the border.

Appendix 4.1: Corruption, State Weakness and Transnational Crime

Country	Score on Index Corruption Indicator (0 = lowest)	Transparency International Ranking (180 being most corrupt)[121]	Overall Index Ranking (1 being weakest)	Narcotics Source or Transit Country?[122]	Human Trafficking Source or Transit Country?[123]	Source, Transit or Facilitating State for Illicit Arms Transfers?[124]	Money Laundering Center?[125]	Center of Piracy?[126]
Somalia	0.00	180	1					X
North Korea	0.24	n/a	15		X	X		
Burma	0.27	178	17	X	X	X	X	
Equatorial Guinea	0.79	171	25					
Afghanistan	0.96	176	2	X			X	
Haiti	0.97	177	12	X			X	X
DR Congo	1.09	171	3					X
Iraq	1.20	178	4					X
Zimbabwe	1.32	166	8					
Nigeria	1.56	121	28	X	X	X	X	X
Bangladesh	1.55	147	48		X			X
Tonga	1.56	138	104					
Turkmenistan	1.58	166	35	X[127]				
Sierra Leone	1.78	158	13					X
Cambodia	1.87	166	34		X		X	
Chad	1.90	173	16			X		
Cote d'Ivoire	1.99	151	10			X		X
Angola	2.06	158	11					X

(continued)

Appendix 4.1: Continued

Country	Score on Index Corruption Indicator (0 = lowest)	Transparency International Ranking (180 being most corrupt)[121]	Overall Index Ranking (1 being weakest)	Narcotics Source or Transit Country?[122]	Human Trafficking Source or Transit Country?[123]	Source, Transit or Facilitating State for Illicit Arms Transfers?[124]	Money Laundering Center?[125]	Center of Piracy?[126]
Papua New Guinea	2.07	151	40		X			
Sudan	2.09	173	6		X	X		
Kyrgyzstan	2.21	166	73			X		
Burundi	2.24	158	5					
Laos	2.34	151	45	X	X			
Venezuela	2.34	158	70	X		X	X	X
Central African Republic	2.30	151	7			X		
Republic of Congo	2.31	158	20	X		X		
Paraguay	2.43	138	75	X			X	
Uzbekistan	2.44	166	36		X			
Total				8	9	10	7	10

Appendix 4.2: Security and Transnational Crime

Country	Rank In Index Security Basket Score (0 = lowest)	Territory Affected by Conflict Indicator Score (0 = lowest)	Overall Index Ranking	Narcotics Source or Transit Country?[128]	Human Trafficking Source or Transit Country?[129]	Destination Country for Illicit Arms Transfers?[130]	Center of Piracy?[131]
Afghanistan	0.00	0.45	2	X		X	
DR Congo	0.28	1.87	3			X	X
Somalia	1.37	0.92	1			X	X
Sudan	1.46	3.06	6		X	X	
Iraq	1.63	3.60	4			X	X
Colombia	1.78	0.00	47	X	X	X	
Nepal	2.94	1.17	22		X		
Burundi	2.95	3.23	5			X	
Sri Lanka	3.38	6.51	56			X	X
Cote d'Ivoire	3.71	4.16	10			X	X
Burma	3.96	5.09	17	X	X		
Algeria	4.04	4.30	57		X		
Philippines	4.16	4.87	58	X	X	X	X
Pakistan	4.69		33		X	X	
Russia	4.83	6.80	65		X	X	
India	4.87	6.32	67	X	X	X	X
Uganda	4.89	6.50	27		X	X	

(continued)

Appendix 4.2: Continued

Country	Rank In Index Security Basket Score (0 = lowest)	Territory Affected by Conflict Indicator Score (0 = lowest)	Overall Index Ranking	Narcotics Source or Transit Country?[128]	Human Trafficking Source or Transit Country?[129]	Destination Country for Illicit Arms Transfers?[130]	Center of Piracy?[131]
Central African Republic	5.06		7			X	
Thailand	5.07		79	X	X		X
Haiti	5.21		12				X
Angola	5.32	6.49	11			X	X
Nigeria	5.37		28	X	X	X	X
Sierra Leone	5.43	5.26	13			X	X
Turkey	5.83	7.21	98		X		
Ethiopia	5.91		19			X	
Indonesia	5.92	7.29	77				X
Guinea-Bissau	5.96	8.72	18	X[132]			
Liberia	6.01	7.22	9			X	
Rwanda		7.94	24			X	
Egypt		8.09	78				
Tajikistan		8.15	42	X[133]			
Republic of Congo		8.47	20			X	
Croatia		8.66	131			X	
Total				**9**	**12**	**22**	**13**

Appendix 4.3: Poverty and Transnational Crime

Country	Gross National Income (GNI) per capita Score (0 = lowest)	Overall Index Ranking	Narcotics Source or Transit Country?[134]	Human Trafficking Source or Transit Country?[135]	Center of Piracy?[136]	Money Laundering Center?[137]
Burundi	0.00	5				
DR Congo	0.03	3			X	
Liberia	0.04	9				
Malawi	0.06	46				
Ethiopia	0.07	19				
Guinea-Bissau	0.08	18	X[138]			
Eritrea	0.09	14				
Somalia	0.12	1			X	X
Sierra Leone	0.13	13			X	
Rwanda	0.14	24				
Niger	0.15	21				
Afghanistan	0.16	2	X			X
Madagascar	0.17	49				
Nepal	0.18	22		X		
Uganda	0.18	27				
Gambia	0.19	51				
Mozambique	0.22	39				
Tanzania	0.23	55			X	X
Togo	0.23	26				

(continued)

Appendix 4.3: Continued

Country	Gross National Income (GNI) per capita Score (0 = lowest)	Overall Index Ranking	Narcotics Source or Transit Country?[134]	Human Trafficking Source or Transit Country?[135]	Center of Piracy?[136]	Money Laundering Center?[137]
Zimbabwe	0.23	8				
Central African Republic	0.24	7				
Tajikistan	0.27	42	X[139]			
Guinea	0.29	23			X	
Mali	0.31	52				
Burkina Faso	0.33	44				
Total			3	2	5	3

Appendix 4.4: Trafficking in Persons: Origin Countries

Country	UNODC Ranking	Index Ranking
Albania	Very high	111
Belarus	Very high	81
Bulgaria	Very high	127
China	Very high	74
Lithuania	Very high	138
Nigeria	Very high	28
Moldova	Very high	88
Romania	Very high	121
Russia	Very high	65
Thailand	Very high	79
Ukraine	Very high	107
Armenia	High	105
Bangladesh	High	48
Benin	High	71
Brazil	High	99
Burma	High	17
Cambodia	High	34
Colombia	High	47
Czech Rep.	High	
Dominican Rep.	High	91
Estonia	High	
Georgia	High	90
Ghana	High	84
Guatemala	High	60
Hungary	High	140
India	High	67
Kazakhstan	High	89
Laos	High	45
Latvia	High	136
Mexico	High	120
Morocco	High	96
Nepal	High	22
Pakistan	High	33
Philippines	High	58
Poland	High	135
Slovakia	High	141
Uzbekistan	High	36

(continued)

Appendix 4.4: Continued

Country	UNODC Ranking	Index Ranking
Vietnam	High	83
Total in bottom 2 Quintiles	**9 of 39 (23.1%)**	
LEGEND:		

	State located in the bottom two quintiles of Index

Appendix 4.5: Trafficking in Persons: Transit Countries

Country	UNODC Ranking	Index Ranking
Albania	Very high	111
Bulgaria	Very high	127
Hungary	Very high	140
Italy	Very high	
Poland	Very high	135
Thailand	Very high	79
Belgium	High	
Bosnia & Herzegovina	High	113
Burma	High	17
Czech Republic	High	
France	High	
Germany	High	
Greece	High	
Kosovo	High	
Macedonia	High	114
Romania	High	121
Serbia	High	108
Slovakia	High	141
Turkey	High	98
Ukraine	High	107
Total in Bottom 2 Quintiles	**1 of 20 (5.0%)**	
LEGEND:		

	State located in the bottom two quintiles of Index

Appendix 4.6: Trafficking in Persons: Destination Countries

Country	UNODC Ranking	Index Ranking
Belgium	Very high	
Germany	Very high	
Greece	Very high	
Israel	Very high	
Italy	Very high	
Japan	Very high	
Netherlands	Very high	
Thailand	Very high	79
Turkey	Very high	98
United States	Very high	
Australia	High	
Austria	High	
Bosnia & Herzegovina	High	113
Cambodia	High	34
Canada	High	
China	High	74
Cyprus	High	
Czech Republic	High	
Denmark	High	
France	High	
India	High	67
Kosovo	High	
Pakistan	High	33
Poland	High	135
Saudi Arabia	High	
Spain	High	
Switzerland	High	
United Arab Emirates	High	
Total in bottom 2 quintiles	**2 of 28 (7.1%)**	

LEGEND:

	State located in the bottom two quintiles of Index

5

ENERGY INSECURITY

We have a serious problem: America is addicted to oil, which is often imported from unstable parts of the world.
—*George W. Bush, State of the Union address, January 31, 2006*[1]

The shocking volatility in world oil prices over the past decade has propelled the issue of energy security to the top of the U.S. and global agenda. Energy is the lifeblood of the world economy—but there are new threats to energy security stemming from higher demand, tighter supply, terrorism, and political instability in energy-producing and transit states. Between 2000 and mid-2008, the cost of a barrel of oil surged 365 percent, doubling in 2007 alone. Oil prices dipped as the world entered a recession, but the underlying dynamics that had been driving prices upward—rising demand in developing economies and falling production from Russia to Mexico—have not changed. Most analysts believe "the era of cheap oil is over."[2] In fact, volatility in energy markets may actually have worsened the long-term outlook, by cutting investment in new projects critical to meeting future demand.

The costs of U.S. energy dependence go well beyond prices at the pump. Revenues from energy exports have emboldened "rogue states," such as Iran, and made countries like Russia and Venezuela more assertive on the world stage. Some petro-states, including Saudi Arabia, have funneled oil dollars to extremist groups. U.S. policies toward oil-rich autocracies and the U.S. military presence in the Persian Gulf—designed at least in part to secure steady oil supplies—breed resentments that fuel groups like al-Qaeda. Rising energy prices could encourage nuclear proliferation, as developing countries seek cheaper alternatives to power their economic growth. Meanwhile, rising energy use in emerging economies has contributed significantly to global warming. U.S. reliance on imported oil has exacerbated each of these foreign policy challenges.

Within the debate on energy security, there is growing emphasis on the role of weak and failed states as energy suppliers. Some of the world's weakest states are increasingly important sources of oil and gas.[3] Nigeria and Angola, for example, are now the United States' fourth- and seventh-largest sources of foreign oil, respectively. In other weak states, including Burma, Chad, and East Timor, recent discoveries may lead to oil and gas booms. But the problems of weak states—internal conflict, political instability, poor governance, and social unrest—can also exacerbate volatility in energy markets. When global supplies are tight, instability and supply disruptions in even marginal producers have an outsize influence, driving up prices and damaging the global economy. In extreme cases, dependence on oil from unstable countries could even require that the United States intervene militarily to secure energy supplies.

As this chapter will argue, the relationship between energy insecurity and state weakness is real but complicated, and the link should not be exaggerated. Weak states *are* more vulnerable to disruptions in energy production and transit. Furthermore, high oil and gas prices tend to fuel corruption and conflict in producer states, while volatility in energy markets may further destabilize weak-state suppliers—reinforcing a vicious cycle of instability and energy insecurity. In general, however, weak states do not pose the greatest threat to U.S. and global energy security; relatively stronger developing countries do.

This chapter begins by analyzing the growing prominence of energy issues in the U.S. national security debate. It then explores the role of fragile states in world energy markets, and evaluates arguments about the dangers posed by these states to energy security. The chapter next focuses on how recent energy trends—and U.S. reliance on supplies from developing countries—may actually exacerbate state weakness and undermine U.S. foreign policy goals. Finally, it underlines the importance of energy-rich "states to watch" for U.S. energy security.

THE GROWING THREAT OF ENERGY INSECURITY

Energy insecurity is increasingly recognized as a potential threat to U.S. economic prosperity, foreign policy, and national security. As gas prices reached historic levels in mid-2008, energy issues grabbed the attention of the U.S. public, media, and policy-makers. During the first half of 2008, Congress held some forty hearings on the oil price shock, and energy security was a central issue in the 2008 U.S. presidential campaign. From climate change to petro-profits, energy concerns dominated the headlines.

Despite recent attention to alternative energy sources, oil will remain the world's dominant source of commercial energy for the foreseeable future. Global oil consumption is about 84 million barrels per day, mostly traded on global markets. In late 2010, notwithstanding a global recession, oil prices were still twice the level of the early 2000s, and they will almost certainly rise again in the medium term. As long as the United States and other major economies depend on fossil fuels, the core elements of energy security will include diverse, reliable, and secure energy supplies and transit routes; ample reserves; and adequate refining and distribution capacity.

Today, virtually all of these components are under strain. Unprecedented global demand for oil and gas has made consuming countries scramble to lock up known reserves. Underinvestment in new oil and gas fields and alternative energy (exacerbated by the recent economic crisis) "is setting the stage for the next price spike."[4] Tight supplies mean that a disruption in supplies anywhere in the world can affect prices everywhere.

Anxiety about energy security is nothing new. Since the Industrial Revolution, energy has played an important role in foreign policy, from the resource grabs of the colonial era to World War II. The quest for energy security has often driven U.S. and European policies in the Middle East, from the 1953 Mossadeq coup to the 1991 Persian Gulf War. Much hand wringing accompanied the oil crisis of the 1970s, when an Arab oil embargo drove up prices and contributed to widespread fuel shortages (and a prolonged economic recession).

During the Nixon administration, the United States found alternative sources of oil, relieving the strain on the U.S. economy and delaying the need to pursue alternative energy technologies. But during the energy crisis of the 1970s, the United States imported roughly 3 million barrels of oil a day; today, it imports more than four times that much. The prospect of a major disruption to world energy supplies thus poses a dramatically greater threat to the U.S. economy.[5]

The economic consequences of the energy crisis for the United States are obvious. Oil dependence takes a steady financial toll through losses to potential GDP. At the height of the recent oil shock, the United States was spending more than $200,000 a minute on foreign oil, or $13 million an hour. In 2005, direct outlays for imported oil accounted for one-third of the United States' $800 billion current account deficit.[6] These massive transfers of wealth to oil-producing regions, including more than $25 billion a year to the Persian Gulf by 2008, have altered the geopolitical landscape, increasing the influence of exporting countries. The growth of sovereign wealth funds in such countries, and their investments in critical sectors of the U.S. economy (e.g., Dubai Ports World), has proven controversial.

High energy prices and dependence on foreign oil also carry security costs for the United States. As Secretary of State-designate Hillary Clinton testified in January 2009, "Energy vulnerability constrains our foreign policy options around the world, limiting effectiveness in some cases and forcing our hand in others."[7] Surging oil prices have also empowered authoritarian regimes, undercutting democracy, reinforcing extremism, and endangering global stability. Iran's status as a major energy producer has reinforced Teheran's leverage in nuclear negotiations, as the Iranian government has repeatedly threatened to cut off exports in retaliation for sanctions. Likewise, President Hugo Chavez of Venezuela, which provides more than 14 percent of U.S. oil imports, has periodically warned of an oil embargo against the United States. Similarly, Russia has at times exploited its dominance of European energy markets in the hopes of weakening Western solidarity. Although a decline in oil prices in late 2008 diminished these countries' short-term leverage, their propensity for playing energy politics is likely to continue over the long term.

There are other risks associated with high energy prices. They may trigger nuclear proliferation by raising the incentives for countries to develop nuclear technology as an alternative energy source. In part due to rising costs of energy, International Atomic Energy Agency (IAEA) officials "have never previously seen such widespread interest in starting a domestic nuclear power industry."[8] Oil exporters may also fund terrorism; Iran has used its oil revenues to support Hamas and Hezbollah, while Saudi Arabia (ostensibly a U.S. ally and the linchpin of the global energy system) has funneled petro-cash to extremists. By one estimate, the Saudi government has spent $70–100 billion over the past three decades in spreading Wahhabi doctrine around the Muslim world. The quest for energy security could also fuel "resource wars" within or between states for control of energy supplies. At the same time, high oil prices diminish the U.S. military's readiness and capability: every $10 increase per barrel of oil raises the U.S. military's operating costs by $1.3 billion per year.[9]

Finally, a tight energy market can contribute to underdevelopment, corruption, political instability, and violence, undermining U.S. interests from Africa to Central Asia. High oil prices are particularly onerous for developing countries, which tend to depend more on imported oil, maintain energy-intensive industries, and use oil less efficiently than advanced industrial nations. For these nations, an oil shock can be devastating. For every $10 increase per barrel of oil, the World Bank calculates, countries with per capita annual income below $300 stand to suffer a 1.47 percent decline in GDP—more than wiping out the value of foreign assistance, in many cases.[10] Rising energy prices could lead to unrest in developing countries.

Energy producers are also at risk of the so-called "resource curse." Natural resources, and specifically oil, are often associated with undemocratic governance, high rates of corruption, and economic underdevelopment. The flood of investments into energy-rich developing countries, from Kazakhstan to Equatorial Guinea, can overheat economies and create asset bubbles, eroding the earning power of local citizens and becoming a source of economic instability over time. As Secretary of State Condoleezza Rice conceded in 2006, heavy U.S. demand for imported fuel has "warped" U.S. diplomacy, strengthening the hand of oil-rich authoritarian governments and complicating the pursuit of U.S. foreign policy objectives (from promoting democracy and development to preventing the spread of WMD).[11]

Today's Energy Crisis

The United States' dependence on foreign oil makes it particularly vulnerable to rising energy costs—which in mid-2008 hit an unprecedented $140/barrel of crude oil. Whatever the temporary effects of the recession, global demand will continue to rise. At the same time, declining output in major producer states like Mexico, Russia, Iran, Venezuela, and Norway shows no sign of being reversed. The economic downturn may actually worsen the long-term problem, curtailing the momentum for investment in new (often more complicated and expensive) oil and alternative energy projects.

Surging Global Demand, Especially for Oil

International competition for limited resources has increased, largely because of emerging economies like China and India. After growing at 1.1 percent annually between 1998 and 2002, global demand for oil accelerated by 2.1 percent annually from 2003 to 2007. Although demand fell slightly in 2008 (for the first time since the 1980s), it began to rise in the second half of 2009 as the global economy recovered. China is now the second-largest oil-importing country, and in 2005, energy consumption in Asia exceeded that in North America for the first time. Global prices may rise further as demand grows in several major oil producers. Indeed, Indonesia recently shifted from a net exporter to a net importer, and Mexico and Iran may follow suit in the coming decade.[12]

Maxed-out Supply, with Minimal Surge Capacity

The discovery and development of new supplies have not kept pace with rising demand. Twenty years ago, global production capacity exceeded demand by 15 percent. But before the economic downturn struck in late 2008, spare capacity was only 2 percent above global daily consumption. While most experts believe there is plenty of oil to be found, many new reserves are in places like the tar sands or the ocean floor, making them difficult and expensive to develop. Volatile oil prices may make some of these projects financially unviable, at least in the short term.

Meanwhile, exploration and production costs for major oil and gas firms have doubled in recent years (largely due to a failure to invest in development when oil prices were low in the 1980s). As a result, production in several major suppliers, including Mexico, Russia, and Venezuela, is far below what experts had once predicted. Even OPEC's production capacity is falling, removing an important a bulwark against supply disruptions. As energy experts Jan H. Kalicki and David L. Goldwyn write, "The danger today is that there will not be enough oil to meet global demand at stable prices—not because America and the world are running out of oil, but because they are running behind on investment."[13]

Thanks to these trends, even small disruptions along the supply chain can have global ramifications. With demand likely to rise as the global economy recovers, this removal of slack in the world oil market will leave prices sensitive to sudden disruptions that prevent—or even threaten to prevent—modest amounts of oil from reaching the global market.[14] In June 2008, Libya threatened to cut its oil production in response to U.S. legislation allowing the United States to sue OPEC members for price manipulation. Although Libya is a fairly minor oil producer (ranking sixteenth globally) and most analysts dismissed its threat, the statement nonetheless helped oil prices rise to a record $142/barrel.[15]

Over time, high energy prices should moderate somewhat, as governments, consumers, and corporations adopt new policies, consumption patterns, technologies, and sources. Oil consumption among OECD countries has in fact been on the decline for several years. After thirty years of inertia, the U.S. government has raised fuel efficiency standards for U.S. automobiles. And the private sector is taking steps not only to reduce its energy use but also to increase its supply, by investing in the extraction of more fossil fuels and the development of less wasteful technologies. Given these innovations in public policy, consumer behavior, investment, and innovation, Daniel Yergin believes that the United States may have passed the point of "peak demand" (at least when it comes to gasoline).[16] Nevertheless, ever-rising global demand coupled with maxed-out production will amplify the price impact of supply interruptions, even in the most marginal producer states.

THE ROLE OF WEAK STATES IN GLOBAL ENERGY MARKETS

Much of the commentary on U.S. energy security has centered on the role of weak states as producer and transit countries. Several critically weak states, such as Iraq and Nigeria, have long been major energy producers; others are important transit states for natural gas. Weak states such as Angola are an increasingly important source of energy supplies for major economies. Moreover, tight global markets have increased the significance and leverage of even relatively minor producers, from Sudan to Azerbaijan.

Weak and Failed States as Energy Suppliers

Weak-state producers are increasingly important to global energy markets. In 2004, the UK Prime Minister's Strategy Unit estimated that some 43 percent of global oil reserves—and 17 percent of global gas reserves—were located in countries "at risk of instability."[17] This is consistent with the Index of State Weakness rankings: approximately 40 percent of the world's oil is produced in countries that rank in the bottom three quintiles of the Index. Eight critically weak states[18] account for nearly 10 percent of global production, and three of these countries (Nigeria, Iraq, and Angola) are among the world's top fifteen oil exporters. Likewise, three of the world's top fifteen natural gas exporters (Turkmenistan, Nigeria and Uzbekistan) are very weak states. States in the third quintile of the Index account for more than 30 percent of world oil production (About 25.5 million bpd) and nearly one-third of global natural gas production, but many of these are "states to watch"—notably Russia, Azerbaijan, Algeria, Libya, Iran, Venezuela, and Indonesia.[19]

As of 2008, critically weak states (primarily Angola, Iraq, Nigeria, Equatorial Guinea and Chad) provided more than 25 percent of all U.S. oil imports—almost as much as Saudi Arabia and Mexico combined (see table 5.1). Angola is now China's biggest source of foreign oil, and more than one-third of China's oil imports come from African states, including Sudan and the Republic of Congo.[20] Europe is also looking to relatively weak states such as Algeria, Azerbaijan, and Nigeria to offset its dependence on Russian energy. Thus, with global demand rising, some of the world's biggest producers—and exporters to the United States—are vulnerable to internal turmoil and instability.

Despite the risks entailed, companies are willing to go to great lengths to unearth energy riches in weak states. State oil companies from China, India, Malaysia, and

Table 5.1 Top 15 Crude Oil Exporters to the United States[21]

Country	Index Ranking	BPD ('000)
Canada	n/a	1,913
Mexico	120	1,219
Saudi Arabia	n/a	1,135
Venezuela	70	962
Angola	11	671
Iraq	4	519
Nigeria	28	457
Brazil	99	365
Kuwait	n/a	251
Ecuador	85	243
Colombia	47	225
Equatorial Guinea	25	167
Algeria	57	142
Russia	65	139
Chad	16	101

LEGEND: Index Ranking

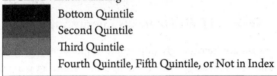

Bottom Quintile
Second Quintile
Third Quintile
Fourth Quintile, Fifth Quintile, or Not in Index

elsewhere are increasingly moving into countries previously deemed too unstable to merit investment, such as Chad. In Papua New Guinea, where major unrest has resulted in the deaths of more than 20,000 people in the past several years, ongoing explorations have uncovered a vast pool of natural gas that may be larger than the United States' annual residential consumption in 2005. "The gold rush is back on," said Andrew V. Boland, an energy analyst at Peters & Company, a Canadian investment firm. "It's like the wild, wild West, all over again."[22]

Some marginal producers have sought to turn this new market clout to their economic and geopolitical advantage. In 2006, Chadian Leader Idriss Deby threatened to terminate the country's 180,000 bpd production unless ExxonMobil and other oil companies paid an additional $100 million in new taxes. "In the not-too-distant past," the *New York Times* reported, such blandishments from a poor, landlocked African country would have been of little concern to oil traders or diplomats. "There was enough oil sloshing around to make up for any shortfall, anywhere. That's no longer the case. In a world where every single barrel counts, the actions of Chad's president could threaten global energy security."[23]

Ironically, growing reliance on oil imports from weak and vulnerable states is partly a function of efforts to diversify sources away from the volatile Persian Gulf, where war, regional competition, and the threat of terrorism have rattled energy markets. For instance, securing reliable access to energy resources in the Gulf of Guinea has been a major focus of U.S. energy policy. Although its reserves pale in comparison to those in the Middle East, West Africa's sweet, low-sulfur oil is comparatively easy to refine and, given its location, transport to the United States. Over the past decade, U.S. and other foreign oil companies have invested some $50 billion in the region. By 2015, the United States may import a full quarter of its oil from the Gulf of Guinea (up from 15 percent in 2005).

But this region is unstable and vulnerable to conflict, with a large organized criminal presence. All of the countries in the Gulf—including Angola, Cameroon, the DRC, Gabon, Equatorial Guinea, and Nigeria—face tremendous governance challenges. Nigeria, a fragile democracy and the fifth-largest exporter of oil to the United States, is beset by grinding poverty, rampant corruption and crime, weak security services, low administrative capacity, and simmering ethnic tensions. Nigeria's production has been repeatedly disrupted by civil unrest, and by the most conservative estimates loses some 100,000 barrels of oil per day to theft and attacks on the country's energy infrastructure[24] (see box 5.1).

The United States has also explored Central Asia and the Caucasus—including Kazakhstan, Uzbekistan, Turkmenistan, and Azerbaijan—as alternative (or at least supplementary) sources of energy. Washington has promoted export pipelines that bypass Russia to prevent Moscow from dominating the flow of energy to Europe, and tried to pry the region's oil and gas reserves open to Western investment. Russia has responded in kind, cozying up to Central Asian autocrats and investing more in the region's oil fields and pipelines that flow north through Russian territory, as opposed to across the Caspian Sea. However, geopolitical competition for the region's reserves could be rendered moot by unrest in the major producing states, several of which face potentially destabilizing political transitions.

Other major exporters facing major security challenges include Iraq, which in the wake of sabotage and insurgency has struggled to restore its oil production to levels prior to the U.S.-led invasion of 2003; and Algeria, a violence-prone state with an active terrorist presence. Angola has emerged as the fastest-growing source of oil exports to the United States, but continues to suffer from the effects of a devastating civil war that ended only in 2002 after killing half a million people. As weak-state producers become more important to global energy markets, instability in these countries could be highly problematic.

Weak and Failed States as Transit Countries

The tightening of global energy markets has increased the geopolitical importance of pipelines. To prevent countries like Iran and Russia from using energy as a political tool, the United States has tried to promote alternative pathways for bringing oil and gas to global markets.

But in many cases, this means seeking transit routes through unstable regions (e.g., Transcaucasia) or vulnerable choke points (e.g., the Straits of Hormuz and Malacca).

Accordingly, weak states that are not even major producers or transit states—but that simply *border* important producers or transit states—could have a significant impact on global energy supplies. In principle, such disruptions could take a variety of forms: terrorist or other attacks on pipelines; attacks on vessels in major choke points; or the spillover of civil war or state collapse in major producing or transit states.

Several states with a recent history of instability are currently important transit countries. Major pipelines run through Russia's unstable northern Caucasus provinces, including Chechnya. The Baku-Tbilisi-Ceyhan (BTC) oil pipeline and its natural gas counterpart, the South Caucasus Pipeline (SCP), are important routes for supplying Europe with Central Asian energy resources that bypass Russia and Iran. But the BTC and SCP pass through Georgia and Azerbaijan, both of which have experienced conflict. Oil from Chad is exported through Cameroon, a weak state. Burma, a critically weak state, is set to become a major transit route for African and Middle Eastern oil en route to southern China. The unstable states of Central Asia are also transit countries for gas destined for China.

In addition to these existing weak-state transit routes, several critically weak states are potentially vital transit countries—but political instability has made pipeline construction infeasible. Two proposed pipelines to supply India provide a case in point. Afghanistan is one of the most geographically and economically viable export routes to the subcontinent, but violence there has derailed several proposed pipeline projects, including the stalled TAPI (Turkmenistan-Afghanistan-Pakistan-India) pipeline. Other plans include an Iran-Pakistan-India (IPI) pipeline to carry Iranian and Central Asian gas through Pakistan's Baluchistan region, but ongoing insurgency there has stalled any such project.[25]

Weak States and Energy Choke Points

Almost half of the world's oil travels by sea, moved by tankers on fixed maritime routes. In 2007, this amounted to 43 million barrels per day. Oil tankers deliver 95 percent of U.S. oil imports—representing 57 percent of total U.S. consumption. For Japan, almost entirely dependent on imported oil, the comparable figure is nearly 100 percent. By 2025, Asia's two emerging giants, China and India, may depend on seaborne foreign oil imports to meet more than two-thirds of their energy needs.[26]

A large percentage of the world's oil supply passes through a small number of choke points—narrow channels along global sea routes—some of which are increasingly vulnerable to piracy and terrorism. The U.S. Department of Energy has designated six "world oil-transit choke points" at risk from these types of attacks. About one-third of global oil production transits these bottlenecks, which include the Straits of Hormuz, Malacca, and Singapore. The latter have long been centers of piracy, although the problem has waned as governments in the region have stepped up efforts to police their waters.

Of possibly greatest concern is the Bab el-Mandab, which connects the Arabian and Red Seas, and through which some 3.3 million barrels of oil pass each day.[27] The Bab el-Mandab is bordered by Somalia, the weakest state in the Index, and Yemen, also a weak state. As noted in previous chapters, Yemen has been the site of terrorist attacks on foreign oil tankers, and each year there are dozens of pirate attacks on vessels in Somali waters (including, in 2008, a successful hijacking of a Saudi tanker carrying some $100 million worth of oil).

WEAK AND FAILED STATES AS A THREAT TO ENERGY SECURITY

While U.S. and global energy security clearly depends on diversifying supplies, the growing role of weak states in global energy markets may complicate efforts to secure reliable supplies. In principle, countries with dysfunctional governance might contribute to global energy insecurity in at least three ways. First, terrorism, political instability, and social unrest (including resource-driven conflicts) may make them unreliable energy suppliers and transit states. Second, poor governance may translate into inefficient economic policies that discourage investments in the energy sector. Finally, the very presence of energy resources within a weak country may, through the dynamics of the "resource curse," exacerbate weakness and instability, not only thwarting U.S. security and development goals but undermining the reliability of the state as a supplier of fossil fuel.

Weak States as Unreliable Energy Suppliers and Transit Countries

Political Instability and Violent Conflict

Weak and failing states are, by definition, more at risk than other states for political instability, which can have adverse effects on global energy security if supplies are disrupted even temporarily. In 2006, the Eurasia Group reported that growing political risk in twelve oil-exporting nations might lead these countries to significantly curtail their collective output of 4.6 million barrels per day—an amount representing 5 percent of total world production and more than any single OPEC state except Saudi Arabia.[28]

The risk that instability and violence will curtail supplies of fossil fuels is highest, of course, in war-torn countries. In addition to disrupting the flow of oil, violence limits investment by major oil companies whose capital and expertise are needed to develop new fields. Insurgents and rebel groups have deliberately targeted oil facilities and workers in Nigeria (see box 5.1), Sudan, Ethiopia, Colombia, Pakistan, and elsewhere. If violence were to erupt again in Georgia, a critical transit state for Caspian oil, exports from the BTC and SCP pipelines could be disrupted, as occurred briefly during the war with Russia in 2008. In Iraq, insurgents and saboteurs were reported to have launched at least 469 attacks on the country's oil infrastructure and personnel by spring 2008. Until recently, these incidents kept postwar Iraqi oil production well below pre-war levels and precluded investment to restore peak production.[29]

Box 5.1: Niger Delta—Center of the Storm

The potential impact of conflict in a producer state on global energy prices may be most apparent in Nigeria, where political instability, ethnic unrest, insurgency, and banditry have taken a heavy toll. Nigeria is the world's twelfth-largest producer and eighth-largest exporter of crude oil, and the source of some 10 percent of U.S. oil imports. Yet its oil production may be as much as 1 million bpd below capacity due to attacks on the region's extraction and transport infrastructure.

A low-level insurgency has raged in the oil-rich Niger Delta for decades, though fighting has intensified dramatically in recent years. The conflict is driven largely by local grievances over the central government's appropriation of the region's oil revenues. The Delta is one of the poorest areas in a country where more than 70 percent of the population lives on less than $1 a day. The rampant corruption that pervades the oil sector—indeed the entire government—at both the local and national levels ensures that the population sees few benefits from the region's oil wealth.[30] Moreover, decades of oil exploration and production have damaged the region's environment, compromising the livelihoods of millions.

Criminality is rampant in the Delta, with frequent kidnappings and attacks on foreigners, particularly oil workers. Local politicians use oil money to fund private militias, which may be employed in racketeering schemes or even used to help rig elections. Sophisticated gangs illegally tap crude oil from pipelines, loading it onto barges and other smaller vessels for transfer to sea-going tankers waiting offshore. Funds from this illegal trade have kept the Delta awash in weapons. One journalist describes violence there as a "three-way struggle" between corrupt government officials, oil companies, and rebels, fueled by both "genuine grievance" and thuggery.[31]

The insurgency escalated after 2003, and particularly following the emergence in 2006 of the well-organized Movement for the Emancipation of the Niger Delta (MEND). Like other groups, MEND has targeted Western oil companies and personnel. Some 200 foreign oil workers were kidnapped in 2007, and 2008 saw near-daily attacks against oil installations, including one assault on a rig 75 miles off the coast. The violence is such that the chief of Total S.A. has acknowledged that his company is "thinking twice" about its investments in Nigeria.[32] In October 2010, MEND rebels detonated car bombs in Abuja, the first time they had taken their campaign out of the delta.

Nigeria does not produce nearly as much oil as the Gulf, but ongoing instability there has nonetheless had a significant impact on global oil prices. Nigeria's oil is sweet, making it particularly valuable, so "Nigeria outages barrel for barrel have more of an impact than additional Saudi output." One bombing of a Shell export facility in 2006 cut the company's local production in half (some 500,000 bpd), forcing it to abandon operations in the western part of the Delta. Attacks on pipelines in April 2008, which cut exports by another 169,000 bpd, helped drive U.S. gas prices above $3.50 for the first time. By summer 2008, Nigerian production was at its lowest level in twenty years, some 35 percent below capacity. Energy expert Daniel Yergin, testifying before the U.S. Congress in mid-2008, said that if the United States wanted to stabilize world energy markets, "Helping bring peace to the Niger Delta would be a major contribution."[33]

Pipelines provide tempting targets for insurgents in weak producer or transit states because they are often insecure and located in remote territory. In many cases, oil companies would rather repair damage to pipelines than invest in proper protection. As of 2005, the United States had spent roughly $99 million to train Colombian security forces to guard the country's largest pipeline, which has been attacked hundreds of times. Experts expect more frequent attacks on pipelines in Africa, where there is little infrastructure protection and where even minor disruptions can cause spikes in global energy prices.[34]

Other transit countries may not be critically weak states, but nonetheless have certain vulnerabilities that could cause supply problems. Turkey, a major transit state for natural gas en route to Europe, provides an example. Although its aggregate score does not make Turkey a weak state, its security score (5.83) falls in the lowest quintile, thanks to ongoing attacks by separatists in Kurdistan—including one that shut down the BTC pipeline for several weeks in August 2008. Russia is also vulnerable to attacks on its infrastructure. Its Druzhba pipeline—the world's longest—supplies Europe with oil by running through the volatile North Caucasus region, site of frequent guerrilla attacks on pipelines. Similarly, Uighur militants in China's western province of Xinjiang have attacked the region's oil infrastructure, and could threaten the 2,600-mile pipeline that China is building through the region to supply Beijing and Shanghai.[35]

Of the thirty energy producers in the bottom three quintiles of the Index, more than two-thirds rank in the bottom quintile for political stability and absence of violence, while nineteen (59.4 percent) score in the bottom two quintiles for territory affected by conflict.

The Index validates the conventional wisdom about potential instability in weak state energy suppliers. More than one-third of all oil production comes from states with significant security challenges (ranking in bottom two quintiles). Four of the world's top producers—Russia, Nigeria, Iraq, and Algeria, which together account for one fifth of world oil production—rank in the bottom quintile for security (see table 5.2) The situation is similar when it comes to natural gas: Three of the world's top fifteen gas exporters (Russia, Algeria, and Indonesia), accounting for some 26 percent of global production, have security scores in the bottom quintile. Of the 30 energy producers in the Index's bottom three quintiles, nearly three quarters (73.3 percent) rank in the bottom quintile for political stability and absence of violence, while 19 (63.3 percent) score in the bottom two quintiles for territory affected by conflict.

Instability in weak states can also threaten supplies or transit routes in neighboring countries. For instance, Colombia's civil war has threatened oil production in neighboring Ecuador, where foreign oil workers have been kidnapped and several pipelines bombed (presumably by Colombian rebels). Even where spillover is unlikely, the mere risk of regional instability may cause oil and gas prices to rise, or investment in energy infrastructure to decline. Thus, it is concerning that seventeen of the world's thirty largest oil producers—(accounting for more than half of global production) and sixteen of the thirty largest gas producers[36]—share borders with states in the bottom two quintiles of the Index (see table 5.3). Admittedly, the risk that instability from conflict or state failure in a neighboring state will place oil production at risk is highly variable. Collapse in North Korea, for instance, is unlikely to appreciably affect Russian oil output.

Table 5.2: Insecurity in Top Oil and Gas Producers

Oil

Production Rank (Oil)	Country	Production ('000 bpd)	Overall Index Rank	Security Basket Score
1	Saudi Arabia	10,782		
2	Russia	9,790	65	4.83
3	USA	8,514	66	6.91
4	Iran	4,174		
5	China	3,973	74	6.85
6	Canada	3,350	120	7.63
7	Mexico	3,186		
8	UAE	3,046	70	7.12
9	Kuwait	2,741	99	7.32
10	Venezuela	2,643	4	1.63
11	Norway	2,466	57	4.04
12	Brazil	2,402	28	5.37
13	Iraq	2,385		
14	Algeria	2,180		
15	Nigeria	2,169		

Gas

Production Rank (Gas)	Country	Production (bcf)	Overall Index Rank	Security Basket Score
1	Russia	23,386	65	4.83
2	United States	20,377	66	6.91
3	Canada	6,037		
4	Iran	4,107		
5	Norway	3,503	57	4.04
6	Algeria	3,055	74	6.85
7	Netherlands	2,990		
8	Saudi Arabia	2,841		
9	Qatar	2,719		
10	China	2,685	35	7.88
11	Turkmenistan	2,490		
12	Indonesia	2,472	77	5.92
13	United Kingdom	2,469		
14	Uzbekistan	2,387	36	6.66
15	Malaysia	2,024	124	8.49

LEGEND: Index Rank

- Bottom Quintile
- Second Quintile
- Third Quintile
- Fourth Quintile
- Top Quintile

Table 5.3: Major Oil Producers with Weak Neighbors

Producer Rank/Country	Production ('000 bpd)	Bordering States in Bottom Two Quintiles of Index
(#1) Saudi Arabia	1,0247	Iraq, Yemen
(#2) Russia	9,874	North Korea
(#4) Iran	4,033	Iraq, Pakistan, Afghanistan, Turkmenistan
(#9) Venezuela	2,670	Colombia
(#10) Kuwait	2,616	Iraq
(#12) Nigeria	2,353	Cameroon, Chad, Niger
(#13) Brazil	2,277	Colombia
(#14) Algeria	2,173	Mali, Mauritania, Niger
(#15) Iraq	2,096	Iran
(#16) Libya	1,844	Algeria, Chad, Niger, Sudan
(#17) Angola	1,768	Democratic Republic of Congo, Republic of Congo
(#19) Kazakhstan	1,444	Turkmenistan, Uzbekistan

Terrorist Attacks on Energy Infrastructure

Limited spare production capacity in the world oil market means that any supply disruptions can have a dramatic impact on the price of oil and growth prospects in oil-importing nations, including the United States. In this environment, attacks by transnational terrorist groups pose a threat to global energy security, although to date relatively few have occurred.

The massive global infrastructure for oil and gas production and delivery creates thousands of targets for terrorist attacks. These include oil and gas fields, wells, platforms, and rigs; refineries and gas processing plants; transportation facilities, including pipelines and pumping stations, terminals and tank ships; oil and gas depots; administrative buildings; distribution centers; and petrol stations.[37] Attacks can range from kidnapping oil workers to blowing up facilities. Even the fear of terrorism can disrupt the global economy. For example, in June 2005, terrorist threats in Nigeria forced the evacuation of the U.S., UK, German, Italian, and Russian consulates. This single event raised fears of economic insecurity in Africa's largest oil producer, and helped drive global oil prices to new highs—over $70 a barrel by mid-August. In recent years, oil traders and industry experts have estimated the "fear premium" generated by the specter of terrorist or criminal attacks on the global oil infrastructure at $8–10 per barrel—approaching $1 billion per day.[38]

Terrorist groups are well aware of these vulnerabilities. In 2004, al-Qaeda called for strikes on oil facilities in the Arabian Peninsula. The following year, an al-Qaeda-affiliated web site released a "Map of Future al Qaeda Operations," which said that terrorists would prioritize attacking oil facilities in the Middle East to draw the United States into "a new quagmire." Senior al-Qaeda strategist Ayman al-Zawahiri reinforced this guidance in a video released in September 2005, in which he instructed, "Focus your operations on oil, especially in Iraq and the Gulf area, since this will cause them to die off."[39] In February 2007, al-Qaeda ordered attacks on oil infrastructure in any country supplying the United States, including Canada and Mexico.

Al-Qaeda and its affiliates have attacked energy infrastructure in major producing states such as Saudi Arabia, Iraq, and Algeria. In Saudi Arabia, a series of al-Qaeda attacks on oil workers' compounds in 2003 and 2004 killed dozens and caused a spike in world oil prices. In February 2006, in the first direct assault on Saudi oil infrastructure, a group linked to al-Qaeda staged an attack on the Abqaiq oil-processing plant— the largest in the world, processing nearly 10 percent of the world's oil supply each day. Although security forces thwarted the attack, the incident caused oil prices to rise. Moreover, terrorists may profit from stealing or trading oil on the black market, as al-Qaeda in Iraq has done.[40]

In Algeria, the world's twelfth-largest oil exporter and the supplier of nearly one-third of Europe's natural gas, terrorist violence has escalated in recent years. The country's main terrorist presence, al-Qaeda in the Islamic Maghreb (AQIM), has declared war on foreign individuals and companies operating in Algeria. At least one AQIM leader has cited the U.S. role in "plundering our oil and planning to get our gas" as a reason for turning against the United States. In December 2006, a bus carrying American and British employees with a Kellogg, Brown & Root joint venture was bombed near Algiers; Russian and Chinese oil and gas personnel have also been targeted.

As described in chapter 2, weak-state producers may be particularly vulnerable to terrorist activity because they lack the resources needed to protect drilling sites, pipelines, and other infrastructure. Many of the thirty energy-producing states ranked in the bottom three quintiles of the Index of State Weakness have been targeted by transnational terrorism, or are known to have a terrorist presence. Al-Qaeda affiliates are reported to have set up training camps across North and West Africa, including in weak-state energy producers such as Algeria, Nigeria, Chad, and Mauritania.[41] In weak states such as Turkmenistan, "a single terrorist attack on the poorly maintained gas infrastructure could...reverberate in the complicated arrangement for Russian gas exports to Ukraine and Europe that depend upon uninterrupted delivery of Turkmen gas."[42]

However, many experts question whether terrorists could really cause severe disruptions to global energy supplies. Only three of the thirty energy-producing states in the bottom three quintiles of the Index (Iraq, Algeria, and Yemen; Saudi Arabia is not ranked) have experienced attacks by transnational terrorists (as opposed to local insurgent groups) on their energy infrastructure. And while these attacks may cause temporary cutoffs and price spikes, none has come close to shutting down oil production in a major state, or has otherwise dramatically disrupted global energy markets.

In fact, major energy producers such as Saudi Arabia and Algeria have increased their investments in securing pipelines and refining facilities. Thus, despite ongoing political violence in Algeria, as of 2008 the country had experienced only three attacks on its energy infrastructure and personnel.[43] Likewise, a debilitating attack on Saudi Arabia's infrastructure is unlikely. The kingdom has developed an extensive system of safeguards to protect its pipelines, ports, and other infrastructure, including through sophisticated electronic surveillance, regular aircraft patrols, and a 30,000-strong guard force. In any case, Saudi Arabia's oil infrastructure is "designed with some redundancy, so that oil could keep flowing despite the destruction of a few facilities."[44] As for local terrorist and insurgent groups, some experts have argued that they are actually unlikely to attack energy targets, which would damage Western interests and cost them support. This may be one reason that there have been relatively few attacks on pipelines in the violent north Caucasus energy corridor.[45]

Likewise, although choke points would seem to be obvious targets for terrorist groups seeking to disrupt global energy supplies, the verdict is out as to whether even a determined terrorist organization would have the ability to exploit this presumed vulnerability (at least in a sustained manner). Admiral Dennis C. Blair, retired U.S. Commander in the Pacific (and former Director of National Intelligence), and University of Michigan professor Kenneth Lieberthal are skeptical, arguing that risks to maritime flows of oil through the world's sea lanes and choke points are vastly over-stated. Modern oil tankers, they wrote in 2007, are less vulnerable to attack from both terrorists and rogue states than conventionally assumed.[46]

In fact, such breezy confidence may be misplaced. The successful Somali pirate attack on a Saudi supertanker in November 2008 suggests that the hurdles for a successful attack may be far from insurmountable, even for a small band of nonstate actors. What *does* seem clear is that the United States and its allies possess sufficient naval power to minimize disruptions to commercial oil traffic from such attacks. Even the Iran-Iraq war (1980–1988), during which some 544 attacks on oil tankers killed more than 400 civilian sailors, failed to disrupt oil shipments (though it did result in a temporary spike in oil prices and a reduction of Gulf oil shipping by 25 percent in the short term).

Social Unrest

Given weak states' tendency to suffer from poor governance, greater repression, higher inequality, and lower growth, weak-state producers would seem more likely than stronger states to see production disrupted by criminal activity, strikes, protests, and other manifestations of social unrest. Strikes and protests have disrupted production in major energy suppliers such as Azerbaijan, Ecuador, and Nigeria, in some cases causing significant spikes in global oil prices.

In Venezuela in 2002–2003, a general strike sparked by opposition to President Hugo Chavez's authoritarian policies—including his replacement of many of the leaders of Petroleos de Venezuela S.A. (PDVSA), the state oil firm, with political allies—caused oil production to fall from 3.2 million barrels per day to less than 100,000 barrels per day. In what Goldman Sachs analysts called "one of the largest shocks in the history of the oil market," some 3 percent of global production went offline, and oil prices spiked 26 percent within weeks. Half of PDVSA's workers took part in the strikes—and were later fired, costing PDVSA most of its managerial and technical expertise. The *Economist* estimated that at least 400,000 bpd in production capacity were permanently lost, as lack of maintenance during the strike ruined critical infrastructure.[47]

As the discussion on the "resource curse" below describes, an influx of oil revenues may itself exacerbate inequality and intensify grievances against oppressive regimes in weak, poor states. In Chad, more than 32,000 civil servants went on a months-long strike in mid-2007, demanding that the government use its oil revenues to increase their salaries. In Algeria, the world's fourth-largest gas exporter, youth unemployment has reached 75 percent and frequent riots "risk triggering wider protests against a political elite slow to turn unprecedented oil wealth into jobs and homes."[48] Likewise, in Pakistan's Baluchistan province, grievances against the government have been fueled by growing poverty and unemployment, despite the enormous revenues from Baluchistan's gas fields—which mostly accrue to the central government. An abrupt end to a resource bonanza can also place strains on regimes that have in the past been able to defuse political pressures through extensive patronage, potentially leading to societal upheaval.

The Index suggests that weak-state energy producers are indeed vulnerable to social unrest. At least twenty-two of the thirty producer states in the bottom three quintiles of the Index have experienced some form of violent social protest in the last decade, including food riots, rampant criminality, and economically motivated unrest. Oil sector strikes have occurred in at least seven of these states (including Iraq, Chad, Nigeria, Gabon, India, Venezuela, and Azerbaijan),[49] although most of these have not caused major disruptions to output. These countries may also be vulnerable to social upheaval due to high levels of income inequality and poor social welfare scores. One-third of the weak-state producers for which data is available are characterized by high or significant inequality (bottom three quintiles), while nearly two-thirds rank in the bottom two quintiles for social welfare scores.

Criminality

Theft of oil and gas from pipelines is not uncommon in weak-state energy suppliers or transit countries. The term "oil bunkering" refers to the practice whereby criminal networks siphon off large volumes of oil from pipelines for sale on the international market. In some countries this enterprise occurs on a shocking scale: the UN Office on Drugs and Crime (UNODC) estimates that smuggling accounts for as much as 35 percent of Nigeria's crude oil exports—some 300,000 barrels a day; others have put the figure as high as 500,000 barrels per day, amounting to a black market bonanza of more than $20 billion per year for criminal organizations.[50]

Given the sophistication required for such illegal schemes, they generally require cooperation of government officials and international syndicates. The UNODC believes that oil bunkering syndicates in the Gulf of Guinea, for instance, draw in West Africans but also Moroccans, Venezuelans, Lebanese, French, and Russians. In addition to driving up costs for energy firms, deterring investment, and removing significant quantities of fuel from legal markets, oil bunkering may finance terrorist groups (as in Iraq), broader criminal networks (as in Mexico), or insurgents (as in the Niger Delta region)—further feeding the cycle of instability and energy insecurity.

Intuitively, oil bunkering would seem most likely in states (or regions of states) with high rates of corruption, weak security services, and low social welfare. But the lawlessness of states experiencing conflict may be the biggest factor in enabling the large-scale theft of oil. Bunkering in Nigeria occurs mostly in the oil-rich but war-torn Rivers State. Perhaps 3 percent of the petrol passing through Colombia's largest refinery is stolen. And Russian officials have accused Chechen rebels of stealing up to one-third of the oil produced in the region, using the profits to purchase weapons.[51]

Theft and bunkering of oil and petroleum products have likewise been common in Iraq, where the government still has limited capacity to safeguard the country's 4,000 miles of pipeline or the rest of its energy infrastructure. Al-Qaeda in Iraq (AQI) and other insurgent groups have hijacked fuel trucks, demanded protection money from those transporting and selling fuel, and even set up their own stations to sell stolen gasoline. Indeed, by early 2008, bunkering and oil racketeering had emerged as AQI's most lucrative "business," earning the organization an estimated $2 million per month. But insurgents are by no means the only actors involved in the trade—they are joined by criminal gangs, tribes, and corrupt Iraqi officials. The consequences for Iraq's security and economic development have been devastating. The Defense Department estimated in 2008 that, in recent years, some 70 percent of the production of Iraq's Baiji refinery (which supplies gasoline, kerosene, diesel, and other fuels to eight Iraqi provinces) vanished into the black market. The total value was some $2 billion.[52]

Poor Governance and Energy Insecurity

If weak energy-producing or transit states are unreliable suppliers for the reasons listed above, energy-rich but poorly governed states are also unattractive targets for investment—limiting exploration and production, and thus the ability of these countries to supply global markets. Inefficient or corrupt bureaucracies, weak rule of law, and misguided policies may deter investors in even the most energy-abundant states, and are particularly dissuasive in countries where reserves are potentially substantial but unproven. Although emerging economies such as China and India are increasingly willing to invest in countries shunned by Western firms, they too face problems in poorly governed states that have delayed or limited their access to energy resources.

Weak states (and some moderately strong states) frequently have bloated bureaucracies and inferior tax regimes, economic policies, and business models, all of which tend to limit foreign investment. Of thirty energy-producing states in the Index's bottom three quintiles, nineteen (63.3 percent) score in the bottom two quintiles for government effectiveness. Bureaucratic inefficiencies have delayed the development of Kazakhstan's Kashagan oil field—potentially the third-largest in the world—by at least two years. Exorbitantly high tax rates and government obstacles have held up construction on the Uzbek portion of a pipeline to supply Central Asian gas to China, and in 2007, the Chinese firm Sinopec pulled out of a $110 million oil exploration deal in Uzbekistan due to unfavorable terms. One senior Western oil executive said, "'No U.S. company would ever agree to invest in Uzbekistan due to excessive government involvement in many key industries and prohibitively high taxes."[53] And in Nigeria, "a near-paralysis in government decision-making...is blocking investment vital for the [oil] industry's long-term health."[54]

Corruption is common in weak states, and may be exacerbated by natural resource revenues. Of the thirty energy producers in the Index's bottom three quintiles, twenty (66.7 percent) rank in the bottom two quintiles for corruption. Corruption and lack of transparency drive up the cost of business for foreign companies and impede the development of a country's energy sector, as officials siphon off oil revenues for themselves rather than investing in exploration, technological innovation, and infrastructure improvements. Indonesia, for instance, is potentially a major oil and gas producer, but has been a net importer of oil since 2005 (and was even forced to withdraw from OPEC in 2008). Although Indonesia is not a critically weak state, its combination of high corruption and weak rule of law (scoring in the second-lowest quintile on both indicators) has made oil companies wary of doing business in the country. Aging infrastructure and lack of new investment have taken a toll on Indonesia's production, which declined from a high of approximately 1.5 million barrels per day in the mid-1990s to only 860,000 barrels per day in April 2008.[55]

Of the thirty producer states in the bottom three quintiles of the Index, twenty-one (70.0 percent) rank in the bottom two quintiles for rule of law. Countries with weak rule of law are risky investment environments, given the possibility that their governments will appropriate foreign firms' assets or otherwise obstruct their operations. Countries that have threatened to expropriate or have actually appropriated firms' assets have driven up oil prices, both by reducing investment and production, and by increasing fears of future expropriations and supply disruptions. Recent years provide multiple examples (see box 5.2).

In poorly governed states where state-owned companies have primary control of a country's oil and gas resources, corruption, cronyism, and weak rule of law may have severe consequences for the efficiency of the energy sector, limiting output as well as needed investments. Uzbekistan's gas sector, for instance, is badly mismanaged; the lack of investment in the country's decrepit gas transport and distribution system caused the loss of some 20 billion cubic meters per year in the 1990s. Western companies have long criticized the "political interference, embezzlement, bureaucracy and incompetence" of Nigeria's National Petroleum Company (NNPC). Largely as a result of these problems, the NNPC has failed "to meet its share of development costs" for joint operations with Western companies such as Shell and Chevron, causing infrastructure problems and threatening long-term supply.[56] However, these problems are also evident in countries that are not critically weak, including Russia, Iran, and Venezuela—which together possess more than 20 percent of the world's oil reserves and about 45 percent of its gas reserves. For similar reasons, production in all three countries is declining (see "The Resource Curse," below).

Partly as a result of poor governance, there has been significant underinvestment in energy-producing developing countries, further exacerbating tight global supplies and contributing to higher energy prices. Of the thirty energy producers in the bottom

---

Box 5.2: Examples of Weak Rule of Law, Underinvestment, and Energy Insecurity

Ecuador: In 2006, the left-wing government of President Rafael Correa of Ecuador (which scores in the second-lowest quintile for corruption and the rule of law) unilaterally abrogated existing production contracts, adopting a new hydrocarbon law that compels foreign oil companies to channel a larger share of revenues to national coffers.

Venezuela: President Hugo Chavez has pressured foreign oil companies to accept higher tax rates and turn over controlling shares in their projects to the state oil company, PDVSA. Companies were often compensated at amounts well below their initial requests. ConocoPhillips, which refused to cede its shares, has reportedly lost more than $4.5 billion, and as of 2009 was still pursuing legal redress.

Kazakhstan: In January 2007, the Kazakh government pressured an international consortium developing the Kashagan oilfield—potentially one of the world's largest—to cede shares to the national oil company, Kazmunaigas, at about half their market value. Later that year, the government passed legislation allowing it to annul natural resource contracts and stripped Italy's ENI (which had led the consortium) of its operating license.

Chad: In August 2006, President Idriss Déby threatened Chevron and the Malaysian firm Petronas with expulsion if they did not pay an additional $100 million in taxes. Although the companies were eventually allowed to stay in Chad, Déby's apparent willingness to shut off production (about 186,000 bpd) sent shivers through oil markets.

Nigeria: Moves by the Nigerian government to "recoup" $1.9 billion in supposedly unpaid revenues and taxes—which some Western analysts say amount to the government's "rewriting the rules and applying them retroactively"—have had a chilling impact on Western investment in the country's oil sector.[57]

---

three quintiles of the Index, at least eleven (36.7 percent) are known to be producing below capacity.[58] The consequences for global energy markets can be dire. The International Energy Agency (IEA) warns, "The immediate risk to supply is not one of a lack of global resources but rather a lack of investment." Likewise, many analysts are concerned that, while there may be ample global reserves of oil, underinvestment means that "we are running out of access to oil."[59]

The Resource Curse: Exacerbating State Weakness and Energy Insecurity

The perverse effects of natural resource abundance in the developing world are well documented. From Azerbaijan to Venezuela, research has demonstrated that nonrenewable resource abundance—coming from oil, gas, and mining—is often exploited for personal profit by state leaders and private corporations, undermining key institutional capacities in already weakened states. It has also bred violent conflict, authoritarianism, economic decline, and environmental degradation. The so-called "resource curse" undermines U.S. development and foreign policy goals around the world. By contributing to instability in weak, energy-producing states, the resource curse threatens U.S. energy security. As energy experts Jan H. Kalicki and David L. Goldwyn note, "America urgently requires new political and economic strategies to address [the] root causes of instability at a time when it must still depend on unstable or badly governed nations for oil."[60]

Petro-Politics

The correlation between dependence on energy resources and undemocratic governance—particularly in weak states—is clear. According to democracy expert Larry Diamond, "There are 23 countries in the world that derive at least 60 percent of their exports from oil and gas and not a single one is a real democracy." In Freedom House's 2007 "Freedom in the World" rankings, more than half of the world's top twenty-five oil producers (and half of the top twenty gas producers) are classified as "not free." Of Freedom House's eight "worst of the worst" countries in 2008, five are energy producers: Burma, Libya, Sudan, Turkmenistan, and Uzbekistan.[61] These trends led journalist Thomas Friedman to coin what he calls the "First Law of Petro-Politics," which says: "As the price of oil goes up, the pace of freedom goes down. As the price of oil goes down, the pace of freedom goes up."[62]

These findings are also borne out by an analysis of the Index of State Weakness. Of thirty energy-rich states in the bottom three quintiles of the Index, twenty-four (80 percent) rank in the in the last two quintiles on political performance, with eleven (36.7 percent) in the bottom quintile. Seven of the world's top fifteen oil producers (and five of the top fifteen gas exporters) are found in the bottom two political quintiles on the Index. This does not include Saudi Arabia, Kuwait, or the United Arab Emirates, none of which is democratic. There are numerous hypotheses for why this correlation exists. Experience shows that massive hydrocarbon revenues frequently eliminate a critical link of accountability between a government and its citizens. Easy resource revenues from petroleum reduce a government's incentive to tax productive activity and, in return, to create effective bureaucratic structures capable of delivering public goods. Natural resource revenues facilitate corruption and the development of patronage networks that consolidate the power of entrenched elites. Staggering levels of wealth flow to the highest levels of government and regime supporters, sharpening inequality and stifling political reform. Natural resource rents also enable dictators to spend disproportionately on the military sector and smother opposition groups.[63] The resource curse thus enables—and gives international leverage to—those weak states that routinely undermine democratic principles. It may also contribute to global energy insecurity since, as described above, corruption and authoritarian governance tends to discourage foreign investment and undermine the efficiency of a country's energy sector.

Resource Rents and Slow Growth

Oil and gas resources have also been linked to slow economic growth rates, inequality, and poverty. The Weak States Index corroborates these findings, with nearly half (fourteen of thirty) of weak state producers scoring in the bottom two economic quintiles, and sixteen of the thirty ranking in the bottom two quintiles for social welfare. One reason may be so-called "Dutch Disease," whereby resource revenues raise a country's exchange rate, hurting competitiveness in non-resource sectors. Other factors may include the volatility associated with commodity prices, which can have especially negative impacts on weak-state economies; and the underdevelopment of agricultural and manufacturing sectors during boom periods in resource-based economies.[64]

As described above, weak energy-producing states are especially likely to suffer from high levels of corruption. Thus, even when oil abundance does produce high growth rates, it too often benefits only a few corrupt elites rather than translating into higher living standards for most of the population. Oil-rich Angola has had one of Africa's highest growth rates since 2005, averaging 17 percent annually—yet its Human Development Index score (a miserable 0.49) and infant mortality rates are worse than the averages for Sub-Saharan Africa. Chad has grown at 9–10 percent in recent years, and Equatorial Guinea has grown on average 23 percent annually for the past decade, yet both countries' populations are among the poorest in the world.[65] The resource curse undermines U.S. development spending and gives leverage to openly corrupt, even kleptocratic countries. For instance, in 2006, total U.S. economic assistance to Nigeria totaled $185.6 million.[66] Meanwhile, the United States imported roughly 1.1 million barrels per day from Nigeria in 2006. With an average oil price of $66 per barrel in 2006, the United States thus spent some $26.5 billion on Nigerian oil, or roughly 140 times the amount of its foreign aid. In a particularly egregious example of the ways in which oil wealth can undermine donor assistance, Chad has flagrantly violated its obligations to the World Bank, which in 1999 agreed to help finance part of the Chad-Cameroon pipeline on the condition that the government use most of the revenues on development projects. In fact, Chad's government used the revenues primarily for military purposes, leading former World Bank President Paul Wolfowitz to freeze Bank loans to Chad. The pipeline project—meant to be a poster child for how the international donors could work with private companies to ensure that Africa's oil benefited its people—instead turned into a major embarrassment.

Some observers fear that high global energy prices will only reinforce poor governance in energy-producing states. Rising demand in emerging economies means that even when Western firms eschew investment in countries such as Sudan or Iran, companies from China, India, Malaysia, and Russia will happily take their place. As Chinese firms have moved into places like Chad, Sudan, Angola, Venezuela, and Burma, they have rarely imposed the sorts of conditions that Western donors do, or felt constrained by the potential for negative press as Western firms might. For instance, no Chinese firms participate in the Extractive Industries Transparency Initiative (EITI), designed to combat corruption and improve governance in resource-rich countries. China's state-owned energy companies can draw on Beijing's resources to outbid Western competitors, and China has offered funding to governments in order to obtain concessions. For these reasons Chinese investments have been criticized as "rogue aid" that undermines multilateral assistance programs and threatens Western development agendas.[67]

Resource Wars

As described above, violent conflict in energy-producing or transit states clearly can hurt global energy security. Unfortunately, the very presence of oil or gas resources within developing countries exacerbates the risk of violent conflict, not least by encouraging armed rebellion to secure control over natural resource rents.

The desire to control oil revenues may have motivated a short-lived military coup in Sao Tome and Principe in 2003—which came immediately on the heels of oil discoveries in the country—as well as a failed coup attempt in Equatorial Guinea in 2005. And the list of civil conflicts fought at least in part over control of oil and gas resources seems endless: Iraq, Colombia, Nigeria, Angola, Burma, Bougainville (PNG), the Republic of Congo, Chad, Pakistan (Baluchistan), and Western Sahara, to name only a few. Sudan's long-festering North-South dispute reflected in large part disputes about how to divide the country's oil resources. Other potential trouble spots include the Gulf of Guinea, where the prospect of oil discoveries has elevated a territorial dispute between Gabon and Equatorial Guinea; and the Caspian Sea, where an ongoing dispute among the littoral states over demarcation has prevented development of the region's vast natural gas reserves.

Even relatively stable countries may face prolonged insurgencies in oil-rich regions, from Russia's north Caucasus region to Indonesia's Aceh and Papua provinces. In India's Assam state, which produces about 15 percent of the country's oil, separatists have bombed pipelines and oil infrastructure. Such dynamics could even arise in the relatively strong state of China, currently the world's fifth-largest energy producer, given ethnic unrest and separatist activity in the western province of Xinjiang (the dominant energy-producing region in the country). In recent years, scholars and experts have debated whether the risk of civil war is actually greater in states with abundant natural resources. Econometric studies suggest that the risk of violent conflict does increase significantly when countries depend on the export of primary commodities, particularly oil. Paul Collier and Anke Hoeffler assess that oil exporters are forty times more likely to be engaged in civil war than countries that are not oil-rich, while James Fearon and David Laitin find that countries dependent on fossil fuel revenues are at least twice as likely to experience civil conflict.[68]

Several factors may explain this correlation. First, the prospect of resource rents may provide an incentive to rebel or secede. Second, wealth from resources may enable rebel groups to finance their operations. Third, resource wealth may lead to poor governance, including high levels of corruption and extortion, generating grievances that lead to rebellion.

An analysis of the Index of State Weakness seems to corroborate these findings; of the thirty energy producers in the bottom three quintiles of the Index, eighteen (60 percent) have experienced violent conflict[69] since 1998; nineteen (63.3 percent) rank in the bottom two quintiles for territory affected by conflict; and twenty-one (70 percent) score in the bottom two quintiles for conflict intensity. The upshot: energy resources may make weak states weaker and more violent, reinforcing the insecurity of global energy supplies.

Even where conflicts have little to do with energy, the growing economic and political clout of weak oil and gas producers raises the prospect of civil and regional conflict.

For instance, the government of Azerbaijan is reportedly spending its oil wealth to build up its military, which could lead to heightened instability in the disputed territory of Nagorno-Karabakh. In Chad, President Idriss Déby has used oil revenues to purchase weapons and vehicles for his military. Likewise, states such as Sudan and Equatorial Guinea have leveraged their status as oil producers to gain arms and military hardware from consumer countries. The costs of these conflicts to the United States go far beyond potential disruptions to energy supplies—oil-related conflicts from Sudan to Baluchistan undermine U.S. regional security and development goals.

There are also financial and, potentially, military costs. Of sixteen current UN peacekeeping missions, six are in states and territories where energy resources are at least one factor in ongoing instability: Chad, Sudan (Darfur and South Sudan), Côte d'Ivoire, Western Sahara, and East Timor. The total approved budgets for these operations in 2008–2009 amounted to more than $7 billion, of which the United States pays nearly one-quarter.[70] Past U.S. and UN interventions from Kuwait to Angola have occurred in oil-rich regions. Moreover, with ever-tightening global energy supplies, energy-related conflicts in producing states such as Nigeria could potentially draw in the United States, militarily or otherwise.

The United States has already significantly expanded its naval presence in the Gulf of Guinea, with almost continuous patrols today compared to nearly none as recently as 2004. In 2007, the United States announced the creation of a separate Africa Command—AFRICOM—in recognition of Africa's growing importance as a major source of U.S. oil imports (as well as a front in the fight against terrorism). And although the possibility of a "resource war" between major powers seems remote, tight global supplies may increase the likelihood of consumer nations such as the United States or China intervening in weak-state producers from Africa to Central Asia.

Thus the potential economic and national security costs of the "resource curse" to the United States range from billions of dollars in "wasted" aid to military interventions to higher energy prices from instability in weak-state producers. The evidence suggests that the very presence of oil and gas wealth tends to fuel local grievances, strengthen corrupt regimes, feed instability and conflict, and entrench poverty. If repression, poor governance, and inequality are catalysts for social unrest, political instability, or civil conflict, the prospects for several significant weak-state energy producers would appear bleak. And if the resource curse exacerbates state weakness in even a few of the current "states to watch"—such as Russia, Azerbaijan, Algeria, Iran, Libya, Venezuela, and Indonesia—the consequences for both international stability and global energy security could be alarming.

"STATES TO WATCH" AND U.S. ENERGY SECURITY

Beyond the dangers posed by weak states to U.S. energy security, some of the greatest threats in the short term may emanate from moderately strong states, including several that rank in the middle of the Weak States Index and are labeled "states to watch." Several of these energy-rich states pose an array of diplomatic, political, and security challenges for the United States. They may also suffer from governance gaps similar to those in weak states that inhibit investment in their energy sectors—further undermining global energy security.

The weakest states—for all their growing clout in an era of tight supply—generally lack the economic weight to pressure foreign firms or deliberately affect global energy markets. In fact, since weak states are more likely to depend heavily on revenues from energy exports, they are much less able than stronger states to engage in "petro-blackmail" (threatening to cut off supplies or appropriate firms' assets for political ends). By contrast, relatively stronger states like Russia, Iran, and Venezuela are better able to use their energy resources for political ends. The United States is concerned that potentially anti-American energy alliances could emerge, from South America (among Venezuela, Bolivia, and Ecuador), to the Shanghai Cooperation Organization (among Russia, China, and the energy-rich Central Asian republics), to a "gas OPEC" (among Russia, Iran, Algeria, and Qatar).[71] These relatively strong (if authoritarian) states are the most likely to damage U.S. energy security.

While corruption, economic mismanagement, and weak rule of law limit investment in weak states' energy sectors, these shortcomings are at least as apparent in several energy-rich "states to watch." From Mexico to Russia to Iran, governance problems have driven up the risks and costs of doing business, deterring much-needed investment and technology transfers—with the result that output in these and other critical producer states has declined dramatically in recent years. Not by coincidence, the creeping authoritarianism of the Venezuelan regime and its growing control of the country's energy sector have coincided with a big drop in investment and output.[72] Likewise, Bolivia has privatized and then (re)nationalized its oil industry three times, confusing and likely deterring investors.

Russia is one of the most dramatic cases of how poor governance can exacerbate tight global energy supplies. Despite Russia's status as a major emerging economy and its vast oil and gas reserves, foreign investment remains at a relatively modest percentage of GDP (2.2 percent)—lower than in neighboring Ukraine. This largely reflects high levels of corruption and vagaries in the rule of law. Corruption in Russia has risen dramatically in recent years: from 2000 to 2008, Russia fell from 82nd to 147th in Transparency International's annual corruption index. Under the presidencies of Vladimir Putin and Dmitri Medvedev, the Kremlin has not only asserted national control over the domestic energy industry, but has forced foreign companies to adhere to increasingly onerous regulations.

Since 2006, the government has used tax and environmental inspections and other tactics to pressure BP and Shell to cede controlling shares in major projects to the state oil and gas companies, Rosneft and Gazprom, underscoring the insecurity of property rights in Russia. BP executives have characterized Russian behavior as a form of "legalized mugging," and one expert says Gazprom's aggressive behavior toward companies like BP and Shell has led to a "torpedoing" of private investment in Russia's energy sector. As a result, despite its vast reserves, production has been declining in Russia since 2003. Rex Tillerson, CEO of ExxonMobil, vented his frustration at a June 2008 meeting of the St. Petersburg Economic Forum, stating baldly, "There is no confidence in the rule of law in Russia today."[73]

Poor governance and economic mismanagement have also led to stagnation and inefficiency in Iran's energy sector. Iran sits atop 16 percent of global gas reserves, but more than 60 percent of these resources remain undeveloped, and its gas exports are modest. Experts estimate that with adequate investment, Iranian oil production could increase from 4 million to 7 million barrels per day. Unfortunately, the country's ruling mullahs have shown themselves entirely unwilling to bear the short-term costs of significant investment, instead "diverting oil profits into a vast, inefficient welfare state."[74]

The regime's political decisions have also deterred investment. Foreign oil companies were expelled during the 1979 revolution; although some have since returned, Iran's oil production is still lower today than it was three decades ago. Thanks to tightened sanctions and perceived political risk—as well as corruption and restrictions on foreign firms—foreign investment has been limited. As a result, Iran lacks both the technology and financial resources to sustain or develop its energy infrastructure. (Experts estimate, for instance, that refinery leakage from aging infrastructure may affect as much as 6 percent of total Iranian oil production.[75]) A similar dynamic is at work in Mexico, the world's sixth-largest oil producer, where output is declining rapidly while the government continues to resist much-needed foreign investment.

Stronger states are also better equipped than weaker ones to move toward nationalization of their energy sectors, a worldwide trend in recent years that could pose major problems for U.S. and global energy security. National oil companies (NOCs) now control more than 80 percent of world oil reserves. While some NOCs are well run (e.g., Saudi Aramco, Norway's Statoil), they have generally been slower than private companies to develop new fields and are more likely to have problems with corruption, underinvestment, and political interference—all of which can lead to supply problems.[76]

The relationship between state weakness and nationalization—and the relationship between nationalization and underinvestment—is complicated. On the one hand, the weakest states generally do not have the financial or technological capacity to nationalize oil and gas production (Chad threatened to do so in 2006, but later relented in negotiations with foreign oil firms). Where they exist, national oil companies in weaker states like Angola tend to seek good relations with foreign firms, whose capital and expertise they need. On the other hand, if/when it does occur in poorly governed states, nationalization is more likely to lead to underinvestment in energy infrastructure, inefficiency, mismanagement and, inevitably, declining production.[77]

Unsurprisingly, given the governance problems in Venezuela and Russia, their state energy companies have performed far worse than Norway's Statoil or Brazil's Petrobras. Russia's state oil and gas firms are heavily politicized, inefficient with their capital, and reluctant to invest in better infrastructure. Partly as a result, growing state control of Russia's energy sector has coincided with declining production levels.

A similar pattern can be seen in Venezuela, where the negative output trajectory of PDVSA parallels a decline in governance. For much of its history, PDVSA ranked as one of the most efficient and best-run NOCs in the world. However, in the late 1990s, the Venezuelan government cut PDVSA's investment budget to divert funds for political purposes. This pattern accelerated after Hugo Chavez came to power in 1999 and wrested control over the previously autonomous company, replacing competent and experienced officials with political cronies and diverting tens of billions in oil revenues to further his political goals. The result, by early 2008, was a drop in output of perhaps 25 percent since Chavez came to power. According to Yergin, the dawn of a new era of high oil prices began with Chavez's "drive to consolidate his control over Venezuela's political system, state-owned oil company, and oil revenues." The decline of oil production in Venezuela, "which had been among the most reliable of exporters since World War II," had a greater impact on global oil supplies than the Iraq war. "Venezuela's output has never fully recovered," he says.[78]

Weaker Than They Appear?

The problems that have limited oil and gas output in countries such as Iran, Russia, and Venezuela—corruption, weak rule of law, authoritarian governance—indicate that these states may be weaker than they appear. All three countries actually score low on telling indicators in the Index of State Weakness, making them each a "state to watch." Other significant energy producers, from Kazakhstan to Bolivia to Azerbaijan, are also not weak states as defined by the Index—but are nonetheless vulnerable to some of the problems facing weak states, which could cause future supply disruptions. Experience suggests, moreover, that heavy dependence on fossil fuel revenues tends to exacerbate those governance gaps that already exist.

Overall, countries in the third quintile designated "states to watch"—notably Russia, Azerbaijan, Algeria, Libya, Iran, Venezuela, and Indonesia—account for more than 30 percent of world oil production (about 25.5 million bpd) and nearly one-third of global natural gas production.[79] Major instability in any one of these countries could have a significant impact on global energy markets. (Saudi Arabia, which is not ranked on the Index, nonetheless clearly suffers from weak institutions, autocratic governance, and security problems of its own, which could have enormous consequences for the world economy if they lead to serious unrest.) As table 5.4 indicates, most of the energy-producing "states to watch" have poor political and security scores—possibly the most troubling indicators for energy security, in terms of the likelihood of supply disruptions due to conflict or instability.

The factors that make these countries states to watch, including their over-dependence on energy exports, mean that a dramatic drop in prices could lead to domestic instability. In Russia, where natural resources—mostly oil and gas—constitute 80 percent of exports and nearly one-third of GDP, the global downturn that struck in late 2008 led the Economist to wonder "whether the regime's political control will crack."[80] Likewise in Venezuela, where oil accounts for more than half of government revenues and the state oil company is a major source of funding for social welfare programs, one journalist wrote that with the drop in energy prices, "At stake are no less than Venezuela's economic stability and the sustainability of [Chavez's] rule."[81] If even one of these or other major producer states is beset by serious political turmoil or conflict, the impact on global energy prices could be dramatic.

Table 5.4: Vulnerabilities of Energy-Producing "States to Watch"

Energy-Producing "States to Watch"	Oil production (Bpd)	Gas Production (tcf)	Overall Index Ranking	Economic Score (0 = lowest)	Political Score (0 = lowest)	Security Score (0 = lowest)	Social Welfare Score (0 = lowest)
Algeria	2173.15	3.108	57	6.83	4.27	4.04	9.13
Bolivia	61.64	.436	64	4.64	5.01	7.77	7.34
Russia	9,875.77	22.623	65	7.14	3.81	4.83	9.04
Iran	4,043.41	3.563	66	5.51	3.32	6.91	9.28
Venezuela	2,666.54	1.014	70	6.01	3.76	7.12	8.44
Indonesia	1,043.70	2.606	77	6.46	5.25	5.92	8.34
Azerbaijan	850.40	.206	80	7.85	3.36	7.06	7.89
India	88.53	1.056-	67	6.72	6.72	4.87	6.79
China	3,900.96	1.763	74	6.89	3.69	6.85	8.21

LEGEND:

- Bottom Quintile
- Second Quintile
- Third Quintile
- Fourth Quintile
- Top Quintile

CONCLUSIONS

The impact of weak but energy-abundant states on U.S. and global energy security is modest but growing. Given its desire to move beyond the Middle East for its oil needs, the United States will likely rely more heavily on small, unstable oil producers in coming decades. World energy markets will continue to tighten over the medium term, as the global economy recovers and demand continues to rise in emerging markets. In this context, even short-term supply disruptions can unsettle global energy markets. Such disruptions are especially likely to occur in weak suppliers and transit countries, given their cocktail of vulnerabilities, including corruption, crime, and susceptibility to violent conflict.

The greatest threat to stable energy supplies from (or through) the weakest states may be violence and political instability, which have disrupted supplies from Nigeria to Colombia. Some two-thirds of the thirty weak-state energy producers in the bottom three quintiles of the Index examined here score very poorly (i.e. in the bottom two quintiles of the Index) for territory affected by conflict and political stability and absence of violence. Given the dynamics of the resource curse in developing countries, this trend is likely to continue. Likewise, thirty-five of the weakest states on the Index border an oil or gas producer, transit state, or choke point; conflict or instability in these countries could threaten regional and global energy supplies.

Other security problems generally associated with weak states, however, may be less of a threat to energy security than is typically imagined. Despite the very real problems of terrorism, piracy, and large-scale oil theft, there is little evidence that any of these problems has caused more than temporary disruptions or price shocks. To date, terrorists have only attacked oil installations in three countries: Yemen, Saudi Arabia, and, on a much smaller scale, Algeria. In contrast, the actions of MEND insurgents in the Niger Delta have been truly damaging to the operations of major oil companies, and almost certainly have been a factor in higher global oil prices in recent years.

Beyond the potential problems weak or poorly governed states could pose to global energy markets, the world's growing dependence on their oil undermines other U.S. foreign policy and security goals. Oil bonanzas in states with weak institutions undermine good governance, development assistance, and democracy promotion. Today, more than two-thirds of the thirty weak-state energy producers in the Index's bottom three quintiles rank in the bottom two quintiles for corruption; a full 70 percent score similarly for rule of law. The governance problems of weak-state oil producers could also affect global energy security if they deter investment or lead to social unrest and instability.

But the problems of insecurity, weak rule of law, corruption, and poor governance are hardly limited to the weakest states. They are also present in some of the world's largest oil and gas producers, including Russia, Algeria, Venezuela, Mexico, and Saudi Arabia—and have been factors in driving down investment and output in many of these countries. In fact, it appears that fairly strong states with governance gaps (including several "states to watch") may still pose the greatest threat to U.S. energy security—they are weak enough to face significant challenges to sustained production, and strong enough to use their resources in the pursuit of (often anti-American) political goals.

Rising dependence on oil from weak and failing states promises to have wider, negative ramifications for the United States. Energy dependence means the United States has few cards on the table regarding its foreign policy goals in such countries. In such a circumstance, energy interests can easily crowd out other priorities, from anti-corruption initiatives to economic development. As in the past, such dependence will continue to complicate U.S. democracy promotion by encouraging the United States to cozy up to authoritarian dictators or shore up already unstable regimes in regions like Africa, the Caucasus, or Central Asia. As the United States seeks to diversify its energy supplies away from volatile Middle Eastern and authoritarian countries—and toward weak states—it may find itself exchanging one set of risks for another.

Appendix 5.1: Weak-State Energy Producers: Potential Disruptions to Investment and Supply in Bottom-Three Index Tiers[82]

Country	Index Ranking	Producing Below Capacity[83]	Potential Causes of Disruptions to Production							Potential Causes of Limited or Declining Investment in Energy Sector		
			Security Score	Political Stability/ Absence of Violence	Territory Affected by Conflict	Attacks on Energy Infrastructure since 1998[84]	Social Unrest Since 1998[85]	Social Welfare Score	Inequality	Government Effectiveness	Corruption	Rule of Law
Iraq	4	X	1.63	1.69	3.6	X	X	6.27	–	1.44	1.2	1.58
Sudan	6		1.46	1.69	3.06	X		4.59	–	3.07	2.09	3.27
Cote d'Ivoire	10		3.71	1.92	4.16		X	3.56	6.13	2.24	1.99	2.77
Angola	11		5.32	5.59	6.49	X		1.45	–	2.89	2.06	3.36
Chad	16		6.18	2.56	9.51	X	X	1.21	–	2.39	1.9	3.18
Burma	17		3.96	5.17	5.09		X	7.07	–	1.78	0.27	2.93
R. Congo	20		6.45	4.52	8.47			3.95	–	2.57	2.31	3.46
Equatorial Guinea	25		7.95	6.41	10			1.91	–	2.52	0.79	3.57
Nigeria	28	X	5.37	2.14	10	X	X	5.24	6.33	3.6	1.56	3.42
Cameroon	29	X	7.54	6.25	10		X	4.07	6.13	3.79	2.68	4.09

Country	Rank												
Yemen	30	X	X	6.43	3.53	8.92		X	4.85	8.43	3.67	3.81	4.2
Pakistan	33	X	X	4.69	2.31	9.56		X	6.13	9.02	4.89	2.71	4.65
Turkmenistan	35			7.88	6.14	9.91			6.75	6.92	2.16	1.58	2.95
Uzbekistan	36		X	6.66	2.26	10		X	7.84	7.74	2.78	2.44	2.96
Mauritania	37			6.38	6.1	10			4.24	7.28	4.52	3.8	5.7
Papua New Guinea	40		X	7.45	4.92	9.43		X	4.08	4.83	3.92	2.07	4.33
East Timor	43			7.74	4.48	10	X	X	5.98	—	4.31	2.87	3.72
Colombia	47		X	1.78	3.02	0	X	X	9.11	3.24	6.42	5.04	5.13
Algeria	57		X	4.04	4.7	4.3	X	X	9.13	8.04	5.35	4.47	5.16
Sao Tome & Principe	61			7.95	7.97	10		X	6.12	—	3.85	4.03	5.59
Gabon	63		X	8.36	7.03	10		X	5.94	—	4.56	3	5.26
Russia	65		X	4.83	5.06	6.8	X	X	9.04	7.09	5.13	3.29	4.39
Iran	66		X	6.91	3.86	10		X	9.28	6.46	4.06	3.84	4.66
India	67		X	4.87	4.83	6.32	X	X	6.79	7.73	6.26	5.08	7.33
Venezuela	70		X	7.12	3.9	10	X	X	8.44	5.39	3.81	2.34	3.09
China	74			6.85	5.92	9.29	X	X	8.21	5.65	6.34	4.01	5.79

(continued)

Appendix 5.1: Continued

Index rank	Potential Causes of Disruptions to Production								Potential Causes of Limited or Declining Investment in Energy Sector		
Indonesia 77	X	5.92	4.06	7.29	X	8.34	8.25		5.26	3.23	4.63
Egypt 78		6.55	4.74	8.09	X	9.03	8.23		5.18	4.41	6.87
Thailand 79		5.07	4.46	10	X	8.51	6.67		7.21	4.92	6.95
Azerbaijan 80		7.06	4.29	8.87	7.89	7.8			4.34	2.52	4.52
Totals in bottom 2 quintiles	11 (36.7%)	24 (80.0%)	22 (73.3%)	19 (63.3%)	13 (43.30%)	22 (73.3%)	16 (53.3%)	5 (16.7%)	19 (63.3%)	20 (66.7%)	21 (70.0%)

LEGEND: Index rank

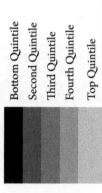

Bottom Quintile
Second Quintile
Third Quintile
Fourth Quintile
Top Quintile

6

INFECTIOUS DISEASE

In the twenty-first century, disease flows freely across borders and oceans....We cannot wall ourselves off from the world and hope for the best, nor ignore the public health challenges beyond our borders.
—*President Barack Obama, May 2009*[1]

There is growing concern that weak and failing states breed new pandemics, thereby endangering global health. Public health has become a fundamental responsibility of the state and a precondition for national security. When fragile states fail to invest in the well-being of their population or to respond to the outbreak of infectious disease, they can become vectors for the spread of disease beyond their borders. As Clive Bell and Maureen Lewis have argued, "failed" or "faltering" states that "cannot or will not perform basic public health functions place the rest of the world at risk."[2] Looking forward, Frederick Burkle predicts that the public health crisis facing many poor countries today "will make state sovereignty a moot point when a fragile nation-state epidemic accelerates...into a continent-wide pandemic."[3]

Claims that weak states today pose the greatest threat to global health seem reasonable. These countries generally lack the resources and institutional capacity to ensure that their citizens have access to even minimal health care—let alone to prevent, detect, and respond to major outbreaks. Not surprisingly, many of the poorest and weakest states—particularly in sub-Saharan Africa—are also those most affected by infectious diseases, from malaria to tuberculosis to HIV/AIDS. Many of the most deadly emerging diseases of recent years, including HIV/AIDS, have originated in very weak states. Moreover, rampant disease is believed to further weaken already fragile states, depleting human capital, intensifying poverty, and in some cases exacerbating insecurity—all of which carry economic and security costs to the region and the world. The result is a "reciprocal spiral dynamic" between weak state capacity and the spread of infectious disease.[4]

And yet, despite the tragic effects of infectious disease in the developing world, the causal link between state weakness and the threat of infectious disease is less clear than often imagined. To begin with, a host of ecological, cultural, and other factors—beyond the question of state fragility—determine the prevalence of certain types of infectious disease. Second, the evidence suggests that only certain kinds of diseases incubated in particular weak states present a serious transnational threat—and many critical diseases are not concentrated in weak states. It is true that corruption, lack of transparency, and insufficient will to tackle public health problems are major enabling factors in the spread of disease. But such deficiencies in both capacity and will can affect stronger developing countries—which are more integrated into the global economy—as well as the weakest states. Finally, the chapter argues that there is little evidence that infectious disease actually leads to violence or state collapse. These findings are not a counsel to ignore the heavy global burden of endemic diseases, but rather a call to prioritize and coordinate the allocation of resources in the fight against infectious disease.

THE GLOBAL THREAT OF INFECTIOUS DISEASE

Historically, infectious disease has posed an existential threat to countless civilizations, spreading across continents without regard to the boundaries of states or empires. The plague that struck Athens during the Peloponnesian War nearly brought the Athenian empire to its knees in a single year—something it took the Spartans twenty-eight years to accomplish. The Black Death (bubonic plague) wiped out one-third of Europe's population in the fourteenth century. The Spanish influenza of 1918 killed tens of millions worldwide—by conservative estimates, some 2 percent of the world's population at the time (and twice the total AIDS toll from the past twenty years).[5]

Yet until recently, most national security practitioners have treated health principally as a domestic policy issue and, internationally, as part of the humanitarian enterprise, subordinate to hard-nosed geopolitics. This neat distinction has largely evaporated as accelerating globalization has blurred the line between domestic and international affairs, while threats from infectious diseases and bioterrorism make clear that we live in an "epidemiologically interdependent world."[6] As never before, the status of public health in any particular state is viewed not only as an indicator of local governance but of vulnerability to pathogens of potentially global significance. Improving global public health is critical to advancing U.S. goals, including protecting U.S. citizens, ensuring global economic growth, alleviating poverty, and advancing human rights.

Globalization and Infectious Disease

Humanity is currently experiencing its fourth great wave of infectious disease. Ten millennia ago, the agricultural revolution precipitated a massive outbreak of epidemic disease. A more sedentary lifestyle, higher population density, closer proximity to domesticated animals, and the appearance of parasitic species (dogs, rodents, insects) in human settlements enabled more pathogens to jump between species. A second great wave crested during classical antiquity, as commercial and military contact among major centers of civilization exposed formerly isolated communities to new diseases and created new vectors (rats, fleas) for the spread of epidemics across the Mediterranean and Asia. The third phase occurred after 1500, as explorers, conquerors, and colonists from Europe brought new pathogens to the Americas, Africa, and Australasia (and sometimes back again), often with devastating results.[7]

At least thirty-nine previously unknown disease agents have emerged or evolved since 1969, including HIV/AIDS, SARS, and the Ebola virus. At the same time, more than twenty well-known pathogens that had been suppressed—including tuberculosis, malaria, and cholera—have re-emerged and spread, often in more virulent and drug-resistant forms. Moreover, "the dynamics of industrialization, globalization, population growth, and urbanization" are facilitating the global spread of infectious disease on a potentially unprecedented scale.[8]

Thus, in recent years, it has become commonplace to say that infectious disease represents a growing threat to the United States and the international community. In 1995, President Clinton's Committee on International Science, Engineering, and Technology first called infectious disease a national security threat. A groundbreaking 2000 report by the National Intelligence Council (NIC) stated that new and reemerging diseases "will endanger U.S. citizens at home and abroad, threaten U.S. armed forces deployed overseas, and exacerbate social and political instability in key countries and regions in which the United States has significant interests." Subsequently, the NIC identified a global pandemic as the single most important threat to the world economy. In recent years, outbreaks of avian influenza, SARS, and the swine flu (H_1N_1) have launched the issue of infectious disease into the headlines—and into the first tier of national security issues. Some experts estimate that a major avian flu epidemic could cause deaths on a scale comparable to the 1918 pandemic.[9]

In addition to the direct threat posed to American lives, infectious disease can have indirect consequences for international security, accelerating instability and undermining the resilience of afflicted states to cope with exogenous shocks, from recession to famine. Experts point to HIV/AIDS, in particular, as an example of a disease that can decimate labor forces and weaken social capital; undermine the readiness of security forces; engender antagonism among diverse groups; further erode already faltering delivery of public services; and reduce the legitimacy of the governing regime in the eyes of its citizens and the international community. According to Andrew Price-Smith, author of *The Health of Nations*, "The relationship between disease and political instability is indirect but real." The stress that outbreaks place on governments may lead to "an increase of chronic sub-state violence and state failure." Price-Smith concludes, "Thus, as disease prevalence increases and the geographical range of pathogens expands, the number of failing states may rise."[10]

Increasing American vulnerability to new and emerging diseases, bioterrorism, and instability in strategic countries due to deteriorating health conditions therein means that public health is critical to U.S. foreign policy goals. Noting that a major flu pandemic could pose a "danger to [the U.S.] homeland," President Bush enacted a multibillion dollar national plan in 2005 and announced the creation of an international partnership to detect and respond to disease outbreaks "anywhere in the world."[11] The 2009 swine flu outbreak prompted the Obama administration to take unprecedented steps to mobilize a national response, drawing on nearly every cabinet agency and requesting $1.5 billion in funding for antivirals, emergency equipment, and vaccine development. Underscoring the potential national security ramifications of a pandemic, swine flu updates were included in the president's daily intelligence briefing throughout the crisis.

The effort to classify infectious disease as a national security issue has not gone unchallenged. Some traditionalists regard this reframing as a blatant attempt by public health officials and others to secure greater resources. Indeed, a bit of perspective is warranted. In broad terms, the trajectory of global public health has moved in a positive direction, with deaths from infectious disease declining over the last century. Nevertheless, infectious diseases remain the leading cause of death worldwide, and are now responsible for 25–26 percent of global deaths (and two-thirds of all deaths in Africa and South Asia), compared to only 0.3 percent from warfare.[12] Among the four horsemen of the Apocalypse, Pestilence still rides tallest in the saddle.

Distinguishing among the Disease "Threats"

In judging the strategic salience of infectious disease, it is appropriate to distinguish among pathogens according to the gravity of the threat they present to the United States and the international system. The *direct* threat posed by a particular infectious disease is a function of four factors: lethality; economic impact of an epidemic; ease and rate of transmission; and potential scope.

Lives Lost. There is huge variation among infectious diseases when it comes to lethality. The deadliest seven infectious diseases, beginning with the most lethal, are acute respiratory infections, HIV/AIDS, diarrheal diseases, tuberculosis, malaria, measles, and Hepatitis B. Despite scary headlines and the public fear they invoke, most new infectious diseases, such as SARS and Ebola, cause few fatalities, numerically speaking.

Economic Impact. Even short-term epidemics can cost billions. The global economic impact of SARS—which killed fewer than 1,000 people—probably exceeded $100 billion. In its first month, the swine flu epidemic cost the Mexican economy alone an estimated $2.2 billion. The economic cost to the United States of a major influenza epidemic has been projected at perhaps $166 billion.[13]

Ease and Rate of Transmission. Some of the most dangerous infectious diseases are those that spread easily and have long, silent incubation periods. Such pathogens include the influenza family of viruses, which can spread very quickly and have the potential to become true pandemics. In contrast, other diseases (such as Ebola) may be horrific on a small scale but are less easily transmitted and therefore pose less of a *global* threat (see box 6.2 below). As HIV/AIDS has shown, certain sexually transmitted infections (STIs) have the potential to become global pandemics. However, they are also naturally slower to spread and (at least in principle) more easily prevented.

Geographic Scope. Waterborne diseases like cholera and dysentery account for 90 percent of infections in developing countries, causing great human suffering and economic losses. At the same time, they typically do not exhibit pandemic potential because of the nature of their transmission (particularly exposure to contaminated water sources) and the relative ease of public health and sanitation interventions in curbing their spread. Similarly, vector-borne diseases tend to be endemic to particular regions, though their geographic range is liable to shift or expand with global warming.

However, even if a particular disease is unlikely to directly affect the United States on a massive scale, it could pose an *indirect* security threat if it destabilizes strategically significant countries where U.S. interests are at stake. Experts have shown that endemic disease is a major factor in economic underdevelopment in many of the poorest countries.[14] In some cases, infectious diseases may also disrupt ecosystems essential to human life, and could in theory contribute to civil unrest or weaken security and political institutions in the worst affected states.

With these criteria in mind, it is useful to consider three categories of infectious diseases as (to varying degrees) prospective national security threats. First, *endemic diseases,* such as malaria, tuberculosis, and measles, continue to plague the developing world and are highly lethal where they occur—and are therefore of concern for humanitarian and development reasons. But they are concentrated in particular regions due to environmental or other factors, and are relatively unlikely to directly affect the United States. A second category of *short-wave pandemics,* such as avian flu, have the potential to rapidly spread worldwide and thus pose a more alarming and immediate national security health threat. Finally, *long-wave global pandemics,* such as HIV/AIDS, may afflict millions, but because their negative effects can take years to materialize, they are easier (at least for developed countries) to prevent and manage.

Endemic Diseases and Drug-Resistant Strains

Many diseases, such as tuberculosis, measles, and polio, barely exist today in the developed world, but they still thrive in many developing countries. Among the most devastating is malaria, which every year kills more than one million people, and affects over 500 million. Malaria can trap families and communities in a downward spiral of poverty: in countries with intense transmission, the disease causes an average loss of 1.3 percent in annual growth, leading to substantial differences in GDP between countries with and without malaria. Endemic malaria can account for as much as 40 percent of public health expenditures and half of all inpatient admissions and outpatient visits.

Other endemic diseases include measles, one of the most contagious diseases in the world and a leading cause of death among young children; and tuberculosis, which caused an estimated 1.6 million deaths in 2005. In both cases, public health interventions are beginning to pay off. Between 2000 and 2006, worldwide deaths from measles fell by 68 percent, and tuberculosis incidence appears to be stable or falling. (However, the declining prevalence of TB is offset by population growth—so the number of new cases annually is still increasing.) Hepatitis B and C also remain highly endemic in the developing world, with some 350 million carriers worldwide. Other, neglected tropical diseases are responsible for about 500,000 deaths annually.[15]

But despite the grim statistics, most do not represent a direct threat to the security of the United States, either in terms of lives lost or significant economic burdens. Instead, bacterial and parasitic diseases thrive in (but are mostly limited to) tropical and under-developed areas. Most malaria victims live in sub-Saharan Africa, although Asia, Latin America, the Middle East, and parts of Europe are also affected. The overwhelming majority (more than 95 percent) of measles deaths occur in countries with per capita gross national income of less than $1,000 and weak health infrastructure. Tuberculosis is concentrated in Africa and Southeast Asia, with more than half a million tubercu-losis deaths in both regions in 2005. Up to 90 percent or more of the world's disease burden from neglected tropical diseases is believed to occur in Africa.[16]

This could change, however, as some of the world's most deadly diseases develop drug-resistant strains and/or spread into new regions (in some cases, as a result of global warming). For instance, malaria has become increasingly resistant to its main treatment, ACT, sparking anxiety among public health experts. Even more concerning is the emergence of multidrug-resistant tuberculosis (MDR-TB) strains, which have been documented in every country surveyed by the World Health Organization (WHO). In the former Soviet Union, the percentage of MDR-TB among new tuber-culosis cases approaches or exceeds a shocking 20 percent. Additionally, some 500,000 cases of extreme drug-resistant tuberculosis (XDR-TB), a virtually incurable form of the disease, have been reported across forty-five countries. The real potential for wide-spread drug-resistance among malaria, tuberculosis, and hepatitis qualifies these particular diseases as international security threats—although perhaps not (yet) the highest-priority ones.[17]

Potential Global Pandemics

Of greatest concern to U.S. public health experts and national security officials are a limited number of diseases with the potential to develop into pandemics—that is, worldwide epidemics. A pandemic occurs when a novel strain of a virus emerges, to which humans have little or no immunity and which can be transmitted in an efficient and sustained manner. These are primarily emerging diseases, most of which are zoo-noses (i.e., an infectious disease transmitted from animals to humans). Most of the catastrophic pandemics that have decimated humanity have been zoonoses, including yellow fever, plague, tuberculosis, smallpox, typhoid fever, HIV, and influenza.[18] In considering the security implications of infectious disease, it is worth examining the origins and impact of two different kinds of pandemics: short-wave/rapid-onset pan-demics, and long-wave phenomena.

Short-wave Pandemics. Certain short-wave, rapid-onset diseases pose possibly the greatest pandemic threat to the United States, given their high rates of lethality and quick transmission rate. Such diseases have the potential to overwhelm national public health systems and, in extreme cases, could lead to the breakdown of security and other state functions.

The emergence and rapid spread of Severe Acute Respiratory Syndrome (SARS) illustrates the challenge of battling infectious diseases in an increasingly globalized world. A new coronavirus to which humans have little immunity, SARS first emerged in China in late 2002. Within six months it had spread to twenty-nine countries, killing more than 900 people. In part because it does not transmit easily from person to person, SARS was relatively quickly contained and killed far fewer people than die each year from common maladies such as pneumonia and flu. Nevertheless, the economic impact was devastating. In East Asia, SARS brought tourism to a standstill and drastically reduced trade, costing the regional economy $20–25 billion. Globally, the direct and indirect costs of the epidemic were "clearly in excess of $100 billion."[19] Today SARS is contained but not eradicated, and there is no vaccine for a disease that could well mutate into a more virulent and lethal form.

But the most worrisome rapid-onset disease with pandemic potential is influenza, which is unmatched when it comes to potential for massive death, economic dislocation, and political instability. The most virulent pandemic of modern times was the so-called "Spanish flu" of 1918–1919, which affected 25–30 percent of the world's population, resulted in an estimated 20–100 million deaths, and caused life expectancy worldwide to drop by ten years or more. In destructive power, the Spanish flu surpassed in one year what the Black Death accomplished in the better part of a century, or that HIV/AIDS wrought in its first twenty-five years. There were more than 500,000 deaths in the United States alone—more Americans than died in the two World Wars, the Korean War and the Vietnam War combined. Were an epidemic similar to Spanish flu to hit the United States today, the U.S. government predicts, at least 90 million Americans would become ill; some two million could die.[20]

Although there is no way to predict precisely when it will strike, most epidemiologists and public health experts consider another flu pandemic "inevitable," even "imminent."[21] Notwithstanding concerns over the recent outbreak of the H1N1 virus (see box 6.1), the most likely source of a virulent, highly contagious strain of influenza originates in birds. In recent years, national security and public health officials have overwhelmingly focused on the H5N1 strain of the Influenza A virus, which first emerged among chickens in China's Guangdong province in 1997. By late 2007, some sixty countries had confirmed H5N1 outbreaks in either animals or humans, including drug-resistant "z" and super-virulent "z+" strains of the virus. So far H5N1 has not demonstrated sustained interhuman transmissibility, but public health officials fear that it will eventually mutate to do so. If H5N1 does acquire this greater transmissibility, it will probably lose some virulence in the process—but this will not necessarily be good news, since diseases that kill half of their victims quickly burn out. The WHO has reported a mortality rate of 72 percent for H5N1, compared with a 2.5 percent rate for the Spanish flu strain.[22]

Although fears of a global influenza pandemic were not borne out during the 2005–2007 avian flu outbreak or the 2009 "swine flu" episode, complacency is hardly warranted. Despite advances in understanding the virus and stockpiling medicine, the world as a whole remains generally unprepared to cope with such a pandemic. The Congressional Budget Office has estimated that in the United States alone, a major flu

---

Box 6.1: H1N1

In March 2009, a new strain of influenza known as H1N1 emerged among Mexican pigs, causing several deaths and prompting a worldwide mobilization against a potential "swine flu" pandemic. The virus quickly spread to more than thirty countries, mostly in Europe, Asia, and North America, infecting some 6,500 people within two months. Hundreds of cases were reported in the United States. For the first time, the WHO raised its warning level to Phase 5, indicating a potential "imminent pandemic." In Mexico, which was hardest hit by the outbreak, tourism ground to a halt and officials effectively shut down Mexico City for five days. During the worst of the crisis, Mexico may have lost as much as $145 million per day.[23] Twenty countries (including Haiti, which rejected food aid from Mexico) banned certain agricultural and livestock exports from the worst-hit countries, including the United States.

To date, H1N1 has proved less deadly than feared—with mortality rates actually lower than for ordinary, seasonal influenza strains, which kill some 30,000 people annually in the United States. Nonetheless, as many health experts were quick to point out, the devastating 1918 influenza pandemic was also initially mild, only to be followed by a much deadlier second wave. Concerns remain that H1N1 could further mutate or combine with other strains in a drug-resistant form. As WHO Director-General Margaret Chan pointed out, H1N1 "may come back...the world should prepare for it."[24]

---

pandemic could kill between 100,000 and 2 million, and result in a loss of 1–4.25 percent of GDP. Poor countries would be hit much harder, with an influenza pandemic on the scale of 1918 killing 62 million people worldwide, 96 percent in the developing world.[25]

Economically, "a [flu] pandemic would trigger a reaction that would change the world overnight."[26] Thanks to modern technology and just-in-time commerce, the global economy is arguably more vulnerable to a major pandemic than ever before. Travel restrictions, quarantines, medical care, and productivity losses could conceivably bring economies to a standstill as workplaces, schools, and public facilities are shut (as in fact occurred on a relatively minor scale in Mexico during the 2009 swine flu outbreak). By some recent estimates, a pandemic on the scale of the 1918 outbreak could result in a 4.8 percent drop in global GDP—a loss of more than $3 trillion.[27]

Given its potential to kill millions and hobble the international economy, a full-bore influenza or other rapid-onset epidemic would place unprecedented stress on leaders, institutions, and communities. In some nations, mounting death tolls and widespread panic could conceivably undermine political authority. Internationally, diplomatic tensions would rise, particularly over access to stockpiles of medication and vaccines. A pandemic could weaken global security by reducing the capacity of militaries, UN peace operations, and police forces worldwide—not to mention infecting world leaders and decimating civil services. Such a prospect is terrifying (and perhaps overly alarmist), but plausible nonetheless. Despite improved contingency and response initiatives worldwide, "no nation can erect a fortress against influenza—not even the world's wealthiest country."[28]

Long-wave Pandemics. Of serious but less immediate concern to U.S. security are long-wave pandemics that have the potential to kill large numbers of people but over a longer period of time. Possibly the most compelling global health challenge the international community confronts today is Acquired Immune Deficiency Syndrome (AIDS), a disease caused by the human immunodeficiency virus (HIV). There is no known cure for HIV/AIDS, which by 2007 had killed more than 25 million people worldwide. In January 2000, the UN Security Council declared the HIV/AIDS virus a "risk to stability and security" in Resolution 1308, marking the first time a global public health issue had been so designated.

Scientists have traced HIV/AIDS to a type of chimpanzee in West Africa, speculating that the virus jumped to humans who hunted the animal for food and came into contact with chimpanzee blood. It then spread gradually to other parts of the world, first attracting widespread attention in the United States in 1981. At the height of the crisis in the mid-1980s, some 150,000 people in the United States were becoming infected every year. In 2002, the NIC published an influential report, *The Next Wave of HIV/AIDS*, describing how the epidemic was globalizing—moving rapidly into Eurasia, including Russia, China, and India.

Indeed, assessments of the epidemic's impact have often tended toward the apocalyptic. As Laurie Garrett wrote in 2005, "Areas of the world that are now witnessing explosive epidemics or are in their second or third wave of HIV infection may well find themselves harder hit—and more deeply transformed—than Europe was by the Black Death." Other respected observers have echoed this sentiment.[29] In late 2007, however, UNAIDS conceded that it had overstated the extent of the epidemic, lowering its estimate for people living with the HIV virus worldwide from 39.5 to 33.2 million. The agency also concluded that the rate of new infections had actually peaked between 1998 and 2001. Few any longer predict an African-style epidemic in Asia.[30]

Despite these downward revisions, the statistics remain staggering. Experts estimate that in 2007, some 2.1 million died of the disease—equivalent to 5,750 deaths a day—and another 2.5 million became infected. Africa has been hardest hit: AIDS is largely responsible for the decline in life expectancies in some thirty-five African countries, most dramatically in Kenya (from 69 to 44), South Africa (68 to 48), Nigeria (65 to 46), Zimbabwe (56 to 33), and Zambia (where average life expectancy has dropped 32.4 years.) Although most of the victims are in the prime of their lives, in the worst-affected countries, AIDS accounts for 50 percent of deaths of children under five years old.[31]

While HIV/AIDS represents the greatest global health emergency in modern times and a tragedy of massive proportions, it is less clear that it poses a significant security threat to the United States and the wider international community. Apocalyptic predictions about the strategic ramifications of the disease have not materialized, and there is scant empirical evidence that the pandemic could cause near-term state failure even in the most afflicted countries.[32] Although still a death sentence for most victims, the invention of sophisticated (but expensive) anti-retroviral treatments means that it no longer need be, particularly in the wealthier global North. As a sexually transmitted infection, HIV spreads much more slowly than influenza, tuberculosis, and other infectious diseases, and is therefore more amenable to human intervention, behavior modification, and medical treatment. Finally, even as the disease ravages Africa and exacts a growing toll in Asia, many parts of the world remain relatively insulated from its effects. This analysis should not be read as a counsel of complacency in the face of perhaps the greatest humanitarian catastrophe in modern times, but the long-wave character of the HIV/AIDS pandemic demands humility in predicting the ultimate global consequences of the disease.

While "infectious disease" loosely defined may not merit the "threat" moniker that contemporary conventional wisdom ascribes, a pandemic with a modest degree of lethality could cause death and disruption on a massive scale. Of the three types of emerging infectious diseases discussed here, rapid-onset, easily transmissible pathogens such as influenza are most likely to directly affect the United States. Their relative speed of transmission could disrupt travel and trade, and sow widespread fear and panic in ways that endemic epidemics and long-wave pandemics like HIV/AIDS never

---

Box 6.2: Ebola Virus: How Great a Threat to the United States?

Viral hemorrhagic fevers are among the most fearsome infectious diseases because of their lethality, gruesome effects on the human body, and unpredictable transmissibility, which combine to induce disproportionate panic. The Ebola virus, a highly lethal pathogen that spreads from wild primates to humans, is a case in point. Death rates can exceed 90 percent, and there is no vaccine or cure. The WHO has termed it "one of the most virulent diseases known to mankind."

Ebola epidemics typically start through the eating of infected animals, usually monkeys, and spread quickly via caregivers and refugees fleeing to escape an outbreak. Over the past decade, Ebola outbreaks have occurred in Sudan, Uganda, Gabon, DRC, and South Africa, typically killing the vast majority of victims. The country hit hardest has been the Democratic Republic of the Congo, where the virus was first discovered more than thirty years ago, and where several outbreaks have occurred in recent years.[33]

The potential for an intercontinental jump via an infected airline passenger or transported wild animal, as popularized in Hollywood movies, remains real and increasingly likely given an incubation period of up to twenty-one days before symptoms emerge. At the same time, it is important not to exaggerate the threat posed by Ebola outside immediate outbreak zones. Ebola outbreaks to date have been largely due to inadequate sterilization in the poorly supplied hospitals of some of Africa's weakest states. Unlike airborne viruses such as tuberculosis or influenza, Ebola is transmitted only through contact with bodily fluids or the skin of infected persons or animals. Thus, even if the Ebola virus spread to a developed country, outbreaks would be unlikely to become epidemics.[34] So, overall, the threat to the United States is fairly remote.

have. Although the latter plague many developing countries on a horrific scale, and are devastating on an individual level, they generally do not pose a direct threat to the United States. However, drug-resistant microbial or vector-borne diseases do merit special attention because of their ability to kill millions globally.

EXPLORING THE FRAGILE STATE–INFECTIOUS DISEASE LINK

Given the potential for certain types of infectious disease to endanger U.S. and international security, the claim that fragile states, rather than strong ones, are likely to be the biggest threat to global health is increasingly common. Emerging infectious diseases often originate in "poor, resource-constrained places where it is more difficult to achieve an effective response."[35] Brower and Chalk argue, "Countries that do not pose an obvious military security danger may be the ones most likely to pose a disease risk owing to poorly developed and underfunded public health systems," which enable the rapid spread of disease within—and beyond—their borders.[36]

On the surface, the notion that weak states incubate and facilitate the spread of infectious diseases seems plausible. Most of the previously unknown disease agents that have emerged in recent decades originated in the developing world. Sub-Saharan Africa in particular stands out for shouldering much of the global burden of infectious disease. The region has only 10 percent of the world's population, but 62.5 percent of the world's fifty-six failed, critically weak, and weak states according to the Index of State Weakness—and accounts for 65 percent of all deaths from infectious diseases.[37]

Such linkages have been made outside of Africa, too. According to the WHO, the global eradication of polio depends on eliminating the disease in four countries where the virus remains endemic—India, Nigeria, Afghanistan, and Pakistan.[38] The last three of these are indisputably weak states, and India has pockets of significant weakness. Malaria death rates are thirteen times higher in fragile states than in other developing countries, and nearly half of people living with AIDS are citizens of fragile states. In fact, among countries in the bottom two quintiles of the Weak States Index, an average of 72.4 percent of people lose years of life to communicable disease, versus 29.8 percent of people in the so-called BRIC countries (Brazil, Russia, India, and China) and only 9 percent of Americans.[39]

It is one thing to assert a correlation between state weakness and the prevalence of infectious disease, but tackling the problem in an efficient and effective way requires precisely identifying the gaps in state capacity and/or will that originate or amplify the threat. Clearly, a state's ability to prevent or mitigate the spread of an infectious disease will depend on variables outside its immediate control. These include ecological factors, such as the nation's climate, and the density and demographics of its population. But other variables—such as the quality of the nation's health care infrastructure and delivery system, its performance in monitoring and managing outbreaks, and its transparency in sharing information with local and international authorities—are very much a function of state capacity and will. The following sections turn to these two dimensions of state fragility.

Capacity

States that cannot (or choose not to) invest in primary health care delivery, preventive measures, or response capabilities lack the means to cope with the epidemics currently in their midst—let alone to detect and contain new outbreaks of diseases with the potential to spread across international borders. Overall, the key capacity-related impediments to addressing infectious disease in weak states appear to be inadequate preventive health care services; weak surveillance, monitoring and diagnostic systems; and poor treatment for victims. The first problem vastly expands the pool of potential (and actual) victims by failing to strengthen their immune systems and improve their general health. The second obstacle slows the recognition of a deadly outbreak, allowing a threatening disease to spread quickly. The third problem greatly increases a disease's lethality and transmissibility, exacting an unnecessary human and economic toll.

The National Center for Medical Intelligence has created a typology of countries by health care status. This scheme reveals gross disparities in health care capacity around the globe (see map in figure 6.1). Almost all (90.9 percent) of the countries where health care status is classified as "unsuitable" are critically weak states, according to the Index of State Weakness.[40] To use another measure, in countries ranking in the bottom two quintiles of the Index, only 73 percent of one-year-olds, on average, received the critical DTP3 vaccination versus 85 percent in the BRIC countries and 96 percent in the United States. (A country's DTP3 immunization rate is considered a strong proxy for the reach and effectiveness of its health care system because the vaccine requires repeated contact with the same cohort of patients.)

The poor performance of many weak states in preventing, detecting, and responding to infectious disease typically reflects underlying capacity gaps in four areas: funding, infrastructure, organization, and human resources. Each of these capacity gaps not only means that these states are more likely to experience poor public health and higher mortality rates in general, but also limits their ability to quickly detect and respond to disease outbreaks—with regional and potentially global implications.

Funding

The world's fragile states invest far less than other countries in the health of their citizens. Global disparities in expenditures are startling (see table 6.1). In 2006, the twenty-eight governments ranked in the bottom quintile of the Index of State Weakness spent an average of about $19 per capita annually on health care, compared with $3,074 in the United States. Per capita health care spending appears to be directly correlated with institutional strength: in 2004 public health spending in relatively stronger states in the third, fourth, and fifth quintiles of the Index of State Weakness was about $95, $175, and $300, respectively.[41]

Obviously states cannot support a functional health care system without financial resources. Cash-strapped states struggle to maintain clinics and laboratories, purchase medicine and equipment, and pay health care providers. Beyond threat-

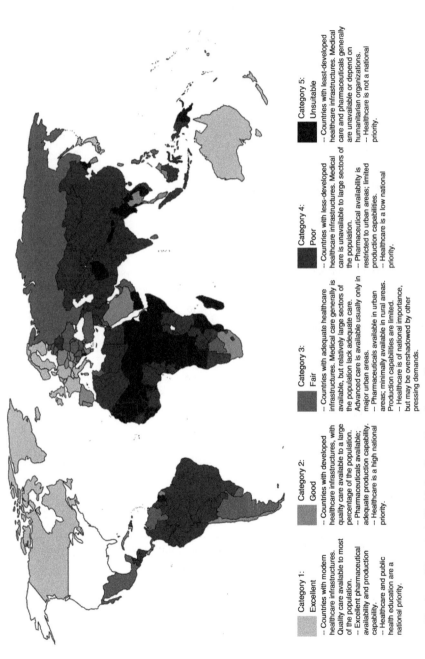

Figure 6.1: Typology of Countries by Health Care Status, December 2002.[42]

Category 1: Excellent
-- Countries with modern healthcare infrastructures. Quality care available to most of the population.
-- Excellent pharmaceutical availability and production capability.
-- Healthcare and public health education are a national priority.

Category 2: Good
-- Countries with developed healthcare infrastructures, with quality care available to a large percentage of the population.
-- Pharmaceuticals available; adequate production capability.
-- Healthcare is a high national priority.

Category 3: Fair
-- Countries with adequate healthcare infrastructures. Medical care generally is available, but relatively large sectors of the population lack adequate care. Advanced care is available usually only in major urban areas.
-- Pharmaceuticals available in urban areas; minimally available in rural areas.
-- Healthcare is of national importance, but may be overshadowed by other pressing demands.

Category 4: Poor
-- Countries with less-developed healthcare infrastructures. Medical care is unavailable to large sectors of the population.
-- Pharmaceutical availability is restricted to urban areas; limited production capabilities.
-- Healthcare is a low national priority.

Category 5: Unsuitable
-- Countries with least-developed healthcare infrastructures. Medical care and pharmaceuticals generally are unavailable or depend on humanitarian organizations.
-- Healthcare is not a national priority.

Table 6.1: Per Capita Public Health Spending in Failed and Critically Weak States

Rank	Country	Overall Score	Per capita public health spending (USD) (2006)
1	SOMALIA	0.52	n/a
2	AFGHANISTAN	1.65	6.00
3	CONGO, DEM. REP.	1.67	2.00
4	IRAQ	3.11	49.00
5	BURUNDI	3.21	1.00
6	SUDAN	3.29	14.00
7	CENTRAL AFRICAN REP.	3.33	5.00
8	ZIMBABWE	3.44	19.00
9	LIBERIA	3.64	6.00
10	COTE D'IVOIRE	3.66	8.00
11	ANGOLA	3.72	62.00
12	HAITI	3.76	29.00
13	SIERRA LEONE	3.77	4.00
14	ERITREA	3.84	4.00
15	NORTH KOREA	3.87	0.00
16	CHAD	3.90	8.00
17	BURMA	4.16	1.00
18	GUINEA-BISSAU	4.18	3.00
19	ETHIOPIA	4.46	4.00
20	CONGO, REP.	4.56	17.00
21	NIGER	4.60	5.00
22	NEPAL	4.61	5.00
23	GUINEA	4.67	3.00
24	RWANDA	4.68	21.00
25	EQUATORIAL GUINEA	4.77	215.00
26	TOGO	4.80	5.00
27	UGANDA	4.86	7.00
28	NIGERIA	4.88	10.00
	UNITED STATES	n/a	3074.00

Source: WHO Statistical Information System (per capita government expenditure on health as percentage (PPP exchange rate), 2006 data).

ening the health of their citizens, funding shortages in weak states have consequences for global health, enabling diseases to flourish. Cambodia is a case in
point: Plagued by corruption and instability, the country spends only $3 per person
per year on health care and suffers from an acute shortage of epidemiologists,
doctors, and nurses. During the 2005 avian flu outbreak, the country's chief of
disease surveillance earned a salary of only $38 a month, shared one Internet line
with his colleagues, and relied on an epidemic alert system consisting of personal
cell phones. The rudimentary level of health and veterinary care in Cambodia has
concerned epidemiologists. In an age of global health threats, notes Klaus Stohr,
the director of the WHO's global influenza program, "The chain is only as strong as
its weakest link."[43]

Infrastructure

Largely due to funding shortages, weak and failing states generally lack the physical
public health infrastructure to ensure the rapid identification, containment, and
suppression of an outbreak. This problem is not always confined to the very weakest
states: In 2000, the NIC implied that a sharp decline in health care infrastructure in the
former Soviet Union was causing a dramatic rise in infectious diseases. Still, as Susan
E. Rice notes, "Of the roughly thirty new infectious diseases that have emerged globally over the past three decades, many—such as SARS, West Nile virus, HIV/AIDS,
hepatitis C, and H5N1 avian flu virus—originated in developing countries that had
rudimentary disease surveillance capability."[44]

Dilapidated infrastructure and ill-equipped clinics without, for example, blood
screening devices, exacerbate epidemics. For instance, Ebola epidemics in Central
Africa have been attributed to "individuals infected with the virus enter[ing] desperately poor hospitals, where dearths of sterilizing equipment and basic protective gear
conspired to offer the virus spectacular opportunities for transmission."[45] Indeed, the
epicenter of an August 2007 Ebola outbreak in Uganda was one of the poorest and
most isolated regions of the country, lacking access to electricity, where a single "over-
stretched hospital treats 65,000 patients with a budget of less than $250,000 in
government funding per year." Some health care workers became infected because
they did not have adequate protective gear.[46]

Infrastructure inadequacies that spawn infectious disease can include poor sanitation, housing conditions, utility access, urban planning, and transportation.[47] Efforts
by WHO and CDC mobile teams in the DRC to suppress Ebola outbreaks were complicated by the decrepit state of DRC's infrastructure after years of war and neglect.[48]
But one of the clearest linkages between weak states and the outbreak of infectious
disease is apparent in the cholera epidemic that swept Zimbabwe in late 2008 and early
2009 (see box 6.4 several pages below). Caused by a bacterial infection spread through
contact with contaminated water and sewage, cholera—which, untreated, can kill half
its victims—frequently appears in squalid slums in the developing world where people
live in extremely close quarters amid mountains of human waste, without access to
clean water. Haiti experienced a similar epidemic in late 2010.

A surveillance network is two-pronged: it depends on first detecting an outbreak, and then correctly diagnosing it. The main capacity gap in many developing countries is on the diagnostic side, as local labs struggle to recognize what kind of pathogen is at the root of an epidemic. Even where local health workers succeed in recognizing a disease outbreak, "many medical facilities in developing countries lack communications equipment and vehicles to alert national officials and transport samples or patients."[49] Another critical gap is the weakness of veterinary services in poor countries, some of which lack the facilities to even test for zoonotic diseases such as bird flu. This is disturbing, since the safest, most cost-effective way to prevent and contain an outbreak of avian influenza in humans is to identify and suppress an epidemic in domesticated animals. In 2006, an H5N1 outbreak was reported in Nigeria's Kaduna State. It spread rapidly across the country, thanks in part to widespread ignorance and misinformation about the disease, treatment, and basic safety measures.[50]

The likelihood of an avian flu pandemic spreading undetected from a very weak state should not be overstated, however. Health officials in developed countries are actually fairly confident that if an outbreak of H5N1 occurs, they will know about—and be able to contain—it fairly quickly, thanks to modern communications technology as well as increased attention to this particular disease. But this does not negate the more general problem of poor surveillance networks in many developing countries and weak states, particularly as it pertains to lesser-known diseases.

Organization: Systems, Policies, and Plans

Having the right infrastructure is important, but it is not nearly enough. Facilities, equipment, supplies, and medicine stocks can be useless if an organizational framework for employing the infrastructure is absent or inadequate. One field expert observes that the health systems in weak states from Afghanistan to Papua New Guinea to Côte d'Ivoire consistently lack policy direction, operational management, coordination, oversight, and critical information.[51] But the problem is not necessarily confined to the weakest states. According to WHO data, of twenty-two target countries for DOTS (Directly Observed Treatment, Short-Course) programs to prevent and treat tuberculosis, "administrative constraints and adverse policy" was a problem in six. This includes some very weak states (Afghanistan, Nigeria, Pakistan, Bangladesh) but also stronger ones (Russia, India).[52]

Many weaker states lack reliable measurements of the resources they devote to public health and the results they achieve. Few of these states, particularly in sub-Saharan Africa, even know how many health workers they have or where those workers are distributed. Thus it can be difficult to determine where the major gaps are in country-level organization to respond to an epidemic. A UN/World Bank bird flu report found in 2007 that 95 percent of the 146 countries surveyed claimed to have a bird flu "plan." But whether all of these states actually have *sound* plans, coordinated with their neighbors and international agencies—let alone the money, manpower, and motivation to implement them in the event of a crisis—is an entirely different question.[53]

The SARS epidemic of 2004 offers a cautionary tale of the potential consequences of poor organization and preparedness. The rapid mobilization of people and resources to detect SARS cases and strengthen quarantines proved critical to controlling the disease, especially in China, Singapore, and Canada. But even most of these relatively developed countries "had not used traditional public health tools such as quarantine and isolation on such a large scale for decades, which slowed the containment."[54] What if, instead of emerging in Hong Kong and spreading to Canada, SARS had originated in Burma and spread to Bangladesh, where health systems are feeble? According to Michael Osterholm, if SARS had hit the developing world its effects would be been exponentially worse: "Instead of one [outbreak] in Hanoi and one in Toronto, we'd have 100 cities like that around the world."[55]

Human Capacity

The best laid plans are meaningless without people to carry them out. But the "talent drain" of health professionals from developing countries is astounding. The problem is particularly acute in sub-Saharan Africa, which bears one-quarter of the global disease burden, but has only 3 percent of the world's health workers. (In Malawi, vacancies in the public health sector approach 90 percent for doctors and 60 percent for nurses.) Today an additional 820,000 doctors, nurses, and midwives are needed in sub-Saharan Africa to provide even the most basic health services. Meanwhile, the number of health workers in sub-Saharan Africa is growing more slowly than the region's population; indeed, the absolute number of physicians could soon begin decreasing. The problem is particularly acute in rural areas.[56]

Insufficient manpower is often compounded by incompetence. In many countries with weak public health systems, the indiscriminate or inappropriate use of antibiotics and other drug therapies is counterproductive, as it can build the resistance of microbes such as tuberculosis and cholera, and enable viral pathogens like malaria to develop drug resistance. Poor medical practices have turned some African hospitals and clinics into "distribution centers" for viral hemorrhagic fevers.[57] The misuse of medical technology can also facilitate the spread of infectious disease via contaminated equipment. A case in point is Egypt, where re-use of needles in hospitals has helped generate the world's highest rate of Hepatitis C. Researchers have also found that due to bureaucratic red tape and other obstacles, in some developing countries health workers may spend only 50–60 percent of their time on productive activities.[58]

Moreover, in large swathes of the developing world, but notably in rural Africa, traditional healers substitute for doctors. These spiritually oriented practitioners generally lack modern medical training, and in some cases their counsel or practices can actually worsen disease outbreaks. In Angola in 2005, an unusually persistent Marburg epidemic that killed 244 of 266 infected people was attributed in part to local healers' use of contaminated needles. In Uganda, it took international officials months to confirm a 2007 Ebola outbreak, thanks to "a variety of logistical and clinical difficulties, not the least being that many locals consult herbalists and traditional healers rather than medical practitioners."[59]

The overall capacity gaps in weak states' health systems—including personnel, infra-structure, and organization gaps—are apparent in assessments by the World Health Organization's DOTS program (see table 6.2).

Will

Poor state performance in delivering public health services is not simply a matter of underlying capacity deficits. It often reflects the unwillingness of defensive, secretive, or isolated regimes to fund public health programs, acknowledge problems, release information, take corrective action, or allow external actors to launch public health interventions. These attitudes impede the containment and suppression of outbreaks, accelerating the rate of infection. From China to South Africa to Central Asia, recent history has demonstrated that "political ignorance, denial, and obduracy compound the risks" of incubating and spreading infectious disease.[60] Unfortunately, in many of the countries at the epicenter of recent disease outbreaks, willful ignorance or misin-formation, a lack of transparency and candor, and resistance to outside intervention have hindered timely and effective response.

Corruption, Undemocratic Governance, and Poor Public Policy

A country's vulnerability is frequently a function of public policy choices, particu-larly the state's investment in basic health services and infrastructure. While donors and NGOs can help pick up the fiscal slack in developing countries, the minimal public health spending by many weak-state regimes raises deeper questions about the state's *will* to serve the public interest. This was graphically evident during a cholera epidemic in Angola in 2006 that sickened 43,000 and killed more than 1,600 people, many of them inhabitants of Luanda's choked shantytowns—where only one in six houses had access to running water. Despite some $16.8 billion in oil revenue in 2006, Angola's corrupt government had not made even modest progress in addressing the country's basic health needs.[61] In this case, the government probably had the resources, but not the will, to bolster its public health sector and prevent the spread of disease.

Logically, it would seem that this problem would be most apparent in undemocratic (or very corrupt) countries. But it can also occur in relatively stable and even fairly well-governed states. For instance, in 2005 fewer than 2 percent of the half million Indians who needed treatment for HIV/AIDS received it. In part, this reflected capacity and resource gaps, but it also pointed to a serious lack of commitment by the state to combat the country's public health crisis (including by improving water and sanitation infrastructure). "AIDS has tested the fragility of a public health system financed by less than one percent of the country's gross domestic product"[62]—a much lower number than for most countries at India's level of development. To be sure, India faces a host of crippling challenges that compete for state funds, but its government nonetheless could—but does not—make the political decision to allocate additional resources to its fight against HIV/AIDS.

Table 6.2: Capacity Gaps in Weak States and Stronger Developing Countries (DOTS Target Countries)

DOTS target country	Index ranking	Lack of qualified staff	Inadequate infrastructure	Weak laboratories
Afghanistan	2	X	X	X
DR Congo	3	X	X	X
Zimbabwe	8	X	X	
Burma	17	X	X	X
Ethiopia	19	X	X	X
Uganda	27	X	X	X
Nigeria	28	X	X	X
Pakistan	33	X	X	X
Cambodia	34	X		
Mozambique	39	X	X	X
Bangladesh	48	X		
Kenya	50	X	X	
Tanzania	55	X	X	X
Philippines	58			
Russia	65			
India	67	X		
China	74	X	X	
Indonesia	77	X		
Thailand	79	X		

(continued)

Table 6.2: Continued

DOTS target country	Index ranking	Lack of qualified staff	Inadequate infrastructure	Weak laboratories
Vietnam	83			
Brazil	99			
South Africa	110	X		X

LEGEND:

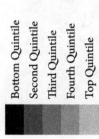

Bottom Quintile
Second Quintile
Third Quintile
Fourth Quintile
Top Quintile

Source: World Health Organization (2004 data).[63]

Ignorance and Misinformation

A state's willful failure to acknowledge an epidemic can condemn its people to death. The refusal until very recently of several South African leaders to acknowledge that the sexually transmitted infection HIV causes AIDS resulted in massive preventable casualties across the country. Even more disturbing were the comments of former South African health minister Manto Tshabalala-Msimang, who recommended olive oil, lemon, beetroot, and the African potato to legions of afflicted South Africans as elements of a healthy diet that could treat the symptoms associated with AIDS. Such official denial caused a crippling delay in the rollout of government-sponsored HIV treatment in South Africa. Likewise, the Angolan government failed to recognize a 2005 Marburg outbreak early on, to explain the virus and its consequences to the public, or to mobilize personnel to deal with the epidemic even several months later— instead leaving the response to NGOs.[64] Similar dynamics have played out with respect to polio in Nigeria (see box 6.3).

Lack of Candor and Resistance to External Intervention

Beyond (deliberate) ignorance, a state's reticence to admit the scope or even the existence of a public health catastrophe can undermine efforts to contain the spread of infectious disease. This phenomenon is common in states that have glaring gaps in political aspects of governance. Authoritarian states that resist transparency and scrutiny, have little concern with democratic accountability, and lack an open media may be reluctant to acknowledge disease outbreaks or to share vital information with other

---

Box 6.3: Polio in Nigeria

The revival and spread of polio from Nigeria to at least sixteen other countries between 2003 and 2005 shows how deliberate ignorance and public misinformation can contribute to national and cross-border epidemics. Thanks to the Rotary International's Global Polio Eradication Initiative, polio was on the brink of eradication by mid-2003. It remained endemic in only a handful of countries, including Nigeria, Niger, Egypt, India, Pakistan, and Afghanistan.

At that time, however, officials in several of Nigeria's northern states abruptly halted immunizations due to rumors that the vaccination program was a Western anti-Muslim conspiracy that would leave those vaccinated sterile or HIV-infected. Teams of vaccinators were frequently attacked. Ultimately tens of thousands of parents refused to have their children vaccinated.

The Nigerian government's failure to enforce its national immunization program in the face of this ignorance allowed the disease to rebound in Nigeria—and spread across a broad swath of Africa and beyond to the Middle East and Asia. By the time the immunization campaign was resumed in 2005, the Nigerian strain of polio had appeared in seventeen countries, including many that had been free of the disease.[65]

governments or international bodies. For instance, there have been allegations that the Ugandan government deliberately concealed an Ebola outbreak in 2007.[66] (The WHO's revised International Health Regulations, which entered into force in 2007, now require all members to report all public health emergencies of potential international concern—but there are no enforcement mechanisms.)

Lack of candor is hardly limited to despotic regimes, however. The initial reactions by Asian governments to both the SARS and avian flu epidemics illustrate stark differences in countries' willingness to confront public health crises openly. In the case of SARS, Chinese leaders lied about the epidemic for months for fear of jeopardizing trade and tourism. By contrast, the government of Vietnam was forthcoming about the H5N1 outbreak from the start—an approach that compensated for some of the shortcomings of its national health sector. Remarkably, Vietnam's performance compared favorably with that of Thailand and Indonesia, both democratic countries, in grappling with bird flu. The Thai government was reluctant to act on early reports of outbreaks in 2004, and its Indonesian counterpart refused to share bird flu strains isolated from cases on its territory. Other states have been guilty of sluggish or haphazard reporting on H5N1 and other infectious diseases within their borders. Azerbaijan reported its first case of bird flu in 2006 "because of international pressure to come clean," said Dr. Juan Lubroth, senior veterinarian at the UN Food and Agriculture Organization (FAO). "We've been repeating over and over to countries that they have to be vigilant, but in most countries it's business as usual."[67]

In a globalized world, deliberate or lazy information gaps are more than inconveniences; they are threats. The refusal of countries like Indonesia to share information about outbreaks has raised questions about the idea of "viral sovereignty." This concept, which the 118-member nonaligned movement has considered endorsing, refers to states' claims that deadly viruses on their territory are their sovereign property, which need not be shared with the WHO or any other international body. As Richard Holbrooke and Laurie Garrett point out, such a concept makes little sense when applied to cross-border pandemics. They write, "Globally shared health risk demands absolute global transparency."[68]

Jealously guarded national sovereignty may impede foreign actors eager to intervene in a country to halt an infectious disease from spreading internationally. For instance, the Burmese junta has effectively forced out the Global Fund for AIDS, Tuberculosis, and Malaria and Médecins Sans Frontières (among other international organizations), vastly reducing treatment and information collection among the Burmese population. This development is especially ominous given Burma's extensive and undocumented cross-border migration with India, China, and Thailand—a potential disease vector.[69] The alternative to official obstruction is often official corruption, as Zimbabwe shows most egregiously. In November 2008, Mugabe's regime was found to have stolen more than $7 million from the Global Fund to Fight AIDS, Tuberculosis, and Malaria— prompting the Global Fund to threaten to withhold $188 million in much-needed aid until it was eventually returned.

The cases of Zimbabwe (see box 6.4) and Burma (see box 6.5), both critically weak states, illustrate how the lack of will on the part of a weak-state government can

---

Box 6.4: Zimbabwe: A Public Health Crisis Amid State Collapse

Perhaps more blatantly than any other government in the world, the brutal regime of Zimbabwean despot Robert Mugabe has actively undermined seemingly every public institution. Mugabe's three-decade rule has destroyed what had been one of the most prosperous countries in Africa. Zimbabwe's economy has shrunk by half in recent years, with inflation rates among the highest in the world, and more than 90 percent of the population lacking formal employment. Observers have warned of the complete collapse of the state.

The consequences of Mugabe's rule for public health in Zimbabwe—which at independence boasted one of Africa's best health care systems—have been equally devastating. Under Mugabe, life expectancy has fallen from 56 to 33 years. This dramatic drop is largely due to the ravages of AIDS, but other aspects of Zimbabwe's health crisis can be directly attributed to the decay of state institutions and infrastructure. The country's economic collapse has drained resources from the already shambolic public health system. Power outages and shortages of nearly every critical supply have rendered the country's medical services virtually "nonexistent."[70] The government's 2006 takeover of Harare's water system from the (opposition-run) city council led to the decay of water and sewage infrastructure in the capital. By 2008, there were no chemicals to purify the water supply, and water was shut off in most parts of the city.

The extent to which Zimbabwe's public health system has been hollowed out was underscored in 2008, when a cholera outbreak infected more than 60,000 people and killed more than 3,000 in a matter of months. Skyrocketing inflation meant that health care workers were unable to afford transportation and stopped coming to work. Strikes by unpaid health workers caused Harare's two largest hospitals to shut down in the midst of the epidemic. As a result, cholera mortality rates were five times higher in Zimbabwe than elsewhere. The following month, at the height of the cholera outbreak, Mugabe announced—without justification—that the epidemic was over.[71]

Zimbabwe's cholera epidemic quickly spread to South Africa, Botswana, and Mozambique—prompting some observers to hope that Zimbabwe's neighbors might finally recognize that the policies of its authoritarian regime could have truly catastrophic costs for the rest of the region. Some even cited Zimbabwe's public health crisis (among other factors) as grounds for the international community to intervene under the mantle of the Responsibility to Protect doctrine. Nonetheless, Mugabe emerged relatively unscathed; in December 2008, South Africa blocked a UN effort to censure the regime.

---

exacerbate a global health crisis. But the response of countries such as China (with SARS) and Indonesia (with H5N1) suggests that the "will" problem can be as acute in stronger developing states as it is in the most fragile countries, particularly if the ruling regimes cling to a monopoly of information and control. Such countries may actually be more inclined and able to resist international pressure to share information. According to the WHO's DOTS program, lack of political commitment has been a barrier to the prevention and treatment of tuberculosis in eight of twenty-two target countries—of which five were critically weak states (Nigeria, Ethiopia, DRC, Zimbabwe,

Mozambique). The rest, however—China, South Africa, and Thailand—are not weak states. This is in contrast to most of the other "barriers" cited by the WHO, for which problems were most acute in the weaker target states (see table above).

Weak State Infectious Disease Multipliers

Certain characteristics of weak states that have little to do with either capacity or will may further contribute to the spread of disease within these states, and the transmission of such diseases beyond their frontiers.

Open Borders

The inability of many weak states to control their frontiers facilitates smuggling and illicit trade, as well as unregulated migration. Such uncontrolled flows of people and goods can intensify the spread of infectious disease, particularly among vulnerable populations such as refugees. In 2004, for example, the virulent $z+$ strain of H5N1 spread to Vietnam via Chinese poultry smugglers. Similarly, experts at FAO believe that the avian influenza virus was probably introduced to Nigeria and Egypt (where the disease is now endemic) not through migratory birds, as in Asia, but via the smuggling of live poultry (most likely from China). Likewise, despite its relative wealth, Thailand's long borders with Laos and Cambodia, which lack "credible" public health systems, result in a regular flow of "odd, and often deadly, infectious diseases."[72]

Violent Conflict

Weak and failing states that descend into warfare typically experience a drastic reduction in health care delivery in conflict-affected zones, with a concomitant rise in infectious diseases. Insecurity and violence degrade a country's health infrastructure, prompt health workers to flee to safer areas, and make travel to health centers difficult and sometimes dangerous. One consequence is that fully 75 percent of epidemics in the last three decades "have occurred in countries where war, conflict, and prolonged political violence have left little or no capacity to respond."[73]

Recent conflicts in DRC, Afghanistan, and Iraq provide dramatic examples of the devastating links between war and disease. In 2008, the International Rescue Committee estimated that some 45,000 Congolese—mostly children—were dying each month, many from infectious disease. Likewise in Afghanistan, the continued insurgency has deprived large segments of the Pashtun population of even rudimentary health care. In Iraq, a cholera epidemic broke out in at least half of the country's provinces in November 2007, spreading through untreated water and raw sewage. "The threat is bad enough in the overcrowded communities of poor countries," writes Mark Drapeau, "but epidemics thrive in war zones."[74]

Beyond depriving populations of health care services, war also introduces new avenues for the spread of infectious disease, potentially endangering global as well as local health. The refugee and internally displaced populations that result from civil wars may serve as disease vectors, spreading pathogens both within and across sovereign borders. "Fragile states and ungoverned spaces, with massive migration and displacement of human populations, represent an 'ideal home' for any future viral mutation and propagation," writes Frederick Burkle. "These diasporic populations risk transmission of disease and resistant organisms that are poorly identified and controlled, while jeopardizing global surveillance required under current international mandates."[75]

The most horrific way in which war may facilitate the spread of infectious disease—particularly HIV/AIDS—is the use of rape as a weapon of war. One unproven but

---

Box 6.5: Burma: State Weakness as an Infectious Disease Multiplier

Burma (Myanmar) is a critically weak state governed by a corrupt and authoritarian military junta. It is beset by civil war; rival gangs; drug, gem, and sex-smugglers; one of the world's poorest populations; and an opium crop second only to Afghanistan's. These dynamics have conspired to make Burma among the hardest-hit countries in Asia for HIV/AIDS and other infectious diseases, and perhaps one of the likeliest sources of a pandemic that could threaten the region and beyond. Long-running internal conflicts and weak health care make Burma "the perfect breeding ground for new, drug-resistant strains of killer diseases such as malaria and TB."[76] Among the most vulnerable groups are eastern Burma's 500,000 internal refugees, the product of a decades-long insurgency, among whom malaria infection rates are as high as 12 percent.

Burma has one of Asia's most severe HIV/AIDS epidemics. The disease is concentrated among prostitutes and intravenous drug users, and is particularly prevalent in Burma's poppy-growing regions. Heroin-smuggling routes tend to be vectors for HIV/AIDS, posing a clear public health threat to Burma's neighbors. Surveys show that almost all of the HIV strains in Southeast Asia originated in northern Burma. The problem has implications for efforts to fight HIV/AIDS globally: according to Laurie Garrett, "Myanmar may be the greatest contributor of new types of HIV in the world."[77] Burma's authoritarian military regime bears responsibility—if not direct culpability—for the HIV/AIDS crisis in Southeast Asia, given its acquiescence (and likely participation) in the country's narcotics industry, which has grown significantly since the ruling junta took power in 1988.

Although many aspects of Burma's weakness have facilitated the spread of infectious disease, perhaps most troubling is the government's willful refusal to tackle the problem. Health spending per capita is only a few dollars per year. Health education is virtually nonexistent, and it is commonplace for people to take malaria medication incorrectly—a problem with potentially global implications, since it can trigger drug immunity.[78] The Burmese regime has denied the severity of cholera and HIV/AIDS epidemics in the country, and has refused to disclose information or grant access to international aid and health workers (an attitude glaringly evident in the junta's glacial response to the aftermath of Cyclone Nargis in May 2008). The regime's lack of transparency has also compounded international efforts to combat avian flu. Given the potential for avian flu to spread rapidly throughout the region, one UN official noted, "the stakes of remaining secretive are tremendous."[79]

plausible account traces the take-off of the HIV/AIDS pandemic to the systematic use of rape in Uganda in the late 1970s. Similar dynamics unfolded in Rwanda, where 80 percent of women suffering rape are reported to have become HIV positive. The collapse of the DRC, where rebels, militia groups, and breakaway army factions continue to rape women on a massive scale, appears to have helped transform that country into a Petri dish for the evolution of numerous strains of the virus.[80]

Militaries from developing countries can also spread infectious disease to new, susceptible populations through their participation in international peace operations, multinational military exercises, and disaster relief missions. Forces deployed from states without extensive vaccination programs and home-country medical monitoring may become infected by pathogens in their area of operation, carrying the disease back to their home countries. The return of Angolan soldiers from the DRC, where they fought in the 1990s, precipitated Angola's HIV/AIDS epidemic. On the other hand, there is little data to suggest that multinational peacekeeping operations actually cause local outbreaks of infectious disease.[81] Moreover, it is possible that warfare, by shutting down borders, trade, and travel, can sometimes reduce the risk of infection.

Disease Breeding Grounds: The Weakest States or Developing Countries?

As with the other transnational threats examined in this volume, capacity and will are critical variables in determining whether a particular fragile state is likely to serve as a host or vector for infectious disease. But although poor governance can certainly worsen the problem, a number of other critical ecological, geographic, cultural, technological, and demographic variables also play a role in making states susceptible to spawning and spreading epidemic disease. Regardless of their institutional strength, some countries are prone to certain diseases due to their climate (e.g., level of rainfall), the variety and habits of indigenous wildlife, and other ecological factors. For instance, one recent study found that the Western Hemisphere was less vulnerable to avian flu outbreaks because its migratory birds do not incubate the H5N1 virus like their Eurasian counterparts.[82]

Today, most countries with environments conducive to the spread of infectious diseases are found in Africa and Asia—but the process of global warming could change this. High temperatures are likely to increase outbreaks of some waterborne and food-borne (diarrheal) diseases. In recent years, malaria has seemed to be climbing mountains where mosquitoes had previously been unable to live, while Dengue and Lyme disease are moving north, and West Nile virus has reached the New World.[83]

The emergence (or reemergence) of infectious diseases often reflects changes in habitation, livelihoods, movement, and land use that bring humans and pathogens into closer contact with one another. Yet the relationship between these exogenous factors and state weakness is less than straightforward. In fact, although the world's weakest states are clearly more vulnerable than developed countries to certain types of disease, in part it is the *development* process itself—rather than state weakness per se—that increases the risk that developing countries will serve as breeding grounds for infectious disease.

As discussed above, moderately strong developing countries may be at least as (or more) likely than the weakest states to actively impede international efforts to combat infectious disease. More than fragile states, these countries have both the ability to resist external intervention and, in some cases, self-serving reasons to do so (concerns about tourism, trade, regional prestige, etc.).

Moreover, although in the long run economic development tends to lead to improved public health, several aspects of the development process—including urbanization, changing demography, and increased links to the rest of the world—may make emerging economies somewhat more likely than the very weakest states to be the source of a global pandemic. As one recent landmark study put it, "Disease emergence is largely a product of anthropogenic and demographic changes, and is a hidden cost of economic development."[84] This argument is borne out by an analysis of countries where recent potential pandemics have originated or spread. As of May 2009, only one country ranking in the bottom two quintiles of the Index—Colombia (#47), itself a relatively developed if insecure state—had ever had any reported cases of either SARS or H1N1. Similarly, only 4.7 percent cases of avian flu had occurred in weak states. (See tables in Appendix.)

Demography. As populations in the developing world grow, humans increasingly exploit marginal or isolated environments, where they (and their livestock) come into contact with previously isolated wild species—and zoonotic diseases.[85] A 1998 Nipah virus outbreak in Malaysia that killed 105 people highlights how the encroachment of people and livestock into new habitats can facilitate the jump of pathogens from wildlife, which have developed immunity, to domestic animals, which have no previous exposure and therefore no immunity. Nipah, for instance, spread from bats to pigs as the bats' habitats were taken over by farms, and then to humans handling infected pigs. At the same time, as more people leave rural areas to seek livelihoods in crowded cities, rapid urbanization accelerates the spread of infectious diseases like tuberculosis, dengue fever, and SARS.

Food Production. Urbanized societies depend on intensified agricultural and livestock production to meet their food needs, increasing humanity's vulnerability to cross-species illnesses. Consider the role of agriculture. As humans modify their environment, they may inadvertently change the transmission ecology of human pathogens; increase their interactions with wildlife, creating new vectors for disease; and provide a stable conduit for human infection via domesticated animals.[86]

More generally, countries with high levels of human interaction with livestock, especially where standards of hygiene regarding animal husbandry are poor, are at special risk of generating and spreading zoonotic diseases. This threat is compounded by economic growth in developing countries, where the International Food Policy Research Institute estimates that animal production will double by 2025. New flu viruses and pandemics have tended to emerge from Asia because of animal husbandry practices in which ducks, chickens, and pigs are raised in close proximity to humans. Moreover, traditional methods of buying livestock at crowded open-air markets—as well as of slaughtering and cooking meat—give Asians high exposure to zoonotic diseases. Meanwhile, modern factory farms, particularly in countries that lack the capacity to regulate sanitation standards, make livestock more susceptible to infectious disease through overcrowding and common feed practices.[87]

Environmental Degradation. The infrastructure projects and corresponding environmental damage that often accompany economic development can destabilize local ecosystems, which can then breed and spread infectious diseases. Deforestation and the expansion of road networks into wilderness have increased human exposure to new zoonotic diseases. Irrigation schemes in Ethiopia implemented to help the country recover from drought have paradoxically caused a sevenfold increase in malaria infection.[88] As these processes accelerate in the developing world, humanity's exposure to new and reemerging lethal diseases will increase substantially.

Travel and Transport. In an age of mass travel and global commerce, a single outbreak in one country can quickly threaten lives and livelihoods across the globe. In particular, the global transport of animals and animal products enables the spread of harmful bacteria, viruses, and fungi. Wildlife markets provide the ideal environment of inter-species, close-quarters interaction for viruses and bacteria to mutate, reproduce, and spread to humans.[89] Of course, these vulnerabilities are likely to be magnified where state regulatory systems are weak and citizens have little access to health care, hygiene education, common vaccines, or antibiotics.

By the year 2000, more than two million people crossed international borders each day, including one million between developed and developing countries. Airfreight exceeded 100 billion ton-kilometers a year. As a result of these trends, a number of formerly local or regional infectious diseases have spread around the globe. AIDS was spread throughout Southern and Central Africa by long-distance truckers, and then globally by air travelers. West Nile virus, a mosquito-borne disease that originated in Uganda, reached New York by aircraft in 1999 and has since spread throughout the continental United States. Similarly, Dengue fever traveled via cargo ships from Southeast Asia to Brazil in the 1990s. It has now become prevalent in South and Central America, enabled by urbanization and high population growth, and is likely to spread to the southern United States in the near future.[90] Were Ebola to spread to a city with a busy international airport (like Johannesburg or Nairobi) it could conceivably leap continents—as SARS did after emerging in 2002 in China.

Although migrants or exports from any country could potentially carry a disease to the United States, developing countries with greater ties to the global economy are probably more likely to serve as disease vectors than the weakest, most isolated states (see box 6.6). This may be one reason why Ebola outbreaks in some of the most remote and impoverished areas of Uganda and the DRC have failed to spread beyond the region. In an exception that proves the rule, HIV/AIDS has spread throughout Southeast Asia from Burma, a critically weak state but one that is linked to the region by an extensive system of heroin and smuggling routes. Although Burma is one of the least developed countries in the world, its Shan state on the border of China's Yunnan province has become a center of the sex and drug trades—and Chinese tourism. Unsurprisingly, HIV/AIDS has spread from Shan state as well.

Box 6.6: Indonesia: The *Relatively* Strong State as Weak Link in Global Public Health

Indonesia presents a good example of a relatively strong state (ranked #77 on the Index of State Weakness) that nevertheless faces a host of dangerous and deadly infectious diseases, including malaria, Dengue, and diarrheal diseases, as well as the world's third-worst tuberculosis infection rate and (in 2008) the fastest growing polio epidemic. Perhaps most alarmingly for the rest of the world, Indonesia has been a major locus of avian flu outbreaks. Despite a decade of robust growth, Indonesia still spends only about 1 percent of its GDP on public health—by far the lowest rate in the region (although the government has taken some steps in recent years to improve the public health sector). Consequently, "Indonesia compares poorly with its neighbors on most conventional measures of health outcomes," including much poorer countries such as Vietnam.[91]

In the summer of 2005, as the country was facing a major polio epidemic, a sudden outbreak of bird flu risked overwhelming Indonesia's already weak public health system. The state lacked a strong monitoring system, laboratories for testing, and basic health supplies such as vaccines and syringes.[92] Moreover, overstretched health authorities have great difficulty monitoring outbreaks across the country's hundreds of islands, mountainous regions, and isolated villages, particularly since local health staff often lack the expertise to verify outbreaks themselves.

Beyond these capacity gaps, however, the Indonesian government has been actively uncooperative in working with international agencies, for instance refusing to share with the WHO or other agencies samples of dozens of deadly H5N1 strains that have infected poultry on its territory. In blatant disregard of its obligations under the 2005 International Health Regulations, Indonesia has also failed to notify the WHO of bird flu outbreaks. In 2008, the government threatened to shut a medical research laboratory of the U.S. Navy on its territory, accusing (without cause) its U.S. employees "of everything from profiteering off its 'sovereign' viruses to manufacturing the H5N1 bird flu in an alleged biological warfare scheme."[93] Corruption has impeded containment efforts as well: "Local officials at times inflated the results [of poultry vaccinations] because they were paid a small bonus by the government for each vaccination recorded," while commercial farmers with ties to senior officials sometimes obstructed inspectors, making it difficult for them to test flocks or report outbreaks.[94] High-level officials who spoke out about the government's failure to respond to avian influenza outbreaks were fired.

Indonesia is hardly among the world's weakest states. And yet, given the country's weak health care system (which reflects government priorities much more than economic constraints) and resistance to cooperation with international bodies on health issues, "International health experts cite Indonesia as one of the weakest links in efforts to head off a potential pandemic."[95]

Infectious Disease as a Cause of State Collapse?

Some argue that the rapid spread of certain infectious diseases could make weak states even weaker—further undermining their capacity to respond to the disease threat, and possibly even leading to state collapse.[96] As far back as the mid-1990s, the CIA added HIV to its "State Failure Watchlist" as a variable contributing to state collapse. In 2003, Secretary of State Colin Powell declared that HIV/AIDS "can destroy countries and, as we have seen, it can destabilize entire regions."[97] If HIV/AIDS (or another pandemic) were to lead directly to social unrest in certain strategic countries—perhaps Russia, Pakistan, or India—the consequences for regional and international security could be significant. However, to date there is little empirical evidence to support most of these arguments.

Analysts have identified several potential causal pathways whereby HIV/AIDS could exacerbate the risk of failure in already weak states. First, there is no question that HIV/AIDS (like malaria and other infectious diseases) has reduced economic growth and undermined development in the hardest-hit states, cutting an estimated 0.3–1.5 percent of GDP per annum in affected countries. The epidemic has had a disproportionate impact on the most productive members of society, including political and business elites, professionals, civil servants, and skilled employees. The labor and productivity costs of dealing with AIDS have also discouraged foreign direct investment.[98]

A second way in which HIV/AIDS could contribute to state fragility is by increasing the risk of violence and instability. In many African countries, HIV/AIDS has produced an "ominous, bottle-shaped population age structure," reflecting a pronounced youth bulge, high child mortality, and an unusually small proportion of older adults. These demographic trends portend ill for social order, given the generally positive correlation between large youth cohorts and a country's propensity for upheaval.[99] Compounding the problem, particularly in Africa, HIV/AIDS has decimated households, undermining traditional coping mechanisms. Moreover, some analysts have suggested that HIV/AIDS could reduce the strength, integrity, and readiness of the military and police, making affected countries more vulnerable. Although accurate infection rates among armed forces are notoriously difficult to obtain, various sources estimate that in some twenty African countries more than 15 percent of the military may be infected.[100]

Finally, in the worst-affected countries, HIV/AIDS could lead to a loss of political legitimacy. The epidemic has strained national budgets and weakened state capabilities, incapacitating bureaucracies though illness or the exigencies of caring for family members with AIDS. UNAIDS has documented the erosion of essential civil service sectors in Africa—especially teachers, hospital workers, and financial-sector employees—as a result of infection. (In 2002, for example, some 300 schools were closed in the Central African Republic because teachers were dead and dying.) In some hard-hit countries, families cannot sustain themselves despite relative abundance at the national level, a phenomenon development experts have termed "new variant famine."[101] FAO predicted in 2009 that another 16 million agricultural workers may die from AIDS by 2020.[102] If these household-level shocks aggregate to create acute food shortages, history suggests that social order could be in jeopardy.

Despite these disturbing trends, there is little empirical evidence to support the theory that HIV/AIDS could precipitate state failure. As the NIC conceded in 2005, "It is not clear if AIDS can be directly tied to state collapse in a way that was feared and anticipated a few years ago."[103] While the economic impact of HIV/AIDS has been noteworthy, macroeconomic modeling of the pandemic indicates that AIDS is not contributing to collapse of the national economy in any state. Nor has it imperiled the legitimacy of ruling regimes in even the hardest hit states. Likewise, it has been difficult to trace spikes in violent crime and decreased social order in afflicted societies to demographic changes wrought by AIDS; and as far as is known, the armies of most afflicted countries survive intact. Indeed, among fragile states, AIDS is neither a common feature nor, for most of them, an issue at all. This less alarmist view reflects a recalibration of HIV/AIDS infection rates; a growing understanding of the dynamics of state collapse; and a dawning awareness that the long-wave nature of the disease (in contrast to a rapid-onset, full-scale pandemic) permits some adaptation and remedial action to mitigate HIV/AIDS' most severe consequences.[104]

CONCLUSION: ASSESSING THE INFECTIOUS DISEASE– WEAK STATES CONNECTION

The inability or unwillingness of a state to prevent, monitor, and treat infectious diseases can expose the entire world to severe consequences. Fragile states clearly present a constellation of institutional weaknesses that make them more vulnerable than stronger countries to public health emergencies. In principle, such weaknesses could transform these states into vectors of infectious disease, including pathogens that pose a pandemic threat to global health. A close look at global patterns, however, suggests that state fragility is only one (relatively unimportant) factor among many in determining where diseases with pandemic potential originate and spread.[105]

Global disease "hot spots"—countries whose population density and growth rate, latitude, climate, and biodiversity make them likely sites for new zoonotic diseases to emerge—include both very weak (Ethiopia, Nigeria, Pakistan) and relatively strong states (Mexico, China, the Philippines). Although HIV/AIDS and malaria (including drug-resistant strains) are concentrated in the world's most fragile states, the list of countries that to date have been most affected by potential pandemics such as avian influenza, SARS, and H1N1 includes only a couple of the world's weakest states, as measured by the Index. Likewise, the highest rates of MDR-TB—which, given its ease of transmission, poses truly pandemic potential—occur in the middle-ranking Central Asian states. So, in part, whether weak states pose the greatest infectious disease threat depends on the level of importance that policymakers attribute to particular diseases.

Inhabitants of the world's weakest states are the most susceptible to certain infectious diseases because weak states have trouble fulfilling their economic, security, and political functions. At the most basic level, poor economic management may limit revenue for health care spending. High levels of violence may decimate health care services and exacerbate the spread of epidemics. Perhaps most critically, the lack of transparent and effective political institutions may distort or delay long-term investments in public health and timely responses to emerging health emergencies. In fact, as this chapter makes clear, gaps in state performance in preventing, detecting, and responding to infectious disease are often less a reflection of objective "capacity" (including budgetary) constraints than of conscious decisions by unaccountable or unresponsive regimes. Such deliberate inaction occurs not only in the world's weakest states (polio in Nigeria) but also stronger ones (SARS in China), and even in promising democracies (bird flu in Indonesia, or HIV/AIDS in South Africa). In principle, such obstructionism could mean the difference between a few culled animals and millions of human fatalities worldwide.

Another conclusion that emerges from the chapter is that stronger developing countries (such as China and Indonesia) may actually pose a bigger infectious disease threat to the United States and the global community than weaker states. The development process itself, while positive overall, may contribute to the spread of infectious disease—particularly as such countries become more integrated into the transportation and trade networks of the global economy. Stronger developing countries may nevertheless possess critical governance gaps (particularly lack of transparency), and be more able to resist external intervention than weaker nations.

Finally, if the pandemic threat from the world's weakest states is arguably overblown, so is the prospect that infectious disease will lead to state failure, even collapse. There is no evidence that infectious disease—including HIV/AIDS, for all its enormous social costs in the worst-affected countries—has actually been a cause of instability or violence, let alone state collapse.

Only by understanding where outbreaks of deadly new and reemerging diseases are occurring and how they become epidemics can the international community act to contain the disease threat. The analysis in this chapter indicates that a pandemic disease with global ramifications could occur almost anywhere—but there is no reason to presume that it will originate in the world's weakest states, rather than in another part of the developing world. To the extent that the most *direct* threat to U.S. security comes from truly global, rapid-onset pandemics, the risks may actually be concentrated in relatively developed countries. Of course, this should not preclude efforts to combat endemic diseases in poor states, given their disastrous economic and human consequences. Regardless of the security implications for the developed world, the humanitarian tragedy is impetus enough to act.

Appendix 6.1: Countries with reported incidences of swine flu, April-May 2009[106]

Country	Overall Index Ranking
Argentina	115
Australia	n/a
Austria	n/a
Brazil	99
Canada	n/a
China	74
Colombia	47
Costa Rica	130
Denmark	n/a
El Salvador	95
France	n/a
Germany	n/a
Guatemala	60
Ireland	n/a
Israel	n/a
Italy	n/a
Japan	n/a
Mexico	120
Netherlands	n/a
New Zealand	n/a
Norway	n/a
Panama	122
Poland	135
Portugal	n/a
R. Korea	n/a
Spain	n/a
Sweden	n/a
Switzerland	n/a
United Kingdom	n/a
United States	n/a

LEGEND: Index Rank

- ■ Bottom Quintile
- ■ Second Quintile
- ■ Third Quintile
- ■ Fourth Quintile
- ■ Top Quintile
- □ Not in Index

Appendix 6.2: Countries with confirmed cases of H5N1, 2003–2009[107]

Country	Confirmed Cases	Overall Index Rank
Azerbaijan	8	80
Bangladesh	1	48
Burma	1	17
Cambodia	8	34
China	38	74
Djibouti	1	38
Egypt	68	78
Indonesia	141	77
Iraq	3	4
Laos	2	45
Nigeria	1	28
Pakistan	3	33
Thailand	25	79
Turkey	12	98
Vietnam	111	83

Totals   **423**   **20 of 423 cases (4.7%) occurred in countries in the bottom 2 quintiles**

LEGEND: Index Ranking

Bottom Quintile
Second Quintile
Third Quintile
Fourth Quintile
Top Quintile

Appendix 6.3: Reported Probable SARS Cases By Country, 2002–2003[108]

Country	Cases	Overall Index Ranking
Australia	5	n/a
Brazil	1	99
Canada	250	n/a
China (incl. Hong Kong)	7083	74
China (Taiwan)	671	n/a
Colombia	1	47

Country	Cases	Overall Index Ranking
Finland	1	n/a
France	7	n/a
Germany	10	n/a
India	3	67
Indonesia	2	77
Ireland	1	n/a
Italy	4	n/a
Korea	3	n/a
Kuwait	1	n/a
Malaysia	5	124
Mongolia	9	97
New Zealand	1	n/a
Philippines	14	58
Romania	1	121
Russia	1	65
Singapore	206	n/a
South Africa	1	109
Spain	1	n/a
Sweden	1	n/a
Switzerland	1	n/a
Thailand	9	79
United Kingdom	4	n/a
United States	75	n/a
Vietnam	63	83
Totals	**8437**	**1 of 8437 cases (.012%) occurred in states in the bottom 2 quintiles**

LEGEND: Index Ranking

	Bottom Quintile
	Second Quintile
	Third Quintile
	Fourth Quintile
	Top Quintile
	Not in Index

7

CONCLUSIONS AND POLICY IMPLICATIONS

In the twentieth century, strategists focused on the world's great industrial heartlands. In the twenty-first, the focus is in the opposite direction, toward remote regions and failing states.

—*9/11 Commission Final Report*[1]

Successful international actions to battle poverty, fight infectious disease, stop transnational crime, rebuild after civil war, reduce terrorism, and halt the spread of dangerous materials all require capable, responsible States as partners.

—*UN High Level Panel on Threats, Challenges and Change (2004)*[2]

Globalization, nonstate actors, and the rise of new transnational threats have raised weak and failed states to the top of the U.S. national security agenda, for reasons beyond simple humanitarian concern. At the same time, the blanket equation of weak states and global threats provides only modest analytic insights and even less practical guidance for policymakers. Each poorly performing country suffers from a distinctive set of pathologies and generates a unique mixture of challenges, of varying gravity. There can be no one-size-fits-all response to addressing either the sources or the consequences of these shortcomings. At a practical level, neither the United States nor its allies have the unlimited resources or attention required to launch ambitious state-building exercises in all corners of the world. U.S. officials will thus need to investigate the sources and consequences of transnational threats better and set priorities about where, when, and how to engage weak states to improve U.S. and international security.

This book has sought to map the intersection between state weakness and particular threats, and to trace those "spillovers" to specific gaps in state capacity or will. As its findings show, the overlap between state weakness and today's most pressing transnational threats is hardly clear-cut, much less universal. It depends on the threat in question, the specific sources and manifestations of state weakness, and the will of

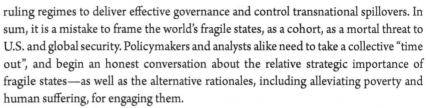

ruling regimes to deliver effective governance and control transnational spillovers. In sum, it is a mistake to frame the world's fragile states, as a cohort, as a mortal threat to U.S. and global security. Policymakers and analysts alike need to take a collective "time out", and begin an honest conversation about the relative strategic importance of fragile states—as well as the alternative rationales, including alleviating poverty and human suffering, for engaging them.

At the same time, the United States, other wealthy world governments, and international agencies need to improve their current policies towards the world's fragile states, which suffer from major shortcomings. A more strategic U.S. approach would include paying greater attention to steps to help prevent deteriorating governance, adjusting U.S. development policy to fragile state contexts, avoiding overly-militarized approaches that undermine long-term stability, and leveraging the contributions of the entire international community.

Finally, the United States and like-minded international partners should seek to cut those links between state fragility and transnational threats that, while hardly universal, do sometimes arise. The conclusion closes by identifying potential points of leverage for reducing the negative global consequences of poor governance in the developing world.

REASSESSING THE CONVENTIONAL WISDOM

Claims about the security risks of fragile states can have a fevered, even breathless quality. USAID asserts: "When development and governance fail in a country, the consequences engulf entire regions and leap across the world. Terrorism, political violence, civil wars, organized crime, drug trafficking, infectious diseases, environmental crises, refugee flows and mass migration cascade across the borders of weak states more destructively than ever before."[3] Of course, under certain conditions, weak and failing states contribute to transnational threats. And some specific ones—namely the production of certain narcotics, maritime piracy, illegal arms trafficking, and some infectious diseases—appear heavily concentrated in the weakest states.

But overall, the connection between weak governance and global (in)security is less straightforward than often portrayed. Although they may be the likeliest sites of pressing humanitarian issues, the vast majority of weak and failing states do not pose a significant threat to the United States. In many cases, stronger developing countries (including several "states to watch") may be at least as likely as the weakest countries to generate negative spillovers. Moreover, for both very weak states and stronger ones, capacity may be less important than political will (or the lack thereof) in determining where a major threat will arise.

The Weakest States vs. other Developing Countries

Interestingly, the very weakest states actually seem *less* likely than other developing (and sometimes developed) countries to incubate certain global threats—in part because they tend to have fewer links to the rest of the world. Transnational terrorists, proliferators, and criminals alike need access to modern communications, transportation, and financial infrastructure, from which the world's weakest (and often poorest) countries are often cut off. Likewise, a terrorist attack may be plotted from remote areas of Somalia or Afghanistan, but its successful implementation will almost certainly require utilizing the infrastructure of cities from Karachi to Hamburg. And as noted in chapter 6, Ebola outbreaks in Central Africa were quickly contained because the regions where they occurred were so remote.

In fact, for the five types of threats examined here, perhaps the most concerning category of countries are "states to watch," which are superficially strong but possess critical "sovereignty holes" (see Appendix 7.2). Such countries enjoy moderate to strong state capacity, making them able to have a major international impact (and in some cases to deliberately challenge U.S. interests) by financing proliferation efforts or terrorist groups, or withholding energy resources from global markets. At the same time, they suffer from significant gaps in governance, increasing the likelihood that they will—inadvertently or not—destabilize regions or facilitate threats from nonstate actors. A few examples can amplify these points.

Consider the threat of WMD proliferation. Among the world's fifty-six weakest states, only two—Pakistan and North Korea—pose a serious proliferation risk. In contrast, multiple "states to watch" (including Iran, Russia, and Syria) either possess or have the means to develop WMD—while lacking the transparency, oversight, and in some cases the resources to ensure that their programs are secure. Similarly, the threat of transnational terrorism is hardly a weak state phenomenon, affecting a number of stronger polities, such as Algeria, Saudi Arabia, and other capable but undemocratic states in the broader Middle East. U.S.-designated "state sponsors of terrorism" tend to be moderately capable authoritarian states, including Iran, Syria, and Libya.

Nor are the main threats to energy security concentrated disproportionately among weak and failing states. Certainly, several important fragile state oil exporters—including Iraq, Angola, and Nigeria—are susceptible to supply disruptions due to political instability or conflict. But most of the world's major energy producers are not weak states. Even if their regimes are repressive or corrupt, their resource wealth enables them to maintain effective security services that can suppress internal conflict and deliver at least minimal levels of social welfare. Of course, some of the governance gaps associated with the "resource curse" (including corruption and lack of accountability) make countries such as Russia, Iran, and Venezuela both "states to watch" and—by driving down investment and production—potential threats to global energy security.

Finally, the world's most developed countries are far from blameless when it comes to enabling the five threats discussed here. The rich world provides markets for contraband as well as banks for transnational money-laundering. Likewise, heavy-handed counternarcotics policies can perversely increase the profits of drug producers and traffickers, undermining already weak governance in source countries. The A.Q. Khan network depended on Dubai, South Africa, and Malaysia as important hubs; in most of the confirmed nuclear smuggling cases, shipments were intercepted in wealthy European countries. The unmistakable implication of these findings is that a state need not be weak to enable global "bads."

Capacity vs. Will

Policymakers must discern whether poor state performance is a function of capacity, will, or both. The previous chapters suggest that inadequate political will may be as important as capacity gaps in enabling the spread of transnational threats from developing countries. Examples include North Korea's refusal to halt proliferation; tolerance for extremist groups in Pakistan, Saudi Arabia, and Yemen; nondisclosure from China and Indonesia on disease outbreaks; Russian and Venezuelan harassment of foreign energy companies; and more generally, the pervasive corruption that makes officials from Guinea-Bissau to Kyrgyzstan reluctant to address criminal activity. Conversely, some relatively weak states have made progress in many of these areas when their leaders are committed to doing so: Liberia in tackling the illegal timber trade, Mali in fighting terrorism, Laos in combating narcotics, and Vietnam on disease reporting.

The problem of inadequate will, of course, may itself be a reflection of certain governance gaps, especially in the political realm. Regimes in states with high levels of corruption, where institutions are unaccountable, are more likely to ignore threats to their own citizens as well as to the international community. They include critically weak states like North Korea or Afghanistan under the Taliban, whose authoritarian or extremist regimes are willing to endure (and whose citizens pay the price of) near total isolation. On the other hand, some of the world's weakest states may also be more susceptible than stronger ones to U.S. or international pressure or incentives to combat transnational spillovers.

Which Weak States Matter?

Fragile states are not equal in terms of how much (or why) the United States cares about them. To determine where U.S. and international engagement is warranted, and to tailor state-building efforts in a manner that mitigates the most salient dangers, policymakers must anticipate which threats are likely to arise from particular countries. Appendix 7.1 summarizes, in an admittedly imperfect and time-bound manner, which fragile states are most worrisome, in terms of their recent connection to transnational terrorism, WMD proliferation, transnational crime, energy insecurity, and infectious disease.

The vast majority of the fifty-six states ranking in the bottom two quintiles of the Index of State Weakness appear to have little if any connection to the global threats considered here. Only four of these states (7.1 percent), for instance, currently have nuclear programs or even minimal stockpiles of weapons-grade fissile material. While a few threats are clearly associated with weak states, such as opium production and piracy, these problems are confined to only a handful of countries. The fifty-six weakest states together supply only about 7 percent of global energy production, so with a few exceptions, disruptions in these countries are unlikely to have a major sustained impact on global markets. And few cases of avian flu or SARS—the diseases which currently have the greatest potential to transform into worldwide pandemics—have been reported in any weak state.

Of course, a handful of weak states clearly do pose significant challenges to U.S. and international security. Somalia, Afghanistan, Pakistan, and Yemen (and to a lesser extent Iraq, Bangladesh, Mali, and Mauritania) are of serious concern as actual or potential terrorist havens. Pakistan and North Korea pose enormous proliferation threats. Afghanistan, Burma, and Laos produce virtually all of the world's opium; Colombia accounts for a majority of global coca production. Most piracy attacks occur off Somalia and Nigeria. Instability in Iraq and Nigeria has already driven up global energy prices; instability in Angola, Uzbekistan, or Turkmenistan could have similar effects. While the institutional weaknesses of these states are only one factor driving these threats, combating them will require an understanding of the dynamics between institutional fragility and transnational risks.

WHICH GOVERNANCE GAPS MATTER?

Where state fragility *does* appear to exacerbate transnational threats, which governance gaps are most relevant? The preceding chapters suggest that political and security variables—notably corruption, weak rule of law, and high levels of violence—are especially conducive to negative spillovers. By contrast, shortcomings in economic development and social welfare are less directly implicated in the transnational security threats covered in this book. Based on the analysis in the preceding chapters, Appendix 7.3 identifies 16 weak states ranked in the bottom 2 quintiles of the Index, as well as another 17 states to watch, that appear of particular concern for their connection to the five threats examined here. The majority of these countries receive very poor scores on political and security components of governance, whereas only about a third score poorly on economic and social welfare indicators.

Corruption appears as a factor in every type of threat examined here. Of the twenty-eight countries ranking in the bottom quintile of the Index for corruption, all but three[4] are known as major centers for at least one type of transnational criminal activity. Likewise, more than 70 percent of the thirty energy producers in the bottom three quintiles of the Index rank very low (in the bottom two quintiles) for corruption, which can undermine investment and fuel resource-based conflicts that interrupt supplies. Corruption may divert government revenues from public health services, enabling the spread of infectious disease. Corruption is implicated in weak law enforcement, including weak policing, inadequate border control, and anemic judicial systems. Weak law enforcement in turn facilitates transnational threats, allowing terrorists, criminals, and traffickers to operate with impunity. Thus, corruption in developing countries, long considered primarily in economic or development terms and rarely a top priority for U.S. policymakers, in fact has significant security ramifications.

Violent conflict is also implicated in many transnational threats. Violence and political instability have disrupted the flow of energy supplies from Iraq to Colombia. Worryingly, more than two-thirds of the thirty energy producers in the bottom three quintiles on the Index score poorly (in the bottom two quintiles) for territory affected by conflict, and for political stability and absence of violence. Refugees fleeing conflict can also serve as transnational disease vectors. Opium- and coca-producing states, pirate havens, and destination countries for illicit arms deals are almost exclusively war-torn countries or those without full control of their territory. Breakaway "state-lets" such as Transdniester, Abkhazia, and South Ossetia have become centers of smuggling, counterfeiting, and arms dealing.

On the other hand, active war zones can pose security and logistical problems for such illicit groups. Criminals (other than rebel groups) tend to shift their operations away from areas where hot conflict threatens trafficking routes. More favorable settings are under-governed, badly governed, or alternatively governed regions, where the local power holders tolerate or even support criminal networks. Although such areas usually *are* governed by some kind of power structure, they are not subject to the same constraints or responsibilities as an effective, sovereign state—making them more likely havens for terrorists or traffickers, whether based on ideological solidarity, profit, or other motivations.

Similarly, weak states suffering from violent conflict offer both opportunities and challenges for transnational terrorist groups. On one hand, Islamist extremists have gained valuable conflict experience in war zones from Iraq to the Balkans to Algeria, and in a handful of cases (Afghanistan in the 1990s, and Somalia since 2006), civil war and state collapse have enabled al-Qaeda-affiliated regimes to take power (in part by promising to establish law and order). But in general, terrorist groups seem to prefer to base their major operations in weak but moderately functional states (or regions of states). Thus weak-state conflict zones appear most dangerous in the handful of cases where they give rise to radical Islamist militias who, if they are able to actually consolidate power, can offer many more benefits to al-Qaeda than a collapsed state would.

Somewhat surprisingly, other characteristics of weak states—particularly economic and social welfare failings—contribute less to the types of threat examined here. Despite common assertions, there is little empirical evidence that poverty is an enabling factor for terrorism at either the micro or macro level (even when only Muslim-majority countries are considered). Poverty and inequality may exacerbate unrest in weak-state energy producers, but bad governance appears to have had a much greater impact in terms of lowering production capacity. And while there is no doubt that states with the lowest social welfare scores are disproportionately affected by many endemic diseases, these are not necessarily the ones that pose the greatest direct threat to the United States. Influenza outbreaks, in contrast, have occurred mostly in wealthier countries like China and Indonesia. More broadly, the poorest states are unlikely to have the financial and other capabilities to directly threaten the United States through arms buildup, support for terrorism, or withholding of energy resources.

Finally, although some critical governance gaps enable transnational threats, the handful of weak and failing states of greatest concern to the United States are problematic largely because of specific attributes that are independent of their weakness. Climate, for instance, plays a role in the susceptibility of many weak states to certain endemic diseases. Haiti—like stronger states in the region—emerged as a drug trafficking route because of its location between South American producers and North American markets. Both the weak states of Central Asia and the relatively stronger countries of the Caucasus and Eastern Europe house arms trafficking thanks to the legacy of the Soviet Union. And terrorist groups exploit weak states primarily when their regimes and/or people are ideologically sympathetic.

In sum, the link between state fragility and transnational threats has often been over-blown. The major transnational threats of the twenty-first century do not emanate dis-proportionately from the weakest states, and not all fragile states deserve the same attention from U.S. policymakers from a strict national security lens. Triage and prior-itization must be the order of the day in determining the level of U.S. attention and resource commitments in any particular country.

THE POLICY CHALLENGE OF FRAGILE STATES

The fact that today's major global challenges are imperfectly linked to institutional shortcomings in the world's weakest states does not absolve U.S. policymakers from crafting more effective policies to engage those countries. The United States retains both a moral and a strategic stake in promoting effective, legitimate states in the devel-oping world.[5] The world's weakest countries are the likeliest sites of mass atrocities, wars, and humanitarian disasters. Promoting states capable of delivering economic growth, human security, and good governance is presumably a worthy goal on its own merits. And in strategic terms, even if only a handful of fragile states pose a direct threat to the United States, understanding the dynamics of state failure and recovery is criti-cal to addressing these risks.

The United States and its international partners need more sophisticated approaches and tools to help ameliorate the underlying causes of state fragility and promote effec-tive states in the developing world. The United States must, of course, engage each fragile state on its own terms, based on a careful assessment of the sources of its dysfunction and the full range of the U.S. interests at stake. There can be no uniform template, nor can the United States be everywhere at once. But any consideration of U.S. interests and policy options should be informed by a broader strategic framework, so that if deteriorating conditions or an emerging threat warrant engagement, the United States will be well positioned to respond.

Formulating a U.S. Fragile States Strategy

For all the rhetorical attention the United States has given to weak and failing states since 9/11, actual U.S. policy towards state fragility has remained reactive, fragmented, militarized, under-resourced, and self-contained. In the wake of the wars in Iraq and Afghanistan, U.S. officials have adopted new doctrines and capabilities designed to help war-torn states recover from violence. In contrast, they have devoted little attention to considering how the United States and its partners might work with responsible local actors to help prevent fragile states from deteriorating toward failure and violence to begin with.

A more effective U.S. fragile states policy will require a "whole of government" approach that draws on all relevant tools of U.S. influence, while leveraging the contributions of international partners and responsible local actors. The State Department's first-ever Quadrennial Diplomacy and Development Review (QDDR), released in December 2010, was a welcome step to begin plugging some of these gaps. "For the past two decades, the U.S. government has recognized that U.S. national security depends on a more effective approach to fragile states," that document notes. "Yet we have struggled with how to understand these challenges and how to organize our civilian institutions to deal with them." A more robust fragile states strategy will require the United States to: elevate prevention over reaction and organize its foreign policy accordingly; improve its intelligence and knowledge about countries at risk; adapt its development aid and policy to fragile state realities; improve the quality of its governance, rule of law, security, and trade assistance; invest in U.S. civilian capabilities needed to balance U.S. military ones; and nurture coordinated, multilateral action to accomplish goals that it cannot achieve on its own.[6]

Elevate Prevention over Reaction—and Organize for It

Current U.S. engagement with fragile states is almost entirely reactive. Policymakers tend to await the outbreak of a major crisis before launching a policy intervention (military or otherwise). Such an approach is far more expensive, in both economic and human terms, than timely preventive action.

The United States can rectify this failing by formulating a government-wide strategy that makes mitigating state fragility a U.S. priority. Such a framework would help define the scale of U.S. ambitions and objectives; discern points of U.S. and international leverage; establish the priority tasks for each phase of engagement and the tactics and instruments to achieve them; apportion responsibilities among U.S. agencies; identify international partners and their prospective roles; and create benchmarks to measure progress. The ultimate aim would be to leverage the entire panoply of U.S. policy instruments in promoting state effectiveness in the world's most challenging institutional environments. To promote coherence, the White House should designate a high-level focal point within the National Security Council for planning and implementing country-specific prevention, mitigation, and post-conflict response efforts.

The United States lacks both the capacity and the motivation to engage every fragile state in a significant manner. National security officials must prioritize U.S. attention and resources based on the national or humanitarian interests at stake. Top-tier countries are those whose fragility poses an actual threat to the lives of Americans. A second tier includes countries where fragility raises few obvious U.S. security concerns, but where the scale of human suffering (at human or natural hands) provides a compelling moral justification for sustained U.S. attention. A third category are fragile states that suffer from some combination of human insecurity, weak institutions, poor economics, and low social welfare, but where the security and humanitarian grounds for more robust U.S. involvement are lacking. Even in such countries, however, the United States can improve the effectiveness of its *existing* policies and resource outlays by tweaking its engagement to reflect the dynamics of fragility.

When it does choose to become heavily engaged, the United States should think soberly about the scale of its aspirations. The experiences of Iraq and Afghanistan demonstrate the hurdles of building war-torn countries into stable, prosperous, democratic states—particularly in the absence of credible, committed, and legitimate local partners. Institution building, it turns out, is hard. It is one thing for external actors to transfer bureaucratic processes and formal organizations; it is quite another to try to rebuild the social trust and respect for the law that are the ultimate foundations for effective and legitimate state institutions. Rather than a gleaming democracy, the realistic goal in many contexts may be "good enough governance"[7]—in the form of a state that is stable, capable of controlling its territory, and legitimate enough to carry out basic functions. U.S. officials may need to target their aid and policy engagement with an eye to making incremental improvements in a few critical institutions, includ-ing—as detailed below—those that are most problematic in terms of security threats and humanitarian suffering.

Improve Fragility Assessments, Intelligence, and Early Warning

The United States must also improve its ability to understand, anticipate, and respond to instability within—and threats from—fragile states. This will require developing a U.S. government-wide methodology to assess fragility in developing countries, expanding intelligence collection and analysis around the world, and creating mecha-nisms to encourage a prompt policy response to impending crises.

The point of departure should be a common understanding among U.S. depart-ments and agencies of the underlying causes and potential consequences of that fra-gility, building on the U.S. government's existing interagency conflict assessment framework. As chapter 1 suggested, each fragile state is unique or (to paraphrase Tolstoy) unhappy in its own way.[8] Even countries ranking closely on the Index have distinctive historical legacies and drivers of instability. States also differ markedly in terms of whether their fragility (and its spillover consequences) owes more to inca-pacity or insufficient political will. Understanding these distinctions is critical to craft-ing effective policies. Where capacity is lacking, the United States and other external actors should help enable states to fill the gaps. Where will is the problem, they should deploy incentives to induce or compel a stronger commitment. Where both are absent, they must try to change the attitudes of the country's leadership while working with reputable nongovernmental actors and civil society.

To complement this effort, the United States should expand its intelligence-gather-ing efforts in pivotal fragile states, as well as promote the sharing of unclassified information among U.S. agencies and with other governments, UN agencies, nongov-ernmental organizations, development professionals, and private sector actors, who are sometimes best positioned to understand local dynamics. Intelligence products will be more relevant to policymakers if they can assess not only the risk of state failure or internal conflict but also its potential impact on specific U.S. interests, such as the stability of oil supplies or the expansion of terrorist threats. Lastly, the president should authorize an automatic triggering mechanism, whereby the National Security Council would direct relevant agencies to formulate a government-wide strategy for any country integral to U.S. interests that enters a predefined danger zone.[9]

Tailor Development Aid and Policy to the Realities of Fragile States

Traditional models of donor engagement are often of limited utility in fragile states, where dysfunctional governance, human insecurity, and poor service delivery compound the challenge of poverty.[10] During 2009–2010, the Obama administration undertook two parallel policy reviews of U.S. development policy. The resulting documents—a Presidential Policy Directive on Global Development and a Quadrennial Diplomacy and Development Review (QDDR)—called attention to the unique development challenges of weak, failing, and war-torn states—without, however, providing detailed guidance for engaging them.[11]

As a first step, the United States should devote a greater proportion of its aid to fragile states. This runs counter to recent donor practice, which has been to channel aid preferentially to so-called "good performers," on the grounds that aid is likely to be more effective in good institutional environments.[12] What U.S. assistance does flow to fragile states is concentrated overwhelmingly in a handful of countries, particularly Afghanistan, Iraq, and Pakistan, as well as several major recipients of HIV/AIDS spending (including Ethiopia and Kenya). Beyond these priority countries, bilateral U.S. aid per capita to fragile states varies enormously, generally running much higher in postconflict countries such as Liberia than in vulnerable (and potentially strategically significant) states like Bangladesh.[13]

The same is true across the wider donor community. According to the OECD, between 2000 and 2007, just five countries—Afghanistan, Cameroon, DRC, Nigeria, and Sudan—received 61 percent of global official development assistance (ODA) delivered to fragile states (see figure 7.1). Moreover, much of this was in the form of debt relief or humanitarian assistance, rather than supporting long-term programs to build resilient institutions. While neither the United States nor any other donor can afford to be everywhere at the same level of funding, such ad hoc selectivity can contribute to the phenomenon of "aid orphans" essentially abandoned by the donor community.[14]

In designing its foreign assistance budget, the United States should follow the lead of the United Kingdom, which decided in summer 2010 to focus a larger percentage of its ODA to fragile states.[15] Certainly, aid to fragile states is a risky proposition, given often high levels of corruption, low absorptive capacity, and sometimes repressive or unresponsive regimes. But so are the costs of allowing such countries to "stew in their own juice."[16] Moreover, evidence suggests that carefully focused foreign assistance can raise growth, lower poverty, improve health and education, and reduce the risk of conflict even where states have weak governance.[17] In general, the United States should treat aid to fragile states like venture capital: liable to have a higher failure rate than typical investments, but potentially higher long-term returns if it succeeds.

The starting point for such aid interventions must be a deep understanding of the political economy of fragility in each recipient country, including the likely impact of aid on local power dynamics and underlying drivers of instability. Where the governing regime demonstrates a commitment to delivering goods to its citizens, the

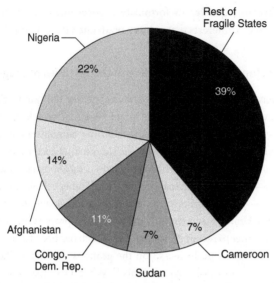

Figure 7.1: Shares of Net ODA to Fragile States 2000–2007 (percentage)
Source: Organisation for Economic Cooperation and Development

United States and other donors should put local officials in the driver's seat. Where a regime's will to do so is negligible, they should support service delivery through non-state actors, while working with local civil society to encourage political reform. But even where they need to bypass the state altogether, donors should attempt to build into the aid framework an eventual regulatory role for the state.[18] Finally, in extreme cases where a totalitarian or autocratic regime holds sway, aid may need to be restricted to humanitarian relief pending an eventual liberalization.

A recurrent dilemma for external actors in fragile states is the trade-off between delivering services rapidly to a needy population and building sustainable national systems to do so in the future. The donor community often exacerbates this predicament by channeling vast quantities of aid through their own service providers, failing to consult local authorities and poaching local talent. In so doing, donor agencies undercut state effectiveness, break the accountability link between citizens and the state, and create long-term dependency on the international community.[19] The United States can foster greater sustainability by aligning its assistance with local priorities, assisting direct service provision by the host state and civil society, and reducing the vast proportion of its aid currently "tied" to U.S.-sourced goods and service providers. It should also explore promising models of decentralized, community-driven development, such as Afghanistan's National Solidarity Program, which allows district councils and local citizens to participate in the design and implementation of projects using modest block grants.

Finally, U.S. methods of evaluating the effectiveness of its foreign assistance programs must be adjusted. Too often, U.S. performance indicators are geared primarily to measure inputs (money spent) or outputs (programs implemented), rather than the impact of programs on conditions on the ground. Establishing appropriate benchmarks for progress is particularly tricky in fragile states, given the lack of base-line data and the multiple goals (including growth, security, and good governance) that donors pursue simultaneously. Given the lack of incentives for honest in-house impact evaluation, the U.S. government should endorse regular monitoring by the Government Accountability Office of the effectiveness of U.S. assistance in fragile states. One model of honest evaluation has been the Special Inspector General for Iraq Reconstruction (SIGIR). In addition to exposing the poor design and mismanagement of billions of dollars of U.S. aid in Iraq, the Special Inspector General has called for the creation of a permanent evaluation agency to manage or oversee reconstruction efforts in conflict zones where the U.S. military is deployed.

Leverage All Policy Tools in a Whole-of-Government Approach

Fragile states pose interconnected security, governance, and development challenges that cannot be addressed with traditional development tools alone. Besides more effective development aid, the United States and other wealthy donors should seek to encourage legitimate and accountable governance, improved security and the rule of law, and balanced economic growth.

Although democracy provides no guarantee of good policy choices, history shows that legitimate, transparent, and accountable institutions that protect individual liberties, allow freedom of speech, and provide checks against abusive power promote political stability, human security, and economic growth. The United States should thus reaffirm its support for democracy assistance with increased resources and a government-wide strategy for democracy promotion. U.S. officials must acknowledge that democratic transitions take time and are often reversed; that elections can be divisive and unpredictable in highly divided (particularly postconflict) societies; and that U.S. policy may appear hypocritical in some cases, given the scope of U.S. national interests.

The United States must also improve its capacity to deliver rule of law and security sector assistance in fragile states. Unlike some Western donors, the United States possesses no constabulary forces to perform missions that fall between peacekeeping and policing in the aftermath of conflict. Nor can it mobilize and deploy adequate numbers of civilian police, criminal investigators, judges, prosecutors, and corrections officers essential to public security and justice. One place to begin is by consolidating all U.S. efforts to advance the rule of law abroad within a single office at the State Department, charged with managing a reserve corps of rule of law experts who could be deployed to crisis zones as temporary federal employees.[20] The United States must also revamp its fragmented approach to security sector reform in fragile and war-torn states. These authorities and programs are currently divided haphazardly among the Departments of Defense, Justice, State, Homeland Security, and USAID, with no clear interagency mechanism to determine programmatic or funding priorities. Moreover, U.S. security initiatives are often poorly integrated into a broader governance and development agenda. Particularly in insurgency contexts, the U.S. goal has been to generate large numbers of security forces—rather than build institutions and inculcate professionalism and democratic accountability.[21]

Fragile states are largely marginalized from the global economy, receiving a tiny share of foreign direct investment and benefiting little from world trade.[22] The United States and other donors should enhance weak states' access to markets, in part by eliminating trade barriers in agriculture, upon which so many fragile states depend. The Overseas Private Investment Corporation should be reformed to promote private U.S. investment in a greater range of labor-intensive manufacturing and assembly sectors (including textiles, apparel, and agribusiness), and U.S. Export-Import Bank capital loan guarantees and export credit insurance should be broadened for U.S. businesses operating in risky transitional contexts. Finally, the United States can press the World Bank and International Monetary Fund to help cushion the macroeconomic impact of economic shocks by helping governments in developing countries hedge against volatility in foreign exchange, interest rates, commodity prices, natural disasters, and extraordinary drought.[23]

Invest in Civilian Capabilities

Chronic underinvestment in the civilian instruments of national power has left the United States ill-equipped to address the long-term causes of state fragility and failure, respond to unforeseen contingencies, and provide critical aid to postconflict states. Although, in the context of the wars in Afghanistan and Iraq, civilian offices were established to address these issues—including the State Department's office of the Coordinator for Reconstruction and Stabilization (S/CRS) and USAID's Office of Military Affairs (OMA)—they have suffered from bureaucratic turf wars, insufficient personnel, unclear mandate, and the constraints of operating as civilian agencies in nonpermissive counterinsurgency environments.[24]

In the absence of civilian leadership, the Pentagon has often filled the vacuum, playing an increasing role not only in postconflict and counterinsurgency contexts but also in conflict prevention and other "shaping" activities to address the roots of instability. Between 2002 and 2008, the Defense Department's share of U.S. security and development assistance surged, while the State Department's steadily declined.[25] In 2005, for the first time, the Defense Department placed "Military Support for Security, Stability, Transition, and Reconstruction (SSTR) Operations" on par with war-fighting as a core military mission.[26] In both Afghanistan and Iraq, commanders in the field became deeply engaged in such activities through the use of Commander's Emergency Response Program (CERP) funds and the activities of provincial reconstruction teams (PRTs), dominated by U.S. soldiers. Finally, the Pentagon's several Regional Combatant Commands have emerged as important platforms for coordinating U.S. government-wide regional security initiatives. This trend is most pronounced in the work of Southern Command (SOUTHCOM), focused on the Western Hemisphere, and the newer Africa Command (AFRICOM).[27]

To avoid the appearance (and perhaps reality) of an overly militarized foreign policy, it is imperative that the expansion of the Defense Department's activities be firmly embedded within a larger U.S. strategy determined within a civilian-led policymaking framework. A first step is to restore some balance between the military and civilian components of U.S. engagement. For the past decade, the U.S. federal budget has been heavily skewed toward military expenditures, shortchanging those components of

America's national security apparatus best equipped to address the roots of weak governance, insecurity, and chronic poverty in the developing world, while forcing the U.S. military to conduct activities that might be more effectively carried out by well-resourced civilians. For all the recent attention to state failure, for example, the United States lacks a single non-humanitarian contingency fund that it can use to deliver aid in response to the specter or outbreak of violent conflict or to support a newly elected democratic government.[28]

Fortunately, influential voices from across the political spectrum have advocated a rebalanced federal budget to adequately fund the international affairs account.[29] During the first two years of the Obama administration, Secretary of State Clinton and Secretary of Defense Gates emerged as the most eloquent voices for ramping up the civilian sides of U.S. global engagement, as well as exploring innovative "pooled" funding arrangements to facilitate U.S. civilian-military cooperation in fragile states.[30] Still, defense expenditures continued to outpace civilian outlays for foreign policy by twelve to one in the Obama administration's budget request for fiscal year 2011, and new fiscal constraints and political realities make it unclear that Congress will rectify this imbalance.[31]

The U.S. government must also develop a civilian workforce to address the challenge of state fragility. This includes constituting an expeditionary cadre of civilian personnel that can deploy and intervene early enough to make a difference in volatile environments; dramatically increasing the number of Foreign Service officers available to the State Department; and restoring USAID's once vaunted technical and professional expertise. Secretary of State Clinton has committed to making such improvements,[32] but progress will require sustained legislative support in a difficult budgetary environment. Beyond funding, Secretary Clinton and her successors must continue efforts to transform State Department culture—traditionally focused on reporting, representing, and negotiating—for the technical and operational skill sets required for twenty-first century diplomats, including by transforming incentives for career advancement.[33]

Pursue Effective International Cooperation

Perhaps most importantly, to bolster fragile states, the United States must leverage the capabilities of international partners who also have interests at stake in improving governance in—and preventing spillovers from—the developing world.[34] Washington should work with other donor countries and institutions—including the OECD, G20 and G8, United Nations, World Bank, IMF, and regional organizations—to forge multilateral consensus on priority global challenges, country-specific requirements for effective state building, the development of joint country plans, and equitable burden sharing in financing and implementing external aid. The United States should offer greater financial and political support to the UN Peacebuilding Commission's Peacebuilding Fund and press for an expansion of the World Bank's Low-Income Countries Under Stress (LICUS) Trust Fund as a multilateral model for delivering help quickly to weak and failing states. In parallel with these steps, multilateral initiatives like the Counter-Terrorism Committee of the UN Security Council, the Financial Action Task Force, and the WHO's International Health Regulations must also be retooled to support capacity-building in weak states, so that the latter can meet their global obligations.

Meanwhile, the United States must expand its support for multilateral peacekeeping efforts. In rare cases, this could involve U.S. military forces (for instance, through NATO). But for the most part, U.S. contributions will include financial and logistical support for UN operations or regional peacekeeping missions. Indeed, the United Nations is being called upon as never before to keep (and at times enforce) peace between warring parties, with approximately 100,000 "blue helmets" in fifteen-odd peacekeeping operations around the globe.[35] The complexity and pace of these undertakings have stretched the modest budget and capacities of the UN Department of Peacekeeping Operations. Too often, Washington has pressed the UN Security Council to endorse ambitious mandates, while sometimes withholding the political and financial support the United Nations needs to get the job done. The White House should insist on realistic mandates and persuade Congress that the best way to optimize the United Nations' performance is for the United States to serve as a reliable (if demanding) supporter of UN peace operations.

It is equally important for the United States to empower and equip regional organizations to monitor brewing conflicts, launch preventive deployments, and undertake multidimensional peace operations. The African Union, in particular, seeks a larger African role in addressing violent conflict on the continent. Meeting these aspirations will require greater U.S. investment in building the capacity and professionalism of African militaries, as well as providing logistical and material support for African Union troop deployments, whose shortcomings were revealed in the Assistance Mission in Sudan (AMIS) deployed to Darfur. An immediate priority should be to extend and expand U.S. support for the valuable Africa Contingency Operations Training and Assistance program, as well as the G8-sponsored Global Peace Operations Initiative, designed to train peacekeeping troops around the world.

Some analysts have proposed expanding the repertoire of the international community beyond UN peace operations, to explore "alternative institutional arrangements," including "de facto trusteeships" and "shared sovereignty" schemes that would provide a check on dysfunctional governance. For these observers, the supposed links between state weakness and transnational spillovers call into question the sanctity of state sovereignty as the bedrock of international order.[36] Arrangements along the lines of "neo-trusteeship" are worth exploring—and in a few cases, such as UN trusteeships in East Timor and Kosovo, have met with relative success—but their potential should not be exaggerated, given their intrusive and controversial nature. One promising example is the Governance and Economic Management Assistance Program (GEMAP) that the donor community imposed on Liberia in 2005, which introduced a "dual key" system in the management of Liberia's revenue collection and expenditures, including the placement of international civil servants in important positions. Such a scheme was possible, however, only because of the extremity of Liberia's prostration after years of war.

As the preceding paragraphs suggest, the United States cannot improve its policy toward the world's fragile states by relying on traditional aid alone. Rather, it must draw on a broad range of national instruments, as well as international partnerships. Addressing the interconnected security, governance, and development challenges of fragile states will require significant integration among—and adaptations by—the historically distinct development, diplomatic, and defense communities within the U.S. government. This agenda will also demand greater patience and a higher tolerance for political risk from the U.S. foreign policy and aid bureaucracies, as well as a larger, more flexible pool of resources from congressional paymasters.

BREAKING THE LINKS BETWEEN
STATE FRAGILITY AND SPECIFIC THREATS

While the United States has a general interest in promoting effective governance and human security in the developing world, its resources and attention for doing so are limited. Beyond extreme humanitarian crises, U.S. policymakers must therefore prioritize those states and particular governance gaps that are most directly linked to global threats with the potential to harm U.S. interests.

Such policies must take into account *why* a particular fragile state matters to the United States, and target the most relevant governance shortcomings. In some countries the primary goal may be to promote economic growth or improve the provision of services; in others it may be simply to ensure that a government can control its borders. Policymakers must also be cognizant of the inevitable trade-offs of short- versus long-term approaches, and of pursuing reforms in certain sectors over others. For instance, the United States may build up a weak state's law enforcement capacity to combat terrorism, but in so doing could bolster an authoritarian regime. Finally, policymakers must keep in mind that the dynamics of transnational threats may undermine governance and state capacity in already weak polities, feeding a self-reinforcing cycle of state weakness and negative spillovers.

Terrorism

Chapter 2 suggests that fragile states are less important to transnational terrorism than is generally assumed. The vast majority of fragile states are unaffected by the global terrorist network affiliated with al-Qaeda, which exploits developed as well as developing countries. The purported benefits of state fragility to transnational terrorists, moreover, are often overstated. Weak developing countries can provide terrorist groups with valuable conflict experience and training opportunities. But they appear to play only modest roles in providing pools of recruits, sources of financing, or targets for operations.

The biggest benefit that a fragile state can provide al-Qaeda and affiliated groups is a safe haven from national or international interdiction—something the network has enjoyed in a small number of troubled, Muslim-majority nations, including Afghanistan, Pakistan, and potentially Yemen and Somalia. The first two have obviously played an outsized role in al-Qaeda's operations, serving as the organizational base or launching pad for virtually every major jihadi plot of the past two decades.[37]

The historical record, however, suggests that the attractiveness of weak states as potential sanctuaries is highly contingent on local conditions. Two core requirements include: (1) weak commitment—and not simply inability—on the part of the central government to take on jihadi groups; and (2) the presence of sympathetic local power wielders and populations willing, for historical, cultural, religious, ideological, and/or pecuniary motivations, to provide terrorist groups with support. Generally speaking, truly "ungoverned" or anarchic zones, like Somalia in the 1990s, offer less predictable (and thus less hospitable) settings for jihadi networks.

These findings suggest several guideposts for charting U.S. policy. Overall, U.S. officials and international partners should be clear-eyed about the modest risks of transnational terrorism emanating from most weak states. There are many chaotic states in the world, but only a handful that might be predisposed to an indigenous *salafi* movement. Al-Qaeda is unlikely to find adequate support among local power brokers in Central Africa, for instance. The United States should probably be less concerned about the possibility that a few terrorists might be operating in any given weak state (e.g., Mali or Mauritania), than by the fact that in a small number of very weak countries (including Afghanistan, Pakistan, Yemen, and Somalia), local movements sympathetic to al-Qaeda have enough of a presence—and popular support—to control at least part of the territory.

Unfortunately, while terrorist havens in areas like the FATA are less the "lawless" zones of Western imagining than "alternatively governed" regions, the United States has much less leverage against nonstate authorities than against national governments. With tribal leaders, for example, the threat of sanctions or aid cut-offs might be meaningless, and any U.S. incentives offered to nonstate actors risk undermining the central state's authority. An effective strategy would use targeted assistance to drive a wedge between transnational terrorist groups and their local hosts, working through central governments (where feasible) to increase their presence in contested regions. Of course, such an approach will require especially careful calibration in areas where central authority has long been resented and rejected, and where an increased state presence (especially if oppressive) could actually increase sympathy for terrorist outfits.

Likewise, an overly militarized response (such as a reliance on drone attacks) does little to address underlying vulnerabilities, while threatening to radicalize local populations. Particularly in Africa, the United States should recalibrate its major counterterrorism assistance initiatives, such as the Trans-Sahara Counterterrorism Partnership (TSCTP) and the Combined Joint Task Force-Horn of Africa (CJTF-HOA). Although these programs were launched with an explicit appreciation of the complex sources of Islamic extremism, they have been carried out primarily by the U.S. military, and the overwhelming focus has been improving the operational effectiveness of foreign security forces—rather than on broader civilian-led efforts to promote democratic governance, address social and economic grievances, and discredit extreme ideologies.

The United States must also be wary of opening itself up to manipulation by ruling regimes seeking to gain access to Western resources or to crush internal dissent by tarring domestic political opponents as members of the global *salafi* jihad—as has occurred, for instance, in Mauritania. In Yemen, Pakistan, and elsewhere, U.S. officials must likewise remain cognizant of the often blurry line between a state's will and its actual capacity to take on transnational terrorist groups, and must tailor responses accordingly.

The United States should also work to incorporate more states into the global struggle against terrorism, which has too often borne a "made in the USA" stamp. In parallel with its own initiatives to train and equip foreign security services, the United States can work with like-minded governments to bolster the capacities of the United Nations, regional organizations, and multilateral partnerships. Priority efforts should include conducting an inventory of all U.S. counterterrorism capacity-building programs; strengthening the UN Security Council's Counter-Terrorism Committee and its Counter-Terrorism Executive Directorate (CTED) to help member states meet their obligations; reinvigorating the G8's Counter-Terrorism Action Group (CTAG) so that it can coordinate capacity-building efforts; prodding the United Nations to integrate the piecemeal counterterrorism-related activities of its multiple programs and agencies; bolstering the resources and activities of the FATF, IMF, World Bank, and other donors to coordinate anti-money-laundering efforts; and strengthening the counterterrorism commitments of regional and subregional organizations, particularly in the developing world (such as the AU, ASEAN, SAARC, and the Organization of the Islamic Conference).[38]

Weapons of Mass Destruction

Chapter 3 identified at least five pathways by which state fragility could facilitate the acquisition of WMD by state or nonstate actors. In principle, a weak state could seek to purchase, steal, or construct WMD; become a target for the theft or diversion of WMD material; provide a transit point for networks trafficking in WMD; serve as a sanctuary for nonstate actors seeking to develop their own weapons; or lose control over its WMD arsenal to nonstate actors as a result of its internal collapse. These are all serious, if not equally plausible, scenarios.

And yet the proliferation threat from fragile states should not be exaggerated. Beyond Pakistan and North Korea—admittedly two of the world's most dangerous countries—few fragile states currently possess WMD-related materials, or appear to be seeking them. On the other hand, the governance gaps of "states to watch," including Russia and Iran, pose serious proliferation concerns. And as the global scope of the A.Q. Khan network revealed, the Achilles' heel of the global nonproliferation regime may be middle- and even upper-middle-income countries that possess technological expertise critical to manufacture nuclear weapons, but that lack the commitment and/or ability to implement export controls and nonproliferation laws.

Breaking the links that do exist between poor state performance and WMD proliferation risks will require ramping up capacity-building and technical assistance; improving the performance of law enforcement and border control agencies in fragile states; combating corruption (especially among frontier guards, customs officials, and guards at nuclear facilities); ensuring that the livelihoods and operational needs of scientists, professionals, and militaries are provided for during periods of economic hardship in nuclear weapons states; and developing contingency plans for nuclear-armed states (namely North Korea and Pakistan) at risk for serious political instability.

Given competing domestic and national security priorities, many weak states (as well as some stronger ones) lack the financial resources or will to meet their nonproliferation obligations.[39] For example, UN Security Council Resolution 1540 (2004) requires all UN members to take legislative and regulatory steps to prevent the transfer of WMD, their means of delivery, and technological know-how from falling into the hands of nonstate actors. Years after its passage, however, implementation lags.[40] The United States and other donor governments can help break these logjams—and help vulnerable countries meet their commitments—by providing focused financial and technical assistance, taking advantage of a mechanism created under Resolution 1540. In addition to multilateral efforts, the United States should expand bilateral assistance programs through the Departments of Energy and Defense. In recent years, these programs have trained border security personnel and installed radiation detection devices at hundreds of border crossings, bridges, and tunnels, and dozens of seaports and airports in some thirty-six countries.[41]

Of course, capacity-building assistance could be rendered meaningless by corruption among border guards, military personnel, scientists, or insiders at nuclear facilities. Thus anticorruption efforts should be a major priority of U.S. nonproliferation programs, particularly in key states that possess (or border) nuclear storage sites and are known to have hosted organized criminal networks (for instance, countries of the Caucasus, Central Asia, and Eastern Europe). The United States and its partners in the international community should prioritize economic assistance and job creation in hard-hit communities with WMD facilities. They can also broaden bilateral training and capacity-building programs for customs and border security agencies in vulnerable countries, and sponsor more robust multilateral initiatives through organizations like the OECD, WTO, and World Customs Organization.

The United States also needs to work with close allies on contingency plans for potential nightmare scenarios—such as the collapse of a nuclear-armed state—that could put nuclear weapons into the hands of terrorists or a rogue faction of the government. The two most plausible cases, Pakistan and North Korea, would present no good options, given the uncertainties of "surgical" air strikes, on the one hand, and the massive costs and risks of an invasion to seize control of the country's nuclear installations and borders, on the other.[42]

Such supply-side measures are critical. But as Braun and Chyba observe, they are inadequate to combat nuclear proliferation in the face of spreading uranium enrichment and nuclear weapons technology, particularly when it comes to states with "especially weak governments." For instance, even sustained financial, regulatory, and technical assistance to weak states "cannot extend a government's authority into territory it does not de facto control." Successful nonproliferation will also require reducing the demand for nuclear weapons through a variety of policies, including security guarantees, economic incentives and sanctions, nuclear fuel arrangements, efforts to bring all nuclear weapons states into the NPT regime, and deemphasizing the role of nuclear weapons in U.S. defense doctrine and international security.[43] Libya, which renounced and dismantled its WMD programs in return for incentives from the West, is a promising example.

Transnational Crime

As chapter 4 underscored, fragile states can provide multiple benefits to transnational criminal networks. These include porous borders, high corruption, spotty law enforcement, weak judicial systems, safe havens from interdiction, and lack of legal economic alternatives, particularly after violent conflict. Moreover, crime itself tends to erode the foundations of effective governance by reducing the will and capacity of ruling regimes to enforce the rule of law and provide other public goods. In extreme cases, the state may become "captured," and the government may essentially defect from international regimes governing criminal activity. Policymakers interested in building effective states must recognize that crime is typically a cause, as well as a consequence, of state fragility—and must be tackled head on in efforts to promote institutions of good governance.

As with jihadi terrorism and WMD proliferation, the connection between state weakness and transnational crime is less clear-cut than imagined. State fragility is closely associated with certain crimes, such as opium and coca production, piracy, illicit arms sales, and certain environmental crimes—but less consistently with others, including intellectual property theft, money laundering, and human trafficking. Generally speaking, criminals prefer to base their activities in dysfunctional rather than truly failed states, and will often assume higher risks to operate in more convenient locations. The recent tribulations of Mexico, a comparatively strong state caught in a deadly war with drug traffickers, highlights this point. The Mexican example also underscores that transnational crime reflects global demand for illicit commodities, including shortsighted and often counterproductive policies of rich-world governments.

Breaking the connections that do exist between transnational crime and state weakness will require sustained bilateral and multilateral engagement to help overcome the commitment and capacity gaps that leave fragile states vulnerable to infiltration by organized criminal networks. Priorities for U.S. and international action include more robust support for anti-corruption measures; strengthening law enforcement, border control, and judicial transparency and capacity; reducing the attraction to criminals of conflict and postconflict environments; and, finally, reexamining the source control approach to the global drug trade.

Addressing transnational crime will require more robust initiatives to target corruption at both the micro (e.g., border guard) and macro (e.g., kleptocratic regime) levels. The former is addressed above, in the discussion of WMD proliferation. In the latter case, the international community needs more effective strategies to combat the involvement of state authorities in organized crime, particularly narcotics trafficking. One possibility is to expand the multilateral sanctions repertoire available to the UN Security Council to combat major organized crime, along the lines of the al-Qaeda/Taliban sanctions committee, to investigate and punish official involvement in criminal activity. Such a confrontational strategy would find little support in the developing world, however, suggesting that the international community will continue to rely primarily on criminal sanctions of judicial institutions,[44] supplemented by more robust monitoring and evaluation mechanisms (as exists in the Inter-American Drug Abuse Control Commission's Multilateral Evaluation Mechanism). Nevertheless, the donor community must make combating criminal and kleptocratic activity by developing country regimes a bigger priority.

The United States and its OECD partners should also take stronger actions to curb the massive illicit financial flows out of developing countries—a drain of wealth that may outpace inflows official development assistance (ODA) by a ratio of ten to one.[45] This will include shutting down international havens for ill-gotten gains—an agenda that the Financial Action Task Force (FATF) has begun to take seriously. One promising mechanism is the joint UNODC-World Bank Stolen Assets Recovery (StAR) Initiative, which provides legal and technical assistance to developing countries to recover and transparently manage stolen assets, and fulfill their obligations under the UN Convention against Corruption. A further measure could be to require that rich-world banks report any deposits that are potentially the result of corrupt practices—as they are already required to do in potential terrorist financing cases.[46]

The international community can also nurture the capacity of fragile states to police their terrestrial and maritime borders. A fundamental premise of the contemporary international system is that sovereign states have the obligation to control the movement of objects and people across national frontiers.[47] But for most states, this vision is a mirage. The United States can begin to rectify this situation by undertaking a thorough interagency study of borders around the world that merit priority attention and by streamlining its multiple bilateral border control assistance programs.[48] In parallel, the United States should cooperate with other wealthy governments to improve the ability of weak states to collectively police their territorial waters against piracy, narcotics trade, human trafficking, migrant smuggling, illegal fishing, oil theft, and other contraband activity.[49]

Current international institutions to combat organized crime are over-stretched and under-resourced. One immediate priority is implementing the frameworks for mutual legal assistance, extradition, law enforcement cooperation, and technical assistance contained in the UN Conventions against Transnational Organized Crime and Corruption. Another is increasing the technical role of the UNODC, which remains constrained by a modest budget (about $100 million) and an overwhelming focus on drugs, to the exclusion of other types of crime.[50]

Chapter 4 underlined the need to combat transnational crime in war-torn states—a task too often left as an afterthought in current practice.[51] UN peacekeeping missions or other international forces should have an explicit mandate to address criminal activity and to share intelligence with international bodies such as INTERPOL and UNODC.[52] Combating crime in post-conflict settings will also require promoting alternative livelihoods. The lessons of Afghanistan, where opium production has exploded following years of eradication efforts—unmatched by serious programs to provide alternative sources of credit and income to poor farmers—are sobering and instructive.[53] The UN Peacebuilding Commission, which is currently taking on

Guinea-Bissau's combustible mix of transnational trafficking networks and chronic political instability, could serve as a useful coordinating mechanism in such efforts.

Finally, the United States and other wealthy countries need to reexamine their own policies and attitudes toward transnational crime. Whether the commodity is drugs, timber, people, or gemstones, cross-border traffic in illicit commodities typically responds to developed world demand (and, in the case of arms trafficking, is largely a product of developed-country industry). Where parallel, licit markets exist (as for gemstones or timber), a partial solution is to establish and strengthen certification schemes, such as the valuable (if flawed) Kimberley Process for certifying diamonds as "conflict-free."[54]

The United States can also work with other governments to curtail the sale of both heavy weapons systems and small arms to poorly governed countries (as well as to increase funding for programs to secure and dispose of weapons stockpiles worldwide, as NATO has done in Ukraine and Moldova, for instance). One positive step would be to endorse the 2001 UN Program of Action on Small Arms and Light Weapons and its follow-up initiatives to manage weapons stockpiles, restrict illegal brokering, and improve efforts to mark and trace weapons.[55] The United States should also consider supporting an extension of the UN register of conventional arms to include small arms and light weapons.

Perhaps most importantly, the time is ripe for the United States to explore alternatives to source control approaches to the global drug trade. Prohibition regimes rest on the proposition that they can be sufficiently punitive to deter perpetrators from offending behavior. Four decades after President Nixon declared a "war on drugs," however, the United States has failed to slow the flow of drugs into the United States.[56] On the contrary, by raising profit margins, U.S. policy has actually increased incentives for cultivation and trafficking, generating enormous rents for drug cartels willing to assume greater risk.

Presuming no near or medium-term change in global prohibition regimes, it is essential that the United States promote a balanced, long-term approach to reducing the production of drugs in source countries. In addition to a heavy emphasis on interdiction, law enforcement, and judicial reform, alternative development must also be a priority. Although eradication must remain an element of any counternarcotics strategy, experience from Bolivia to Afghanistan suggests that single-minded focus on it can risk a backlash.[57] In the latter, selective eradication has risked driving farmers into the arms of insurgents, while letting rich traffickers escape and pushing production elsewhere.[58]

Energy Insecurity

Increased reliance on fossil fuels from poorly governed and conflict-prone countries makes state fragility a growing factor in global energy security. At least in theory, political instability, violence, and social unrest can threaten the predictability of supplies by endangering production and transit, leaving world energy markets vulnerable to sudden price shocks. However, as chapter 5 describes, there is little evidence that such disruptions are occurring on a scale that would have a sustained impact on global prices (with the possible exceptions of Iraq and Nigeria).

On the other hand, the rampant corruption, weak rule of law, and poor economic and business policies that characterize many weak state energy producers (as well as some stronger ones, including Russia, Venezuela, Mexico, and Iran) have exacerbated tight global energy markets by discouraging investment and driving down production. Moreover, the windfalls from natural resource bonanzas can paradoxically prove more a curse than a blessing to already fragile states, reinforcing authoritarian governance, crowding out other productive forms of economic activity, and exacerbating violent conflict between groups competing for lucrative revenue streams.

Breaking the links between governance gaps (including in states to watch) and energy insecurity will require a four-pronged approach. First, the United States government should identify global hotspots where poor governance could cause disruptions to energy supplies. Second, to ward off the "resource curse," U.S. development and investment policies should promote equitable growth in resource-rich states. Third, the United States and other OECD countries should support efforts by businesses and civil society organizations to promote the rule of law in resource-rich states. Finally, U.S. policies must be aware of the risks of pursuing energy sources in authoritarian weak states, given the potential for repressive governance to devolve into political instability—and potential future energy disruptions. Of course, more broadly, real energy security will require the U.S. government—and public—to take serious steps toward developing alternative energy sources.

The United States should begin by comprehensively mapping global energy markets, routes, and supply networks to pinpoint where dysfunctional governance could potentially have a major impact on production or transit. Such an analysis would focus not only on currently fragile states but on other states with worrisome underlying political, economic, and security dynamics. On this basis, the United States and its allies could increase security assistance to target countries to enable them to protect energy infrastructure—or, in extreme cases, could undertake direct military intervention.

The United States should also collaborate with international partners to help ensure that energy windfalls in weak states do not exacerbate corruption, inequitable development, authoritarian governance, and violent conflict. This agenda should include campaigning for worldwide endorsement of the OECD Convention on Bribery of Foreign Public Officials in International Business Transactions, and for full implementation of the OECD's Public Sector Integrity Assessment Framework, which sets standards for rich-world companies and governments alike.

Rich-world governments must also promote transparent revenue management in the exploitation of natural resources, both on the part of national governments and Western-domiciled corporations involved in these sectors. The UK-sponsored Extractive Industries Transparency Initiative (EITI), for example, works with some thirty resource-rich developing countries to improve transparency in public revenue management. Another worthwhile initiative is the "Publish What You Pay" campaign, which encourages multinational corporations to reveal their payments to local authorities, so that civil society groups and the broader public in these countries can monitor how such revenues are spent. In parallel, the IMF or World Bank should formulate guidelines for developing countries to manage their resource revenues, both to minimize the impact of price shocks and to prevent the buildup of massive funds that might prove tempting to corrupt or populist governments—as has occurred in Venezuela and Azerbaijan.[59]

In many poorly governed states, establishing genuine rule of law will be a long-term process requiring the development of a robust civil society, stronger judicial and law enforcement institutions, a political system of checks and balances, and democratic accountability. The United States and other donor countries can and should support initiatives in each of these areas. In countries like Russia, Kazakhstan, or Bolivia, the problem is less about general rule of law than about ensuring that contracts are upheld, property rights respected, and competent and impartial third-party enforcement mechanisms are available.[60] The United States should encourage such efforts where they are occurring, and press for them where they are not—emphasizing that they will pay economic dividends without necessarily intruding on (at least in the short term) a regime's prerogatives in other areas.

Finally, The United States needs to recognize the long-term costs of its strategy of enabling authoritarian regimes in energy-producing countries. The fate of the shah of Iran is a classic example of how shortsighted policies to ensure access to energy resources may sow seeds of instability and radicalism—and lead to future supply disruptions. This does not imply abandoning bilateral or business relationships in undemocratic states. But U.S. policies should find a balance that promotes better governance and long-term stability without antagonizing host regimes.

Infectious Disease

As the rapid emergence and spread of the H1N1 virus in 2009 vividly revealed, we live in an epidemiologically interdependent world. The growing ability of natural (as well as man-made) pathogens to travel quickly to all corners of the earth has led many to portray the world's fragile states as the weak link in securing global public health. Given their dilapidated primary care infrastructure, inadequate surveillance and reporting systems, and meager preventive and response capabilities, such countries seem ideal vectors (as well as victims) for the next great plague.

And yet as chapter 6 underscores, the relationship between state fragility and infectious disease is far from straightforward. Most of the endemic diseases that afflict the "bottom billion" pose little immediate threat outside the developing world—making them a humanitarian, but not necessarily a security, concern for the United States. Nor is there compelling evidence that the burden of infectious disease (including HIV/AIDS) has been a significant factor in instability or state failure, even in the hardest-hit countries. Finally, when it comes to generating rapid-onset pandemics—from SARS to avian influenza to "swine flu"—the countries of greatest concern may actually be better performing nations that have extensive links with the global economy but possess important governance gaps.

Nevertheless, it is clear across a wide range of developing countries that shortcomings in state capacity can facilitate the emergence, persistence, and spread of infectious disease. Such gaps—including meager investment in basic public health, lack of technical capacity to detect and contain outbreaks, inadequate management and planning systems for coping with health emergencies, and the absence of qualified professionals—have repeatedly stymied prompt public health responses to epidemics, from avian influenza in Cambodia to Ebola in Central Africa. And yet poor state performance is often more a question of commitment than inherent capability. Governing regimes in developing countries have repeatedly exacerbated infectious disease threats by condoning massive corruption and mismanagement of national health systems; concealing the scope of public health emergencies; promoting public ignorance and misinformation; and resisting external offers of support. Over the past decade, for example, unproductive attitudes on the part of regimes in Nigeria, China, South Africa, Indonesia, and Zimbabwe have undercut efforts to grapple with (respectively) polio, SARS, HIV/AIDS, avian influenza, and cholera.

The United States can take steps to help break the links between weak state capacity or will, on the one hand, and the threat of infectious disease, on the other. First, it should identify developing states of greatest concern for global pandemics and work with other governments to target aid accordingly. While such predictions are no easy task, a good place to start is with low-ranking countries that have recently experienced epidemics of the world's most dangerous diseases. This cohort includes states weak enough to have serious capacity (and in some cases political) gaps that prevent them from recognizing or responding to outbreaks, yet which are sufficiently linked to regional or international trade networks that an outbreak on their territory poses a significant global risk. Such countries include Vietnam, Cambodia, Nigeria, Egypt, Bangladesh, Burma, and Pakistan, all of which have seen (limited) avian flu outbreaks.

Second, the United States should, with other wealthy donors, invest in improving health care delivery in weak states, with an emphasis on building up overall health systems rather than focusing on single diseases (such as HIV/AIDS or malaria). Important steps will include providing financial and technical support to train additional health professionals, prioritizing the expansion of cadres of community health workers in rural areas; and expanding military-to-military health partnerships with developing countries, which have proven among the most useful U.S. instruments to help weak states improve health delivery capabilities.[61] Strengthening a weak state's overall health care delivery system will pay dividends in the event that a dangerous outbreak *does* occur within its borders, improving the odds that it will be recognized and contained.[62] The Obama administration has taken an important step in launching a Global Health Initiative, focused on building responsive health care systems, which will help developing countries to respond to a wide range of health contingencies.

Third, U.S. health sector assistance should target gaps in disease surveillance and response systems in fragile states, to enable them to detect, identify, and contain potential pandemics. The United States currently promotes emergency detection in developing countries through the Department of Defense's Global Emerging Infections Surveillance and Response System (GEIS), which includes laboratories in Jakarta,

Cairo, Bangkok, Lima, and Nairobi. Additional measures should include embedding teams of response and containment experts in at-risk countries; mutual aid agreements for sharing intelligence, research, diagnostics, personnel, vaccines, and antibiotics; and assistance for building networks of research institutions and centers for disease control.[63] One multilateral mechanism through which such assistance could be coordinated is the Global Outbreak Alert and Response Network (GOARN), a WHO-led technical collaboration of institutions and networks that pool human and technical resources with the aim of rapidly identifying, confirming, and responding to outbreaks of international importance.

Fourth, the international community should encourage greater transparency in developing countries' health reporting—and failures to report outbreaks and share information should be taken seriously at the political level. The Bush administration incorporated this principle into its International Partnership on Avian Pandemic Influenza (IPAPI), developed in concert with the WHO.[64] The challenge now is to ensure its consistent implementation. The WHO's newly revised International Health Regulations, which took effect in June 2007, are meant to prod countries to improve their surveillance and reporting of disease outbreaks. They represent a major step forward in the normative framework for disease reporting, but the WHO cannot enforce compliance. The United States should therefore make such reporting a priority in bilateral relations, and propose travel warnings and other penalties for countries that do not comply.

CONCLUSION

The first decade of the twenty-first century drove home a reality of contemporary international life: it is no longer possible for the world's richest and most powerful nation to remain indifferent to the fate of the planet's impoverished, insecure, and misgoverned countries. In many ways, this represents a paradigm shift away from traditional conceptions of U.S. national security, with profound implications for the U.S. foreign policy agenda. Developments in a handful of fragile states could have truly significant strategic consequences; these include North Korea, Pakistan, and Iraq.

But many other weak states also play an important regional or international role; the spillover effects of state weakness in Kenya, Nigeria, Ethiopia, Sudan, Yemen, Colombia, or Somalia, for instance, could have (or have had) considerable ramifications for the United States or other wealthy countries. Other strategically significant countries, such as Algeria, Iran, or Lebanon, are marginally stronger, but face many of the problems of fragile states and are at risk for further instability. Moreover, the governance gaps of several stronger states, from Russia to India to Mexico, can carry major costs for U.S. interests. A nuanced understanding of the dynamics of state weakness is therefore critical to crafting balanced U.S. policies.

At the same time, some perspective is in order. Not every weak and failing state is an Afghanistan in the making. The hard truth is that some of the worst cases of state failure may actually have little strategic impact on the United States, whatever the local or regional spillovers. Witness the decade-long implosion of the Democratic Republic of the Congo, which despite its almost unbelievable human costs has gone practically unnoticed in the United States. As the preceding chapters have illustrated, precise and informed analysis is needed to determine which fragile states represent an actual or potential direct threat to U.S. interests. Policymakers should be realistic in assessing both the threats that emanate from weak states, and the potential for a U.S. response (of whatever variety) to have a meaningful impact.

Likewise, policymakers' options and decisions must be informed by an understanding of which interests are at stake in particular fragile or collapsed states. It is appropriate, indeed desirable, for the United States or other wealthy countries to act on the basis of moral or humanitarian concerns. But overall policies, as well as the resources allocated to implement them, will inevitably be subject to strategic calculations.

Generally speaking, the United States is more likely to act decisively to help mitigate state fragility in countries where vital interests are seen to be at stake. In engaging these countries, the United States will often face a trade-off between broad-based and narrowly tailored policies—that is, between a broad governance and development agenda to build effective state institutions and more limited interventions designed to address specific transnational threats. For instance, focusing donor resources on building up disease surveillance and diagnostic systems in developing countries (which makes sense from the point of view of combating major pandemics) does little to address the public health crises facing many of these countries. Likewise, bolstering security forces in poorly governed weak states, which may be critical to addressing terrorist and criminal threats, may entrench authoritarian regimes and even lead to instability in the longer term. Thus, while the new paradigm of weak states as potential "threats" has elevated these countries to the top of the U.S. and international security agendas, that same lens may also encourage a shortsighted and unsustainable approach to promoting effective statehood in the developing world.

Finally, state weakness—and the spillover effects it sometimes generates—cannot be understood merely in an "us/other" framework, in which weakness "out there" create problems for "us here." As the book has documented, state weakness is often a function, at least in part, of sins of omission or commission by wealthy-world governments, corporations, and citizens—not least when it comes to sustaining markets for illicit goods. In the end, the afflictions of weak states are "our" problem too—both because they can generate spillover effects that can affect us directly and because they are inhabited by fellow human beings who have a moral and humanitarian claim on our conscience.

Appendix 7.1: Are Weak States Really a Threat?

Rank on Index	Country	Presence of al-Qaeda or affiliates[65]	Nuclear Weapons or Weapons-Grade Fissile Material Stockpiles[66]	"Major" Narcotics Source Country[67]	Incidence of Piracy[68]	"Major" Money Laundering Center[69]	Major Energy Producer[70]	Outbreak Site for H5N1, SARS or H1N1[71]
1	SOMALIA	X			X			
2	AFGHANISTAN	X		X		X		
3	CONGO, DEM. REP.				X			
4	IRAQ	X					X	X
5	BURUNDI							
6	SUDAN	X					X	
7	CENTRAL AFRICAN REP.							
8	ZIMBABWE							
9	LIBERIA							
10	COTE D'IVOIRE						X	
11	ANGOLA						X	
12	HAITI					X		
13	SIERRA LEONE							
14	ERITREA							
15	NORTH KOREA		X					
16	CHAD						X	
17	BURMA			X		X	X	

(continued)

Appendix 7.1: Continued

Rank on Index	Country	Presence of al-Qaeda or affiliates[65]	Nuclear Weapons or Weapons-Grade Fissile Material Stockpiles[66]	"Major" Narcotics Source Country[67]	Incidence of Piracy[68]	"Major" Money Laundering Center[69]	Major Energy Producer[70]	Outbreak Site for H5N1, SARS or H1N1[71]
18	GUINEA-BISSAU							
19	ETHIOPIA							
20	CONGO, REP.						X	
21	NIGER	X						
22	NEPAL							
23	GUINEA				X			
24	RWANDA							
25	EQUATORIAL GUINEA						X	
26	TOGO							
27	UGANDA	X						
28	NIGERIA	X	X		X	X	X	X
29	CAMEROON						X	
30	YEMEN	X					X	
31	COMOROS							
32	ZAMBIA							
33	PAKISTAN	X	X	X		X	X	X
34	CAMBODIA					X		X

#	Country							
35	TURKMENISTAN						X	
36	UZBEKISTAN	X	X				X	
37	MAURITANIA	X					X	
38	DJIBOUTI							X
39	MOZAMBIQUE							
40	PAPUA NEW GUINEA						X	
41	SWAZILAND							
42	TAJIKISTAN	X						
43	EAST TIMOR						X	
44	BURKINA FASO							
45	LAOS			X				X
46	MALAWI							
47	COLOMBIA			X		X	X	X
48	BANGLADESH	X			X			X
49	MADAGASCAR							
50	KENYA	X			X	X		
51	GAMBIA							
52	MALI	X						
53	LESOTHO							
54	SOLOMON ISLANDS							
55	TANZANIA				X			

(*continued*)

Rank on Index / Country	Presence of al-Qaeda or affiliates[65]	Nuclear Weapons or Weapons-Grade Fissile Material Stockpiles[66]	"Major" Narcotics Source Country[67]	Incidence of Piracy[68]	"Major" Money Laundering Center[69]	Major Energy Producer[70]	Outbreak Site for H5N1, SARS or H1N1[71]
56 SRI LANKA				X			
Totals in Bottom Quintile (critically weak states)	7 (25.0%)	2 (7.1%)	2 (7.1%)	4 (14.3%)	4 (14.3%)	9 (32.1%)	2 (7.1%)
Totals in Bottom 2 Quintiles (Weak States)	15 (26.8%)	4 (7.1%),	5 (8.9%)	8 (14.3%)	8 (14.3%)	18 (32.1%)	8 (14.3%)
Additional Observations	Al Qaeda presence is particularly high in five countries (Somalia, Afghanistan, Iraq, Yemen, and Pakistan) including three of the weakest states.	Most worrisome are Pakistan and North Korea, accounting for about 100 nuclear weapons, 0.05% of highly enriched uranium stocks worldwide, and enough plutonium for 10-20 nuclear weapons	Afghanistan, Burma, Laos, and Colombia account for 100% of global opium production and 72% of world coca production.[72]	Four countries (Somalia, Nigeria, Bangladesh, and Tanzania) accounted for 177 of 293 attacks (60.4%) in 2008		Six countries (Iraq, Angola, Nigeria, Pakistan, Turkmenistan, and Uzbekistan) account for about 7.7% of global oil production and about 6.5% of global natural gas production.	States in the bottom two quintiles accounted for 20 of 423 cases (4.7%) of H5N1, and only 1 of 8437 cases (.012%) of SARS.

LEGEND: Index Ranking

Bottom Quintile
Second Quintile

Appendix 7.2: States to Watch and Transnational Threats

Rank on Index	Country	Presence of al-Qaeda or affiliates	Nuclear Weapons or Weapons-Grade Fissile Material Stockpiles	"Major" Narcotics Source Country	Incidence of Piracy	"Major" Money Laundering Center	Major Energy Producer	Outbreak Site for H5N1, SARS or H1N1[73]
57	ALGERIA	X	X				X	
58	PHILIPPINES	X			X	X		X
59	SYRIA	X	X			X	X	
60	GUATEMALA			X		X		X
61	SAO TOME & PRINCIPE							
62	CUBA							
63	GABON						X	
64	BOLIVIA			X				
65	RUSSIA	X	X			X	X	X
66	IRAN	X	X			X	X	
67	INDIA	X	X	X	X	X	X	X
70	VENEZUELA			X		X	X	
74	CHINA	X	X			X	X	X
75	PARAGUAY			X		X		

(continued)

Appendix 7.2: Continued

Rank on Index	Country	Presence of al-Qaeda or affiliates	Nuclear Weapons or Weapons-Grade Fissile Material Stockpiles	"Major" Narcotics Source Country	Incidence of Piracy	"Major" Money Laundering Center	Major Energy Producer	Outbreak Site for H5N1, SARS or H1N1[73]
77	INDONESIA	X			X	X	X	X
78	EGYPT	X					X	X
79	THAILAND	X				X	X	X
80	AZERBAIJAN	X					X	X
81	BELARUS		X					
82	NAMIBIA							
86	LIBYA	X	X				X	
98	TURKEY		X			X		X
103	MICRONESIA							
104	TONGA							

MARSHALL ISLANDS

Totals						
Al-Qaeda and affiliates are present in 12 states to watch, (48.0%) particularly Algeria, Indonesia, and the Philippines.	9 (36%) states to watch account for more than half the world's nuclear weapons[74] and for about half of highly enriched uranium outside the U.S.[75]	5 (20%) states to watch account for about 12.7% of world coca production.[76]	3 (12.0%) states to watch account for 43 of 293 attacks (14.7%) in 2008.	11 (44.0%) states to watch are "major" money laundering centers.	13 (52%) states to watch account for about 34.1% of global oil production, and 38.4% of worldwide natural gas production.	10 (40.0%) states to watch accounted for 292 of 423 cases (69.0%) of H5N1 and 7,112 of 8,437 cases (84.3%) of SARS.

LEGEND: Index Rank

Third Quintile
Fourth Quintile

Appendix 7.3: States of Concern
(i.e. countries from the previous tables which are of "major" concern—that is, highlighted—for at least one threat area; or have some degree of connection to 2 or more threats.)

Rank on Index	Country	Economic Score	Political Score	Security Score	Social Welfare Score	GNI per capita	Government Effectiveness	Rule of Law	Corruption	Conflict Intensity	Territory Affected by Conflict	Political Stability
1	SOMALIA	0	0	1.37	0.7	226	0	0	0	0.72	0.92	0.37
2	AFGHANISTAN	4.51	2.08	0	0	271	2.33	1.43	0.96	1.54	0.45	1.45
11	ANGOLA	5.42	2.67	5.32	1.45	1980	2.89	3.36	2.06	5.09	6.49	5.59
15	NORTH KOREA	0.52	0.95	7.28	6.73	n/a	1.42	3.38	0.24	10	10	6.22
17	BURMA	4.72	0.89	3.96	7.07	n/a	1.78	2.93	0.27	2.58	5.09	5.17
28	NIGERIA	5.39	3.51	5.37	5.24	640	3.6	3.42	1.56	7.05	10	2.14
30	YEMEN	5.8	3.64	6.43	4.85	760	3.67	4.2	3.81	8.99	8.92	3.53
33	PAKISTAN	6.58	3.52	4.69	6.13	770	4.89	4.65	2.71	8.24	9.56	2.31
35	TURKMENISTAN	3.05	1.4	7.88	6.75	1700	2.16	2.95	1.58	10	10	6.14
36	UZBEKISTAN	5.2	1.78	6.66	7.54	610	2.78	2.96	2.44	10	10	2.26
37	MAURITANIA	6.23	4.34	6.38	4.24	740	4.52	5.7	3.8	10	10	6.1
45	LAOS	5.88	2.56	7.98	5.71	500	3.72	4.3	2.34	10	10	6.56
47	COLOMBIA	5.84	5.79	1.78	9.11	2740	6.42	5.13	5.04	2.58	0	3.02
48	BANGLADESH	6.08	3.97	6.55	5.98	480	4.02	4.54	1.55	10	9.95	3.06
50	KENYA	5.77	4.72	6.95	5.15	580	4.36	4.22	2.59	9.97	9.5	4.25

55	TANZANIA	6.38	5.41	8.08	3.89	350	5.49	5.59	4.55	10	10	6.37
57	ALGERIA	6.83	4.27	4.04	9.13	3030	5.35	5.16	4.47	5.72	4.3	4.7
58	PHILIPPINES	6.18	5.59	4.16	8.4	1420	6.34	5.58	3.5	4.43	4.87	3.84
59	SYRIA	4.62	2.76	7.49	9.67	1570	3.38	5.36	3.61	10	10	4.73
60	GUATEMALA	5.63	4.66	6.65	7.65	2640	4.44	4.09	3.49	9.19	8.83	4.86
64	BOLIVIA	4.64	5.01	7.77	7.34	1100	4.36	4.42	3.68	10	10	4.61
65	RUSSIA	7.14	3.81	4.83	9.04	5780	5.43	4.39	3.29	4.45	6.8	5.06
66	IRAN	5.51	3.32	6.91	9.28	3000	4.06	4.66	3.84	9.87	10	3.86
67	INDIA	6.72	6.72	4.87	6.79	820	6.26	7.33	5.08	4.43	6.32	4.83
70	VENEZUELA	6.01	3.76	7.12	8.44	6070	3.81	3.09	2.34	10	10	3.9
74	CHINA	6.89	3.69	6.85	8.21	2010	6.34	5.79	4.01	9.41	9.29	5.92
75	PARAGUAY	4.78	4.5	8	8.5	1400	3.81	4.34	2.43	10	10	5.66
77	INDONESIA	6.46	5.25	5.92	8.34	1420	5.26	4.63	3.23	8.66	7.29	4.06
78	EGYPT	6.34	4.09	6.55	9.03	1350	5.18	6.87	4.41	9.62	8.09	4.74
79	THAILAND	7.14	5.3	5.07	8.51	2990	7.21	6.95	4.92	8.87	10	4.46
80	AZERBAIJAN	7.85	3.36	7.06	7.89	1850	4.34	4.52	2.52	9.33	8.87	4.29
86	LIBYA	6.84	2.45	8.12	9.77	7380	3.87	4.85	2.85	10	10	7.33
98	TURKEY	7.32	6.53	5.83	9.06	5400	7.05	7.08	5.94	7.9	7.21	5.25

(*continued*)

Appendix 7.3: Continued

Rank on Index	Country	Economic Score	Political Score	Security Score	Social Welfare Score	GNI per capita	Government Effectiveness	Rule of Law	Corruption	Conflict Intensity	Territory Affected by Conflict	Political Stability
Total in Bottom Quintile		7 (21.20%)	10 (30.3%)	14 (42.40%)	4 (12.10%)	3 (9.10%)	7 (21.20%)	9 (27.30%)	12 (36.40%)	14	13 (39.4%)	11 (33.3%)
Total in Bottom Two Quintiles		13 (39.40%)	24 (72.7%)	25 (75.80%)	12 (36.4%)	12 (36.40%)	16 (48.50%)	22 (66.7%)	20 (60.10%)	20 (60.10%)	19 (57.8%)	24 (72.7%)

LEGEND: Index Rank

Bottom Quintile

Second Quintile

Third Quintile

Fourth Quintile

Top Quintile

NOTES

Introduction

1. Condoleezza Rice, remarks at the Launch of the Civilian Response Corps (Washington, DC: U.S. Department of State, July 16, 2008).
2. Barack Obama, remarks to the Chicago Council on Global Affairs (April 23, 2007).
3. Susan E. Rice, Corinne Graff, and Carlos Pascual, eds., *Confronting Poverty: Weak States and U.S. National Security* (Washington, DC: Brookings Institution, 2010); Commission on Weak States, and U.S. National Security "On the Brink: Weak States and U.S. National Security" (Washington, DC: Center for Global Development, 2004). Susan E. Rice, "The New National Security Strategy: Focus on Failed States," Brookings Policy Brief no. 116 (Washington, DC: Brookings Institution, February 2003). Chester A. Crocker, "Engaging Failing States," *Foreign Affairs*, 82/5 (September/October 2003): 32–44. "Failed States: Fixing a Broken World," *Economist* (January 29, 2009). Roxana Tiron, "Weak Countries Pose Threat, Pentagon Says," *The Hill* (April 29, 2009). On this conventional wisdom, see Stewart Patrick, "Weak States and Global Threats: Assessing Evidence of 'Spillovers,'" World Paper no. 73 (Washington, DC: Center for Global Development, January 3, 2006), 3.
4. From Francis Fukuyama, *State-Building: Governance and World Order in the 21st Century* (Ithaca, NY: Cornell University Press, 2004), 92; Hillary Clinton, Testimony to Senate Foreign Relations Committee (January 13, 2009); Robert Gates, remarks to U.S. Global Leadership Campaign annual conference (Washington, DC: July 15, 2008).
5. See J. Brian Atwood, "Suddenly, Chaos," *Washington Post* (July 31, 1994): C9; Robert D. Kaplan, "The Coming Anarchy," *Atlantic Monthly*, 273/2 (February 1994): 44–76.
6. Richard N. Haass, "Sovereignty: Existing Rights, Evolving Responsibilities," Remarks to the School of Foreign Service and the Mortara Center for International Studies, Georgetown University (January 14, 2003); *National Security Strategy of the United States of America* (Washington: White House, 2002). Also see Liana Sun Wyler, *Weak and Failing States: Evolving Security Threats and U.S. Policy*, CRS Report for Congress (Washington: Congressional Research Service, August 28, 2008).

7. *National Security Strategy of the United States of America* (Washington, DC: White House, 2006).
8. George Tenet, "The World Wide Threat in 2003: Evolving Dangers in a Complex World," testimony before the Senate Select Committee on Intelligence (February 12, 2003); Central Intelligence Agency, "Possible Remote Havens for Terrorists and Other Illicit Activity," [map (unclassified)], May 2003; Stephen D. Krasner and Carlos Pascual, "Addressing State Failure," *Foreign Affairs*, 84/4 (July/August 2005): 153–163; USAID, *Fragile States Strategy* (Washington, DC: USAID, February 2005); Hillary Clinton, testimony to the Senate Foreign Relations Committee, January 13, 2009; Hillary Rodham Clinton, "Leading through Civilian Power," *Foreign Affairs*, 89/6 (November/December 2010): 13–24.
9. Michèle Flournoy, "Rebalancing the Force: Major Issues for QDR 2010," remarks at the Center for Strategic and International Studies (April 29, 2009).
10. Department of Defense, *National Defense Strategy of the United States of America* (June 2008), 3.
11. Robert Gates, "A Balanced Strategy," *Foreign Affairs* (January/February 2009).
12. See European Union, *A Secure Europe in a Better World: European Security Strategy* (Brussels: European Union, 2003), 11; Prime Minister's Strategy Unit (PMSU), *Investing in Prevention: An International Strategy to Manage Risks of Instability and Improve Crisis Response* (London: PMSU, February 2005); UK Prime Minister's Office, *A Strong Britain in an Age of Uncertainty: The National Security Strategy* (London: Stationary Office, 2010); *Canada's International Policy Statement: A Role of Pride and Influence in the World* (Ottawa: Canadian International Development Agency, 2005); *Australian Aid: Promoting Growth and Stability—White Paper on the Australian Government's Overseas Program* (Canberra: Australian National Aid Agency, 2006).
13. Kofi Annan, remarks at the Council on Foreign Relations, New York, December 16, 2004. See also *A More Secure World: Our Shared Responsibility*, Report of the Secretary-General's High-Level Panel on Threats, Challenges and Change (New York: United Nations, 2004), 9.
14. Lee Hamilton, Comments at Woodrow Wilson International Center for Scholars Symposium on "The Dangerous Connection—Failed and Failing States, WMD, and Terrorism" (April 25, 2005); OECD DAC Development Ministers and Heads of Agencies, *Principles for Good International Engagement in Fragile States and Situations* (Paris: OECD, 2007); Patrick Meagher, "Service Delivery in Fragile States: Key Concepts, Findings and Lessons" (Paris: OECD, 2008). OECD DAC, *Supporting Statebuilding in Situations of Conflict and Fragility* (Paris: OECD, 2011).
15. Stewart Patrick, " 'Failed' States and Global Security: Empirical Questions and Policy Dilemmas," *International Studies Review* 9/4 (December 2007): 644–662.
16. Peter Bergen and Laurie Garrett, "Report of the Working Group on State Security and Transnational Threats" (Princeton, NJ: Princeton Project on U.S. National Security, September 2005); Gregory F. Treverton, "Understanding the Links between Security and Development: Probing the Connections," paper presented at the Annual Bank Conference on Development Economics, World Bank, Amsterdam, May 23–24, 2005.
17. Barack Obama, remarks to the Chicago Council on Global Affairs, April 23, 2007.
18. See, for instance, Leslie Gelb, "It's Time to 'Go to Strength' on Foreign Policy," *Wall Street Journal* (March 21, 2009); Gary T. Dempsey, "Old Folly in a New Disguise: Nation Building to Combat Terrorism," *Policy Analysis*, 429 (March 21, 2002); John Mearsheimer, *The Tragedy of Great Power Politics* (New York: W.W. Norton, 2001).
19. Bergen and Garrett, "Report of the Working Group on State Security and Transnational Threats," 17.
20. Patrick, " 'Failed' States and Global Security."

21. General William "Kip" Ward, "AFRICOM and African Security Challenges," Remarks at the Atlantic Council, September 29, 2009. The White House, National Strategy for Combating Terrorism (Washington, DC, February 2003), 22.

22. Stewart Patrick, "Weak States and Global Threats: Fact or Fiction?" *The Washington Quarterly*, 29/2 (Spring 2006): 27–53.

23. UK Prime Minister's Strategy Unit, *Investing in Prevention* (London: Prime Minister's Strategy Unit, 2005).

24. David Albright and Corey Hinderstein, "Unraveling the A.Q. Khan and Future Proliferation Networks," *The Washington Quarterly*, 28/2(Spring 2005): 111–128.

25. Susceptibility to infectious disease is an exception here, being more closely correlated with low social welfare (and particularly public health) investments.

Chapter 1

1. Susan E. Rice, "A New Course in the World, a New Approach at the UN," Remarks at the Center on International Cooperation at New York University, August 12, 2009.

2. Robert M. Gates, "Helping Others Defend Themselves: the Future of U.S. Security Assistance," *Foreign Affairs*, 89/3 (May/June 2010): 2–6.

3. This book uses these two terms interchangeably.

4. See, respectively, Robert D. Kaplan, "The Coming Anarchy," *The Atlantic* (February 1994): 44–76; Samuel P. Huntington, *The Clash of Civilizations and the Remaking of World Order* (New York: Simon and Schuster, 1998), 321; J. Brian Atwood, "Suddenly, Chaos," *Washington Post* (July 31, 1994), C9.

5. See Condoleezza Rice, "Promoting the National Interest," *Foreign Affairs*, 79/1 (January-February 2000): 45–62; Bernard L. Finel, "What is Security? Why the Debate Matters," *National Security Studies Quarterly*, 4/4 (Autumn 1998): 1–18; Michael Mandelbaum, "Foreign Policy as Social Work," *Foreign Affairs*, 75/1 (January-February 1996): 16–32.

6. Adam Garfinkle, "A Conversation with Condoleezza Rice," *The American Interest*, 1/1 (Autumn 2005): 49–50. See also Bruce Jones, Carlos Pascual, and Stephen John Stedman, *Power and Responsibility: Building International Order in an Era of Transnational Threats* (Washington: Brookings Institution Press, 2009), 3–20; Martin Wolf, "The Fate of Failed States is our Shared Responsibility," *Financial Times* (February 23, 2005): 15.

7. Rice, "A New Course in the World, a New Approach at the U.N."

8. See Francis Fukuyama, *State-Building: Governance and World Order in the 21st Century* (Ithaca: Cornell University Press, 2004); James D. Fearon and David D. Laitin, "Neotrusteeship and the Problem of Weak States," *International Security*, 28/4 (Spring 2004): 5–43; Stephen D. Krasner, "Governance Failures and Alternatives to Sovereignty," Stanford University Center on Democracy, Development, and the Rule of Law, Working Paper no.1 (Palo Alto: Stanford University, November 2, 2004).

9. World Bank, Office of the President, "Fragile States: 'Toughest Development Challenge of Our Era,'" [online] (September 19, 2008) <http://go.worldbank.org/B1MIX6GLT0>, accessed February 8, 2010.

10. See Craig Burnside and David Dollar, "Aid, Policies and Growth," *American Economic Review*, 90/4 (September 2000): 847–868. The U.S. Millennium Challenge Account (MCA), created in 2003, embodies this selective approach, directing aid to countries that "rule justly, promote economic freedom, and invest in people."

11. OECD-DAC International Network on Conflict and Fragility, "Ensuring Fragile States are Not Left Behind," Summary Report (March 2009).

12. Charles Call, "The Fallacy of the 'Failed State,'" *Third World Quarterly*, 29/8 (2008): 1491–1507; Charles Call, "Beyond the 'Failed State': Seeking Conceptual Alternatives," Paper presented at the 49th Annual Convention of the International Studies Association, San Francisco, CA, March 26, 2008.

13. Daniel Lambach, "Close Encounters in the Third Dimension: The Regional Effects of State Failure," in *State Failure Revisited I: Globalization of Security and Neighborhood Effects*, INEF Report 87, ed. Daniel Lambach and Tobias Diebel, 32–50 (Duisburg: Institute for Development and Peace, University of Duisburg-Essen, 2007). Robert Jackson, *Quasi-States: Sovereignty, International Relations and the Third World* (Cambridge: Cambridge University Press, 1990). Ali Mazrui, "Africa Entrapped: Between the Protestant Ethic and the Legacy of Westphalia," in *The Expansion of International Society*, ed. Hedley Bull and Adam Watson, 289–308 (Oxford: Clarendon Press, 1984).

14. Mick Moore, "Rich World, Poor World," *Boston Review* (December 2004/January 2005).

15. Hendrik Spruyt, *The Sovereign State and Its Competitors* (Princeton, NJ: Princeton University Press, 1994); Christopher Clapham, "The Challenge to the State in a Globalized World," *Development and Change*, 33/5 (December 2002): 775–795.

16. Alan James, *Sovereign Statehood: The Basis of International Society* (London: Allen and Unwin, 1986).

17. Hedley Bull, *The Anarchical Society: A Study of Order in World Politics* (London: Macmillan, 1977), 36–37. See also James Mayall, "The Legacy of Colonialism," in *Making States Work: State Failure and the Crisis of Governance*, ed. Simon Chesterman, Michael Ignatieff and Ramesh Thakur (Tokyo: United Nations University, 2005), 36–58.

18. Hedley Bull and Adam Watson, eds., *The Expansion of International Society* (Oxford: Oxford University Press, 1984), 430.

19. Robert Jackson, and Carl Rosberg, "Why Africa's Weak States Persist: The Empirical and the Juridical in Statehood ," *World Politics*, 35, 1 (1982): 22.

20. Christopher Clapham, "The Global-Local Politics of State Decay," in *When States Fail: Causes and Consequences*, ed. Robert I. Rotberg (Princeton: Princeton University Press, 2004), 79.

21. Tobias Debiel et al., "Between Ignorance and Intervention: Strategies and Dilemmas for External Actors in Fragile States," Policy Paper 23 (Bonn: Development and Policy Foundation, 2005), 4. See also Alberto F. Alesina, Janina Matuszeski, and William Easterley, "Artificial States," NBER Working Paper no. 12328 (Cambridge, MA: National Bureau for Economic Research, 2006).

22. Tanisha M. Fazal, "State Death in the International System," *International Organization*, 58 (Spring 2004): 311–344.

23. Sebastian von Einsiedel, "Policy Responses to State Failure," in *Making States Work: State Failure and the Crisis of Governance*, ed. Simon Chesterman, Michael Ignatieff and Ramesh Thakur, (Tokyo: United Nations University, 2005), 13–35; I. William Zartman, ed., *Collapsed States: The Disintegration and Restoration of Legitimate Authority* (Boulder: Lynne Rienner Publishers, 1995).

24. Charles Tilly, "War Making and State Making as Organized Crime," in *Bringing the State Back In*, ed. Peter Evans, Dietrich Reuschemeyer and Theda Skocpol, 169–191 (Cambridge: Cambridge University Press, 1985).

25. This Section (pages 26–36) draws on *The Index of State Weakness in the Developing World*, which the author created with Susan E. Rice, then Senior Fellow at the Brookings Institution.

26. More than forty systems exist for ranking governance; see Marie Besançon, "Good Governance Rankings: The Art of Measurement," World Peace Foundation report no. 36 (Cambridge, MA: World Peace Foundation, 2003).

27. "Political Instability Task Force," [online], January 19, 2010 <http://globalpolicy.gmu.edu/pitf/>, accessed February 8, 2010.

28. Commission on Weak States and U.S. National Security, "On the Brink: Weak States and U.S. National Security" (Washington: Center for Global Development, 2004).

29. On USAID's model, see USAID, "Measuring Fragility: Indicators and Methods for Rating State Performance" (June 2005). On DFID's approach, see "Why We Need to Work More Effectively in Fragile States," (London: DFID, 2005): 27–28; Michael Anderson et al., "Measuring Capacity and Willingness for Poverty Reduction Strategies in Fragile States," DFID PRDE Working Paper no. 6 (London: Department for International Development, January 2005). LICUS countries are determined by low scores on the World Bank's Country Policy and Institutional Assessments (CPIA). The 2008 CPIA ratings can be accessed online at:<http://web.worldbank.org/WBSITE/EXTERNAL/EXTABOUTUS/IDA/0,,contentMDK:21359477~menuPK:2626968~pagePK:51236175~piPK:437394~theSitePK:73154,00.html.>

30. The Fund for Peace and *Foreign Policy*, "The Failed States Index 2009," *Foreign Policy* [online], (July/August 2009) <http://www.foreignpolicy.com/articles/2009/06/22/the_2009_failed_states_index>, accessed February 8, 2010; Carleton University, "Country Indicators for Foreign Policy," [online], (January 27, 2010) <www.carleton.ca/cifp>, accessed February 8, 2010; Ashraf Ghani, Clare Lockhart and Michael Carnahan, "Closing the Sovereignty Gap: An Approach to Statebuilding," Overseas Development Institute Working Paper no. 253 (London: Overseas Development Institute, 2005); Mo Ibrahim Foundation, "The Ibrahim Index," [online], (October 5, 2009) http://www.moibrahimfoundation.org/en/mifindex/ibrahimIndex>, accessed February 8, 2010; Monty G. Marshall and Jack Goldstone, "Global Report on Conflict, Governance and State Fragility 2007," *Foreign Policy Bulletin* 17/1 (March 2007): 3–21.

31. J. Joseph Hewitt, Jonathan Wilkenfeld, and Ted Robert Gurr, *Peace and Conflict 2008: Executive Summary* (College Park: University of Maryland Center for International Development and Conflict Management, 2008).

32. Susan E. Rice and Stewart Patrick, *Index of State Weakness in the Developing World* (Washington: Brookings Institution Press, 2008); also available online at http://www.brookings.edu/reports/2008/02_weak_states_index.aspx.

33. This includes all low, lower middle, and upper middle income countries as calculated by the World Bank Atlas method.

34. See DFID, "Why We Need to Work More Effectively in Fragile States"; USAID, "Fragile States Strategy" (Washington: USAID, 2005); and OECD-DAC International Network on Conflict and Fragility.

35. For more on the rationale for selecting these twenty indicators, on the underlying data sources, on country coverage, and on aggregation methods, please consult the technical annex in Rice and Patrick, *Index of State Weakness*, 29–37.

36. Since there is no widely accepted formula to definitively assess the relative contribution of each of the four areas to state weakness, any unequal weighting system would be open to criticism that it reflected the arbitrary biases of the researchers.

37. Low-income countries are defined by the World Bank as having a per capita GNP below $975 (in 2008). In addition to Malawi, the ten poorest countries are Somalia, Democratic Republic of the Congo, Burundi, Liberia, Sierra Leone, Eritrea, Ethiopia, Guinea-Bissau, and Rwanda.

38. While there is a strong positive relationship between countries' scores on most individual indicators and their overall performance on the Index, this does not hold for four of the twenty indicators: coups, inflation, GDP growth, and inequality. By contrast, overall weakness is most strongly associated with the indicators of government effectiveness, child mortality, recent conflict, and GNI per capita. Together, these four indicators explain some 50 percent of variation in country scores.

39. See Nicholas van de Walle, *Overcoming Stagnation in Aid-Dependent Countries* (Washington: Center for Global Development, 2005).

40. See Andrew Rosser, "The Political Economy of the Resource Curse: A Literature Survey," Institute for Development Studies Working Paper no. 268 (Brighton: Institute for Development Studies, 2006).

41. Marina Ottaway, "Rebuilding State Institutions in Collapsed States," in *State Failure, Collapse and Reconstruction*, ed. Jennifer Milliken (Oxford: Blackwell, 2003), 245–266.

42. See, among others, Monty G. Marshall, "Fragility, Instability, and the Failure of States: Assessing the Sources of Systemic Risk," Council on Foreign Relations Working Paper (New York: Council on Foreign Relations, 2008); Paul D. Williams, "State Failure in Africa: Causes, Consequences and Responses," *Africa South of the Sahara 2009* (New York: Routledge: Europa Regional Surveys of the World, 2008), 20–28; Jennifer Milliken, ed., *State Failure, Collapse, and Reconstruction* (Malden, MA: Institute for Social Studies, 2003); David Carment, "Assessing State Failure: Implications for Theory and Policy," *Third World Quarterly*, 24/3 (June 2003): 407–427.

43. Robert H. Bates et al., "Political Instability Task Force Report: Phase IV Findings" (McLean, VA: Science Applications International Corporation, 2003).

44. Mats Berdal and David Malone, eds., *Greed and Grievance: Economic Agendas in Civil Wars* (Boulder: Lynne Rienner Publishers, 2000); Karen Ballentine and Jake Sherman, *The Political Economy of Armed Conflict: Beyond Greed and Grievance* (Boulder: Lynne Rienner Publishers, 2003).

45. Susan L. Woodward: "Fragile States: Exploring the Concept," FRIDE Working Paper (Madrid: Fondación para los Relaciones Internacionales y el Diálogo Exterior, 2006).

46. Homi Kharas, "The Whiplash Effect," *Foreign Policy* (July/August 2009); "Trying to Weather the Storm," *Economist* (October 30, 2008).

47. Seven of the ten countries most dependent on export of non-oil primary commodities are weak states: Uganda, Ethiopia, Niger, Malawi, Rwanda, Chad and Burundi (World Bank, *Global Economic Prospects 2009*, World Bank Development Prospects Group (Washington: World Bank, 2008), 99).

48. As much as one-third of GDP growth in developing countries in recent years may be attributed to investment and capital inflows. See *Global Economic Prospects 2009*.

49. "The People Crunch," *Economist* (January 15, 2009).

50. Kofi Annan, "Time of Crisis and Opportunity," *Huffington Post* (January 27, 2009).

51. Niall Ferguson, "The Axis of Upheaval," *Foreign Policy* (March/April 2009); Robert Raffaele, "US Intelligence Director Warns of Economic Crisis Effects on Global Political Stability," *VOA News* (February 26, 2009).

52. Paul Collier and Anke Hoeffler, "The Challenge of Reducing the Global Incidence of War," Copenhagen Consensus Challenge Paper (Copenhagen: Copenhagen Consensus Center, 2004).

53. Paul Collier and his colleagues thus aptly label civil war "development in reverse." See Collier et al., *Breaking the Conflict Trap: Civil War and Development Policy* (Washington: World Bank and Oxford University Press, 2003).

54. Overall, more than half of the states classified by UNHCR as "major" sources of refugees in 2007 (28 of 46, or 60.9 percent) are weak states. (UNHCR, *2007 Global Trends: Refugees, Asylum Seekers, Returnees, Internally Displaced and Stateless Persons*, Field Information and Coordination Support Section (FICSS) Report (Geneva: UNHCR, 2008).

55. The PTS measures political violence and terror on the basis of two different sources: the yearly country reports of Amnesty International and the U.S. State Department Country Reports on Human Rights Practices. See Political Terror Scale, "About the Political Terror Scale" [online], (December 13, 2009) <http://www.politicalterrorscale.org/about.html>, accessed February 8, 2010.

56. DFID, "Why We Need to Work More Effectively in Fragile States," 9.

57. Paul Collier, *The Bottom Billion: Why the Poorest Countries are Failing and What Can Be Done about It* (Oxford: Oxford University Press, 2007).

58. World Health Organization, *World Health Report 2005 – Make Every Mother and Child Count*, Office of Family-Child Health (Geneva: World Health Organization, 2005).

59. Andrew Branchflower, "How Important Are Difficult Environments to Achieving the MDGs?" DFID PRDE Working Paper no. 2 (London: Department for International Development, 2004).

60. Stewart Patrick and Kaysie Brown, "Fragile States and U.S. Foreign Assistance: Show Me the Money," Center for Global Development Working Paper no. 96 (Washington: Center for Global Development, 2006); Victoria Levin and David Dollar, "The Forgotten States: Aid Volumes and Volatility in Difficult Partnership Countries," 1992–2000, summary paper for the DAC Learning and Advisory Partnership on Difficult Partnerships (Washington: World Bank, 2004); Mark McGillivray, "Aid Allocation and Fragile States," Discussion Paper Number 2006/01 (Helsinki: UNU-WIDER, January 2006), 11–12.

61. Lambach, "Close Encounters"; Myron Weiner, "Bad Neighbors, Bad Neighborhoods: An Inquiry into the Causes of Refugee Flows," *International Security*, 21/1 (Summer 1996): 5–42.

62. Table is based on the Center for Systemic Peace's regional warfare and governance trends, 2000–2005.

63. Warfare totals (on a 0-60 scale) are based on fatalities and casualties, social impact of violence, resource depletion, and destruction of infrastructure and population dislocations. See Center for Systemic Peace, "Global Conflict Trends," [online], (September 22, 2009) <http://www.systemicpeace.org/conflict.htm>, accessed 8 February 2010.

64. Fernanda Faria and Patricia Magalhaes Ferreira, *An Adequate EU Response Strategy to Address Difficult Situations of Fragility and Difficult Environments*, Study for the Portuguese Presidency of the EU (Maastricht: European Center for Development Policy Management, 2007).

65. Paul Collier and L. Chauvet, "Presentation to the DAC Learning and Advisory Process on Difficult Partnerships" (Paris, November 5, 2004).

66. *CIA World Factbook* (July 2008 estimates).

67. Richard F. Grimmett, "Instances of Use of United States Armed Forces Abroad, 1798–2007," CRS Report for Congress (Washington: Congressional Research Service, January 14, 2008). According to Grimmett's data, the United States deployed military forces to the following countries in the bottom two quintiles of the Index: Afghanistan (1998) (2001-), Burundi (1994), Cambodia (1997), Central African Republic (1996), R. Congo (1997), Cote d'Ivoire (2002), Djibouti (2004), East Timor (1999–2003), Eritrea (2004), Ethiopia (2004), Guinea-Bissau (1998), Haiti (1990s) (2004), Iraq (early 1990s, 1998–99, 2003-), Kenya (1998, 1999, 2004), Liberia (1990, 1998, 2003), Rwanda (1994, 1996), Sierra Leone (1992, 1997, 2000), Somalia (1992-), Sudan, (1998), Tanzania (1998), Yemen (2000, 2004), Democratic Republic of the Congo/Zaire (1991, 1996). In addition, the United States has in recent years conducted both drone strikes and special operation in Pakistan.

68. France and the EU have also deployed forces to Cote d'Ivoire and DRC, respectively, and the United Kingdom sent troops to Sierra Leone.

69. The UN has deployed to: Angola, Burundi, Central African Republic, Chad, Democratic Republic of the Congo, Cote D'Ivoire, Republic of Congo, Ethiopia, Eritrea, Liberia, Rwanda, Sierra Leone, Somalia and Sudan.

70. UN General Assembly, "A/10841: General Assembly Adopts Peacekeeping Budget of Nearly $7.8 billion for period July 1, 2009 to June 20, 2010" (June 30, 2009); U.S. General Accounting Office, *UN Peacekeeping: Estimated US Contributions, Fiscal Years 1996–2001*, (Washington: General Accounting Office, February 2002).

71. U.S. Department of Homeland Security, Yearbook of Immigration Statistics, *Office of Immigration Statistics Report* (Washington: U.S. Department of Homeland Security, 2008).

72. There are six sites in Colombia, and two in Kenya. Both countries rank near the top of the second quintile on the Index. See U.S. Department of Defense, Base Structure Report FY 2007 [online] <http://www.defenselink.mil/pubs/BSR_2007_Baseline.pdf>, accessed February 8, 2010. These figures do not include alleged U.S. military installations in Pakistan.

73. *CIA World Factbook* (July 2008 estimates).

74. Samuel Bazzi, Sheila Herrling and Stewart Patrick, "Billions for War, Pennies for the Poor: Moving the President's FY 2008 Budget from Hard Power to Smart Power," (Washington: Center for Global Development, March 16, 2007).

75. UNHCR, 2007 *Global Trends*.

76. Countries scoring a 4 or 5 on the Political Terror Scale. For more information about PTS methodology, see "About the Political Terror Scale."

77. Grimmett, "Instances of Use of United States Armed Forces Abroad."

78. Pakistan is not included in the CRS 2007 report.

Chapter 2

1. Barack Obama, "The War We Need to Win" (Washington, DC: Woodrow Wilson International Center for Scholars, August 1, 2007).

2. Cited in Glenn Kessler, "This Year, Bush Takes a Different Tone with the U.N.," *Washington Post* (September 15, 2005).

3. "Fighting Terrorism at Gleneagles," *New York Times* (July 5, 2005). Tochi Drezen and Philip Shishkin, "Mideast Peril Growing Concern: Terrorist Haven in 'Failed States,' Instability in Afghanistan, Iraq and Lebanon Raise Risk that US Seeks to Address," *Wall Street Journal* (September 12, 2006).

4. Definition adapted from several sources, including: Bruce Hoffman, *Inside Terrorism* (New York: Columbia University Press, 1999).

5. U.S. State Department Country Reports on Terrorism (2008): Chapter 6.

6. Marc Sageman, *Understanding Terror Networks* (Philadelphia: University of Pennsylvania Press, 2004).

7. Barack Obama, Press Conference (January 14, 2009).

8. James J.F. Forrest, "The Final Act: Ideologies of Catastrophic Terror," Paper prepared for Fund for Peace conference on Threat Convergence: New Pathways to Proliferation? (2006).

9. Bruce Hoffman, "Does Our Counter-Terrorism Strategy Match the Threat?" (Testimony presented before the House International Relations Committee, September 29, 2005). Bruce Riedel, "Al-Qaeda Strikes Back," *Foreign Affairs*, 86/3 (May/June 2007): 24–40. "Declassified Key Judgments from *Trends in Global Terrorism: Implications for the United States*," National Intelligence Estimate (Washington, DC: Director of National Intelligence, April 2006).

10. Scott Shane, "Rethinking Our Terrorist Fears," *New York Times* (September 26, 2009).

11. Dennis C. Blair, "Annual Threat Assessment of the Intelligence Community for the Senate Select Committee on Intelligence" (Testimony presented before the Senate Intelligence Committee, February 12, 2009). Karen DeYoung and Walter Pincus, "Al-Qaeda's Gains Keep U.S. at Risk, Report Says," *Washington Post* (July 18, 2007).

12. The data and analysis in this section rests heavily on research by Alexander Pascal.

13. The latter two groups joined forces in 2009 under the name al-Qaeda in the Arabian Peninsula and were apparently behind the foiled Christmas bombing that year of a U.S. airliner.

14. George Joffé, cited in "A Real Network of Terror?" *Economist* (September 11, 2008).

15. A. Rabasa et al., *Beyond al-Qaeda: The Global Jihadist Movement* (Santa Monica, CA: The RAND Corporation, 2006): 79. Groups listed by the State Department are included as al-Qaeda affiliates if the description of the entities included explicit reference to any relationship (ideological, operational, etc.) to al-Qaeda. Table 2.1 is a rough approximation, given the dynamic and shifting landscape of global terrorism—and the fact that relations among groups tend to be shrouded in secrecy or exaggerated for political effect. The potential for alliances among like-minded organizations and the apparent momentum toward a networked global jihad justifies erring on the side of inclusiveness.

16. White House, *National Security Strategy of the United States of America* (2002).

17. John J. Hamre and Gordon R. Sullivan, "Toward Post-Conflict Reconstruction," *Washington Quarterly*, 25/4 (Autumn 2002): 85.

18. Bruce Hoffmann, "Overwhelm. Divide. Spread. Bankrupt. Diversify. Al-Qaeda's New Grand Strategy," *Washington Post* (January 10, 2010): B1.

19. Monty G. Marshall, "Global Terrorism: An Overview and Analysis," Center for International Development and Conflict Management (College Park: University of Maryland, September 12, 2002): 25.

20. The Prime Minister's Strategy Unit, Assessment, (Mimeo) (March 1, 2004).

21. Edward Newman, "Weak States, State Failure, and Terrorism," *Terrorism and Political Violence* (2007): 463–488.

22. Table adapted from Daniel Byman, *Deadly Connections: States that Sponsor Terrorism* (Cambridge: Cambridge University Press, 2005): 11.

23. Matthew Levitt, "Iran and Syria: State Sponsorships in the Age of Terror Networks," in *Confronting Terrorism Financing*, American Foreign Policy Council (Lanham, MD: University Press of America, 2005). Daniel L. Byman, "The Changing Nature of State Sponsorship of Terrorism," Brookings Institution Saban Center for Middle East Policy Analysis Paper, no. 16 (May 2008).

24. Robert D. Lamb, "Ungoverned Areas and Threats from Safe Havens," Final Report of the Ungoverned Areas Project, prepared for the Office of the Undersecretary of Defense for Policy (November 2007): 26–27.

25. Dan Byman, *Deadly Connections: States That Sponsor Terrorism*, 15; 221–224.

26. U.S. State Department Country Reports on Terrorism (2006).

27. Mark Landler, "Clinton Is Sharply Critical of Pakistan on Terrorism," *New York Times* (October 30, 2009). Mark Mazzetti and Eric Schmitt, "U.S. Says Agents of Pakistan Aid Afghan Taliban," *New York Times* (March 26, 2009).

28. Cited in Ed Henry, "White House Report Critical of Pakistan's Activity against Militants," *CNN.com* (October 6, 2010).

29. Pamela Constable, "U.S. Says Taliban Has a New Haven in Pakistan," *Washington Post* (September 29, 2009).

30. Ulrich Schneckener, "How Transnational Terrorists Profit from Fragile States," *SWP Research Paper* (May 2004).

31. Hamlin B. Tallent, "Eliminating Terrorist Sanctuaries" (Testimony presented to the Congressional Committee on International Relations on March 10, 2005): 18.

32. Abu Bakr Naji, *The Management of Savagery: The Most Critical Stage through Which the Umma Will Pass*, trans. William McCants, Combating Terrorism Center (West Point, May 23, 2006): 15–16. Douglas Farah, "Jihadists Now Targeting Africa," (December 19, 2006) <http://www.douglasfarah.com/article/66/jihadists-now-targetting-africa>.

33. Dana Priest, "Iraq New Terror Breeding Ground: War Created Haven, CIA Advisers Report," *Washington Post* (January 14, 2005): A1.

34. Reuters, "Afghanistan Says Foreign Fighters Coming from Iraq," (February 4, 2009). Tom Regan, "Report: Al-Qaeda Using Iraq as Terrorist Training Ground," *Christian Science Monitor* (July 3, 2006).

35. "Al-Qaeda on the March," *Economist* (May 21, 2009).

36. Economist Intelligence Unit, *Country Report: Yemen* (London: Economist Intelligence Unit, November 2005). International Crisis Group, "Yemen: Coping with Terrorism and Violence in a Fragile State" (January 8, 2003).

37. Henrik Urdal, "The Demographics of Political Violence: Youth Bulges, Insecurity, and Conflict," *Too Poor for Peace? Global Poverty, Conflict and Security in the 21st Century*, eds. Lael Brainard and Derek Chollet (Washington, DC: Brookings Institution, 2007): 90–100. Paul Collier, "Doing Well Out of War: An Economic Perspective," *Greed and Grievance: Economic Agendas in Civil Wars*, edited by Mats Berdal and David M. Malone (Boulder, CO: Lynne Rienner, 2000): 94.

38. Alexander D. Newton, quoted by Eric Schmitt, "U.S. Training in Africa Aims to Deter Extremists," *New York Times* (December 13, 2008).

39. Marc Sageman, *Understanding Terror Networks* (Philadelphia: University of Pennsylvania Press, 2004). Also see Anna Simons and David Tucker, "The Misleading Problem of Failed States: A 'Socio-Geography' of Terrorism in the Post-9/11 Era," *Third World Quarterly*, 28/2 (2007): 387–401.

40. Richard A. Oppel, Jr., "Foreign Fighters in Iraq Are Tied to Allies of U.S.," *New York Times* (November 22, 2007). Dexter Filkins, "Foreign Fighters Captured in Iraq come from 27, Mostly Arab Lands," *New York Times* (October 21, 2005).

41. Christian Caryl, "Al-Qaeda: The Uzbek Branch in Pakistan," *New York Review of Books Blog* (November 4, 2009), <http://blogs.nybooks.com/post/233160623/al-qaeda-the-uzbek-branch-in-pakistan>.

42. Olivier Roy, *Globalized Islam: The Search for a New Ummah* (London: Hurst, 2004).

43. Sageman, *Understanding Terror Networks.*

44. List of individuals detained by the Department of Defense at Guantanamo Bay, Cuba, from January 2002 through May 15, 2006 <www.defenselink.mil>.

45. Andrea Elliott, "A Call to Jihad, Answered in America," *New York Times* (July 11, 2009).

46. Austin Merrill, "Letter from Timbuktu," *Vanity Fair* online exclusive (September 10, 2007) <http://www.vanityfair.com/politics/features/2007/09/sahara200709>.

47. U.S. State Department, "Patterns of Global Terrorism" (2002–2003) and "Country Reports on Terrorism" (2004–2007). National Counterterrorism Center. Raphael Perl, "Trends in Terrorism: 2006," *Congressional Research Service Report* (2006): 3–7.

48. Gretchen Peters, *Seeds of Terror* (New York: Thomas Dunne Books, 2009): 10.

49. William K. Rashbaum, "U.S. Charges 3 Malians in Drug Plot," *New York Times* (December 19, 2009): A5.

50. Douglas Farah, "Al-Qaeda's Use of Commodities and Natural Resources" (unpublished paper). Douglas Farah, *Blood from Stones* (New York: Broadway, 2004). Although challenged by the CIA and FBI, Farah's assertions have been substantiated by independent sources. Global Witness, "For a Few Dollars More: How al-Qaeda Moved into the Diamond Trade" (April 2003). Nicholas Cook, "Diamonds and Conflict: Background, Policy, and Legislation," *Congressional Research Service Report* (2003): 7–10, 25–26.

51. Background paper prepared for the UN High Level Panel on Threats, Challenge and Change (mimeo). On the official UN document, see S/2003/1070, p. 24.

52. William Wechsler, "Strangling the Hydra, Targeting AQ's Finances," *How Did This Happen?* eds. Gideon Rose and James F. Hoge, Jr. (New York: PublicAffairs, 2001). See also Sidney Weintraub, "Disrupting the Financing of Terrorism," *Washington Quarterly*, 25/1 (Winter 2002).

53. Craig Whitlock, "Diverse Sources Fund Insurgency in Afghanistan," *Washington Post* (September 27, 2009).

54. Simons and Tucker, "The Misleading Problem of Failed States."

55. As Hassan Nasrallah, a Hezbollah leader, explained in a televised interview shortly after the Israeli-Lebanon war in 2006: "We are not a replacement for the state. But when the state is absent we have to take up the slack." Edward Cody, "Lebanon Left to Face Most Basic of Issues," *Washington Post* (September 10, 2006): A1.

56. Jane Perlez, "Taliban Leader Flaunts Power inside Pakistan," *New York Times* (June 6, 2008).

57. David H. Shinn, "Domestic or International Terrorism? A Dysfunctional Dialogue" (presented to a symposium organized by the National Defense University on "Africa: Vital to U.S. Security?," November 2005).

58. Sabrina Tavernise, "Islamic Schools in Pakistan Fill a Void, While Fueling Militancy," *New York Times* (May 4, 2009).

59. Peter Bergen, "A Discussion of Some of the Underlying Causes of Al Qaeda Terrorism," paper prepared for New America Foundation Conference on Security, Prosperity, and America's Purpose: Strategic Choices for the 21st Century (Washington. DC: September 6–7, 2005, <http://www.americaspurpose.org/downloads/working_group_papers.pdf>. Robert Pape, "Suicide Terrorism and Democracy," *Policy Analysis* No. 582 (Washington, DC: CATO Institute): 12–13.

60. "Taliban 'Out-Governing' Afghan Govt," Australian Broadcasting Corporation (August 31, 2009).

61. Andrew Exum, "No Place to Hide," *New Republic* (March 31, 2009).

62. Michael Innes, ed., *Denial of Sanctuary: Understanding Terrorist Safe Havens* (Westport, CT: Praeger, 2007).

63. 9/11 Commission, "Final Report of the National Commission on Terrorist Attacks on the United States" (Washington, DC: Government Printing Office, 2004):365–367. Peter Bergen, "The Front: The Taliban-Al-Qaeda Merger," *New Republic* (October 19, 2009).

64. Carlotta Gall and Ismail Khan, "Taliban and Allies Tighten Grip in Northern Pakistan," *New York Times* (December 11, 2006). "Facing al-Qaeda: With the Terrorists Growing Stronger, Their Sanctuary in Pakistan Must Be Eliminated," *Washington Post* (July 19, 2007).

65. National Intelligence Council, "Possible Remote Havens for Terrorists and Other Illicit Activity" (Unclassified CIA map with text, 2003.)

66. Defense analysts have now expanded the "ungoverned" concept to include under-governed areas where the state performs some functions; mis-governed areas where it empowers illicit actors; contested areas where nonstate actors fill the governance void; and non-physical, functional havens (such as communications networks, social customs, or legal norms) that terrorists can exploit. Lamb, "Ungoverned Areas and Threats from Safe Havens," 18.

67. Richard J. Norton, "Feral Cities: The New Strategic Environment," *Naval War College Review* 56/4 (2003).

68. For an excellent conceptual survey, see Anne L. Clunan and Harold A. Trinkunas, eds., *Ungoverned Spaces: Alternatives to State Authority in an Era of Softened Sovereignty* (Stanford: Stanford University Press, 2010).

69. Eric Schmitt, "As Africans Join Iraqi Insurgency, U.S. Counters with Military Training in their Lands," *New York Times* (June 10, 2005).

70. Peter Bergen, "The Front: The Taliban-Al-Qaeda Merger," *New Republic* (October 19, 2009). Blair, "Annual Threat Assessment," 3–6.

71. Lamb, "Ungoverned Areas and Threats from Safe Havens," 30.

72. Anne Clunan and Harold Trinkunas, "Conceptualizing Ungoverned Spaces: Territorial Statehood, Contested Authority and Softened Sovereignty" (Paper presented at Naval Postgraduate School Conference on Ungoverned Spaces, August 2007): 1–4.

73. William B. Farrell and Carla M. Komich, "USAID/DCHA/CMM Assessment: Northern Mali," (Washington, DC: Management Systems International, July 2004). Eric Schmitt, "U.S. Training in Africa Aims to Deter Extremists," *New York Times* (December 13, 2008).

74. Karin Brulliard, "Radical Islam Meets a Buffer in West Africa," *Washington Post* (December 21, 2009): A1. Nicholas Schmidle, "The Saharan Conundrum," *New York Times Magazine* (February 15, 2009).

75. Lamb, "Ungoverned Areas and Threats from Safe Havens," 18.

76. Byman, *Deadly Connections*, 187–188.

77. Scott Wilson and Anne E. Kornblut, "White House Considers Narrower War Effort," *Washington Post* (October 2, 2009).

78. Anthony Cordesman, cited in Peter Baker and Eric Schmitt, "Afghan War Debate Now Leads to Focus on Al-Qaeda," *New York Times* (October 7, 2009).

79. For Guantanamo detainees, see http://projects.washingtonpost.com/guantanamo/>. For foreign fighters in Iraq, see tables already cited in the chapter.

80. Table considers only links between the states listed here and the Al Qaeda-linked global *salafi* jihad. Thus connections between, for instance, Iran and Hezbollah are not reflected. In addition, it reflects the subjective and partial (and possibly politically influenced) views of the U.S. State Department as expressed in its 2002–2009 Country Reports on Terrorism.

81. They include the possibility, for instance, that al-Qaeda was profiting from the diamond trade out of Liberia, DRC, and Angola, or may have transited through Uganda or Tanzania.

82. George W. Bush comments at UN Summit on Financing for Development, March 22, 2002, Monterrey, Mexico. <http://www.pbs.org/newshour/bb/international/jan-june02/aidmoney_3-22a.html> Blair cited in Colbert I. King, "Homegrown Hatred," *Washington Post* (July 16, 2005).

83. Sageman, *Understanding Terror Networks*. Alan B. Kreuger and Jitka Laeckova, "Education, Poverty, Political Violence and Terrorism: Is There a Causal Connection?" National Bureau of Economic Research Working Paper No. 9074 (July 2002).

84. Alan Kreuger and David Laitin, "Kto Kogo: A Cross-Country Study of the Origins and Targets of Terrorism," *Terrorism, Economic Development, and Political Openness*, eds. Philip Keefer and Norman Loayza (New York: Cambridge University Press, 2007). As historian Walter Lacquer points out, "In the 49 countries currently designated by the United Nations as the least developed hardly any terrorist activity occurs." Walter Lacquer, *No End to War: Terrorism in the Twenty-First Century* (New York: Continuum, 2003): 11.

85. Alan B. Kreuger, *What Makes a Terrorist: Economics and the Roots of Terrorism* (Princeton: Princeton University Press, 2007).

86. Robert A. Pape, "Suicide Terrorism and Democracy."

87. Andrea Elliott, "Where Boys Grow Up to Be Jihadis," *New York Times Magazine* (November 25, 2007). Jenifer Bremer and John D. Kasarda, "The Origins of Terror: Implications for U.S. Foreign Policy," *The Milken Institute Review* (Fourth Quarter 2002).

88. Ahmed Rashid, *Descent into Chaos* (New York: Penguin, 2008): 15–16.

89. Ken Menkhaus, "Somalia: State Collapse and the Threat of Terrorism," *Adelphi Paper* No. 364 (London: International Institute for Strategic Studies, 2004): 71–73; 78–80.

90. Mark Mazetti, "U.S. Aborted Raid on Qaeda Chiefs in Pakistan in '05," *New York Times* (July 8, 2007).

91. Spencer S. Hsu and Walter Pincus, "US Warns of Stronger Al-Qaeda: Administration Report Cites Havens in Pakistan," *Washington Post* (July 12, 2007): A1.

92. Simons and Tucker, "The Misleading Problem of Failed States."

93. "Al-Qaida's (Mis)Adventures in the Horn of Africa," Harmony Project (West Point: Combating Terrorism Center, 2007): 24.

94. Menkhaus, "Somalia: State Collapse and the Threat of Terrorism," 67–69.

95. Kenneth J. Menkhaus, "Constraints and Opportunities in Ungoverned Spaces: The Horn of Africa," in Innes, ed., *Denial of Sanctuary*, 67–82.

96. "Al-Qaida's (Mis)Adventures in the Horn of Africa," 14–15.

97. "Al-Qaeda on the March," *Economist* (May 21, 2009).

98. Eric Schmitt and Jeffrey Gettleman, "Qaeda Leader Reported Killed in Somalia," *New York Times* (May 2, 2008).

99. "President Obama's Speech on Afghanistan and Pakistan," *U.S. News and World Report* (March 27, 2009), http://politics.usnews.com/news/articles/2009/03/27/president-obamas-speech-on-afghanistan-and-pakistan.html?PageNr=3.

100. David S. Morgan, "Gibbs on Afghanistan: Not Nation-Building," CBS News online, (December 1, 2009) <http://www.cbsnews.com/blogs/2009/12/01/politics/politicalhot-sheet/entry5848072.shtml>.

101. Blair, "Annual Threat Assessment," 7.

102. Robert F. Worth, "Yemen Emerges as Base for Qaeda Attacks on U.S.," *New York Times* (October 29, 2010).

103. Steven Erlanger, "Yemen's Chaos Aids Evolution of al-Qaeda Cell," *New York Times* (January 3, 2009): A1.

104. Sheila Carapico, "No Quick Fix: Foreign Aid and State Performance in Yemen," *Short of the Goal: U.S. Policy and Poorly Performing States*, eds. Nancy Birdsall, Milan Vaishnav, and Robert L. Ayers (Washington, DC: Center for Global Development, 2006).

105. "The World's Next Failed State?" *Economist* (September 10, 2009).

106. Associated Press, "Yemen Suffers Turmoil on Multiple Fronts," (September 17, 2009).

107. Michael Mullen quoted in Eric Schmitt and David E. Sanger, "Some in Qaeda Leave Pakistan for Somalia and Yemen," *New York Times* (June 11, 2009).

108. Robert F. Worth, "Yemen's Deals with Jihadists Unsettle the U.S.," *New York Times* (January 28, 2008).

109. Ibid. Robert F. Worth, "Saudis Issue List of 85 Terrorism Suspects," *New York Times* (February 4, 2009).

110. Worth, "Yemen's Deals with Jihadists Unsettle the U.S." Robert F. Worth, "For Yemen's Leader, a Balancing Act Gets Harder," *New York Times* (June 21, 2008).

Chapter 3

1. Kennedy comments cited by Deputy Secretary of State James B. Steinberg in address to Carnegie Endowment Nonproliferation Conference, April 6, 2009, <http://www.carnegieendowment.org/files/npc_steinberg.pdf>.

2. See the "Threat Convergence" Project of the Fund for Peace, described at <http://www.fundforpeace.org/web/images/pdf/threatconvergence_april06.pdf>.

3. Allison MacFarlane, "All Weapons of Mass Destruction Are Not Equal," *Audit of the Conventional Wisdom* (Cambridge, MA: MIT Center for International Studies, July 2005).

4. Chaim Braun and Christopher F. Chyba, "Proliferation Rings: New Challenges to the Nuclear Nonproliferation Regime," *International Security*, 29/2 (Fall 2004): 6.

5. William J. Broad and David E. Sanger, "Restraints Fray and Risks Grow as Nuclear Club Gains Members," *New York Times* (October 15, 2006). World Nuclear Association, "World Nuclear Power Reactors 2007–09 and Uranium Requirements" (April 1, 2009).

6. Andrew Grotto, "Defusing the Threat of Radiological Weapons: Integrating Prevention with Detection and Response," Center for American Progress (July 2005): 1–2.

7. Biological agents with weapons potential include bacterial diseases (e.g., anthrax, brucellosis, glanders, plague, Q fever, Rocky Mountain spotted fever, tularemia, and typhus); viral diseases (e.g., smallpox, viral encephalitis, African hemorrhagic fevers, South American hemorrhagic fevers, and Rift Valley, Lassa, and yellow fever viruses); fungal diseases (e.g., rice blast, rye stem rust, and wheat stem rust); and biological toxins (e.g., botulinum toxin, enterotoxin B, epsilon toxin, ricin, and shiga toxin).

8. S. Trevisanato, "The 'Hittite Plague,' An Epidemic of Tularemia and the First Record of Biological Warfare," *Medical Hypotheses,* 69/6 (2007): 1371–1374. Also see George W. Christopher et al., "Biological Warfare: A Historical Perspective," *Journal of the American Medical Association,* 275/5 (1997).

9. Charles C. Mann, *1491: New Revelations of the Americas before Columbus* (New York: Knopf, 2005).

10. Christopher F. Chyba and Alex L. Greninger, "Biotechnology and Bioterrorism: An Unprecedented World," *Survival,* 46/2 (Summer 2004): 143–144.

11. "World at Risk: The Report of the Commission on the Prevention of Weapons of Mass Destruction Proliferation and Terrorism" (New York: Random House, December 2008): 8. Benjamin Friedman, "Homeland Security," *Foreign Policy,* 149 (July/August 2005).

12. Adrienne Mayor, *Greek Fire, Poison Arrows and Scorpion Bombs: Biological and Chemical Warfare in the Ancient World* (New York: Overlook, 2003).

13. Jonathan Tucker, *War of Nerves: Chemical Warfare from World War I to Al Qaeda* (New York: Anchor, 2006).

14. Paul F. Walker and Jonathan B. Tucker, "The Real Chemical Threat," *Los Angeles Times* (April 1, 2006).

15. William J. Broad and David E. Sanger, "Restraints Fray and Risks Grow as Nuclear Club Gains Members," *New York Times* (October 15, 2006).

16. Quoted in Michael Crowley, "The Stuff Sam Nunn's Nightmares Are Made Of," *New York Times Magazine* (February 25, 2007).

17. National Intelligence Council, *Global Trends 2025: A Transformed World* (November 2008): 62.

18. William Langewiesche, *How to Get a Nuclear Bomb, Atlantic Monthly* (December 2006).

19. National Intelligence Council, *Global Trends 2025,* 67. "World at Risk," xv.

20. U.S. National Intelligence Council, "The Terrorist Threat to the U.S. Homeland," National Intelligence Estimate (July 2007).

21. David Mosher, "Vulnerability of Russian and FSU Nuclear Establishments to Terrorism" (Presented at Fund for Peace conference, Threat Convergence: New Pathways to Proliferation, November 30, 2006).

22. This section builds on David Albright, "Terrorists' Acquisition of Nuclear Weapons: The Dangerous Synergy between Weak States and Illicit Nuclear Procurement" (Presented at Fund for Peace conference Threat Convergence: New Pathways to Proliferation, November 30, 2006).

23. Quoted in Mark Landler, "UN Official Sees a 'Wal-mart' in Nuclear Trafficking," *New York Times* (January 23, 2004).

24. Christopher Clary, "Dr. Khan's Nuclear WalMart," *Disarmament Diplomacy,* No. 76 (March/April 2004): 31–36.

25. Michael Bronner, "100 Grams (and Counting...): Notes from the Nuclear Underworld," Harvard University Belfer Center for Science and International Affairs (June 2008): 1–2.

26. Bronner, "100 Grams (and Counting)."

27. Lyudmila Zaitseva quoted in Lisa Trei, "New Database Tracks Illicit Trafficking of Nuclear Material Worldwide," *Stanford News Service* (March 5, 2002). ElBaradei quoted in "Gone Missing," *New York Times* (November 2, 2008). For incidents of lost or stolen fissile material, see International Atomic Energy Agency Illicit Trafficking Database 2007 Fact Sheet (September 1, 2008) and International Atomic Energy Agency, "Combating Illicit Trafficking in Nuclear and other Radioactive Material," IAEA Nuclear Security Series no. 6 (2007): 126.

28. Hajder Nizamani and Arjun Dutta, "Smuggling of Uranium from India: Stories Persist," *WMD Insights* (June 2006).

29. IAEA, "Combating Illicit Trafficking in Nuclear and other Radioactive Material," 127. Robert Orttung and Louise Shelley, "Linkages between Terrorist and Organized Crime Groups in Nuclear Smuggling: A Case Study of Chelyabinsk Oblast," Policy Memo No. 392 (Washington, DC: Program on New Approaches to Russian Security, 2005).

30. "A Hero at Home, A Villain Abroad," *Economist* (June 19, 2008).

31. Douglas Frantz and Catherine Collins, *The Man From Pakistan: The True Story of the World's Most Dangerous Nuclear Smuggler* (New York: Hachette, 2007): xv.

32. Jeffrey Lewis quoted in Joby Warrick, "Nuclear Ring Was More Advanced Than Thought, U.N. Says," *Washington Post* (September 13, 2008).

33. Stephen P. Cohen, "Fractured Pakistan: Potential Failure of a Nuclear State," (Presented at Fund for Peace conference Threat Convergence: New Pathways to Proliferation, November 30, 2006).

34. Charles D. Ferguson, "Preventing Catastrophic Nuclear Terrorism," Council Special Report No. 11 (New York: Council on Foreign Relations, March 2006). See also Joby Warrick, "Pakistani Nuclear Security Questioned," *Washington Post* (November 11, 2007).

35. Matthew Bunn, "Securing the Bomb 2008," Harvard University Belfer Center for Science and International Affairs, Project on Managing the Atom (November 2008): 101.

36. Lyudmila Zaitseva and Kevin Hand, "Nuclear Smuggling Chains: Suppliers, Intermediaries, and End-Users," *American Behavioral Scientist*, 46/6 (February 2003).

37. Bunn, "Securing the Bomb 2008," vi, 90–91.

38. Michael Berletta, Amy Sands, and Jonathan Tucker, "Keeping Track of Anthrax," *Bulletin of the Atomic Scientists*, 58/3 (May/June 2002): 57–62. William Broad, "A Nation Challenged: Germ Bank Security," *New York Times* (October 23, 2001). Joby Warrick, "Soviet Germ Factories Pose New Threat," *Washington Post* (August 20, 2005).

39. Some speculate on a secret Pakistani agreement to transfer nuclear weapons to Saudi Arabia should Iran go nuclear. Arnaud de Borchgrave, "Pakistan, Saudi Arabia in Secret Nuke Pact," *Washington Times* (October 22, 2003).

40. Michael O'Hanlon, "Dealing with the Collapse of a Nuclear-Armed State: The Cases of North Korea and Pakistan," The Princeton Project on National Security (September 2005). Also see David E. Sanger, "Pakistan Strife Raises U.S. Doubt on Nuclear Arms," *New York Times* (May 4, 2009). Paul B. Stares and Joel S. Wit, "Preparing for Sudden Change in North Korea," Council Special Report No. 42 (Washington, DC: Council on Foreign Relations, January 2009).

41. William J. Broad, "Hidden Travels of the Atomic Bomb," *New York Times* (December 8, 2008).

42. There are two main types of nuclear weapons: an implosion device (which requires plutonium) and a gun-type device (which uses uranium). The latter is much easier in principle for a nonstate actor to build.

43. David E. Sanger, "Nuclear Ring Reportedly Had Advanced Design," *New York Times* (June 15, 2008).

44. Peter D. Zimmerman and Jeffrey Lewis, "The Bomb in the Backyard," *Foreign Policy* (October 10, 2006). William Langewiesche, "How to Get a Nuclear Bomb," *Atlantic Monthly* (December 2006).

45. Chaim Braun and Christopher F. Chyba, "Proliferation Rings: New Challenges to the Nuclear Nonproliferation Regime," *International Security*, 29/2 (Fall 2004): 5–6, 22.

46. National Intelligence Council, *Global Trends 2025*, 67.

47. David Sanger, "So, What about Those Nukes?" *New York Times Magazine* (November 11, 2007). Also see Sharon Squassoni, "Closing Pandora's Box: Pakistan's Role in Nuclear Proliferation," *Arms Control Today*, 34/3 (April 2004): 8–13; Frantz and Collins, *The Man from Pakistan*, 201.

48. Ashton B. Carter, William J. Perry, and John M. Shalikashvili, "A Scary Thought: Loose Nukes in North Korea," *Wall Street Journal* (February 6, 2003). Michael A. Levi, "Deterring State Sponsorship of Nuclear Terrorism," Council on Foreign Relations Special Report No. 39 (New York: Council on Foreign Relations, 2008): 5–9.

49. "The Terror Next Time?" *Economist* (October 4, 2001).

50. National Intelligence Council, *Global Trends 2025*.

51. Countries with known or suspected biological weapons programs are North Korea, Pakistan, Algeria, Syria, Cuba, Russia, Iran, China, Egypt, and Israel. Biological weapons programs have been ended in Iraq, France, United Kingdom, South Africa. Countries with known chemical weapons programs or facilities include Russia, United States, India, North Korea, Serbia, and Bosnia. Those with suspected/likely chemical weapons programs are Iran, Sudan, Egypt, Israel, Syria, Algeria, Kazakhstan, Burma, Pakistan, Saudi Arabia, South Africa, Taiwan, and Vietnam. And those that have ended chemical weapons programs include South Korea, Albania, France, Iraq, United Kingdom, Indonesia, China, and Libya. Sharon A. Squassoni, "Nuclear, Biological, Chemical Weapons and Missiles: Status and Trends," Congressional Research Service Report (2005).

52. The fifteen are Algeria, Philippines, Syria, Cuba, Russia, Iran, India, Venezuela, China, Indonesia, Egypt, Thailand, Belarus, Vietnam, and Ghana.

53. Broad, "Hidden Travels of the Atomic Bomb."

54. Michelle Smith and Charles Ferguson, "France's Nuclear Diplomacy," *International Herald Tribune* (March 11, 2008).

55. The four are Angola, Iraq, Somalia, and North Korea. (The other 3 are Lebanon, Syria, and Egypt).

56. Nuclear Threat Initiative, "Highly Enriched Uranium: Who Has What?" (Monterey, CA: James Martin Center for Nonproliferation Studies, October 2008). George Perkovich, Jessica T. Mathews, Joseph Cirincione, Rose Gottemoeller, and Jon B. Wolfsthal, "Universal Compliance: A Strategy for Nuclear Security," (Washington, DC: Carnegie Endowment for International Peace, June 2007). Data taken from the International Atomic Energy Agency and Institute for Science and International Security, U.S. Department of Energy.

57. Jeffrey Fleishman, "Sting Unravels Stunning Mafia Plot," *Philadelphia Inquirer* (January 12, 1999).

58. Bunn, "Securing the Bomb 2008," 38.

59. Joby Warrick, "Custom-Built Pathogens Raise Bioterror Fears," *Washington Post* (July 31, 2006).

60. Associated Press, "Slovak Arrests Show Shadowy Market," (November 29, 2007). Zaitseva and Hand, "Nuclear Smuggling Chains," 827.

61. Thomas C. Reed and Danny B. Stillman, quoted in Broad, "Hidden Travels of the Atomic Bomb."

62. Michael Wines, "Break-in at Nuclear Site Baffles South Africa," *New York Times* (November 15, 2007).

63. According to estimates from the International Institute for Strategic Studies.

64. Ivan Watson, "Radioactive Cargo on Train to Iran Investigated," NPR.org (January 31, 2008) <http://www.npr.org/templates/story/story.php?storyId=18582342>.

65. Moises Naim, *Illicit: How Smugglers, Traffickers, and Copycats Are Hijacking the Global Economy* (New York: Anchor Books, 2005): 44.

66. On financial motivations, see Zaitseva and Hand, "Nuclear Smuggling Chains," 824, 826–828.

67. Zaitseva and Hand, "Nuclear Smuggling Chains," 824–825. Matthew Bunn, "The Threat: Anecdotes of Nuclear Insecurity," Nuclear Threat Initiative (January 16, 2004) <http://www.nti.org/e_research/cnwm/threat/anecdote.asp>.

68. Bunn, "Securing the Bomb 2008," 27, 23.

69. Nathan Busch, "China's Fissile Material Protection, Control, and Accounting: The Case for Renewed Collaboration," *Nonproliferation Review,* 9/3 (Fall/Winter 2002).

70. Graham Messick and Michael Karzis, "Nuke Facility Raid an Inside Job?" CBS News (November 23, 2008).

71. Zaitseva and Hand, "Nuclear Smuggling Chains," 830, 832.

72. Langewiesche, "How to Get a Nuclear Bomb," *Atlantic Monthly* (December 2006). Nikola Krastev, "FBI Breaks Weapons-Smuggling Ring Linked to Russia, Caucasus," *Radio Free Europe* (March 16, 2005). Misha Glenny, *McMafia: A Journey Through the Global Criminal Underworld* (New York: Knopf, 2008): 338.

73. Busch, "China's Fissile Material."

74. Frantz and Collins, *The Man from Pakistan,* 264, 271

75. Broad, "Hidden Travels of the Atomic Bomb."

76. Langewiesche, "How to Get a Nuclear Bomb."

77. Bunn, "Securing the Bomb 2008," x, 7, 27–29. Also see Chris Chyba, "Russia's Poison Gases," *New York Times* (October 30, 2002).

78. Frantz and Collins, *The Man from Pakistan,* 123–124.

79. Bunn, "Securing the Bomb 2008," 98.

80. Ibid, 17.

81. "World at Risk," 3.

82. Nuclear Threat Initiative, "Who has what: HEU" (updated October 2008).

83. As of June 2007. Perkovich et al, "Universal Compliance" (2007), based on data from IAEA and Institute for Science and International Security, U.S. Department of Energy.

84. Braun and Chyba, "Proliferation Rings," 13. Robin Wright and Joby Warrick, "Purchases Linked N. Korean to Syria," *Washington Post* (May 11, 2008).

85. David Albright, "Shipments of Weapons-Usable Plutonium in the Commercial Nuclear Industry," (Washington, DC: Institute for Science and International Security, January 3, 2007): 15. Also see Albright, "Terrorists' Acquisition of Nuclear Weapons."

86. Bunn, "Securing the Bomb 2008," 4, 41, 51.

87. Ibid, 39.

88. Busch, "China's Fissible Material."

89. Watson, "Radioactive Cargo on Train to Iran Investigated."

90. Gene Aloise, "Combating Nuclear Smuggling: Challenges Facing U.S. Efforts to Deploy Radiation Detection Equipment in Other Countries and in the United States," (Testimony for the House Committee on Homeland Security, June 21, 2005).

91. Konstantin Kemularia, quoted in Molly Corso, "Georgia: Uranium Smuggling Highlights Border Security Concerns," Eurasianet.org (March 1, 2007) <http://www.eurasianet.org/departments/insight/articles/eav030107a.shtml>.

92. Bunn, "100 Grams (and Counting)," preface.

93. Michael Bronner, "When the War Ends, Start to Worry," *New York Times* (August 16, 2008).

94. 140 of 192 UN member states had passed implementing legislation as of November 2009. States in the bottom two quintiles that had not submitted reports as of 2009 were: Somalia, Democratric Republic of Congo, Central African Republic, Zimbabwe, Liberia, Côte d'Ivoire, Haiti, Chad, Guinea-Bissau, Ethiopia, Guinea, Rwanda, Equatorial Guinea, Togo, Comoros, Zambia, Mauritania, Mozambique, East Timor, Swaziland, Malawi, Gambia, Mali, Lesotho, Solomon Islands. UN 1540 Committee legislative database is available online at <http://www.un.org/sc/1540/legisdatabase.shtml>.

95. Gene Aloise, quoted in Bryan Bender, "Georgia Chaos Halts Nuclear Security Effort," *Boston Globe* (August 19, 2008).

96. Lawrence Scott Sheets and William J. Broad, "Smuggler's Plot Highlights Fear over Uranium," *New York Times* (January 25, 2007).

97. Quoted in Sheets and Broad, "Smuggler's Plot Highlights Fear over Uranium."

98. Bronner, "100 Grams (and Counting)," 5–6.

99. Georgian government claims, and GAO quoted, in Bender, "Georgia Chaos Haults Nuclear Security Effort."

100. Richard Weitz, "After the Georgia War: Part Two: Regional U.S. Nonproliferation Programs Complicated," *WMD Insights* (November 2008).

101. Associated Press, "Slovak Arrests Show Shadowy Market" (November 29, 2007).

102. Of the sixteen incidents, six occurred in Germany; three in the Czech Republic; two in Russia; two in Georgia; and one each in Lithuania, Bulgaria, and France. There were also two incidents of lost nuclear materials in the United States and Japan. IAEA, "Illicit Trafficking Database, 1993–2007" (2007 Factsheet).

103. Robin Wright and Joby Warrick, "Purchases Linked N. Korean to Syria," *Washington Post* (May 11, 2008).

104. Albright, "Terrorists' Acquisition of Nuclear Weapons," 1–2.

105. Commission on the Intelligence Capabilities of the United States Regarding Weapons of Mass Destruction, "Report to the President of the United States" (March 31, 2005): 273.

106. Frantz and Collins, *The Man from Pakistan*, 269. "World at Risk," 10.

107. Joby Warrick, "Pakistan's Nuclear Security Questioned," *Washington Post* (November 11, 2007).

108. Albright, "Terrorists' Acquisition of Nuclear Weapons," 1–2.

109. Alexandros Petersen, "Negotiating a Black Hole," Guardian.co.uk (June 7, 2008). <http://www.guardian.co.uk/commentisfree/2008/jun/07/eu>.

110. "David Albright, "Terrorists' Acquisition of Nuclear Weapons."

111. National Intelligence Council, *Global Trends 2025*, 67.

112. Busch, "China's Fissile Material."

113. National Intelligence Council, *Global Trends 2025*, 63.

114. "World at Risk," xxiii. Also see "The World's Most Dangerous Place," *Economist* (January 3, 2008). Cohen, "Fractured Pakistan."

115. Sanger, "So, What about Those Nukes?"

116. "The Terrorism Index: A Perfect Nightmare," *Foreign Policy* (September/October 2007).

117. Cohen, "Fractured Pakistan."

118. David Albright and Paul Brannan, "Update on Khushab Plutonium Production Reactor Construction Projects in Pakistan," ISIS Imagery Brief (Washington, DC: Institute for Science and International Security, April 23, 2009).

119. Sanger, "So, What about Those Nukes?" Also see Ferguson, "Preventing Catastrophic Nuclear Terrorism," 13.

120. John Brennan quoted in Warrick, "Pakistani Nuclear Security Questioned."

Chapter 4

1. High Level Panel Research Staff, "Evaluating Collective Responses to Corruption and Transnational Crime," background paper prepared for the Vienna meeting of the UN Secretary General's High Level Panel on Threats, Challenges and Change (2004): 1–3.

2. Prime Minister's Strategy Unit discussion document (PPT mimeo) (2004): 8.

3. United Nations Office of Drugs and Crime, "United Nations Convention on Transnational Organized Crime and the Protocols Thereto" (Vienna: UNODC, 1998).

4. Ethan A. Nadelman, "Global Prohibition Regimes: The Evolution of Norms in International Society," *International Organization* 44/4 (1990): 479–526.

5. David T. Courtwright, *Forces of Habit: Drugs and the Making of the Modern World* (Cambridge, MA: Harvard University Press, 2001): 34–35, 152.

6. *Illicit Financial Flows and Criminal Things: States, Borders and the Other Side of Globalization*, eds. Willem van Schendel and Itty Abraham (Bloomington: Indiana University Press, 2005).

7. Report of the High-Level Panel on Threats, Challenges, and Change, *A More Secure World: Our Shared Responsibility* (New York: United Nations, 2004): 53. Comparisons to GDP are based on CIA World Factbook 2007 estimates, using GDP at PPP over $300 million.

8. Peter Andreas, Comments at 49th Annual Meeting of the International Studies Association (San Francisco, CA, March 26–29, 2008).

9. Figures on illegal drugs from *A More Secure World*, 49. Statistics on counterfeit goods are a 2007 OECD estimate, cited by the World Intellectual Property Association, "An Overview: 2007": 24. Money laundering estimates are based on Michel Camdessus, "Money Laundering: The Importance of International Countermeasures," Address before the Financial Action Task Force (Paris, February 10, 1998). Figures for human trafficking are from Moises Naim, *Illicit: How Smugglers, Traffickers, and Copycats are Hijacking the Global Economy* (New York: Anchor Books, 2005): 88. Statistics for the illegal small arms trade, cigarette smuggling, and unrecorded oil sales are from Raymond W. Baker, *Capitalism's Achilles Heel: Dirty Money and How to Renew the Free Market System* (Hoboken, NJ: John Wiley and Sons, Inc., 2005). Figures for the illegal timber trade are from UK Department

for International Development, "Crime and Persuasion: Tackling Illegal Logging, Improving Forest Governance" (November 29, 2007). Revenues from trafficking in endangered species are from the U.S. Department of Justice, as cited in Charles W. Schmidt, "Environmental Crimes: Profiting at the Earth's Expense," *Environmental Health Perspectives* (January 23, 2004). Data for art and antiquities theft is from the Federal Bureau of Investigation Art Theft Program, available at <http://www.fbi.gov/hq/cid/arttheft/art-theft.htm>.

10. On criminal networks, see Louise Shelley, "Identifying, Counting and Categorizing Transnational Criminal Organizations," *Transnational Organized Crime* 5 (1999): 1–18. Phil Williams, "Transnational Criminal Networks," in *Networks and Netwars: The Future of Terror, Crime and Militancy*, eds. John Arquilla and David Ronfeldt (Santa Monica: RAND, 2001). UN Office on Drugs and Crime, "Transnational Organized Crime in the West African Region" (New York: UNODC, 2005): 21–22.

11. Misha Glenny, *McMafia: A Journey Through the Global Criminal Underworld* (New York: Knopf, 2008): 248–249. James Cockayne, "Transnational Organized Crime: Multilateral Responses to a Rising Threat," Coping With Crisis Working Paper Series (New York: International Peace Academy, April 2007): 4.

12. "Actual Causes of Death in the United States, 2000," *Journal of the American Medical Association*, 291/10 (March 10, 2004). U.S. Office of National Drug Control Policy, "The Economic Costs of Drug Abuse in the United States, 1991–2002" (Washington, DC, December 2004). John R. Wagley, "Transnational Crime: Principal Threats and U.S. Responses," Congressional Research Service Report for Congress (Washington, DC: Congressional Research Service, March 20, 2006): 5. Glenny, *McMafia*, 166.

13. UNODC, "Organized Crime and Corruption Are Threats to Security and Development: The Role of the United Nations System" (April 2004): 19.

14. Carrie Johnson, "U.S. Charges Three in Narcoterrorism Case," *Washington Post* (December 19, 2009): A2. Neil McFarquhar, "Near Timbuktu, Mali Tackles Al-Qaeda and Drug Traffickers," *New York Times* (January 2, 2011): 6.

15. Louise I. Shelley, "The Nexus of Organized International Criminals and Terrorism" (May 20, 2004). David E. Kaplan, "Paying for Terror: How Jihadist Groups Are Using Organized Crime Tactics—and its Profits—to Finance Attacks on Targets around the Globe," *US News and World Report* (December 12, 2005).

16. White House, "International Crime Control Strategy" (May 1998). U.S. Department of Justice, "Law Enforcement Strategy to Combat International Organized Crime" (April 2008).

17. *A More Secure World*, 49–50. European Council, "A Secure Europe in a Better World: European Security Strategy" (Brussels: European Union, 2003): 4–5.

18. White House, "National Security Strategy of the United States of America" (2006): 33. For a British view, see <http://www.cabinetoffice.gov.uk/media/cabinetoffice/strategy/assets/sa_wfs_extract.pdf>. Cabinet Office, "The National Security Strategy of the United Kingdom: Security in an Interdependent World" (London: The Stationery Office, 2008): 12–13. UN High Level Panel Research staff document, p. 7.

19. John P. Sullivan and Robert J. Bunker, "Drug Cartels, Street Gangs, and Warlords," in *Non-State Actors and Future Wars*, eds. J. P. Sullivan and Robert J. Bunker, (London: Frank Cass, 2003).

20. Bartosz H. Stanislawski and Margaret G. Hermann, "Transnational Organized Crime, Terrorism, and WMD," discussion paper prepared for conference on Non-State Actors,

Terrorism, and Weapons of Mass Destruction (College Park: Center for International Development and Conflict Management, University of Maryland, October 15, 2004).

21. U.S. Government Interagency Working Group, "International Crime Threat Assessment" (2000): 124.

22. Quoted in Nico Colombant, "West Africa's Drug Circulation Increases, Worrying Officials," *Voice of America* (June 18, 2007). Phil Williams, "The Global Implications of West African Organized Crime," Input Paper, West Africa Assessment Project (May 2004): 24.

23. C. J. Chivers, "Heroin Seizes Turkmenistan, a Nation Ill Equipped to Cope," *New York Times* (July 11, 2007).

24. *Illicit Financial Flows and Criminal Things*, eds. Schendel and Abraham, p. 4.

25. This section draws on James Cockayne, "Transnational Organized Crime: Multilateral Responses to a Rising Threat," Coping with Crisis Working Paper Series (New York: International Peace Academy, April 2007). See also James Cockayne and Adam Lupel, "Introduction: Rethinking the Relationship between Peace Operations and Organized Crime," *International Peacekeeping*, 16/1 (February 2009): 4–19, especially 11.

26. Erica Marat, "Impact of Drug Trade and Organized Crime on State Functioning in Kyrgyzstan and Tajikistan," *China and Eurasia Forum Quarterly* 4/1 (Johns Hopkins University Central Asia-Caucasus Institute & Silk Road Studies Program, 2006).

27. Cockayne, "Transnational Organized Crime," p. 8.

28. Douglas Farah, "Al Qaeda's Use of Commodities and Natural Resources" (Unpublished paper, 2006). Raphael Perl, "Drug Trafficking and North Korea: Issues for U.S. Policy," Congressional Research Service Report (January 25, 2007). Raphael Perl and Dick K. Nanto, "North Korean Counterfeiting of U.S. Currency," Congressional Research Service Report (March 22, 2006).

29. Tom Farer, "Conclusion: Fighting Transnational Organized Crime: Measures Short of War," in *Transnational Organized Crime in the Americas*, ed. Tom Farer (New York: Routledge, 1999): 251.

30. Somalia, Myanmar, Iraq, Haiti, Afghanistan, Sudan, Guinea, Chad, Equatorial Guinea, Democratic Republic of the Congo, Zimbabwe. Transparency International, "2008 Corruption Perceptions Index" (September 22, 2008) .

31. Quote is from Naim, *Illicit*, 143. Monte Reel, "Paraguayan Smuggling Crossroads Scrutinized," *Washington Post* (August 3, 2006). CIA, "Possible Remote Havens for Terrorists and Other Illicit Activity" (2003).

32. Ronald D. Asmus and Bruce P. Jackson, "The Black Sea and the Frontiers of Freedom" *Policy Review* No. 125 (June/July 2004). Peter Finn, "Probe Traces Global Reach of Counterfeiting Ring: Fake $100 Bills in Maryland Tied to Organized Crime in Separatist Enclave," *Washington Post* (November 26, 2006).

33. Willem van Schendel, "Spaces of Engagement: How Borderlands, Illegal Flows and Territorial States Interlock," in *Illicit Financial Flows and Criminal Things*, eds. Schendel and Abraham, 46.

34. World Customs Organization Columbus Programme, "WCO Trends and Patterns Report—A Capacity building Estimate" (June 2007): 9–10.

35. Antonio Maria Costa, "Cocaine Finds Africa," *Washington Post* (July 29, 2008).

36. Ibid.

37. Ahmed Rashid, *Descent into Chaos: The United States and the Failure of Nation Building in Pakistan, Afghanistan, and Central Asia* (New York: Viking, 2008), 318. UN Office on Drugs and Crime, "Afghanistan Opium Survey 2007" (August 2007).

38. Bureau for International Narcotics and Law Enforcement Affairs, "2008 International Narcotics Control Strategy Report (INCSR)," (Washington, DC: State Department March 2008): 497.

39. Peter Andreas, "Illicit International Political Economy: The Clandestine Side of Globalization," *Review of International Political Economy*, 11/3 (August 2004): 650. Paul Collier, "Rebellion as a Quasi-Criminal Activity," *Journal of Conflict Resolution*, 44/6 (2000): 839–853. William Reno, "Shadow States and the Political Economy of Civil War," in *Greed and Grievance: Economic Agendas in Civil Wars*, eds. Mats Berdal and David Malone (Boulder: Lynne Rienner, 2000), 43–68.

40. UNODC, "Transnational Organized Crime in the West African Region," 21.

41. Stephanie A. Blair, Dana Eyre, Bernard Salomé, and James Wassertrom, "Forging a Viable Peace: Developing a Legitimate Political Economy," *The Quest for Viable Peace: International Intervention and Strategies for Conflict Transformation*, eds. Jack Covey, Michael J. Dziedzic, and Leonard R. Hawley (Washington, DC: U.S. Institute of Peace, 2005). *Combating Serious Crimes in Post-Conflict Societies: A Handbook for Policymakers and Practitioners*, ed. Colette Rausch (Washington: United States Institute of Peace, 2007), 8.

42. Author interview with chief of Haitian National Police Mario Andresol, Port-au-Prince, January 2007.

43. World Bank, 2007.

44. Based on Transparency International, "2008 Corruption Perceptions Index."

45. Robert Perito and Greg Maly, "Haiti's Drug Problem," United States Institute of Peace Briefing (June 2007). Also see International Crisis Group, "Reforming Haiti's Security Sector" (September 18, 2008).

46. Stevenson Jacobs, "Haiti's President Says U.S. Not Doing Enough to Help Fight Narcotics Trade," *Associated Press* (January 8, 2007).

47. These countries are listed in a European Commission report on counterfeiting hotspots (October 4, 2006).

48. According to the UNODC. Other estimates place the figure considerably higher, at $500–900 billion. Wagley, "Transnational Crime: Principal Threats and U.S. Responses," 5. Estimates of drug market as share of GDP are based on CIA World Factbook 2007 estimates of GDP (at PPP).

49. Office of National Drug Control Policy web site, (accessed October 21, 2008) <http://www.whitehousedrugpolicy.gov/>. Jeffrey A. Miron, "The Budgetary Implications of Drug Prohibition" (Cambridge, MA: Harvard University, December 2008).

50. Bureau for International Narcotics and Law Enforcement Affairs, "2008 International Narcotics Control Strategy Report (INCSR)," 21. UNODC figures are from UN Office on Drugs and Crime, "World Drug Report: 2007" (Vienna: UNODC, 2007).

51. According to the 2008 International Narcotics Control Strategy Report, major precursor countries are Argentina, Germany, South Korea, Brazil, India, Taiwan, Canada, Mexico, Thailand, Chile, Netherlands, United Kingdom, China, Singapore, and the United States.

52. UN Office on Drugs and Crime, "Is Poverty Driving the Afghan Opium Boom?" Discussion Paper (March 2008). Likewise in Pakistan, considered "poppy free" in 2001, opium production apparently rose in the tribal regions in tandem with a growing insurgency.

53. Sources: 2008 INCSR, 2008 UNODC World Drug Report

54. Most cannabis is produced locally, for domestic consumption. These countries produce cannabis for export.

55. By the 2008 U.S. International Narcotics Control Strategy Report (INCSR). The U.S. State Department's 2008 INCSR designates major producers and/or transit countries as: Afghanistan, the Bahamas, Bolivia, Brazil, Burma, Colombia, Dominican Republic, Ecuador, Guatemala, Haiti, India, Jamaica, Laos, Mexico, Nigeria, Pakistan, Panama, Paraguay, Peru, and Venezuela.

56. The figures are even worse in southeastern Europe, where countries "intercept less than 2% of their opiate trade." UNODC, "UNODC Reveals Devastating Impact of Afghan Opium," Press Release (October 21, 2009).

57. Other estimates of Taliban profits from the drug trade range widely, from $70 million to $400 million annually.

58. UNODC statement cited in Richard A. Oppel, Jr., "U.N. Agency Finds Evidence of Drug Cartels Forming in Afghanistan," *New York Times* (September 2, 2009). Peter Finn, "Gates Urges NATO to Take on Afghan Drug Traffickers," *Washington Post* (October 10, 2008).

59. "A Tidal Wave of Crime," *Economist* (June 22, 2000). Also see Glenny, *McMafia*, 119.

60. Bureau for International Narcotics and Law Enforcement Affairs, "2008 International Narcotics Control Strategy Report" (INCSR): 186, 366, 620.

61. UNODC figures are from UN Office on Drugs and Crime, "World Drug Report: 2008" (Vienna: UNODC, 2008). Vivienne Walt, "Cocaine Country," *Time* (June 27, 2007).

62. UNODC, "An Assessment of Transnational Organized Crime in Central Asia" (New York: UNODC, 2007): 51. "A Caribbean Crime Wave," *Economist* (March 20, 2008). Vladimir Fenopetov, "The Drug Crime Threat to Countries Located on the 'Silk Road,'" *China and Eurasia Quarterly*, 4/1 (2006): 5–13. Costa, "Cocaine Finds Africa." James Cockayne and Phil Williams, "The Invisible Tide: Towards an International Strategy to Deal with Drug Trafficking in West Africa," International Peace Institute Coping with Crisis Policy Paper series (October 14, 2009).

63. United States Joint Forces Command, "2008 Joint Operating Environment: Challenges and Implications for the Future Joint Force" (November 25, 2008), 36.

64. International Crisis Group, "Guinea-Bissau: In Need of a State," Africa Report No. 142 (July 2, 2008).

65. "Guinea-Bissau, Pusher's Paradise," *Economist* (June 7, 2007).

66. Walt, "Cocaine Country."

67. Adam Nossiter, "Fragile Nation in Disarray Holds Few Hopes for Vote," *New York Times* (June 28, 2009).

68. *Migrant smuggling*, a related crime, refers to the illegal movement of undocumented foreign nationals across state borders. Unlike trafficking, it operates on the basis of consent— although the terms of passage may be dangerous or degrading—and does not involve the ongoing exploitation of a trafficked individual following arrival at the final destination. In practice, the distinctions may blur.

69. The 800,000 figure is from the U.S. Department of State 2008 "Trafficking in Persons Report", citing "USG-sponsored research completed in 2006."

70. U.S. Department of State, "Trafficking in Persons Report 2006" (June 2006): Introduction. Also see William Finnegan, "The Countertraffickers." *New Yorker* (May 5, 2008). Caroline Moorehead, *Human Cargo: A Journey among Refugees* (New York: Henry Holt, 2006), 98.

71. This section relies primarily on data from UNODC's report, "Trafficking in Persons: Global Patterns" (April 2006), *http://www.unodc.org/documents/human-trafficking/*

HT-globalpatterns-en.pdf supplemented by the annual U.S. "Trafficking in Persons Report", compiled by the State Department. The UN report identifies the main countries of origin, transit, and destination, generating three separate lists that assign countries to one of five categories ("very high," "high," "medium," "low," and "very low"), depending on incidence of reporting. The State Department's annual report gives countries a single overall classification—Tier 3 (worst), Tier 2/Watch List, Tier 2, and Tier 1—according to whether that nation is "a country of origin, transit, or destination for *significant* numbers of victims of severe forms of trafficking in persons." Both UNODC and the State Department omit a number of developing and transitional countries and depend on information supplied by host governments. Moreover, the criteria for placing countries in tiers remains opaque in the case of UNODC and somewhat arbitrary in the case of the State Department, and U.S. tier designations are also acutely susceptible to broader political and diplomatic considerations.

72. The eleven "very high" origin countries are Albania, Belarus, Bulgaria, China, Lithuania, Moldova, Nigeria, Romania, Russia, Thailand, and Ukraine. Albania, Bulgaria, Hungary, Poland, Italy, and Thailand are the 6 "very high" transit countries; the 14 "high" transit states are Belgium, Bosnia, Burma, Czech Republic, France, Germany, Greece, Kosovo, Macedonia, Romania, Serbia, Slovakia, Turkey, and Ukraine.

73. The twelve are Burma, Chad, Cuba, Eritrea, Iran, Mauritania, North Korea, Sudan, Swaziland, Syria, Zimbabwe, and Fiji. The other Tier 3 countries are Kuwait, Malaysia, Niger, Papua New Guinea, and Saudi Arabia. U.S. Department of State, "Trafficking in Persons Report 2009" (June 2009).

74. "Guns and the City" *Small Arms Survey* 2007 (Geneva: Graduate Institute of International Studies, 2007): Section 3. *Running Guns: The Global Black Market in Small Arms*, edited by Lora Lumpe (London: Zed, 2000): 2.

75. Douglas Farah, "War and Terror Inc." *Washington Post* (September 23, 2007). Douglas Farah and Stephen Braun, *Merchant of Death: Money, Guns, Plans, and the Man Who Makes War Possible* (Hoboken, NJ: John Wiley & Sons, 2007), 15. *Small Arms Survey* estimates global illicit trade in SALW at $1 billion, compared to licit trade of $4 billion. "Counting the Human Cost," *Small Arms Survey* 2002 (Geneva: Graduate Institute of International Studies, 2002): Section 3.

76. 90 percent figure is from "Big Damage," *Economist* (June 12, 2001).

77. Naim, *Illicit*, 57–58. Peter Landesman, "Arms and the Man," *New York Times Magazine* (August 17, 2003).

78. "Small Arms Trade Transparency Barometer 2008," *Small Arms Survey* (2008).

79. Naim, *Illicit*, 51–53. C. J. Chivers, "Ill-Secured Soviet Arms Depots Tempting Rebels and Terrorists," *New York Times* (July 16, 2005).

80. Farah and Braun, *Merchant of Death*, 77.

81. Peter Reuter and Edwin M. Truman, *Chasing Dirty Money: The Fight against Money Laundering* (Washington, DC: Institute for International Economics, 2004). Also see Raymond W. Baker and Jennifer M. Nordin, "Toolbox: Dirty Money," *The American Interest* (September/October 2006).

82. Jack Blum, "Offshore Money," in *Transnational Crime in the Americas*, ed. Tom Farrer (New York: Routledge, 1999): 57–84.

83. Economists have generally relied on one of two estimation techniques to gauge the scale of global money laundering. See Friedrich Schneider, "The Size of Shadow Economies in 145 Countries from 1999 to 2003," *Brown Journal of World Affairs*, 11/2 (2005): 114.

84. See Camdessus, "Money Laundering." The CIA World Factbook (2007) estimates world GDP at $54.62 trillion (based on official exchange rates), or $65.61 trillion at PPP. World Bank figures are from the World Bank and UNODC, "Stolen Asset Recovery (StAR) Initiative: Challenges, Opportunities, and Action Plan," (September 17, 2007). Narcotics figures are from Jack Blum, Michael Levi, Thomas Naylor, and Phil Williams, "Financial Havens, Banking Secrecy and Money Laundering," (Vienna: UNODC, 1998).

85. Countries named to the Non-Cooperative Countries and Territories (NCCT) list have included: the Bahamas, Burma, Cayman Islands, Cook Islands, Dominica, Egypt, Grenada, Guatemala, Hungary, Indonesia, Israel, Lebanon, Liechtenstein, Marshall Islands, Nauru, Nigeria, Niue, Panama, Philippines, Russia, St. Kitts and Nevis, St. Vincent & Grenadines, and Ukraine. Burma, the last country to remain on the list, was removed in 2006. Also see Jonathan M. Winer and Trifin J. Roule, "Fighting Terrorist Finance," *Survival*, 44/3 (Autumn 2002).

86. They were: Afghanistan, Burma, Cambodia, Colombia, Haiti, Kenya, Nigeria, and Pakistan. The survey of money laundering and financial crimes produced annually by the State Department as Part 2 of its International Narcotics Control Strategy Reports (INCSR) relies on inputs from the Financial Crimes Enforcement Network (FinCEN) of the Department of Treasury.

87. William F. Wechsler, "Follow the Money," *Foreign Affairs* (July/August 2001).

88. Reuter and Truman, *Chasing Dirty Money*, 162–163.

89. Naim, *Illicit*, 143. "Features of an Ideal Financial Haven" are from UNODC, *Financial Havens, Banking Secrecy and Money Laundering* (1998).

90. Raymond W. Baker and Jennifer M. Nordin, "While Dirty Money Flows, the Poor Stay Poor," *International Herald Tribune* (April 13, 2005). For another estimate, see Dev Kar and Devon Cartwright-Smith, "Illicit Financial Flows from Developing Countries: 2002–2006," Global Financial Integrity (2008).

91. Warren Hoge, "Countries to Get Help Recovering Stolen Assets," *New York Times* (September 7, 2007).

92. Overall figures for environmental crime cited by UNEP Executive Director Klaus Toepfler, in United Nations Environmental Program, "UNEP's Action to Meet the Challenge of Illegal Trade in Chemicals" (2005). Figures for the trade in endangered species are from the Environmental Investigation Agency, "Environmental Crime: Our Planet, Our Problem," Briefing to the 17th meeting of the United Nations Commission on Crime Prevention and Criminal Justice (April 14–18, 2008). Also see William Clark, "Poaching American Security: Impacts of Illegal Wildlife Trade," Testimony before the U.S. House of Representatives Committee on Natural Resources (March 5, 2008).

93. "Down in the Woods," *Economist* (May 23, 2006). Figure of $15 billion (also cited by OECD and World Bank) is from "Crime and Persuasion: Tackling Illegal Logging, Improving Forest Governance," UK Department for International Development (DfID) (November 29, 2007).

94. "An African Dumping Ground," *New York Times* (October 4, 2006). Lydia Polgreen and Marlise Simons, "Global Sludge Ends in Tragedy for Ivory Coast," *New York Times* (October 2, 2006).

95. Environmental Investigation Agency, "Borderlines: Vietnam's Booming Furniture Industry and Timber Smuggling in the Mekong Region" (March 2008). Ellen Nakashima, "For Timber Trade, Many Routes Lead Through Singapore," *Washington Post* (April 1, 2006).

96. Phrase appears on website of the Basel Action Network (BAN), an NGO that monitors the environmental impact of trade in toxic wastes, products, and technologies.

97. Environmental Investigation Agency, "Demanding Deforestation" (December 2008). "Down in the Woods," *Economist.*

98. On trafficking in endangered species, see Naim, *Illicit,* 163. Environmental Investigation Agency, "How Ivory from 11,000 Elephants Has Disappeared into China's Black Market" (July 14, 2008). "Africa's Vanishing Apes," *Economist* (January 10, 2002).

99. "The Most Dangerous Seas in the World," *Economist* (July 19, 2008). "Swimming against the Tide" (August 3, 2006). For more on illegal fishing, see Sharon LaFraniere, "Europe Takes Africa's Fish, and Boatloads of Africans Follow," *New York Times* (January 14, 2008).

100. Schmidt, "Environmental Crimes."

101. Findings on CITES implementation are cited in Schmidt, "Environmental Crimes." On Democratic Republic of the Congo, see "Down in the Woods," *Economist,* and Global Witness, "DRC's Forests" (December 2007).

102. Raffi Khatchadourian, "The Stolen Forests: Inside the War on Illegal Logging," *New Yorker* (October 6, 2008).

103. Stephen R. Glaster, "Poaching American Security: Impacts of Illegal Wildlife Trade," Testimony before the U.S. House of Representatives Committee on Natural Resources (March 5, 2008).

104. James Kanter, "Indonesia Officials Unveil a Deal to Protect Forests," *New York Times* (October 9, 2008). "Call of the Wild," *Economist* (March 6, 2008).

105. $15 billion figure for illegal logging is from Khatchadourian, "The Stolen Forests." See Global Witness, "A Choice for China: Ending the Destruction of Burma's Frontier Forests" (October 1, 2005). Global Witness, "Timber, Taylor, Soldier, Spy" (June 15, 2005).

106. Global Witness, "Cambodia's Family Trees: Illegal Logging and the Stripping of Public Assets by Cambodia's Elite" (June 2007).

107. "IMB Reports Unprecedented Rise in Marine Hijackings," International Chamber of Commerce Commercial Crime Services (January 16, 2009).

108. "The Most Dangerous Seas in the World," *Economist* (July 19, 2008). Also see "Somali Pirates Demand Ransom for Saudi Oil Tanker," *Telegraph* (November 19, 2008).

109. "The Most Dangerous Seas in the World," *Economist.*

110. Figures for piracy are compiled by the Piracy Reporting Center of the International Chamber of Commerce International Maritime Bureau. The Center defines maritime piracy and armed robbery as "an act of boarding or attempting to board any ship with the apparent intent to commit theft or any other crime and with the apparent intent or capability to use force in the furtherance of that act."

111. Figures are compiled from: International Chamber of Commerce International Maritime Bureau, "Piracy and Armed Robbery Against Ships," Annual Report (2007). International

Chamber of Commerce, "IMB Piracy Report Highlights Trouble in African Waters" (July 10, 2008). International Chamber of Commerce, "IMB Reports Unprecedented Rise in Maritime Hijackings" (January 16, 2009).

112. Marc Lacey, "Waters That Prompt Fear from the Toughest of Sailors," *New York Times* (July 3, 2006). Ellen Knickmeyer, "On a Vital Route, a Boom in Piracy," *Washington Post* (September 27, 2008). For figures on Somali hijackings, see "IMB Issues Latest Quarterly Piracy Report," Baird Maritime (October 25, 2009).

113. These findings are consistent with the work of Donna Ninic, who finds that piracy off the coast of Africa is closely correlated with a state's loss of the monopoly on the use of armed force. Donna J. Ninic, "State Failure and the Re-Emergence of Maritime Piracy," Presented at the 49th Annual Convention of the International Studies Association (San Francisco, CA: March 26–29, 2008).

114. Zimbabwe, Turkmenistan, Tonga, and Burundi. (Turkmenistan is known as a transit state for Afghan heroin, but is not cited as a "major" transit state by the UNODC or INCSR).

115. Glenny, *McMafia*, 205.

116. El Paso Mayor John Cook, quoted in James C. McKinley, Jr., "Two Sides of a Border: One Violent, One Peaceful," *New York Times* (January 22, 2009).

117. Marc Lacey, "In Drug War, Mexico Fights Cartels and Itself," *New York Times* (March 30, 2009).

118. United States Joint Forces Command, "2008 Joint Operating Environment," 36. Dennis Blair, quoted in Mark Landler, "Clinton Reassures Mexico about Its Image," *New York Times* (March 27, 2009). Manuel Perez Rocha, "Mexico: Neither a Failed State nor a Model," *Foreign Policy in Focus* (February 23, 2009).

119. Lacey, "In Drug War, Mexico Fights Cartels and Itself."

120. Mark Landler, "Clinton Says U.S. Feeds Mexico Drug Trade," *New York Times* (March 25, 2009). James C. McKinley, Jr., "U.S. Is Arms Bazaar for Mexican Cartels," *New York Times* (February 26, 2009).

121. Transparency International, "2008 Corruption Perceptions Index." Rankings are out of 180.

122. Based on Bureau for International Narcotics and Law Enforcement Affairs, "International Narcotics Control Strategy Report: 2008" (INCSR) "major" countries and UN Office on Drugs and Crime, "World Drug Report: 2008."

123. Countries ranked as "high" or "very high" as origin and transit states in UNODC, "Trafficking in Persons: Global Patterns," or listed as "worst offenders" or in third (bottom) tier of States in the U.S. Department of State, "Trafficking in Persons Report, 2008."

124. Based on literature review.

125. Based on Bureau for International Narcotics and Law Enforcement Affairs, 2008 International Narcotics Control Strategy Report (INCSR).

126. Countries experiencing four or more attacks since 2003, based on International Chamber of Commerce International Maritime Bureau data.

127. Turkmenistan is not listed as a "major" transit state by the Bureau for International Narcotics and Law Enforcement Affairs, 2008 International Narcotics Control Strategy Report (INCSR), but is known as a transit state for Afghan heroin.

128. Based on Bureau for International Narcotics and Law Enforcement Affairs, 2008 International Narcotics Control Strategy Report (INCSR) "major" countries and UN Office on Drugs and Crime, "World Drug Report: 2008."
129. Countries ranked as "high" or "very high" origin and transit states in UNODC, "Trafficking in Persons: Global Patterns," and countries listed as "worst offenders" or in the third (bottom) tier of states in the U.S. Department of State, "Trafficking in Persons Report 2008."
130. Based on Farah and Braun, *Merchant of Death*, and broader literature review.
131. Countries experiencing four or more attacks since 2003, based on International Chamber of Commerce International Maritime Bureau data.
132. Guinea-Bissau is known as a major transit state for cocaine, although it is not listed as a "major" drug transit country in the Bureau for International Narcotics and Law Enforcement Affairs, 2008 International Narcotics Control Strategy Report (INCSR).
133. Tajikistan is known as a transit state for Afghan opium/heroin, although it is not listed as a "major" drug transit country in the Bureau for International Narcotics and Law Enforcement Affairs, 2008 International Narcotics Control Strategy Report (INCSR).
134. Based on "major" countries in the Bureau for International Narcotics and Law Enforcement Affairs, 2008 International Narcotics Control Strategy Report (INCSR) and UN Office on Drugs and Crime, "World Drug Report: 2008."
135. Countries ranked as "high" or "very high" origin and transit states in UNODC, "Trafficking in Persons: Global Patterns," and countries listed as "worst offenders" or in the third (bottom) tier of states in the 2008 U.S. State Department Trafficking in Persons Report.
136. Countries experiencing four or more attacks since 2003, based on International Chamber of Commerce International Maritime Bureau data.
137. Bureau for International Narcotics and Law Enforcement Affairs, 2008 International Narcotics Control Strategy Report (INCSR).
138. Guinea-Bissau is known as a major transit state for cocaine, although it is not listed as a "major" drug transit country in the Bureau for International Narcotics and Law Enforcement Affairs, 2008 International Narcotics Control Strategy Report (INCSR).
139. Tajikistan is known as a transit state for Afghan opium/heroin, although it is not listed as a "major" drug transit country in the Bureau for International Narcotics and Law Enforcement Affairs, 2008 International Narcotics Control Strategy Report (INCSR).

Chapter 5

1. Cited in Dan Collins, "Bush: U.S. Must Break Oil 'Addiction,'" *CBSnews.com* (February 1, 2006) <http://www.cbsnews.com/stories/2006/01/31/politics/main1260701.shtml>.
2. International Energy Agency (IEA), "Executive Summary," *World Energy Outlook* 2008 (Paris: OECD/IEA, 2008), 15.
3. Carlos Pascual, "The Geopolitics of Energy: From Security to Survival" (Washington: Brookings Institution, January 2008).
4. Philip C. Adams, quoted in Jad Mouawad, "Oil Closes below $50, Lowest Price since May 2005," *New York Times* (November 21 2008); Fatih Birol, remarks at *World Energy*

Outlook 2008 Launch Event, Center for Strategic and International Studies, Washington, DC, November 24, 2008; Jad Mouwad, "Rising Fear of a Future Oil Shock," *New York Times* (March 27, 2009).

5. Energy Information Administration (EIA), "Imports by Area of Entry," [online], (June 29, 2009) <http://tonto.eia.doe.gov/dnav/pet/pet_move_imp_dc_NUS-Zoo_mbblpd_a. htm>, accessed February 8, 2010; Council on Foreign Relations, "National Security Consequences of U.S. Oil Dependency," Independent Task Force Report no. 58 (New York: Council on Foreign Relations, 2006).

6. Energy Security Leadership Council, *Recommendations to the Nation on Reducing U.S. Oil Dependence* (Washington: Energy Security Leadership Council, December 2006), 17. Data taken from prepared statement by Milton Copulos before the U.S. Senate Committee on Foreign Relations, *Energy Diplomacy and Security: A Compilation of Statements by Witnesses*, 109th Congress, 2nd session (June 2006), 46.

7. Hillary Clinton, Prepared remarks, Senate Confirmation Hearing, January 13, 2009.

8. Joby Warrick, "Spread of Nuclear Capability Is Feared," *Washington Post* (May 12, 2008), A1.

9. $1.3 billion figure is from David B. Sandalow, *Freedom from Oil: How the Next President Can End the United States' Oil Addiction* (New York: McGraw Hill, 2008). Estimates of Saudi Arabia's support for Wahhabist groups are from George P. Shultz and R. James Woolsey, "The Petroleum Bomb," *Mechanical Engineering*, 127/10 (October 1, 2005), 30–34.

10. U.S. Senate Foreign Relations Committee, *Energy Diplomacy and Security* (Washington, DC: June 2006), XIII.

11. Condoleezza Rice, testimony to the Senate Foreign Relations Committee (2006), cited in Peter Ogden, "The Energy Warp: New Security Strategy Can Reduce the Negative Effect of Oil Dependence on Foreign Policy," (Washington: Center for American Progress, March 20, 2007); Peter Maass, *Crude World: The Violent Twilight of Oil* (New York: Knopf, 2009).

12. In 2008 the International Energy Agency estimated that demand for oil would grow by roughly 20 percent by 2030, despite higher prices and lower GDP growth (IEA, "Executive Summary," 4). Figures for rising demand from 1998–2007 are from Daniel Yergin, "Oil at the Break Point," Prepared Testimony, U.S. Congress Joint Economic Committee Hearing, "Oil Bubble or New Reality: How Will Skyrocketing Oil Prices Affect the U.S. Economy?" June 25, 2008. Figures for China and Asia are from Erica Downs, *China*, Foreign Policy Studies Energy Security Series (Washington, DC: Brookings Institution, December 2006).

13. Jan H. Kalicki and David L. Goldwyn, eds., *Energy and Security: Toward a New Foreign Policy Strategy* (Washington, DC: Woodrow Wilson Center Press, 2005), 2–3; "Double, Double, Oil and Trouble," *Economist* (May 29, 2008).

14. Jason S. Grumet, prepared statement, cited in Senate Foreign Relations Committee, *Energy Diplomacy and Security* (Washington: June 2006), 26.

15. Javier Blas and Andrew Ward, "Libya's Oil Cut Threat Sends Out Jitters," *Financial Times* (June 27, 2008).

16. Daniel Yergin, "Oil at the Break Point," (June 25, 2008).

17. United Kingdom Prime Minister's Strategy Unit, *Investing in Prevention* (London: Prime Minister's Strategy Unit, 2005).

18. Iraq, Sudan, Angola, Cote d'Ivoire, Chad, Republic of Congo, Equatorial Guinea, and Nigeria.

19. Production and export figures throughout the chapter are based on 2008 EIA data (U.S. Energy Information Administration, "International Petroleum (Oil) Production," [online] <http://www.eia.doe.gov/emeu/international/oilproduction.html>, accessed February 8, 2010.). Saudi Arabian and Chinese production is not included in these figures.

20. Downs (2006), 31.

21. Energy Information Administration, February 2009 data.

22. Charles Duhigg, "Big Game? An Enron Survivor Hunts for Riches," New York Times (January 21, 2007).

23. Jad Mouawad, "Once Marginal, But Now Kings of the Oil World," New York Times (April 23, 2006).

24. Will Connors, "New Attacks on Pipelines in Delta Region of Nigeria," New York Times (September 17, 2008).

25. Gal Luft, "Iran-Pakistan-India Pipeline: The Baloch Wildcard," Energy Security, [online newletter], (January 12, 2005) <http://www.iags.org/no115042.htm>, accessed February 8, 2010.

26. Dennis Blair and Kenneth Lieberthal, "Smooth Sailing: The World's Shipping Lanes are Safe," Foreign Affairs, 86/3 (May/June 2007): 83–90.

27. U.S. Energy Information Administration, "World Oil Transit Chokepoints" [online], (January 2008) <http://www.eia.doe.gov/cabs/World_Oil_Transit_Chokepoints/Background.html>, accessed February 8, 2010. Other important passages include the Panama Canal and the Panama Pipeline; the Suez Canal and the Sumed Pipeline; and the Turkish/Bosporus Straits.

28. Jad Mouawad, "Once Marginal, But Now Kings of the Oil World."

29. Brookings Institution, "Iraq Index" [online], (May 29, 2008) <http://www.brookings.edu/saban/iraq-index.aspx>, accessed February 10, 2010.

30. Human Rights Watch report, quoted in Jad Mouawad, "Growing Unrest Posing a Threat to Nigerian Oil," New York Times (April 21, 2007).

31. Graham Bowley, "One Reason Gas Is Emptying Your Wallet: Nigeria." New York Times (June 29, 2008).

32. "The Slippery Business of Oil," Economist (June 28, 2008); Lydia Polgreen, "Niger Delta Rebels Say They Hit Another Pipeline in 'Oil War,'" New York Times (September 20, 2008).

33. Adam Robinson and Daniel Yergin quoted in Bowley, "One Reason Gas Is Emptying Your Wallet;" Jad Mouawad, "Gas Reaches $3.50, with Little Hope for Relief," New York Times (April 22, 2008); "Nigeria Attacks Boost Oil Price," BBC News (May 26, 2008).

34. Gal Luft, "Pipeline Sabotage Is Terrorist's Weapon of Choice," IAGS Pipeline & Gas Journal (March 28, 2005). On Colombia, see U.S. Government Accountability Office, "Security Assistance: Effort to Secure Colombia's Cano Limon-Covenas Oil Pipeline Have Reduced Attacks, But Challenges Remain," Report to Congressional Requesters (Washington: GAO, September 2005).

35. Jehangir Pocha, "China Pipeline Raises Ethnic Strife," Boston Globe (November 5, 2006).

36. According to EIA 2005 data.

37. Steinhausler et al., "Security Risks to the Oil and Gas Industry," Strategic Insights, VII/1 (Monterey, CA, February 2008).

38. Luft, "Pipline Sabotage"; "What If?" *Economist* (May 27, 2004). Figures from 2005 Nigeria attacks are from James J. F. Forest and Matthew V. Sousa, *Oil and Terrorism in the New Gulf: Framing U.S. Energy and Security Policies for the Gulf of Guinea* (Plymouth: Lexington Books, 2007), 114.

39. Al Zawahiri quoted in Stephen Ulph, "Al Zawahiri Encourages Targeting of Gulf Oil," *Terrorism Focus*, 2/23 (December 13, 2005). Map of Future al Qaeda Operations quoted in James S. Robbins, "No Blood for Oil," *National Review* (July 12, 2005).

40. Hassan M. Fattah, "Suicide Bombers Fail to Enter Saudi Oil Plant," *New York Times* (February 25, 2006); Lennox Samuels, "Al Qaeda Nostra," *Newsweek* [online feature], (May 21, 2008) <http://www.newsweek.com/id/138085>, accessed February 10, 2010.

41. Forest and Sousa, *Oil and Terrorism in the New Gulf.*

42. Peter K. Baev, "Reevaluating the Risks of Terrorist Attacks against Energy Infrastructure in Eurasia," *China and Eurasia Forum Quarterly*, 4/2 (2006): 33–38.

43. Geoff D. Porter, "Islamist Terrorism and Energy Sector Security in Algeria," *Terrorism Focus*, 5/12 (June 21, 2007).

44. "Terrorism and Oil," *Washington Post* (June 3, 2004).

45. Baev, "Reevaluating the Risks."

46. Blair and Lieberthal, "Smooth Sailing."

47. "Chavez's Battle to Keep the Oil Flowing," *Economist* (July 31, 2003); "Venezuela's Oil Crisis," *Economist* (February 6, 2003).

48. Integrated Regional Information Networks, "Chad: Month Two of Strike Threatens People More Than Government," [online], (June 4, 2007) <http://www.irinnews.org/Report. aspx?ReportId=72526>, accessed February 8, 2010; William Maclean, "Algeria Riots Pose Risk of Wider Unrest," *Reuters* (June 1, 2008).

49. Strikes have also occurred in Ecuador, which at #85 on the Index is just out of the 3rd quintile.

50. UN Office of Drugs and Crime, *Transnational Organized Crime in the West African Region* (Vienna: UNODC, June 2005), 4.

51. "The Curse of the Vigilantes," *Economist* (April 21, 2001); Roman Kupchinsky, "Chechnya: Stolen Oil and Purchased Guns," *Radio Free Europe/Radio Liberty* (October 25, 2005).

52. Richard Oppel, "Iraq's Insurgency Runs on Stolen Oil Profits," *New York Times* (March 16, 2008).

53. International Crisis Group, *Uzbekistan: Stagnation and Uncertainty*, Asia Briefing no. 67 (Brussels: International Crisis Group, August 22, 2007), 5. On Kazakhstan, see "Exxon attacks Kazakh Oil Field Delays," *Financial Times* (July 1, 2008).

54. Matthew Green, "Nigeria's Oil Militants Take Their Fight beyond the Delta," *Financial Times* (July 1, 2008).

55. "Indonesia Considers Temporarily Pulling out of OPEC," *Associated Press* (May 6, 2008).

56. "Nigerian Oil Giant NNPC Will Become Real Company: President," *Agence France Presse* (May 17, 2008); Matthew Green, "State Group Faces Overhaul as Nigeria Weighs Plans to Boost Oil Output," *Financial Times* (August 8, 2008); International Crisis Group, "Uzbekistan: Stagnation and Uncertainty," Asia Briefing no. 67 (Brussels: International Crisis Group, August 22, 2007), 4.

57. "Conoco Earnings Drop Sharply on Asset Losses in Venezuela," *Associated Press* (July 26, 2007); Carola Hoyos, "Exxon Attacks Kazakh Oil Field Delays," *Financial Times* (July 1, 2008); "The Slippery Business of Oil."

58. Based on EIA Country Analysis Briefs (updated for 2007 and 2008).

59. Marianne Kah, quoted in Roger Lowenstein, "What's Really Wrong with the Price Of Oil," *New York Times* (October 19, 2008). IEA quote is from "Executive Summary," 3.

60. Kalicki and Goldwyn, *Energy and Security,* 2; Michael L. Ross, "What Do We Know about Natural Resources and Civil War?" *Journal of Peace Research,* 41/3 (May 2004): 337–356.

61. Larry Diamond, *The Spirit of Democracy: The Struggle to Build Free Societies Throughout the World* (New York: Times Books, 2008); Economist Intelligence Unit, "African Free-for-all?" *Economist* (August 30, 2007). In Freedom House's *Freedom in the World* 2007, oil producers classified as "not free" are Saudi Arabia (#1 oil producer), Russia (#2), Iran (#4), China (#5), UAE (#8), Algeria (#14), Iraq (#15), Libya (#16), Angola (#17), Kazakhstan (#19), Qatar (#20), Azerbaijan (#23), Oman (#25). Gas producers classified as "not free" are Russia (#1 gas producer), Iran (#4), Algeria (#5), Saudi Arabia (#10), Turkmenistan (#12), Uzbekistan (#13), China (#14), UAE (#15), Qatar (#16), Egypt (#19). See Freedom House, *The Worst of the Worst: The World's Most Repressive Societies* (2009). Freedom House's 2008 report, *Nations in Transit* 2008, emphasized the rise of "petro-authoritarianism" in Central Asia.

62. Thomas Friedman, "The Democratic Recession," *New York Times* (May 7, 2008).

63. See Terry L. Karl, *The Paradox of Plenty* (Berkeley: University of California Press, 1997); James D. Fearon, "Primary Commodity Exports and Civil War," *Journal of Conflict Resolution,* 49 (2005).

64. Jeffrey Sachs and Andrew M. Warner, "Natural Resource Abundance and Economic Growth," NBER Working Paper No. 5398 (Cambridge, MA: National Bureau of Economic Research, 1995); Collier, *The Bottom Billion,* 39.

65. Economist Intelligence Unit, "African Free-for-all?" On Angola, see "Angola's Uncertain Future," *Economist* (November 16, 2007).

66. USAID, Overseas Loans and Grants, "Nigeria: Country Ten-Year Page."

67. Moises Naim, "Rogue Aid," *Foreign Policy* (March-April 2007).

68. Paul Collier and Anke Hoeffler, "Greed and Grievance in Civil War," Policy Research Working Paper 2355 (Washington: World Bank Development Research Group, May 2000); Fearon and Laitin, "Ethnicity, Insurgency, and Civil War," *American Political Science Review,* 97/1 (2003). See Ibrahim Elbadawi and Nicholas Sambanis, "How Much War Will We See? Explaining the Prevalence of Civil War," *Journal of Conflict Resolution,* 46/3 (2002): 307–334.

69. Conflict defined as at least 1,000 battle deaths per year. Data from the International Peace Research Institute (Oslo). (See http://www.prio.no/sptrans/-634415636/1946–2006_cumulative.pdf). Nineteen (59.4 percent) rank in the bottom quarter of countries listed in the 2008 Global Peace Index (see <http://www.visionofhumanity.org/gpi/results/rankings.php>)

70. UN Department of Peacekeeping Operations, March 31, 2009.

71. See Andrew E. Kramer, "With Russia's Help, Gas-Producing Countries Try to Be More Like OPEC," *New York Times* (December 23, 2008).

72. Romero; "Trouble in the Pipeline," *Economist* (May 8, 2008).

73. Tillerson, quoted in Gideon Rachman, "Respect for the Law Is in Russia's Interest," *Financial Times* (June 10, 2008). Vladimir Milov, "How Sustainable Is Russia's Future as an Energy Superpower?" Remarks at the Carnegie Endowment for International Peace, Washington, D.C. (March 16, 2006). "Smoke and Mirrors," *Economist* (February 28, 2008).

74. Roger Stern, "Iran Actually Is Short of Oil," *International Herald Tribune* (January 8, 2007); *EIA Iran Energy Profile* (October 2007); Lionel Beehner, "Tehran's Oil Dysfunction,"

Council on Foreign Relations Backgrounder, [online] (February 16, 2007) <http://www.cfr.org/publication/12625/>, accessed February 10, 2010.

75. Stern, "Iran Actually Is Short of Oil"; Economist Intelligence Unit, "Polishing the Shop Window," *Economist* (February 6, 2007).

76. "Oil's Dark Secret," *Economist* (August 10, 2006).

77. Robert Pirog, "The Role of National Oil Companies in the International Oil Market," CRS Report for Congress (Washington: Congressional Research Service, August 21, 2007).

78. Yergin, "Ensuring Energy Security;" "Trouble in the Pipeline," *Economist* (May 8, 2008).

79. EIA, 2007 data.

80. "Boom to Bust and Worse," *Economist* (December 16, 2008).

81. "Trouble in the Pipeline."

82. Table analysis based on the 30 states in the bottom three quintiles of the Index which are significant energy producers (defined as producing at least 80,000 bpd of oil, or with at least 0.5 tcf of natural gas reserves), or where significant recent discoveries have been reported (e.g. Mauritania, East Timor, Sao Tome & Principe, Papua New Guinea). The analysis does not take into account major energy producers not ranked on the Index, including Saudi Arabia, Kuwait, Qatar and UAE.

83. Based on assessments in EIA Country Analysis Briefs, updated 2007 and 2008.

84. Terrorist or guerilla attacks, based on news reports.

85. Based on news reports. Seeks to capture captures economically- or socially-motivated violent protests (e.g. food riots), and rampant criminality, but not armed rebellion, protests linked to conflicts, political protests or peaceful demonstrations.

Chapter 6

1. Barack Obama, Statement by the President on Global Health Initiative (May 5, 2009).

2. Clive Bell and Maureen Lewis, "The Economic Implications of Epidemics Old and New," Working Paper No. 54, (Washington, DC: Center for Global Development, 2004): 31.

3. Frederick M. Burkle, Jr., "Pandemics: State Fragility's Most Telling Gap?," in *Global Strategic Assessment*, edited by Patrick Cronin (Washington, DC: NDU, 2009) 105–107.

4. Andrew T. Price-Smith, "Downward Spiral: HIV/AIDS, State Capacity, and Political Conflict in Zimbabwe," *Peaceworks*, 53 (July 2004): 13–14.

5. Robin A. Weiss and Anthony J. McMichael, "Social and Environmental Risk Factors in the Emergence of Infectious Diseases," *Nature Medicine Supplement* 10/12 (December 2004).

6. David P. Fidler and Nick Drager, "Health and Foreign Policy," *Bulletin of the World Health Organization* (September 2006): 697.

7. Charles C. Mann, *1491: New Revelations of the Americas before Columbus* (New York: Knopf, 2005).

8. Robin A. Weiss and Anthony J. McMichael, "Social and Environmental Risk Factors in the Emergence of Infectious Diseases," *Nature Medicine Supplement*, 10/12 (December 2004). Elisabeth Rosenthal, "WHO Urges Effort to Fight Fast-Spreading New Diseases," *New York Times* (August 27, 2007). One study published in *Nature*—the most comprehensive ever—identified 355 different emerging infectious diseases (EIDs) between 1940 and 2004, and remarked that the rate of new EID events accelerated considerably over that time (Jones et al., "Global Trends in Emerging Infectious Diseases," *Nature*, 451/21 [February 2008]: 990). "Emerging" diseases are those that are recently discovered; are caused by long-standing

pathogens that have evolved; have jumped from their traditional host (e.g., Lyme disease); or have expanded their geographic range (e.g., West Nile virus). "Reemerging" diseases are familiar pathogens controlled in the past but now rapidly increasing in incidence or geographic distribution (e.g., tuberculosis, Dengue fever).

9. National Intelligence Council, "The Global Infectious Disease Threat and Its Implications for the United States" (January 2000). "Mapping the Global Future," Report of the National Intelligence Council's 2020 Project (December 2004).

10. Andrew Price-Smith, *The Health of Nations* (Cambridge, MA: MIT Press, 2002): 15.

11. U.S. State Department, "Nation, World Must Prepare for Pandemic Flu, Bush Says," (November 1, 2005).

12. United Nations Environment Program, "Geo Year Book: An Overview of Our Changing Environment" (2005): 72.

13. Figure of $2.2 billion from Agustin Carstens, quoted in Associated Press, "Swine Flu Outbreak Costs Mexico $2.2 Billion," (May 5, 2009). Figure of $166 billion is from CDC, cited in Laurie Garrett, "The Next Pandemic?" *Foreign Affairs* (July/August 2005).

14. Malaria in Africa is a case in point. Jeffrey Sachs, *The End of Poverty* (New York: Penguin Books, 2004): 58.

15. World Health Organization, Measles Factsheet (December 2007) <http://www.who.int/mediacentre/factsheets/fs286/en>. David H. Molyneux, Peter J. Hotez, and Alan Fenwick, "Rapid-Impact Interventions: How a Policy of Integrated Control for Africa's Neglected Tropical Diseases Could Benefit the Poor," *PLoS Medicine*, 2/11 (October 11, 2005): e336.

16. Ibid.

17. Nicholas D. Kristof, "A Killer without Borders," *New York Times* (December 7, 2008).

18. On zoonoses, see Jones et al, "Global Trends in Emerging Infectious Diseases," 992. Kruse et al., "Wildlife as a Source of Zoonotic Infections," *Emerging Infectious Diseases*, 10/12 (December 2004).

19. Dennis Pirages, "Containing Infectious Disease," in Worldwatch Institute, *State of the World 2005: Redefining Global Security* (New York: W. W. Norton, 2005). World Bank, "The World Bank Responds to SARS," (June 4, 2003). National Intelligence Council, "SARS: Down But Still a Threat" (August 2003).

20. Claudia Alvarado de la Barrera and Gustavo Reyes-Taran, "Influenza: Forecast for a Pandemic," *Archives of Medical Research*, 36 (2005): 629. Barack Obama and Richard Lugar, "Grounding a Pandemic," *New York Times* (June 6, 2005); Garrett, "The Next Pandemic?" 52–53. Homeland Security Council, "National Strategy for Pandemic Influenza" (November 2005).

21. Alvarado de la Barrera and Reyes-Taran, "Influenza: Forecast for a Pandemic."

22. Michael T. Osterholm, "Is the Bird Flu Threat Still Real and Are We Prepared?" (Transcript of event held in Washington, DC, at the Council on Foreign Relations, on April 23, 2007).

23. Hugh Collins and Jose Enrique Arrioja, "Mexico's Economy Set for More Damage as Flu Wanes," *Bloomberg* (May 4, 2009).

24. "Feeling a Bit Better?" *Economist* web edition (May 4, 2009).

25. Congressional Budget Office, "A Potential Influenza Pandemic: Possible Macroeconomic Effects and Policy Issues" (December 8, 2005; revised July 27, 2006). Garrett, "The Next Pandemic?" C. J. L Murray, A. D. Lopez, B. Chin, D. Feehan and K. H. Hill, "Estimation of Potential Global Pandemic Influenza Mortality on the Basis of Vital Registry Data from the 1918–1920 Pandemic: A Quantitative Analysis," *Lancet*, 368/9554 (2006): 2211–2218.

26. Michael T. Osterholm, "Preparing for the Next Pandemic?" *Foreign Affairs* (July/August 2005).

27. "The Cost of Flu," *Economist* (April 30, 2009).

28. Garrett, "The Next Pandemic?"

29. Laurie Garrett, "The Lessons of HIV/AIDS," *Foreign Affairs* (July/August 2005). National Intelligence Council, "The Next Wave of HIV/AIDS: Nigeria, Ethiopia, Russia, India and China" (September 2002). Mark Schneider and Michael Moodie, "The Destabilizing Impacts of HIV/AIDS," (Washington, DC: Center for Strategic and International Studies, May 2002). Nicholas Eberstadt, "The Future of AIDS," *Foreign Affairs* (November/December 2002).

30. Donald G. McNeil, Jr., "A Time To Rethink AIDS's Grip," *New York Times* (November 25, 2007).

31. UNAIDS, "2007 AIDS Epidemic Update" (November 19, 2007). UNAIDS/World Health Organization, "Global HIV Prevalence Has Leveled Off," Press Release (November 20, 2007).

32. Pieter Fourie, "The Relationship between the AIDS Pandemic and State Fragility," *Global Change, Peace & Security,* 18/3 (2007).

33. Andrew Ehrenkranz, "Ebola Rising," Newsweek.com (December 6, 2007) <http://www.newsweek.com/id/74101>.

34. See Fred Guteri, "You Don't Want This Going Places," Newsweek.com (December 10, 2007) <http://www.newsweek.com/id/74942>. Laurie Garrett and Scott Rosenstein, "Missed Opportunities: Governance of Global Infectious Diseases," *Harvard International Review* (Spring 2005).

35. William Newbrander, "Rebuilding Health Systems and Providing Health Services in Fragile States," MSH Occasional Paper No. 7 (2007): 6.

36. Jennifer Brower and Peter Chalk, *The Global Threat of New and Reemerging Infectious Diseases: Reconciling U.S. National Security and Public Health Policy* (Santa Monica, CA: RAND, 2003): xviii.

37. National Intelligence Council, "The Global Infectious Disease Threat."

38. UN Office for the Coordination of Humanitarian Affairs, "Pakistan: Opposition to Anti-Polio Drive Weakens," *IRIN Humanitarian News and Analysis* (November 13, 2007).

39. Based on the World Health Organization's Statistical Information System's years of life lost calculations, available at <http://www.who.int/whosis/indicators/compendium/2008/1llr/en/index.html>. For infectious disease rates in weak and failing sates, see Newbrander, "Rebuilding Health Systems and Providing Health Services in Fragile States."

40. The scheme ranks nations in five categories based on resources and priority devoted to public health, quality of health care delivery, access to drugs, and capacity for surveillance and response. National Intelligence Council, "Typology of Countries by Health Care Status," DI Cartography Center (2003), <http://memory.loc.gov/cgi-bin/query/h?ammem/gmd:@field(NUMBER+@band(g3201e+ct001291))>.

41. Per capita health spending for bottom-quintile states is based on WHO Statistical Information System, per capita government expenditure on health (PPP exchange rate), 2006 data, available at <http://apps.who.int/whosis/data/Search.jsp?countries=%5bLocation%5d.Members)>.

42. "Typology of Countries by Health-Care Status," map created by Central Intelligence Agency Cartographic Center (December 2002), archived at <http://memory.loc.gov/cgi-bin/query/h?ammem/gmd:@field (NUMBER+@band(g3201e+ct001291))>.

43. Alan Sipress, "Hunting Bird Flu on the Cheap in Cambodia," *Washington Post* (March 23, 2005).

44. Susan E. Rice, "Poverty Breeds Insecurity" in *Too Poor for Peace?* eds. Lael Brainard and Derek Chollet (Washington, DC: Brookings Institution Press, 2007): 41.

45. Garrett and Rosenstein, "Missed Opportunities."

46. Ehrenkranz, "Ebola Rising." Andrew Ehrenkranz, "Ebola Epicenter," Newsweek.com, (December 11, 2007) <http://www.newsweek.com/id/76935>.

47. Frederick M. Burkle, Jr., "Globalization and Disasters: Issues of Public Health, State Capacity, and Political Action," *Journal of International Affairs* (2006).

48. Craig Timberg, "Congo's Ebola Outbreak Could Be Worst in Years," *Washington Post* (September 19, 2007).

49. National Intelligence Council, "SARS: Down But Still a Threat" (August 2003).

50. Lydia Polgreen, "Nigeria Tries TV Jingles, Anything to Chip Away at Ignorance of Spreading Bird Flu," *New York Times* (February 26, 2006).

51. Newbrander, "Rebuilding Health Systems and Providing Health Services in Fragile States," 9.

52. WHO, "Planning and DOTS Implementation." Online at <http://www.who.int/tb/publications/global_report/2004/07_results2/en/>.

53. See UN and World Bank (December 1, 2007); Michael D. Conway et al., "Addressing Africa's Health Workforce Crisis," *McKinsey Quarterly* (November 2007).

54. National Intelligence Council, "SARS: Down But Still a Threat." Also see Weiss and McMichael, "Social and Environmental Risk Factors in the Emergence of Infectious Diseases."

55. Rob Stein, "SARS Exposed World's Weak Spots," *Washington Post* (June 15, 2003).

56. Conway et al., "Addressing Africa's Health Workforce Crisis."

57. Pirages, "Containing Infectious Disease."

58. Christoph Kurowski et al., "Human Resources for Health: Requirements and Availability in the Context of Scaling-Up Priority Interventions in Low-Income Countries: Case Studies from Tanzania and Chad," London School of Hygiene & Tropical Medicine Working Paper (2004). On Egypt, see Weiss and McMichael, "Social and Environmental Risk Factors."

59. Sharon LaFraniere, "Specialists Say 'Healers' in Angola Are Helping to Spread Deadly Virus," *New York Times* (April 25, 2005). Ehrenkranz, "Ebola Rising."

60. Weiss and McMichael, "Social and Environmental Risk Factors."

61. Sharon LaFraniere, "In Oil-Rich Uganda, Cholera Preys upon Poorest," *New York Times* (June 6, 2006). Craig Timberg, "Cholera Spreading Rapidly in Angola," *Washington Post* (May 18, 2006).

62. Somini Sengupta, "Spread of AIDS in India Outpaces Scant Treatment Effort," *New York Times* (May 27, 2005).

63. WHO, "Planning and DOTS Implementation."

64. Mark Gevisser, *Thabo Mbeki: The Dream Deferred* (Capetown: Jonathan Ball Publishers, 2007). Sharon LaFraniere and Denise Grady, "Stalking a Deadly Virus, Battling a Town's Fear," *New York Times* (April 17, 2005).

65. Celia W. Dugger and Donald G. McNeil, Jr., "Rumor, Fear and Fatigue Hinder Final Push to End Polio," *New York Times* (March 20, 2006). Craig Timberg, "Nigeria Picks Up the Pace in War against Polio: Two-Year Delay Let Disease Spread," *Washington Post* (August 24, 2005).

66. Ehrenkranz, "Ebola Epicenter."

67. Juan Lubroth, quoted in Elisabeth Rosenthal and Donald G. McNeill, Jr., "A Worrisome New Front," *New York Times* (February 12, 2006). Also see National Intelligence Council, "SARS: Down But Still a Threat."

68. Richard Holbrooke and Laurie Garrett, "'Sovereignty' That Risks Global Health," *Washington Post* (August 10, 2008).

69. Open Society Institute, "The Gathering Storm: Infectious Diseases and Human Rights in Burma" (July 2007).

70. Karin Brulliard, "Zimbabwe's Cholera Crosses Borders," *Washington Post* (December 5, 2008).

71. Celia W. Dugger, "Cholera Is Raging, Despite Denial by Mugabe," *New York Times* (December 12, 2008).

72. Michael Specter, "Nature's Bioterrorist," *New Yorker* (February 28, 2005). Also see Elisabeth Rosenthal, "Virus That Causes Bird Flu May Be Spread by Smuggling," *New York Times* (April 15, 2006). Garrett, "The Next Pandemic?" 19.

73. Burkle, Jr., "Fragile States and Ungoverned Spaces." Kent Ranson et al., "Promoting Health Equity in Conflict-Affected Fragile States" (London: London School of Hygiene & Tropical Medicine, February 3, 2007): vi.

74. Mark Drapeau, "A Microscopic Insurgent," *New York Times* (December 4, 2007). International Rescue Committee report cited in Chris McGreal, "War in Congo Kills 45,000 People Each Month," *Guardian* (January 23, 2008).

75. Burkle, Jr., "Fragile States and Ungoverned Spaces." Also see Bell and Lewis, "The Economic Implications of Epidemics Old and New," 31.

76. Ed Cropley, "Malaria, Drug-Resistant TB Flourish in Myanmar," *Reuters* (May 30, 2007).

77. Garrett, "The Lessons of HIV/AIDS." Garrett, "HIV and National Security." Chris Beyrer et al., "Overland Heroin Trafficking Routes and HIV-1 Spread in South and South-East Asia," *AIDS*, 14/1 (January 7, 2000).

78. Cropley, "Malaria, Drug-Resistant TB Flourish in Myanmar."

79. Alan Sipress, "Experts Fear Burma Is Ill-Equipped to Handle Bird Flu," *Washington Post*, (January 15, 2006).

80. Laurie Garrett, "HIV and National Security: Where Are the Links?" (New York: Council on Foreign Relations, 2005). Jeffrey Gettleman, "Rape Epidemic Raises Trauma of Congo War," *New York Times* (October 7, 2007).

81. Jean-Paul Chretian et al., "The Importance of Militaries from Developing Countries in Global Infectious Disease Surveillance," *Bulletin of the World Health Organization* (2007).

82. Jones et al., "Global Trends in Emerging Infectious Diseases," 992.

83. David Brown, "As Temperatures Rise, Health Could Decline," *Washington Post* (December 17, 2007).

84. Jones et al., "Global Trends in Emerging Infectious Diseases," 991.

85. William B. Karesh and Robert A. Cook, "The Human-Animal Link," *Foreign Affairs,* 84/4 (2005): 38–39. Weiss and McMichael, "Social and Environmental Risk Factors."

86. Jessica M.C. Pearce-Duvet, "The Origin of Human Pathogens: Evaluating the Role of Agriculture and Domestic Animals in the Evolution of Human Disease," *Biological Reviews,* 81 (2006): 378–379.

87. Garrett "The Next Pandemic?" National Intelligence Council, "SARS: Down But Still a Threat." Osterholm, "Preparing for the Next Pandemic?" and "Is the Bird Flu Threat Still Real and Are We Prepared?"

88. British Broadcasting Company, "Irrigation Increases Malaria Rates" (September 10, 1999). Christopher Joyce, "Deforestation Boosts Malaria Rates, Study Finds," National Public Radio (January 5, 2006).

89. The Wildlife Conservation Society estimates that annual traffic in live wild animals involves roughly 4 million birds, 640,000 reptiles, and 40,000 primates, and that "at least a billion direct and indirect contacts among wildlife, humans and domestic animals results from the handling of wildlife and the wildlife trade annually." Karesh and Cook, "The Human-Animal Link."

90. Rice, "Poverty Breeds Insecurity," 43–44.

91. IPEA/World Bank, "Spending for Development: Making the Most of Indonesia's New Opportunities," *Indonesia Public Expenditure Review* (2007): 54. Tuberculosis rates are from World Health Organization, "Global Tuberculosis Control Report" (2008).

92. Allen Sipress, "Indonesia Stretched to the Limit in Battle against Two Diseases," *Washington Post* (November 6, 2005).

93. Holbrooke and Garrett, "'Sovereignty' That Risks Global Health" (August 10, 2008).

94. Alan Sipress, "UN Urging Indonesia to Take Stronger Action against Bird Flu," *Washington Post* (October 23, 2005).

95. Ibid.

96. Andrew Price-Smith, *The Health of Nations*. Garrett, "The Lessons of HIV/AIDS."

97. Colin L. Powell, Remarks at the Global Business Coalition on HIV/AIDS Annual Dinner (Washington, DC, June 12, 2003).

98. Figure for impact of AIDS on GDP is from Fourie, "The Relationship between the AIDS Pandemic and State Fragility." Laurie Garrett, "The Lessons of HIV/AIDS."

99. Richard P. Cincotta, Robert Engelman, and Daniele Anastasion, *The Security Demographic: Population and Civil Conflict after the Cold War* (Washington, DC: Population Action International, 2003): 62–69. Henrik Urdal, "The Demographics of Political Violence: Youth Bulges, Insecurity, and Conflict," in *Too Poor for Peace?*, eds. Lael Brainard and Derek Chollet (Washington, DC: Brookings Institution Press, 2007).

100. Garrett, "HIV and National Security." Paul Collier, et al. *Breaking the Conflict Trap: Civil War and Development Policy* (Washington, DC: World Bank, 2003).

101. Alex de Waal and Alan Whiteside, "New Variant Famine: AIDS and the Food Crisis in Africa," *Lancet*, 362/9391 (October 11, 2003): 1234–1237.

102. UN Food and Agriculture Organization, Impacts of HIV/AIDS, web site accessed May 12, 2009.

103. National Intelligence Council, "Mapping Sub-Saharan Africa's Future" (March 2005): 2.

104. Fourie, "The Relationship between the AIDS Pandemic and State Fragility." Tony Barnett, "A Long-Wave Event: HIV/AIDS, Politics, Governance, and 'Security': Sundering the Intergenerational Bond," *International Affairs*, 82/2 (2006): 304.

105. See map of global distribution of risk of an emerging infectious disease event, in Jones et al. (February 2008) p. 993.

106. World Health Organization, "Influenza A (H1N1)" Update 26 (May 12, 2009).

107. World Health Organization, Epidemic and Pandemic Alert and Response, H5N1 (May 6, 2009).

108. World Health Organization, Cumulative Number of Reported Probable Cases of SARS from November 1, 2002 to July 11, 2003.

Chapter 7

1. *The 9/11 Commission Report: Final Report of the National Commission on Terrorist Attacks upon the United States* (New York: W.W. Norton, 2004), 367.
2. *A More Secure World: Our Shared Responsibility, Report of the High-Level Panel on Threats, Challenges and Change* (New York: United Nations, 2004).
3. USAID, "Foreign Aid in the National Interest: Promoting Freedom, Security, and Opportunity" (Washington, DC: U.S. Agency for International Development, 2002).
4. Zimbabwe, Tonga, and Burundi. Turkmenistan is known as a transit state for Afghan heroin, but is not cited as a "major" transit state by the UN Office on Drugs and Crime or the International Narcotics Control Strategy Report.
5. This section draws on Stewart Patrick, "U.S. Policy Toward Fragile States: An Integrated Approach to Security and Development," *The White House and the World: A Global Development Agenda for the Next U.S. President,* ed. Nancy Birdsall (Washington, DC: Center for Global Development, 2008): 327–353.
6. U.S. Department of State, *Leading through Civilian Power: The First Quadrennial Diplomacy and Development Review* (Washington, DC, 2010) 122. For a survey of U.S. efforts and those of Western governments, see Stewart Patrick and Kaysie Brown, *Greater Than the Sum of Its Parts? Assessing "Whole of Government" Approaches to Fragile States* (New York: International Peace Academy, 2007). OECD/DAC, *Whole of Government Approaches to Fragile States* (Paris: OECD: 2006).
7. Marilee S. Grindle, "Good Enough Governance: Poverty Reduction and Reform in Developing Countries." *Governance: An International Journal of Policy, Administration, and Institutions,* 17/4 (October 2004): 525–548.
8. Simon Chesterman, Michael Ignatieff, and Ramesh Chandra Thakur, *Making States Work* (New York: United Nations University Press, 2005).
9. On weaknesses of the current system of "watch lists," see Paul B. Stares and Micah Zenko, "Enhancing U.S. Preventive Action," Council Special Report No. 48 (New York: Council on Foreign Relations, October 2009).
10. USAID, "Service Delivery in Fragile Situations: Key Concepts, Findings, and Lessons," OECD/DAC Discussion Paper (Washington, DC: U.S. Agency for International Development, 2008). OECD/DAC, "Principles for Good International Engagement in Fragile States" (Paris: OECD, 2007) <http://www.oecd.org/document/48/0,3343,en_2649_33693550_3523 3262_1_1_1_1,00.html>.
11. The White House, "Fact Sheet: U.S. Global Development Policy" (September 22, 2010), <http://www.whitehouse.gov/the-press-office/2010/09/22/fact-sheet-us-global-development-policy>. U.S. Department of State, *Leading through Civilian Power,* xii–xv, 15–16, 121–158.
12. Craig Burnside and David Dollar, "Aid, Policies, and Growth," *American Economic Review,* 90 (September 2000): 847-68. This is the philosophy behind the Millennium Challenge Account (MCA). The Presidential Policy Directive on Development of September 2010, points in the same direction, calling for aid to be targeted to countries with responsible governments and favorable conditions for development. The White House, "Fact Sheet".
13. For 2008, Liberia received $161.6 million ($47.5 per capita); East Timor: $23.3 million ($21.2 per capita); Yemen: $17.6 million ($0.74 per capita); Bangladesh: $105.0 million ($0.67 per capita). Figures are from the FY09 Foreign Affairs Congressional Budget Justification/Request by Region (online at <http://www.state.gov/documents/organization/101448.pdf>) Per capita/population figures are from *CIA World Factbook,* 2009 estimates.

14. Plausible aid orphans in recent years include Burundi, the Central African Republic, Congo Republic, the Democratic Republic of the Congo, and Niger. Jonathan M. White, "No Development without Security," Brussels Forum Paper Series (Washington, DC: German Marshall Fund, 2009).

15. Nicholas Watt, "Protests as UK Security Put at Heart of Government's Aid Policy," *The Guardian* (August 29, 2010).

16. Chauvet and Collier, "Development Effectiveness in Fragile States: Spillovers and Turnarounds," Center for the Study of African Economies, Oxford University, January 2004. http://www.jica.go.jp/cdstudy/library/pdf/20071101_09.pdf.

17. David Dollar and Victoria Levin, "The Increasing Selectivity of Foreign Aid: 1984–2002," World Bank Policy Research Working Paper No. 3299 (May 6, 2004). Mark McGillivray, "Aid Allocation and Fragile States," United Nations University Discussion Paper No. 2006/01 (January 2006): 11–12.

18. USAID, "Service Delivery in Fragile Situations." OECD/DAC Principles for Good International Engagement in Fragile States.

19. Ashraf Ghani and Clare Lockhart, *Fixing Failed States* (New York: Oxford University Press, 2008).

20. Robert Perito, Mike Dziedzic, and Beth C. Degrasse, "Building Civilian Capacity for U.S. Stability Operations: The Rule of Law Component," U.S. Institute of Peace, April 2004, http://www.usip.org/files/resources/sr118.pdf

21. Improving U.S. support for security sector reform is a key theme of the QDDR released in December 2010. See U.S. Department of State, *Leading through Civilian Power.*

22. In 2007, the world's fragile states received just 3.4 percent of the $586 billion in FDI to developing countries and accounted for only 3 percent of developing country merchandise exports. Commission of the European Communities, "EU 2009 Report on Policy Coherence for Development" (September 2009). Transatlantic Taskforce on Development, "Toward a Brighter World: A Transatlantic Call for Renewed Leadership and Partnerships in Global Development" (Washington, DC: German Marshall Fund, 2009). White, "No Development without Security."

23. On these proposals, see Nancy Birdsall, "Righting the Three-Legged Stool: Why Development Matters and What the Next President Should Do about It," in *The White House and the World: A Global Agenda for the Next U.S. President,* ed. Nancy Birdsall: 1–42. Theodore H. Moran and C. Fred Bergsten, "Reforming OPIC for the 21st Century," International Economics Policy Briefs (Washington, DC: Institute for International Economics, 2003). Edward Miguel, "Poverty and Violence: An Overview of Recent Research and Implications for Foreign Aid," in *Too Poor for Peace? Global Poverty, Conflict, and Security in the 21st Century,* eds. Lael Brainard and Derek Chollet. (Washington, DC: Brookings Institution, 2007).

24. For more detail, see Stewart Patrick, "The U.S. Response to Precarious States: Tentative Progress and Remaining Obstacles to Coherence," in *Diplomacy, Development and Defense: A Paradigm for Policy Coherence* eds. Stefani Weiss, Hans-Joachim Spanger, and Wim van Meurs (Gutersloh: Bertelsmann, 2009): 54–104.

25. Gordon Adams, "The Role of Civilian and Military Agencies in the Advancement of America's Diplomatic and Development Objectives" (Testimony before the Subcommittee on State, Foreign Operations and Related Programs of the House Committee on Appropriations, March 5, 2009).

26. Department of Defense, "Military Support for Stability, Security, Transition, and Reconstruction (SSTR) Operations," Directive 3000.05 (November 28, 2005).

27. Report of the Task Force on Non-Traditional Security Assistance, "Integrating 21st Century Development and Security Assistance" (Washington, DC: Center for Strategic and International Studies, January 2008). George Withers, Adam Isacson, Lisa Haugaard, Joy Olson, and Joel Fyke, "Ready, Aim, Foreign Policy" (Washington, DC: Washington Office on Latin America, March 2008).

28. Commission on Weak States, and U.S. National Security "On the Brink: Weak States and U.S. National Security" (Washington, DC: Center for Global Development, 2004.).

29. Robert Gates, "Tools of Persuasion and Inspiration" (Speech before the U.S. Global Leadership Campaign, July 15, 2008). See Richard L. Armitage and Joseph S. Nye, "A Smarter, More Secure America," Center for Strategic and International Studies Commission on Smart Power (Washington: CSIS, 2008), 63–67.

30. Hillary Rodham Clinton, "Leading through Civilian Power," *Foreign Affairs* 89/6 (November/December 2010), 13–18. Robert M. Gates, "A Balanced Strategy," *Foreign Affairs* 88/1 (January/February 2009).

31. In December 2009, Congress passed a $636 billion defense spending bill (including supplementals, but not the cost of the Afghanistan surge). According to the Office of Management and Budget, the FY2010 budget for the "U.S. State Department and Other International Programs" was $53.9 billion, of which $36.5 billion was for foreign assistance. White House Office of Management and Budget, "U.S. Department of State and Other International Programs," President's Budget Fact Sheets <http://www.whitehouse.gov/omb/fy2010_department_state/>.

32. Clinton, "Leading through Civilian Power,".

33. Stimson Center and Academy of Diplomacy, "A Foreign Affairs Budget for the Future: Fixing the Crisis in Diplomatic Readiness" (October 2008).

34. Patrick and Brown, *Greater Than the Sum of Its Parts?*

35. Department of Peacekeeping Operations, "Monthly Summary of Military and Police Contributions to United Nations Operations," accessed September 2010, http://www.un.org/en/peacekeeping/contributors/documents/Yearly06.pdf.

36. Stephen D. Krasner, "Governance Failures and Alternatives to Sovereignty," Center on Democracy, Development, and the Rule of Law Working Paper (November 2, 2004). Robert O. Keohane, "Political Authority after Intervention: Gradations in Sovereignty," in *Humanitarian Intervention: Ethical, Legal and Political Dimensions,* eds. J. L. Holzgrefe and Robert O. Keohane (New York: Cambridge University Press, 2003).

37. Peter Bergen, "The Front: The Al Qaeda-Taliban Merger," New Republic online (October 19, 2009) <http://www.tnr.com/article/world/the-front>.

38. Eric Rosand, "Global Terrorism: Multilateral Responses to an Extraordinary Threat," International Peace Academy Coping with Crisis Working Paper Series (April 2007). Eric Rosand, Alistair Millar, and Jaspn Ipe, "Building Stronger Partnerships to Prevent Terrorism: Recommendations for President Obama," (Washington, DC: Center on Global Counterterrorism Cooperation, January 2009).

39. Brian Finlay and Elizabeth Turpen, "The Next 100 Project: Leveraging National Security Assistance to Meet Developing World Needs" (Washington, DC: Stimson Center and Stanley Foundation, 2009), 2–4.

40. Eric Rosand, "Global Implementation of Security Council Resolution 1540—An Enhanced UN Response Is Needed," Center on Global Counterterrorism Cooperation, Policy Brief (October 2009).

41. Michael Bronner, "100 Grams (and Counting…): Notes from the Nuclear Underworld," Harvard University Belfer Center for Science and International Affairs (June 2008): 9.

42. Michael O'Hanlon, "Dealing with the Collapse of a Nuclear-Armed State: The Cases of North Korea and Pakistan," The Princeton Project on National Security <http://www.wws. princeton.edu/ppns/papers/ohanlon.pdf>.

43. Chaim Braun and Christopher F. Chyba, "Proliferation Rings: New Challenges to the Nuclear Nonproliferation Regime," *International Security*, 29/2 (Fall 2004): 43–47. Allison MacFarlane, "All Weapons of Mass Destruction Are Not Equal," Audit of the Conventional Wisdom (Cambridge: MIT Center for International Studies, July 2005).

44. James Cockayne and Phil Williams, "The Invisible Tide: Towards an International Strategy to Deal with Drug Trafficking through West Africa," International Peace Institute Policy Paper (October 2009): 27.

45. Dev Kar and Devon Cartwright-Smith, "Illicit Financial Flows from Developing Countries: 2002–2006" (Washington, DC: Global Financial Integrity, December 2008).

46. Paul Collier, *The Bottom Billion: Why the Poorest Countries Are Failing and What Can Be Done about It* (Oxford: Oxford University Press, 2007).

47. Willem van Schendel, "Spaces of Engagement: How Borderlands, Illegal Flows, and Territorial States Interlick," *Illicit Flows and Criminal Things: States, Borders, and the Other Side of Globalization*, eds. Willem van Schendel and Itty Abraham (Bloomington: Indiana University Press, 2006), 59.

48. Commission on Weak States, "On the Brink," 57.

49. A successful model is the Africa Partnership Station, a U.S. naval flotilla in the Gulf of Guinea.

50. James Cockayne, "Transnational Organized Crime: Multilateral Responses to a Rising Threat," International Peace Institute Coping with Crisis Working Paper Series (April 2007).

51. See *Combating Serious Crimes in Post-Conflict Societies: A Handbook for Policymakers and Practitioners*, ed. Collette Rausch (Washington, DC: U.S. Institute of Peace Press, 2006.)

52. James Cockayne and Daniel Pfister, "Peace Operations and Organized Crime," International Peace Institute Working Paper Series (April 2008).

53. See Barnett R. Rubin and Omar Zakhilwal, "A War on Drugs, or a War on Farmers?" *Wall Street Journal* (January 11, 2005). Juan Forero, "Colombia's Coca Survives U.S. Plan to Uproot It," *New York Times* (August 19, 2006).

54. Global Witness, "The Kimberley Process" <http://www.globalwitness.org/pages/en/the_ kimberley_process.html)>.

55. See C.J. Chivers, "U.S. Position Complicates Global Effort to Curb Illicit Arms," *New York Times* (July 19, 2008).

56. Ted Galen Carpenter, *Bad Neighbor Policy: Washington's Futile War on Drugs in Latin America* (New York: Palgrave Macmillan, 2003). Misha Glenny, "The Lost War," *Washington Post* (August 19, 2007): B1.

57. Larry Rother, "Bolivian Leader's Ouster Seen as Warning on U.S. Drug Policy," *New York Times* (October 23, 2003). Juan Forero, "Turbulent Bolivia Is Producing More Cocaine, the U.N. Report." *New York Times* (June 15, 2005).

58. Glenny, "The Lost War." James Risen, "Poppy Fields Are Now a Front Line in Afghanistan War," *New York Times* (May 16, 2007): A1.

59. Collier, Bottom Billion, 140–150.

60. Thomas Carothers, "The Rule of Law Revival," *Foreign Affairs* (March/April 1998).

61. Michael D. Conway et al., "Addressing Africa's Health Workforce Crisis," *McKinsey Quarterly* (November 2007). Jean-Paul Chretien et al., "The Importance of Militaries from Developing Countries in Global Infectious Disease Surveillance," *Bulletin of the World Health Organization*, 85 (2007): 177.

62. David Brown, "Africa's Polio Efforts Aiding Bird Flu Fight," *Washington Post* (February 12, 2006).

63. Jennifer Brower and Peter Chalk, *The Global Threat of New and Reemerging Infectious Diseases: Reconciling U.S. National Security and Public Health Policy* (Santa Monica, CA: RAND, 2003), xviii. Michael T. Osterholm, "Preparing for the Next Pandemic?," *Foreign Affairs* 84/4 (2005): 36.

64. Homeland Security Council, "National Strategy for Pandemic Influenza: Implementation Plan" (May 2006).

65. Based on 2003–2008 U.S. Department of State Country Reports on Terrorism.

66. Assessments of quantities of HEU and Plutonium by state are from the Nuclear Threat Initiative, "Who has what: HEU" (updated October 2008); Perkovich et al, "Universal Compliance" (2007), based on data from IAEA and Institute for Science and International Security, U.S. Department of Energy.

67. Based on 2009 U.S. International Narcotics Control Strategy Report, data from 2006–2008.

68. Based on data from the International Maritime Bureau; countries listed are those experiencing at least 5 attacks from 2006-2008. Highlighted countries experienced at least 20 attacks total in these years.

69. 2008 INCSR.

70. Based on U.S. Energy Information Administration data. Countries listed are those which produce at least 80,000 bpd of oil, or with at least 0.5 tcf of natural gas reserves, or where significant recent discoveries have been reported (e.g. Mauritania, East Timor, Sao Tome & Principe, Papua New Guinea).

71. Data is from the World Health Organization: "Epidemic and Pandemic Alert and Response" (May 6, 2009); "Cumulative Number of Reported Probable Cases of SARS from November 1, 2002 to July 11, 2003"; and "Ifluenza (H1N1) Update 26" (May 12, 2009).

72. 2009 INSCR.

73. Highlighted countries are those in which more than 2 dozen cases of H5N1 and/or SARS were reported.

74. Based on figures from Robert S. Norris and Hans M. Kristensen, "U.S. nuclear forces, 2008," *Bulletin of the Atomic Scientists* 64:1 (March/April 2008): 50–53; Norris and Kristensen, "India's nuclear forces, 2005," *Bulletin of the Atomic Scientists* 61:5 (September/October 2005): 73–75.

75. Based on figures from the Nuclear Threat Initiative, "Who has what: HEU" (updated October 2008).

76. 2009 INSCR.

INDEX